Structural Economics in China:
A Three-Dimensional Framework
for Balanced Growth

Structural Economics in China:

A Three-Dimensional Framework for

Balanced Growth

Xiang Junbo

Published by

Enrich Professional Publishing (S) Private Limited
16L, Enterprise Road,
Singapore 627660
Website: www.enrichprofessional.com
A Member of Enrich Culture Group Limited

Hong Kong Head Office:
2/F, Rays Industrial Building, 71 Hung To Road, Kwun Tong, Kowloon, Hong Kong, China

Beijing Office:
Rm 1108A, Culture Plaza, No. 59 Zhongguancun St., Haidian District, Beijing, China

English edition © 2013 by Enrich Professional Publishing (S) Private Limited
Chinese original edition © 2009 China Renmin University Press

Translated by Yang Yanfei and Li Lulu

All rights reserved. This book, or parts thereof, may not be reproduced in any form or by any means, electronic or mechanical, including photocopying, recording or any information storage and retrieval system now known or to be invented, without prior written permission from the Publisher.

ISBN (Hardback)	978-981-4298-38-4
ISBN (ebook)	978-981-4298-39-1 (pdf)
	978-981-4298-64-3 (epub)

This publication is designed to provide accurate and authoritative information in regard to the subject matter covered. It is sold with the understanding that the publisher is not engaged in rendering legal, accounting, or other professional service. If legal advice or other expert assistance is required, the services of a competent professional person should be sought.

Enrich Professional Publishing is an independent globally minded publisher focusing on the economic and financial developments that have revolutionized new China. We aim to serve the needs of advanced degree students, researchers, and business professionals who are looking for authoritative, accurate and engaging information on China.

Contents

Foreword vii

Introduction xi

Chapter 1   An Overview of Structural Economics 1

Chapter 2   The Theory of the Evolution of Economic Structure 29

Chapter 3   The Theory of the Imbalance of Economic Structure 51

Chapter 4   The Interaction of the Evolution of
Economic Structure and the Resource Environment 73

Chapter 5   Evolution and Imbalance of
China's Investment and Consumption Structures 97

Chapter 6   Evolution and Imbalance of China's Industrial Structure 123

Chapter 7   Evolution and Imbalance of China's Financial Structure 153

Chapter 8   Evolution and Imbalance of
China's Regional Economic Structure 187

Chapter 9   Evolution and Imbalance of
China's Balance of Payments Structure 213

Chapter 10 Integrated Analysis of the Imbalance of
China's Economic Structure 239

Contents

Chapter 11 Strategic Orientation of
China's Economic Structural Adjustment 279

Notes 315
References 329
Index 339

Foreword

As a sub-discipline of economics, the emergence of structural economics is quite a recent phenomenon. I did not hear of the saying of structural economics until 1990s; instead, what crossed my mind was structuralism in economics. The founder of economic structuralism is Raúl Prebisch, the renowned left-wing economist and director of Economic Commission for Latin America. Structural economics is a school of development economics which emphasizes structural features of an economy, rather than a sub-discipline in economics. Lance Taylor, professor of Harvard University, published his eminent book *Structuralist Macroeconomics* in 1983. He made his purpose clear at the beginning of the book, "In an economy, if its system and behaviors of its members make some particular pattern of resource allocation and evolution much more likely to happen, then that economy has a structure." In other words, any economy features a specific system with members of not only economic people, but also political and social people. Economic theories should not simply be the problem concerning the maximization of a series of relationships among economic people or the set of discussions of solutions to those problems. However, Taylor did not specialize in the system and structure of a particular economy. Though his book *Structuralist Macroeconomics* once captured people's attention, it has never been accessible to the mainstream of economics. It was in 1990s that structural economics officially came into being. In 1992, Faye Duchin of New York University, U.S., published a paper *Industrial Input-Output Analysis: Implications for Industrial Ecology*, in which she claimed that structural economics is a detailed and classified description of the entire economy from the perspective of its specific and observable components and their relationships. Actually, in 1988 Duchin published a book with structural economics as the theme—*Structural Economics: Measuring Change in Technology, Lifestyles, and the Environment* (Washington, D.C., Island Press, 1988). In that monograph, she surveyed into the residential lifestyles, technological selection and their impacts on the use of resources by combining the qualitative approaches based on input-output analysis and the quantitative one based on social accounting. The latest book entitled with structural economics may be Thijs ten Raa's *Structural Economics* (Routledge, 2004, Tilburg University, Netherlands). Raa believed that the economic structure contains three elements: technologies, endowments and preferences. The task of structural economics is to provide a national accounting framework comprised of those three elements and analyze problems, based on

Foreword

this framework, such as what effect the increase in the proportion of the service industry will have on the speed of economic growth. His *Structural Economics*, to a great extent, is the further development and application of Leontief's input-output analysis. Besides, it is found in various articles that discussions in terms of research objects of structural economics. For example, Bob Williams claimed that structural economics aims to study what influence the uneven distribution of the stock (capital) and flow (income) of the wealth will exert on the overall economic operation. In general, there is an immense amount of literature on economic structures, and terms such as structural change, structural imbalance, structural adjustment and structural reform have been frequently employed in economics. However, as expressed by Mr Xiang Junbo, theoretical studies on structural economics has not yet developed into an independent discipline by now, though the theory of structural economics possesses a strong historical accumulation.

China has accomplished an average annual GDP growth rate of 9.8% in the past three decades, and became the world's third largest economy with its GDP surpassing Germany in 2007. Despite a strong economic growth, structural problems of China's economy are exacerbating. The most crucial problem China faces is whether China's rapid economic growth is sustainable. It is no exaggeration to say that whether China's economic growth can sustain depends on whether its economic structure can be improved in time. From China's current economic reality, it seems that the inclusive problem of its economic structure consist of two sub-problems, which are, what kind of growth to pursue (which can be regarded as the problem of the growth quality) and how to optimize the ratio of various elements in the economic system. In addition, a series of problems in institutional economics behind those structural issues require further studies.

The purpose of economic growth is to raise people's living standards. However, the growth of the gross domestic product cannot be equaled to the improvement of common welfare. The measurement of living standards should be based on the economic welfare, a broader concept. Not every economic activity accounted into GDP can improve the national welfare; sometimes these activities may even produce counter-effects, which are exemplified by the environmental pollution issues. For example, profligate waste of resources precludes the possibility of the future improvement of the national welfare. As for China, another important issue is that due to substantial foreign capital inflow, the GDP growth may thus, to a large degree, represent the growth of the foreign national welfare, rather than the growth of China's own national welfare. What is the target mode of economic growth? How can we measure it?

Foreword

What kind of institutional arrangement will secure the economic growth biasing toward the maximization of the national welfare? These problems have yet to be resolved by Chinese economists.

Chinese academia conducted discussions on issues in terms of the gross social product and the proportion of the two old divisions in the 1950s and 1960s. The pursuit of the speed of economic growth led to the unbalanced proportion of the two old divisions, which in turn caused a great volatility in the economic growth, and consequently pushed China's national economy to the verge of collapse. Since the reform and opening-up, with China's rapid economic development, the proportional imbalance has turned into a more complicated structural imbalance, which is featured in the investment-consumption imbalance and international payments imbalance. China's investment rate rose from 38.2% in 1978 to 42.1% in 2007, whereas the consumption rate fell from 62.1% to 49% during the same period. The increasing investment rate indicates a rising production capacity. However, with the declining consumption rate, the excessive production capacity can only be absorbed through further improving the investment rate or via export; while the improvement of the former in turn propels the further increase of capacity. Obviously, the growth mode of absorbing the production capacity of excessive steel by establishing more steel plants is not sustainable. With the expansion of economic scale, it is difficult for China to absorb a huge surplus capacity via export. The structural imbalance of international payments is another important evidence for China's structural imbalance. Trade surplus means capital export. In order to pursue the optimal resource allocation, China, as a developing country, should deploy more resources to domestic consumption and investment, rather than to the low-yielding financial assets like U.S. treasury bonds. China's economy heavily depends on external demands. The unexpected shock to its economy caused by the current global economic downturn fully illustrates that the export-driven growth pattern is not sustainable.

Without the economic growth over the past three decades, there is no remarkable success in today's China. However, China, which has already gotten rid of the "poor and blank" status, should seriously reflect on what the development direction and growth pattern is that it needs to follow. At the same time, we must also recognize that only with constant restructuring can China continue ahead along the path of sustainable growth. Both the growth targets and the institutional and structural basis for achieving sustainable economic growth are the most important subjects in Chinese economic studies. Although these issues are covered in the traditional political economics, development economics, economic growth theories, macroeconomics, microeconomics,

Foreword

industrial economics and institutional economics, it seems that no economic discipline has yet specialized in the above problems. Mr Xiang Junbo's *Structural Economics* sets structural problems in the economic system as objects of study and explores "rules of changes of economic structure in the process of economic growth and their roles in the resource allocation," which is a very meaningful attempt.

Xiang has conducted a comprehensive summary of China's structural imbalance in his book *Structural Economics*. In his opinion, there are currently five major structural imbalances in China: the structural imbalance between investment and consumption, the imbalance of industrial structure, the imbalance of financial structure, the imbalance of the regional economic structure and the imbalance of the international payments structure. Xiang makes a detailed, in-depth analysis of the causes, evolution and solutions of the imbalances.

Considering the development of physical theories, Einstein pointed out that the complete system of theoretical physics is comprised of concepts, basic principles regarded as effective to these concepts (also known as basic assumptions, basic postulates, basic laws, and so on) and conclusions deduced by logical reasoning. The most fundamental part of a theory is the concepts and basic assumptions which are as few as possible in numbers and cannot be further simplified in logic. The construction of a complete system of economic theories and an economic discipline should roughly follow such a principle. Measured by the above principle, we can see that, even though China has accumulated abundant materials of structural economics, the final establishment of China's structural economics still entails endeavors of Mr Xiang Junbo and other scholars interested in that.

Yu Yongding
February 9, 2009

Introduction

Since the 1980s, with the speeding up of technological advancement and the deepening of the global economic integration as well as the aggravation of the imbalance and the instability of the economic development of all countries, the imbalance of the economic structure has become a common phenomenon. Meanwhile, the risks hidden in the economy, the society, as well as in the resource environment have increased. Sustainable development is seriously challenged; while the theory of the traditional economy seems helpless. Establishing a theoretical system for structural economics is the inner motivation to solve those practical problems and the inner call for the theoretical innovation.

The current international financial crisis is the deep reflection of the imbalance of the global economic structure. Since its outbreak in April, 2007, the U.S. subprime crisis has been evolving into a global and overall crisis. Despite dedicated efforts and bail-out plans, the worsened trend has not been curbed, yet further expanded into a global economic crisis. At present, the influence of the crisis on the world's economy has not bottomed out. Why would the seemingly regional subprime crisis cause so much global economic and financial turmoil? The current interpretations level accusation against the excessive financial innovation, encouragement of speculation due to asymmetry of incentive and restraint mechanisms, and the moral hazard within rating agencies. Objectively speaking, these interpretations are convincing to some extent because they explain the reasons for the financial crisis outbreak from some specific perspectives. However, none of them gives sufficient attention to the nature of the subprime crisis causes — the imbalance of the economic structure. Based on historical experience, whether in developed or developing countries, the economic causes of the crisis can be traced back to the imbalance of the economic structure. In fact, the outbreak, spread and deepening of the subprime crisis originated from the excessive consumptive financial growth mode in the U.S. Ultimately, the subprime crisis is still a typical financial crisis caused by the structural imbalance.

Currently, the United States is undertaking a consumption-driven mode. Both the U.S. government and its people are over-optimistic, which is manifested in a manner of maintaining excessive consumption pattern through a wholesale borrowing. In recent years, the U.S. savings rate has been declining, with even negative figures appearing in some years. Until 2007, the total

Introduction

savings and the net savings in the U.S. had dropped to 14%, and 1.7% to the GDP respectively. The personal debt had accumulated to the sum of 40 years' debt volumes prior to 2002. In order to stimulate the debt-driven consumption of both households and governments, the U.S. had to continue the increase the issue of currency and maintain relatively low interest rates. With the existing structural imbalance in the U.S. economy, it brought excessive liquidity to the financial system, encouraged excessive financial innovations, and consequently led to the excessive asset price inflation and the prevalence of market speculation, eventually resulting in a serious imbalance of both virtual and real economic structures. According to the statistics, the U.S. subprime housing loans amounted to approximately USD1.7 trillion before the financial crisis, but more than USD7 trillion mortgage-backed securities (MBS) were released, and the derived collateralized debt obligations (CDO) and credit default swaps (CDS) were worthy of tens of trillions dollars. In fact, the excessive expansion of the financial derivative instrument not only became the "accomplice" to the asset price bubble but also evolved into a "ringleader." The crisis is actually a wholesale banking crisis occurring in the global financial center caused by financial derivatives. Therefore, its amplifying effect and lethality are greater than that of a banking crisis in the general sense.

Moreover, in order to maintain the over-consumption and make up for insufficient domestic savings, the United States must continuously absorb foreign savings through trade deficit and external debt. On the one hand, the U.S. over-consumption growth pattern created huge external demands for the emerging economies, yet at the same time it formed a huge structural imbalance. In 2007, the U.S. trade deficit was USD819.4 billion. On the other hand, the United States also became the world's biggest debtor relying on its dollar's status as the international currency. Its global foreign exchange reserves were mainly in China and other emerging market economies while the debts were concentrated in the United States and a few other developed economies. In 2007, the U.S. imported about USD1 trillion in foreign capital to finance its deficit with the average imported figure of USD4 billion every working day. In reality, due to the trust of the dollar, emerging market economies were willing to invest substantial foreign exchange reserves in U.S. treasury bonds and other financial assets. As a result, the dollars the U.S. used to export its trade deficit circulated back in the form of financial account surpluses, through which the U.S. received a huge amount of seigniorage and had drawn a large number of foreign savings; but at the same time exacerbated its asset price bubble, and worsened the existing imbalance of the structures of the global finance, investment and consumption. Thus, the U.S. over-consumption growth pattern

Introduction

not only caused imbalance between the real and virtual economic structures due to the structural imbalance between domestic savings and investment, but also induced a global trade and financial structural imbalance. In other words, as the U.S. economy continued to expand its consumption debts, the global economy would become increasingly vulnerable. Once the U.S. over-consumption pattern exceeded the maximum tolerance the global economy could endure, global economic and financial crisis would occur. That is why the humble "sub-prime butterfly" flapping its wings would result in such a global financial and economic crisis.

The volatile political situation and ever-growing social risks in some regions and countries are also the deep-seated reflection of the imbalance of the economic structure. Currently, there still exists the imbalance in the global economic growth and a large gap between rich and poor. In formulating the rules for the market economy, the absolute power of the developed countries and the weak position of the developing countries will generate the conflicts between them. Meanwhile, the imbalance of the economic structure within some countries is also the root of social conflicts. In the late 1960s, Latin American countries became the world's most inequitable income distribution areas due to the uneven economic development, a widening wealth gap and the strict social hierarchy; thus these potential social risks expanded into a serious social crisis in which people's basic living conditions were seriously undermined — the states were chaotic and all the social and economic achievements destroyed overnight. For the past few years, a serious economic development imbalance existed between China's urban and rural areas, which were manifested in a widening income gap and an unhealthy social security system. Compared with other countries, China's expenditure in education, health, and social security occupies only about 10% of the total GDP, lower than the 16% in the U.S., 30% in France, and the 20% in Poland, Russia, Iran, Brazil, and other countries. At present, China's Gini coefficient has reached the level of 0.5—higher than the international warning level of 0.4. Therefore, the social instability and the risks caused by the imbalance of the economic structure are still the long-term social problems of the future.

The resource and environmental problems are the concentrated expression of the economic structural imbalance. Since the industrial revolution, human society has gone after the short-term interests at the cost of environmental resources. Global warming is caused by the excessive consumption of resources and ecological degradation of the environment, continuous rising concentrations of the atmospheric carbon dioxide and other greenhouse gases due to the extensive economic development mode. Meanwhile, with the surge

Introduction

in population and massive deforestation in many countries, forest coverage has constantly decreased, intensifying land desertification and a serious setback of the environment. In addition, industrialization in some countries has led to a dramatic increase of harmful gaseous emissions such as sulfur dioxide, resulting in the acid rain phenomenon and frequent accidents of grave environmental pollution, which will bring a devastating disaster to the living environment of human society. For a long time, despite the rapid economic growth, China had actually taken an extensive economic development pattern, but the situation of high input, consumption, pollution and low quality benefit is very serious, leading to the imbalance in a rapid development of the heavy industries mainly in steel, non-ferrous metals, building materials, machinery and chemistry. The excessive consumption and irrational use of resources brought about the intense supply of vital recourses as coal, steel, oil and other, economic development, leading to an increasingly evident situation that economic development is restrained by resources and the environment. Recently, although China has stepped up environmental protection efforts, the environmental situation is as grim as before and the emission of pollutants is large as usual. Pollution is still at a very high level. Environmental quality in some areas continues to deteriorate. Water, air, and soil pollution in urban areas is still very serious with emergence of the trend that spreads to rural areas, which has become a serious threat to the basic living environment and sustainable development. Therefore, the resources and the environmental risk caused by the economic structural imbalance deserve attention.

Why are the economic structural problems so important? What's the relationship between the economic and social structure, resources and environment? Why has the structure had such an enormous impact on the economic and social development impact? This requires a systematic and in-depth discussion at the theoretical level. From the perspective of economic theory history, the structural theory has not been involved in the mainstream economics, with only some intermittent studying traced along the development of economic theory but without a complete and rigorous system. Classical economics discusses the power of economic growth from the perspective of production structure, but has not established a complete analytical basis. Structural analysis disappeared from the new classical economists' vision after the "Marginal Revolution." After WWII, the structuralism of the development economics studied the structural problems for the developing countries, based on their path choices to industrialization. But it cuts off the organic relations with the developed countries, mainly using system analysis and description of analytical methods which are difficult to establish a rigorous theoretical

Introduction

paradigm. Ever since the 1970s, the economic structure has mainly used empirical research or experience in analysis, such as "multi-national standard industrial structure," which lacks basic theoretical support. Recently, the term "structural economics" appeared in the western economic circles, which were not theoretical achievements but studies based on relevant methodologies. For example, some used the input-output method to analyze the problems of industrial structure. It can be seen that research on the structural economics are seriously lagging behind the practical needs, which makes the economic theory unable to explain the changeable economic phenomena and solving the complex structural problems. Under the current circumstances, the global financial crisis urges research on the economic structure, which promotes the establishment of structural economics. Certainly, the establishment and development of the structural economics are both challenging and innovative research, and are also common tasks that the domestic and international economic circles should undertake. Unremitting efforts, knowledge accumulation and sustainable innovation are necessary in shaping structural economics into a more comprehensive and more systematic discipline. I have worked in the university, governmental departments, central bank, and commercial bank for years, and have been dedicated to the structural and institutional studies. Since 2004, while working in the People's Bank of China, I have had a chance to observe the Chinese economy at a higher and broader level. Having accumulated the experience and knowledge of macroeconomic research and policy analyses, and systematic and in-depth thinking of the structural economic issues, I realized the importance, urgency and difficulty of researching these problems. In recent years, through continuous theoretical exploration of structural economics, I became confident that it would help broaden my thinking and clarify the theoretical errors so as to better analyze and study the practical problems.

This book fully explored and created the theoretical system of structural economics. Sustainable development, which is currently the common pursuit both at the global and national levels, is manifested in a manner of coordinated development among the economic, social, and resource environment, which can be summarized as "three-dimensional balance." Under the guidance of this theory, this book, which was aimed at solving the economic structural imbalance and achieving sustainable development, created a theoretical framework of structural economics, including the theories of economic structural evolution, theories of economic structural imbalance, and theories of interaction between economic structural evolution and resource environment, which constituted the theoretical basis of this book. However, structural economics is a broader-defined system, thus this book may only be able to cover some specific areas. It

Introduction

has definite focuses, clear targets and specific research objectives, rather than general abstraction or theoretical preaching. Additionally, it emphasizes the problem-oriented analysis of the economics theories, which is the distinctive feature of this book. The theoretical system of structural economics is a multi-disciplinary integration and innovation, which is inclusive of not only the theoretical advantage of the structuralism in development economics but also the sustenance of various disciplines, including institutional economics, population economics, environmental and resource economics and sustainable development economics. Thus, it can be seen that the structure of this theory system of economics is an integration.

This book emphasizes the empirical analysis and the application value of the disciplinary construction. With the aim of disciplinary construction, studying and analyzing the Chinese economic structural imbalance thus contains a great potential. China is the biggest developing country in the world, and the potential candidate for the practice of the structural economics. Since the reform and opening-up, the Chinese productivity got a quick release, and the economic growth has maintained a high speed. However, at the same time, the Chinese non-equilibrium reform and development path, and its extensive growth pattern lead to the aggravation of the economic structural imbalance. As an open developing power, China has become the focus of the global economic structural imbalance. Therefore, the research on the imbalance problems in the process of economic structural evolution is quite necessary. As Premier Wen said, "there are substantial problems in the Chinese economy which are still unstable, unbalanced, uncoordinated and unsustainable structural problems." If the Chinese economic structural imbalance cannot be effectively solved in a timely manner, China will suffer a greater economic and social cost in the future, or even a severe crisis. Therefore, a comprehensive study on the theories of structural economics seems part-and-parcel. How to strengthen the academic discussions on the Chinese economic structural imbalance, and how to make China's economy maintain a sustainable and coordinate expansion are two outstanding topics. Under the guidance of the structural economic theories, this book elaborates the evolution and imbalance of the economic structure during the 30-year reform and opening-up, ranging from the investment consumption structure, industrial structure, and financial structure to the regional economic structure and balance of payments structure. It initially proposed a measure to examine the level of the economic structural imbalance, and came to many important empirical conclusions. As the study results indicated, accompanied with rapid economic growth, China's economic structural imbalance, which evolved from mild to severe, continued exacerbating from 1992 to 2007.

Introduction

Therefore, viewing China's economy from a structural perspective has a unique theoretical and practical significance.

The rigorous and scientific academic research is requisite to formulate effective policies and measurements. This book emphasizes the internal relations between the academic research and policy analysis, which was the starting point in writing this book. It systematically analyzes the general regularity of the evolution of the economic structure, objectively assesses its level, features and risks, and has found that the extensive economic development mode was the culprit of this structural imbalance. As one of the largest developing countries, China's economic structural imbalance is related to its unique and complicated backgrounds, including industrialization, marketization and urbanization, and thus the task of the economic structural adjustment and optimization is epic and difficult. Under the current global financial crisis, the unduly export-dependent economic growth pattern is not sustainable. China must obtain a strategic economic restructuring by the transformation of economic development, from the extensive development mode of "high energy consumption, high emission and high pollution" to the intensive development mode of "low energy consumption, low emissions and low pollution," thus promoting the coordinated economic, social, and environmental development, and ultimately reaching the "three-dimensional balance." This book, in which the basic ideas and principles of the economic restructuring are proposed, is based on the systematic theoretical analysis and panoramic empirical analysis. For different time points in the future, the adjustment path of the Chinese economic structure should find the best binding point between the economic growth and structural optimization in the target conditioned area, and this binding point should satisfy the following conditions: economic growth rate should be close to the potential economic growth rate; economic structure has been constantly optimized, and Pareto Optimal has been achieved in the resource allocation. The future collection of these points constitutes the optimal path for the adjustment of the China's economic restructuring. To achieve this path, this book puts forward five strategies for the adjustment of China's economic restructuring based on fundamental research and international crosswise comparison, and discussed the idea, denotation and internal relation of every adjustment strategy. The five strategies are: the structural adjustment strategy of low-carbon economy; the structural adjustment strategy of consumer-oriented economy; the structural adjustment strategy of market-oriented finance; the structural adjustment strategy of coordinated regional economy; and the structural adjustment strategy of management balance and balance of payments. These policies and proposals are aimed to resolve the risk of the economic structure,

Introduction

and to achieve the internal organic unity of the economic, social and resource environment. At present, though, China's economy is facing many difficulties and contradictions, and is particularly under the severe impact of the global financial crisis. However, judging from the long period of economic growth, China is still in the starting phase of economic development, in which supply is relatively abundant and demand is also relatively strong. The global industrial structure is accelerating and upgrading, and the economic structure is showing a non-equilibrium tendency that evolves to the high class, which offers its economy a rare opportunity for further expansion. Therefore, as long as the economic structure adjustment achieves the expected results, the fundamentals of China's future economic development will still be full of hope, and the sustainable development of the Chinese economy will be entirely reachable.

Hopefully, this book will promote China's economic growth; and I hope to deeply discuss it with the experts at home and abroad. The research achievements are still exploratory, and they need to be continuously developed and perfected via deeper research and practices. As a discipline, structural economics is still structurally immature, and there is certainly a large gap between the sublimation of the discipline and its present research. In theory, theoretical conclusions from the specific to the general should be strengthened, so as to achieve theoretical innovation; in practice, the dynamic monitoring and pre-warning research of the structural problems should be deepened, the international comparative research of the structural problems should be strengthened, and the policy analysis of the research on the structural problems should be constantly improved, so as to refine and enrich them in the process of practice. In my opinion, structural economics is extensive and profound, and this book serves as a modest spur to induce experts and readers to come forward with their valuable contributions. I sincerely hope we can work together to promote the construction and development of structural economics.

Xiang Junbo
February 1, 2009

Chapter 1

An Overview of Structural Economics

STRUCTURAL ECONOMICS IN CHINA

Historically, economic development includes both economic growth as well as the evolution and optimization of the economic structure. Since the collapse of the Bretton Woods System in the 1970s, the imbalance in economic structure has gradually become a global concern. With expanding economic globalization and the continuous adjustment to the pattern of international division of labor, the imbalance in economic structure has become not only a shackle restraining overall economic development, but also a major cause of economic and/or political crisis. The 2008 financial turmoil, triggered by the U.S. subprime mortgage crisis, reflects the deep-seated worldwide imbalance in the economic structure. It is of great theoretical and practical importance to systematically extend studies into and establish a theoretical system for structural economics especially under current circumstances, which are dominated by an increasingly complex structural contradiction and a plunged economy.[1] This book contributes to establishing such a theoretical system for structural economics through disciplinary studies.

Basic Concepts of Structural Economics

When a discipline is established, its core concepts at all levels, which involve both inter-connections and distinctions, should be clearly defined otherwise misunderstandings and errors will occur. Concepts such as *Structure*, *Economic Structure*, *Structural Economy* and *Structural Economics* are comprehensively analyzed and compared in this chapter, and form the basis of the general theoretical system for structural economics.

The "structure"

Definition

Structure is a concept with profound implications. A wide variety of basic structures with mutual interdependence, interaction and restraint constitute the very fabric of this vast planet. Research into structure stems from the philosophy of structuralism, which focuses on analyzing the overall composition of various elements and their inter-relationships. Jean Piaget, a Swiss psychologist, in his book *Structuralism*, summarized the common features of structuralism in terms of physics, psychology and economics. Piaget believed that structure is the combination of the relation between and the inter-dependence of its members then characterized by the relationships of individual elements with the entirety.[2] As the most fundamental concept in structural economics, structure refers to the interaction of different elements in a system.

An Overview of Structural Economics

Whether in the field of natural sciences or of humanities and social sciences, structural analysis is more comprehensive in reflecting the nature and regularity of all things, especially compared with aggregate analysis, and therefore the concept of structure is fundamental to scientific research.

Features

Any structure is an organic unity. Generally speaking, a structure features the following three typical traits. First, structure is integrated. Structure is the combination of several elements and individuals in accordance with certain rules; it is not a simple total or sum but the reflection of the inter-dependent relationships between the various elements and individuals. Second, structure is self-adjusted. The system of structure has the inherent ability to self-adjust; therefore every structure under external influence possesses the function for feedback and, in order to adapt to changes in the external environment, structure can adjust itself within a certain range to secure its evolution toward a specific direction. However, that function of self-adjustment will be weakened or even veer out of control when the internal or external environment is inharmonious or inadaptable. Third, structure is transformable. When quantitative changes of elements in a structural system accumulate to a certain degree, the structure will experience transformations in terms of its function and property, which may also alter its evolutionary trajectory.

The economic structure

Definition

Economic structure is the core concept in the human social and economic system. Due to its complexity, the economic structure has to be understood and defined in various dimensions. The American economist Lance Taylor claimed that "an economic system, if the behaviors of its members and institutions have gradually developed into some certain patterns in the process of the allocation of resource, it is regarded to have a structure."[3] French economist François Perroux defined the economic structure as "specific proportions and relations of an economic system determined by time and space dimensions existing in the framework of given technological, sociological and institutional characteristics." Jan Tinbergen, the renowned Dutch economist and first Nobel laureate in economics, believed that the economic structure is the sum of unobservable features of reactions to changes in the economic system.[4]

STRUCTURAL ECONOMICS IN CHINA

Marxist economics defines economic structure from a different perspective, deeming "the totality of the relations of production constitutes the economic structure of a society."[5] Opinions varied among domestic scholars in the interpretation of the economic structure based on Marxist theory. For example, the *Dictionary of Political Economy* describes it in two ways: first, the totality of social relations of production represented by the ownership structure of the means of production; and second, the compositions and structures of all sectors in the national economy and all aspects of social reproduction.[6] At the same time, many economists define economic structure from angles of interconnection between various elements and sectors in the national economy.

The author believes that economic structure consists of the fundamental connections and proportional relationships between its constituent parts formed during resource allocation. It reflects not only the attribute connections between economic systems, but also the quantitative relationships of the components within those systems in terms of their variations and functions.

Research status

The economic structure occupies an important position in the structural system as a whole, a position that specifically manifests in two aspects. First, economic structure plays a vital role in the entire structural system because economy is the material basis for the progress and development of human society, the comprehensive reflection of productivity, and the structure of production relations. Second, the evolution of economic structure is the result of interactions within the environmental and human social systems; its evolution is governed by the process of the human system transforming the natural one as well as the harmony between humans and nature.

The structural economy

Definition

As a special economic pattern, the structural economy, corresponding to the aggregate economy, refers to the totality of the results and process of resource allocation of all constituent parts in the economic system. Due to the complexity of sectors in the economic system, structural economy can be analyzed from many perspectives, such as sectors in the national economy, links in the social reproduction chain, spatial composition and the like. For instance, in terms of the national economy, the structural economy can be categorized into agricultural economy, industrial economy and service economy. In terms of social reproduction, it can be classified as investment economy and consumption economy. And in terms of spatial composition, it can be assorted into regional economy, urban-rural economy, et cetera. Therefore, patterns displayed by the structural economy are complex and manifest themselves in the manner of mutual connections and restrictions.

Structural economy exerts a significant influence on economic growth and development as well as total social output, and thereby promotes social progress through adjusting the efficiency of resource allocation. Joseph Stiglitz, the U.S. economist and Nobel laureate, claimed that the U.S. followed the evolutionary pattern of an agricultural economy becoming an industrial economy and then a service economy. The nature of that structural change features an adjustment process of resource configuration from low productivity sectors to high productivity sectors.[7]

Differences between the structural economy and the aggregate economy

Being the two basic operating patterns in an economic system, the structural economy and the aggregate economy are inter-complimentary. The structural economy is a more specific and fundamental economic pattern and is built on the aggregate economy. Compared with the aggregate economy, it has three characteristics: first, it represents the quality and efficiency of the economic operation, while aggregate economy reflects the quantity and scale of operating the social economic system. Second, it shows the adjustment and optimization processes of the economic structure, focusing on long-term transformation in the economic system, while the aggregate economy concentrates on the process of the scale accumulation. Third, it often manifests changes in quality with discontinuous and non-additive characteristics, while the aggregate economy features the contrary. Therefore, the measurement of the structural economy, compared with aggregate economy, seems complex and epic.

Economic structure and structural economy

Economic structure and structural economy are separate concepts and there are fundamental differences between the two. The former is a pattern belonging to the structural system, whereas the latter is a state in the operation of the economic system. However, the two concepts are also intrinsically related: first, both are important components in the economic system, representing the fundamental characteristics within and rules of the economic operation; and, from a long-term perspective, economic development shows the constant evolution of the economic structure as well as the enrichment of the structural

STRUCTURAL ECONOMICS IN CHINA

economy. Second, in a certain stage of development, the economic structure of a country or a region determines the details and pattern of its structural economy, the two being interdependent and complimentary. And third, changing trends in the economic structure determine the structural economy. As the economic structure is determined by the productivity and production relations during a given period of time (and there are objective laws directing the actions of productivity and production relations), so the economic structure inevitably determines the structural economy in the country or region.

Structural economics

Structural economics is a new discipline and it is an applied discipline that poses structural problems in the economic system as a research subject. Structural economics specializes in changing the rules of economic structure in the course of economic growth as well as the mechanism of that influence on the resource allocation process against the backdrop of the constant imbalance within the global economic structure and the ever increasing pressure on resources and the environment.

Structural economics is a theoretical innovation for new historical conditions. As a newly-emerged and independent discipline, it is fundamentally different from previous structural economic theory. The former is an independent discipline with a system of basic concepts, theoretical assumptions, and research framework, whereas the latter is a branch of development economics, focusing on economic growth strategies and policy-making in under-developed countries. Structural economics features openness and inclusiveness wherein developing and developed countries are studied collectively, which exceeds the fundamental research scope of development economics. At the same time, structural economics takes sustainable development as its research purpose and economic structure as its main object, but it does not confine itself to those problems concerning resource allocation in the economic structure system. Instead, it emphasizes internal relations between the operation of the economic structure system and sustainable development. Therefore, the structure of structural economics actually has two aspects: first, it refers to various structural connections within the economic system, including the investment-consumption structure, the industrial structure, the financial structure, the regional economic structure, the international balance of payments structure, etcetera, all of which form the building blocks of structural economic research. Second, it refers to the structural connections formed by the economic system and the resource and environmental system. Resources and environment are the most basic requisites for material production and for one's self-development. When economic development reaches a certain level, conflicts will rise between the economic system and the system of resources and the environment. Structural imbalances will follow and people will struggle to strike a balance between the economic and the environmental.

Thus it is clear that studies of economic structure within structural economics is not self-contained but involves research into the evolution, optimization and adaptability to external environments under the framework that resources and the environment are the most fundamental binding conditions and interactive objects. Therefore, structural economics is no longer structural economics of old, but a multi-disciplinary integration and innovation involving the economics behind economic structure, population, environment, sustainable development, and so on.

Dynamics Behind and Sources of Building Structural Economics

With the ongoing evolution of economy and society, the economic structure has become increasingly complex and the contradiction between the economic system and the resource environment system has become acute. Therefore, existing economic theories and research methodologies may no longer be able to explain these newly emerged problems. Thus, based on related studies, it is significantly meaningful to systematically build structural economics.

The practical needs of solving the economic imbalance

Since the 1980s and the economic convergence characterized by the globalization of manufacture, investment, trade, and finance, each country's trade and financial openness have increased remarkably but the growing global economic structural imbalance has been taken as inevitable throughout this economic development.

In recent years, the imbalance in the global economic structure manifests itself as a form of the trade structure imbalance. In February, 2005, the President of the International Monetary Fund (IMF), Rodrigo de Rato, officially proposed the term "global imbalance" to refer to the concept that one country has a substantial trade deficit against a few particular countries.[8] Structural imbalance in global trade has become a tough, global challenge and may create still unknown long-term impacts.

STRUCTURAL ECONOMICS IN CHINA

The imbalance of the global trade structure contributes to the aggravation of imbalances in the global industrial structure and capital structure. Collectively, the changes of the international labor division, comparative advantage, and opportunity cost generate the global industrial staggered transfer, thereby aggravating the "hollowing out" effects of the traditional sunset industries in developed countries as well as the low degree and convergence of the industrial structure in developing countries. Global capital flow involves developed countries transferring capital into developing countries by purchasing equipment and raw materials as well as employing labor for transnational manufacturing, thus bringing huge capital inflow to these labor-intensive industries and providing quick returns and stable revenues. In return, developing countries will normally exert regulations on foreign exchange policies and tend to accumulate large foreign exchange reserves with which to purchase bonds issued by developed countries, thus facilitating capital backflow to the developed countries. Due to the vulnerability of the economic and financial systems in developing countries however, international hot money tends to take advantage of this inflow-backflow process to conduct large-scale speculation, which deteriorates the balances in global capital flow.

The direct consequence of economic structural imbalance is the increasing but still potential risks to global economic development. Based on historical experience, the root of the current economic crisis can be traced back to economic structure imbalance, in developed and developing countries. For example, the real culprit behind Japan's economic stagnation in the 1990s was problems in its economic structure; making the asset price bubble that induced the subsequent depression merely a fuse. Specifically, because the economic structure problems changed the fundamental components of macroeconomics, the problems caused the asset price bubble to burst, which induced massive panic selling of private portfolios and ultimately resulted in a destructive economic crisis. Moreover, in the late 1990s, economic liberalization and internal economic structure adjustments were not synchronized due to the ignorance of economic restructuring hidden in the rapid economic development of Southeast Asia. When the risks spread to the economic operation, foreign capital swiftly fled and the Southeast Asian financial crisis exploded. Since the outbreak of the U.S. subprime crisis in August 2007 and despite the ever-increasing bailout efforts by governments, the crisis has intensified reactively and has developed into a global economic bust. The causes of this subprime crisis are varied but are manifested in the unduly financial innovation and the regulation lag. Generally though, the root cause is still the economic structure imbalance, that is, the financial structure imbalance caused by the over-expansion of virtual financial

An Overview of Structural Economics

assets, the imbalance between investment and consumption structure brought by excessive consumption, and the imbalance of the global economic structure created by the international financial system.

At present, the growing structural imbalance in the global economy is also reflected in the hidden risk of resource depletion and environmental degradation. As early as in 1972, it was proposed in the United Nations Conference on the Human Environment that "there will be a water crisis in the wake of the current oil crisis." The British newspaper *The Independent* reported in 2006 that "half of the world's 500 rivers are severely depleted " and much of the world, in both rural and urban areas, is facing a water shortage crisis.[9] Moreover, with the surge in population and a continuation of (and in some countries an increase in) deforestation, land desertification is intensifying. In addition, industrialization has dramatically increased harmful gas emissions such as sulfur dioxide, resulting in more frequent acid rain and climate change.

Thus, governance of the economic structure and the imbalance therein is of global concern and must be a long-term undertaking, involving not only the macroeconomic variables in industry, investment, consumption, finance, technological progress, institutional innovation, etc., but also external factors such as the resources and the environment. The interaction between the variables produces a complex hierarchical structure, which, coupled with information asymmetry and uncertainty, makes the economic structure imbalance harder to tackle. Therefore, the problem must be analyzed and solved from a theoretical yet practical way.

Requirements for the innovation of economic theory

Theories facilitate the solution of problems. Abundant research and related theoretical achievements on economic structure and problems in the structural economy have been accumulating yet still lag behind the real demands of economic development. Therefore, now is the optimum opportunity to establish structural economics.

Historical foundations of theories on structural economy

Studies on structural economy have gone through three developing phases.[10]

The exploratory phase

From the second half of the 18th century to the first half of the 19th century, classical economists studied structural issues together with economic growth theories. Adam Smith, the British political economist, divided all social work

STRUCTURAL ECONOMICS IN CHINA

into "productive" labor and "unproductive" labor in order to explain the economic growth. He argued that, in addition to the obvious relationship with labor productivity, the improvement of a country's wealth is closely related to the proportions between productive and unproductive labor forces. The summation presumed that national income will increase year on year if productive labor takes up more portions in the annual national income. Thus he advocated an increase in productive labor coupled with a decrease in unproductive labor to increase a country's wealth and income. Moreover, based on the two basic assumptions of a progressive income: a decrease in the agricultural sector and an ever-increasing labor surplus; fellow Briton David Ricardo proposed a two-sector model comprised of the agricultural and manufacturing industries. As economic growth follows the law of diminishing returns, the economy of various departments will eventually stagnate as they develop to a certain level.

The deepening phase

From the 1940s to the 1960s, the "structuralist" school emerged from classical economics, which studied various evolutionary strategies in developing countries via structural analysis. The structuralist analysis employs a dual-structure theory, also known as the Latin American structuralist theory, with reference to the theory of balanced and unbalanced growth. The renowned American economist W. Arthur Lewis designed the analytical framework for the dual economic structure which theorized and specified the problem of rigid structure in developing countries,[11] which became the most influential theory of the structuralism of the development economics. The representative of structuralism, Argentine development economist Raúl Prebisch put forward the structural hypothesis of world economic "center-periphery" pattern to explain the structural imbalance in the world economic order. He argued that the price of industrial products was higher than that of agricultural products due to products of industry having a higher income elasticity of demand, which consequently deteriorates the trading conditions of developing countries and the result of this structural evolution was the strengthened dependence of underdeveloped "peripheral" economies on advanced "central" economies. Therefore, he surmised that developing countries should adopt the strategy of import-substitution industrialization.[12]

Structuralist development economics also conducted in-depth research on the optimization of structure, proposing theories of both balanced and unbalanced growth. The theory of balanced growth advocated a simultaneous

An Overview of Structural Economics

and large-scale investment in all the structural departments of a national economy in order to curb the vicious circle of poverty. American development economist Paul Rosenstein-Rodan was the originator of the Big Push Model theory, which proposed a proportional allocation of investment into various social sectors, thereby transferring an enterprise's external economic efficiency into an internal efficiency of society so as to achieve economic growth and development.[13] Another American, Ragnar Nurkse, extended his vicious circle of poverty concept to demonstrate the necessity of implementing a balanced growth strategy in developing countries. He believed that balanced growth is one way to accelerate development and this can be produced through the multiplier effects of investment.[14] The aspirations of developing countries to pursue balanced growth are called into doubt by some economists due to a general lack of funds with which to conduct comprehensive, large-scale investments. American development economist Albert O. Hirschman put forward the unbalanced development strategy of economic structure in his book *Economic Development Strategy* (1958). He decided that a "correlation effect" prevailed between national economic sectors, meaning an inter-dependent and inter-influential relationship existed among various industries in a national economy. Hirschman's concept included "forward linkage" and "backward linkage" and so, based on the principle "optimization of induced investment," concluded that developing countries should prioritize industries with the largest linkage effect in the industrial structure of their national economy.

The extension phase

After the 1970s, empirical studies into structural transformations made significant progress. The famous Italian economist Luigi L. Pasinetti explicitly defined "structural transformation" as the constitution, proportion, and relationship that constitute the characteristics of the economic system in space and time.[15] While the American economist Hollis B. Chenery defined it as a "change constituted by demand, production, trade and employment which reflects a transfer in the patterns of resources allocation led by the raise of income level."[16] Fellow American Moises Syrquin gave the definition "structural transformation is the relative importance of all the economic sectors, while industrialization is its center process."[17]

Analytical methods used in empirical studies in economic structural transformation also became increasingly enriched and the American economist and statistician Simon Kuznets subsequently divided the national economy into three sectors (agriculture, manufacturing and services) according to differences

STRUCTURAL ECONOMICS IN CHINA

in the demand function and production function. His studies showed that growth in manufacturing outweighed that of the service sector. He also analyzed the structural changes in growth processes in an attempt to show the dynamic transformation process of the economic structure. Chenery implemented Kuznets' idea of structure in his attempt to find the standard structure in the process of economic development, which could then be taken as a basic policy principle in the coordination of economic development in all countries. Chenery, in his book *Patterns of Development, 1950–1970*, proposed a "transformation" concept having discovered that structural changes are accelerated during some economic development phases. In his book *Structuralist Macroeconomics: Applicable Models for the Third World*, Lance Taylor established a mathematical macro-model in structuralism that explained institutional structure and its internal causal connection in macro-theories, which represented the features of functional configuration widespread in developing countries.

Since the 1980s, the computable general equilibrium (CGE) model[18] has been applied to economic structure studies to link industries within various economic sectors, thus exceeding the input-output model and reinterpreting previous structure theories. Since the 1990s, some economists have applied structuralist analysis onto the fully-fledged market economies, creating dynamic structural research, which gradually escalates structure economy studies to quantifiable and elaborate levels. According to the American economist Edmund Phelps, economic structure is affected by investment and consumption as well as other practical factors and may foster a new equilibrium based on the interaction between abundant micro-structural factors.

The dilemma and innovation dynamic of the development of economic structure theory

Classical economics looked for the dynamic to spur economic growth from the perspective of production structure, but it never established a comprehensive analytical framework and after the Marginal Revolution, structural analysis approaches were abandoned by neoclassical economists. Structuralist development economics studies structural problems found on the path of industrialization in underdeveloped countries and thereby severs the organic link between developing and developed countries and makes it difficult to establish a standard theoretical model. Since the 1970s, empirical analyses of economic structural problems have made significant progress and have summarized features of the development of the agricultural, industrial, and service sectors, and proposed the "multi-national standard industrial structure" at different developing phases. But, as elaborate and comprehensive as the research was, no united theory has been formed.

Economic structure theory has not been developed into an independent subject in Western economic circles and this poses two problems. The first is that the theory seriously lags behind practice: new situations and problems arising from society's economic expansion cannot be explained by what the "multi-national standard" implies. The second is that the mainstream status of neoclassical economics has seriously hampered any deepening of the economic structure theory. Neoclassical economics adopts marginal analysis to discover the equilibrium point of the economic operation and wealth accumulation approaches in a balanced market model. The neoclassical school of economics attempted to establish an integrated theory connecting macro- and micro-economics, but this analytical framework overlooked the relationships between resources and the environment and between developed and developing countries as well as any evolution and imbalance in the economic structure. This new era calls for the establishment of an independent discipline: a discipline of structural economics which integrates the entire economic structure with the ability to analyze and solve current structural contradictions.

After the 1990s, Western scholars began to break the ceiling of the development economics. Some researchers absorbed factors such as technology and the environment into the analysis of economic structure, thereby creating this so-called "structural economics." In her 1998 book on structural economics, Faye Duchin[19] established a basic economic analysis framework and demonstrated how to use it to analyze technology, lifestyle, and environmental issues. Thijs ten Raa[20] aimed to combine the finances and structure of an economic entity, thereby integrating the budget with economic analysis and applying national accounts to the economic model via an input-output analysis.

The Research Framework of Structural Economics

As a direct descendant of modern economics, structural economics aims at sustainable economic development. It has specific research objectives and methodologies and is formed around a relatively independent theoretical framework.

Research objective

At present, the world economy is in major transition: from unsustainable development to sustainable development, the latter being the objective of structural economics.

STRUCTURAL ECONOMICS IN CHINA

Sustainable development is the basic objective of structural economics

Since the 1960s, people started seeking new development modes. The famous British historian Arnold Toynbee stated that the decline or extinction of human civilizations is directly or indirectly related to disharmony between man and nature, with the destructive use of resources due to the population explosion, land reclamation and excessive deforestation cited as the main sources of disharmony.[21] The concept of sustainable development was formally proposed by the United Nations Environment Program (UNEP) as "the coordinated development of the economy, society and environment, [and] refers to development that meets contemporary needs without endangering future generations."[22] This concept defines, in theory, the interrelation between economic development and environmental protection. Individuals, especially those living in less-developed countries, should set limits as to the use of resources when pursuing economic growth. Sustainable development relates to fundamental changes in production mode, lifestyle and values, which have included ecological sustainability, economic sustainability, and social sustainability. Ecological sustainability is the prerequisite, economic sustainability is the basis, and social sustainability is the goal. The core idea is sound economic development should be based on ecological sustainability, social justice, and individuals' active participation in their own decision-making processes. Thus, in a broad sense, sustainable development is the study of achieving coordinated relations between mankind, between man and resources, and man and nature. These relations form the research method and objective of structural economics.

Three-dimensional balance represents the sustainable development

The aforementioned sustainable development defines the relationship between the economy, society and the resource environment. These are the three constituent dimensions of sustainable development in which economic growth, the income gap and environmental pollution are measured, as shown in Fig. 1.1.

In the horizontal dimension, with the X-axis (economic growth) as the independent variable and the Z-axis (social income distribution gap) as the dependent variable; as the average income rises, the social income distribution gap shows an inverted U-curve, as is shown in *OCA* plane (Curve 1). Taking the X-axis (economic growth) as the independent variable and the Y-axis (environmental pollution) as the dependent variable, it is demonstrated that economic development contributes to a rise in average income and the subsequent change in environmental pollution will manifest in an inverted

U-curve, as is shown in *OBA* plane (Curve 2). In the three-dimensional area of the *X, Y* and *Z* axes, the social income distribution gap and environmental pollution are indirectly determined by Curve 1 and Curve 2, so the relationship between the economy, society and the resource environment should remain contained within a three-dimensional space formed by Curve 1 and Curve 2. If variations in the relationship exceed the tolerance of the system, it will cause a significant risk to future development. Furthermore, the three-dimensional balance refers to the co-adaptation and mutual promotion of the economy, society and the resource environment and this is arguably the concrete manifestation of sustainable development.

Fig. 1.1.   Illustration of the relationship between the economy, society and the environment

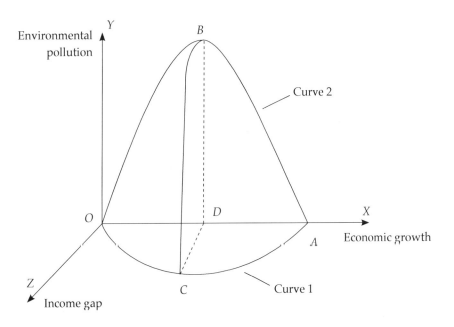

First, the economy, society and the resource environment are interdependent, and they collectively form a co-existing system for man's survival and development. They are mutually endogenous variables or constrained variables. The economic development of this co-existing system is one aim, but economic development cannot exceed the maximum capacity of the resource environment

STRUCTURAL ECONOMICS IN CHINA

and so the distribution of economic achievements should be fair and efficient. Second, the internal structure of the economy, society and the resource environment as a whole should be mutually adaptive. The economic structure is constantly evolving and the upgrading of the economic structure will promote the transformation of the social structure, and consequently spur strong demands on the resource environment. In other words, sustainable development is a complex objective function, and only when all the three dimensions are optimized can the objective function be achieved. Third, the economy, society and the resource environment are mutually reinforcing and form a dynamic balance. For the same reason that knowledge and technology are cumulative, development between individuals and groups is competitive. This competition contributes to a continuous improvement in productivity, which will promote the reform of production relations, which will positively promote the development of the productivity. On the other hand, economic development will comprehensively promote resource conservation and environmental improvement and the changes in the methods of resource consumption and environmental protection awareness will facilitate the restructuring of the productivity structure, thus promoting economic restructuring and economic growth. Therefore, based on the fundamental interests and inter-generational equity, the three-dimensional balance must constantly promote the co-adaptation and mutual promotion between people and society, as well as man and nature, and consequently achieve a harmonious, dynamic and balanced system for sustainable development.

The three-dimensional balance system is a dynamically open system and is also the result of checks and balances between various forces, which can be divided into two basic types. The first is a positive force that enhances sustainable development and the second, is a negative force that hinders such development. Positive forces include technological progress, institutional innovation, new resources or energies, and environmental protection measurements while negative forces include the shortage of resources, environmental degradation, and the ever-increasing income distribution gap. Positive and negative forces continuously impact and act on the three-dimensional balance system. If the positive forces prevail, then the three-dimensional balance is consolidated but otherwise, an imbalance may be created which risks systematic chaos. In the modern three-dimensional balance system, economic risks are often represented as financial risks. Finance is the core of the economy and is also its most vulnerable component. The current international financial crisis is the embodiment of an economic development imbalance; social risk is often manifested in the huge income gap that eventually exceeds the level of social tolerance and thus may trigger a social crisis; the risk to the resource environment is generally expressed as resource bottlenecks and environmental degradation. Natural resources and the environment are in essence the basis for the survival and development of human beings but our natural resources are mostly non-renewable and the deterioration of the ecological environment is often difficult to repair. "As scientific observations show, with the large-scale use of fossil fuels following the industrial revolution, the atmospheric concentration of carbon dioxide and other greenhouse gases continues to rise. This is a major cause to global warming, which involves glaciers retreating, sea levels rising, and the increase of extreme weather events, all of which produce a severe threat to the human survival."[23] Therefore it can be concluded that the risks to the three-dimensional balance system includes financial risks, the polarization of rich and poor, resource bottlenecks, and environmental degradation.

From the perspective of sustainable development, there are two basic mechanisms in the economic operation, namely the dynamic and the balancing. The dynamic mechanism is the basis for the sustainable economic growth. Without positive dynamics, economic development would suffer stagnation, or even regression. However, if these dynamics are out of balance, greater destruction will be created as the dynamic grow recklessly. In China's contemporary history, the "Great Leap Forward" (*da yue jin*) that led to economic and social chaos teaches a valuable lesson in engaging those two complementary mechanisms. Without a rational balancing mechanism, the effects of the dynamic mechanism could be reversed and curb the onward march of society, which undermines sustainable development. Therefore, in this modern economic climate, the three-dimensional balance principle should be adopted resolutely and employed constantly in the formulation of sustainable development strategies.

Research content

Research subjects of structural economics

The research subjects in structural economics are the structural phenomena of the economic system and their regularities, including the following three levels.

Regularity of the evolution of economic structure

Regularity of the economic structure evolution is the most basic research content of structural economics. The evolution of the modern economic structure consists of two basic dimensions: one dimension is the evolution of the social reproduction circulation structure, which takes the evolution

STRUCTURAL ECONOMICS IN CHINA

of industrial structure as its core. It includes the four basic links, namely production, circulation, distribution and consumption. The production structure is determined by the investment structure, and constrained by the industrial structure. Economic behaviors such as saving, consumption and investment are developed in the process of product circulation and value distribution. Besides, these behaviors determine two basic economic structures, namely the investment consumption structure and the financial structure, which also involve the contradiction and unity between the real economy and the fictitious economy. The other dimension is the spatial structure of social reproduction, which consists of two levels: the first level is the inter-regional urban-rural economic structure; the second level is the international economic structure, namely the economic connections and the structurally proportional relations forged by investment, trade and other economic activities between countries or regions, mainly manifesting in the structural relations of the international balance of payments. Spatial structure, which reflects the centralized or scattered trend of socio-economic space, is the regional combination of human economic activities, and an important complementation to the modern economic structure. Generally, the main contents of the modern economic structure can be summarized in the investment consumption structure, the industrial structure, the financial structure, the regional economic structure, and the structure of the international balance of payments. The research objective of structural economics is to study the regularities of evolution in different economic structures, and their internal relations.

Relationship between evolution of economic structure and economic growth

Relationship between the economic structure evolution and economic growth are the second level of structural economics studies. The evolution of economic structure will alter resource allocations, thus affecting economic growth. The driving force behind economic growth comes from production factors, including labor, capital, technology, and management, which are also the basis for social reproduction. Social reproduction refers to processes in which various labor forces use physical capital to produce innovative activities, material products and services. These processes reflect economic growth and wealth accumulation, and are influenced by technological and institutional innovations and external factors. However, when the economic structural imbalance emerges, economic growth, social equity, the ecological environment, and other aspects will be affected and damaged over time. Therefore, the key to studying structural economics is to analyze the mechanism and underlying causes of the economic structural imbalance and discuss appropriate adjustment and correction mechanisms.

An Overview of Structural Economics

Relationship between evolution of economic structure and the sustainable development

The internal relationship between economic structure evolution, the resource environment, and the social system is the underlying content of structural economics. Resource structure involves the intrinsic link between the basic elements, including land, climate, mineral products, and energies. Environmental structure refers to the allocation relationship between these various environmental elements. The structure and interrelation between the environmental elements function as a constraint on environmental material exchanges and energy flows. The use and input of energy and land resources constitute the basic elements of the production process, and environment provides the space and conditions essential for economic activities. The relation between the resource environment and the economic structure is so complicated that structural economics needs to analyze these internal connections; connections such as the impact of economic structure evolution on the environment and the constraint put on the economic structure adjustment by the resource environment. In addition, the evolution of structural economics will have significant impact on the social structure; and in particular changes in the income distribution and the regional economic structures, which will affect social stability and interest patterns of all social classes. And, resource and environmental issues will also cause social problems. Therefore, the study of the relationship between the economic structural system, the resource environment and the social system are important academic basis to the structural economics.

The logical framework of this book

This book aims to create a theoretical system for the structural economics and takes the evolution, imbalance, and strategic adjustment of China's economic structure as the specific subject for empirical research. Therefore, this book will systematically expound the evolution of China's economic structure in the 30 years since the reform and opening-up. It will also measure the degree of the imbalance of China's economic structure, and finally will propose strategies for adjustment.

Fig.1.2 denotes that technological progress and institutional innovation are the basic driving forces behind the evolution of economic structure. The two innovative variables and traditional production factors (labor, physical capital, natural resources, etc.) constitute the basic elements of modern economic growth. Economic growth and restructuring are interdependent and interrelated. According to the classification of economic structural evolution in this book, modern economic adjustment involves five main areas: the investment consumption structure, the industrial structure, the financial structure, the regional economic structure and the international balance of payments structure. In the course of economic structural evolution, the economic structure will evolve from non-equilibrium to imbalance, and bring potential risks to the economic, social, and resource environment systems. Therefore, the core content of this book is to survey into the evolution and imbalance of the economic structure. This study on evolution and imbalance in the economic structural system aims to analyze the sustainability of economic development and propose relevant adjustment strategies.

Fig. 1.2.   The logical framework

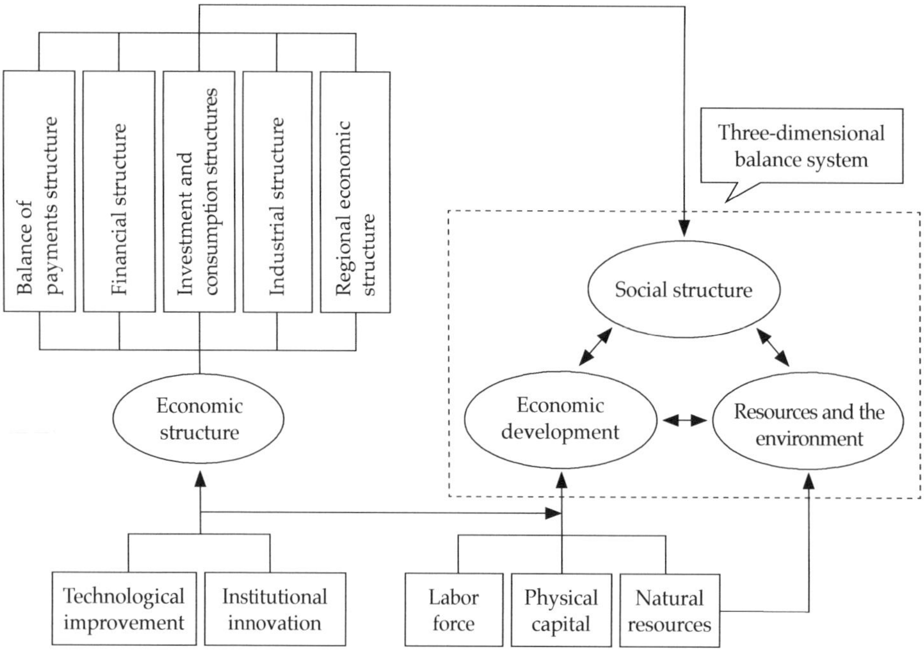

Research methodologies

Structural economics has developed from prior structural economic theories, institutional economics, environmental and resource economics, sustainable development economics, etc., and its research methodologies are integrated with the methodologies of the above disciplines. In line with the research objective, the main research methodologies of structural economics can be summarized as follows.

Statistical analysis

Statistical analysis is the basic tool for studying structural economics. It is classified into two sub-categories. First, studying the composition proportions and variation features of the economic structures via analyzing the statistical indicators; second, studying the quantitative features of interdependence and the mutual impact between economic structures by means of the input-output method, the social accounting matrix (SAM), and other specialized methods.

The indicators employed to study the composition and variations of the structures include the structural indicators, strength indicators, proportional indicators, and dynamic indicators, etc. Structural indicators reflect the proportional relationship between various constituent components; strength indicators reflect the proportional relationship between two different but intrinsically linked indicators; proportional indicators reflect the quantitative proportion between two indicators; and dynamic indicators reflect the developing speed and trends of all indicators. In the study of structural relationships, the average index and variation index can also be used to manifest the quantitative characters of various parts of the structure and the rules of structural variations.

The input-output method and the SAM are specific for structural analysis. The input-output method is a quantitative analysis of input-output interdependence and variation features between various components of the economic system. The core content for input-output structure analysis focuses on technological and economic ties via consumption coefficients between products and industries or between industries, which thereby evaluates the rationality of economic structures.

SAM[24] is the matrix form of the national accounting system, and it can be seen as a matrix expression of transactions in the socio-economic system. Based on the input-output table, SAM completely expresses the processes of production, income, consumption, and capital accumulation in different entities in the form of the symmetric matrix, and it aims to reflect internal relations and structural relations in the socio-economic system. SAM aims to examine the structural relations in the economic system from different perspectives in terms of elements, households, institutions, etc., and, at the same time, provides the foundation for evaluations such as growth and income distribution.

Institutional analysis

Institutional analysis is the application of institutional economics in the analysis of structural economics. Institutional economics can be classified in its old and new versions. The original institutional economics studies institutional problems in economics using philosophical and sociological methods; neo-institutional economics[25] is marked by the transaction-cost paradigm and has close theoretical connections with original institutional economics, neoclassical economics and Marxist economics. With the assistance of the neoclassical analysis system, neo-institutional economics achieves a qualitative leap and initiates a number of sub-branches. Both versions of institutional economics have recognized the institution's dominant role in economic operation and advocated to improve social and economic welfare, as well as improving the institution itself to achieve greater efficiency in the allocation of resources.

Institutional analysis is also an important research methodology for structural economics. The institution plays an indispensable role in the process of the transformation of economic structures. Institutional analysis emphasizes the importance of institutional constraints in the behaviors of individuals and the whole society during structural transformation. More generally, structural economics regards the institution as an important endogenous variable in the transformation of economic structures. It covers two aspects: first, analyzing the contribution of institutional innovation to the economic structure transformation and economic growth; and second, analyzing the internal mechanism between institutional innovation and the evolution of economic structure. In structural economics, institutional factors mainly refer to factors within economic institutions, including the institutions of property rights, finance, taxes and subsidies, etc. In addition, institutional factors also include political, social, demographic, cultural, and environmental aspects.

In neo-institutional economics, institutional analysis methodology includes the analysis of evolution and behavior. Evolution analysis argues that the evolution of the human social system, as with other biological evolutions, reflects a historical development process. Institutions evolve when the foundation and the environment that they rely upon, change, or, alternatively, when transaction costs change. Behavior analysis places an emphasis on studying the behavior of economic agents. According to neo-institutional economics, the rational choice for economic agents and the 'game'[26] played via their different economic interests are the root causes for changing transaction costs and promoting institutional changes. These methods and ideas that characterize neo-institutional economics provide the analyses of structural evolution and the unbalanced situation from a very valuable methodological basis.

An Overview of Structural Economics

Game analysis

The evolutionary process of the economic structure is essentially a game of interests between economic agents; thus, the game analysis has broad prospects of application in the analysis of structural economics. The long-term cooperation discussed in *Game Theory* has the most profound influence and impact on changes and transformations of the entire economic structure. For instance, farmers may cooperate and manage certain common resources (such as pasture and water). In economic and social life, many interactions are long term and some are even indefinite in length; when a competitive enterprise makes a decision about production and price, it must take into consideration the past behaviors of its competitors. This long-term, cyclical interaction inevitably changes the economic structure, and thereby exerts significant influence on its transformation.

Various stages of the economic game are interdependent, and this causes the decision-making process of a rational game player to be influenced by both past experience and future uncertainties. Patterns of behaviors, such as reward, punishment, and the transmission or leakage of information, can be seen as a multi-stage, dynamic game and the analysis of this multi-stage; dynamic game as played by economic entities can then be used to analyze and explain economic behaviors and phenomena, which in turn alters the economic structure.

In addition, the economic evolutionary game theory (EGT), developed on the basis of the biological EGT, studies 1) the balance of strategies and behaviors within human economic activities, and 2) the process of adjustment and convergence to a state of balance. Therefore, the evolution of the economic structure can also be regarded as a kind of "adaptive evolution" to some extent.

Econometric model

With the continuous development of econometric technology, econometric models are increasingly used in the structural analysis of the economic system. Econometric models, as the name suggests, are equations of the quantitative relationship between economic phenomena and their main factors. According to the quantity of equations, econometric models can be divided into the single equation model and the simultaneous equation model. The single-equation econometric model aims to study the relationships between economic phenomena in the form of an equation. It is widely used to analyze the intrinsic relationship between economic structure and economic growth and between the environment and living standards, etc. However, many structural economic theories are based on a set of economic relations, and hence many equations are required to describe the relationship among variables. In this case we may use

STRUCTURAL ECONOMICS IN CHINA

the simultaneous equation model. The simultaneous equation model is used to study the relationship between various structural variables within the complex structure of economic relations. It may be applied to verify and develop economic theories and also for analysis, forecasting, and decision-making. At present, the CGE model within simultaneous equations has a broad application in structural research. The CGE is based on the input-output model, it is boosted when the price regulating mechanism is added and becomes deformed when it is integrated into the rigid structure. On a technological level, the CGE model, with nonlinear equations and endogenous prices added to the input-output model, overcomes the deficiency of the econometric model, which is limited to the macroeconomic aggregate, and offsets disadvantages of the input-output model, which places too much emphasis on structural rigidity. In addition, this model to some degree introduces the assumption of rational agents as well as the production and demand functions in neoclassical theory, and includes the price mechanism as a variable for balanced adjustment. It analyzes the industrial linking structure in the market mechanism to provide a strategic guide for the transformation of industrial structures.

The Application of Structural Economics

The theoretical innovation in structural economics needs to systematically summarize the basic features of the evolution of the global economic structure and abstract them into the basic theory. As a developing country in which structural problems are relatively prominent, China urgently needs to establish structural economics. Therefore, China should accomplish something in this field and make its own contribution; although, conversely, the best application of structural economics is to analyze and research the existing problems in the China's economic structure and then propose solutions to these problems from the disciplinary perspective. And at the same time, however, China should analyze, and amend related theories when required, which cumulatively will benefit the enrichment, development of the theories in structural economics.

Problem orientation

Since the 1990s, Chinese economic growth has been driving in the fast lane but the structural imbalance is growing due to factors that include the economic development mode and economic reform. Premier Wen Jiabao has made it clear that huge structural problems still dampens a healthy growth of China's economy. China's economic structural imbalance is primarily represented in

An Overview of Structural Economics

an uncoordinated industrial structure, a below-par proportion in the added value of tertiary industry, an irrational investment consumption structure, a high investment rate—but slow growth in the consumption level, a skewed international balance of payments, overheated credit expansion, excessive monetary circulation, unbalanced inter-regional, urban and rural economic development, an ever-widening income gap, an underdeveloped social security system and low living standards, and, finally, high energy and resource consumption and environmental pressures. As Premier Wen Jiabao pointed out, "the condition of long-term high input, high consumption, high pollution and low output and low efficiency has not fundamentally changed; and China's major pollutants, including the demand for chemical oxygen and sulfur dioxide emissions, rank high in the world. If these problems are not tackled, economic development cannot be sustainable."[27]

The IMF supports the global trade imbalance plan. It aims to shrink the trade surplus in other economies in order to balance the U.S. deficit,[28] in which China is the most important target. Biased and unfair as it may be, it does show that China's economic structure imbalance has escalated into an international concern. Therefore, it is urgently necessary to strengthen research on the imbalances in the process of economic structural evolution for it is directly related to the sustainable development of China's economy and long-term social stability.

Application value

Structural economics has a wide range of applications in China, mainly employed in two aspects, solving practical economic problems and generating theoretical innovations:

First, structural economics is of important theoretical significance for the solution of China's current economic structure imbalance. It is possible to systematically analyze and solve the current structural imbalance within the process of current economic operation. Since reform and opening up, China has achieved remarkable, sustainable, and rapid economic growth. However, the entry into WTO brought about the structural imbalances. At present, many areas in China feature different structural imbalances. For example, imbalances in the investment consumption structure, the regional economic structure, and the international balance of payments structure are growing and are in need of urgent treatment. It is important to grasp the evolutionary regularity of China's economic structure so as to solve structural imbalances and make the economy develop in a sustainable and healthy manner. The fundamental way to tackle economic structure imbalances is to transform the economic growth

STRUCTURAL ECONOMICS IN CHINA

pattern from the extensive mode to the intensive one, which requires to change the mechanism of macroeconomic policies and policy implementation from the combination of aggregate and structural policies to the coordination of monetary and fiscal policies, from the interface of demand management and supply management to the active cooperation between the central and the local governments, and from the integration of macro-policy and micro-policy within domestic policy and the international balance of payments. Realizing all these transformations requires a systematic and comprehensive adjustment to the current economic structure based on theoretical guidance from structural economics. Besides, China's economic structure imbalance can also be solved purely on the basis of structural economics. Learning from previous international solutions to economic structure imbalances, the path-selection and implementation intensity of solutions will be determined by the degree of the imbalance. For nations that have serious structural imbalances that will inevitably lead to economic crisis, the solutions must be highly targeted in order to re-balance the structure to within the bearable range for sustainable development. Correspondingly, for those who have been trapped by some moderate structural imbalances that will not substantially damage the economic growth, self-adjustment should be achieved by applying the market mechanism.

Second, structural economics is part-and-parcel of improving research on economics and establishing a theoretical system for China's economic circle. On one hand, structural economics can rationally and systematically explain China's non-equilibrium economic growth. There is no theory to systematically and comprehensively interpret the reason for economic growth up to now. China's reform and opening up is gradual and during this process, there must be continuous adjustment of the accompanying economic structure. Evolution of the economic structure, is the crucial aspect of structural economics, is also a major motivation for China's economic growth. On the other hand, structural economics can contribute to the development of China's economic theories. It is one of the important tasks in economics circles to systematically research China's structure imbalance from a theoretical perspective. Currently, theoretical research on structural imbalance does exist but they remain unsystematic and sporadic. For example, research into the skewed international balance of payments needs to link with related theoretical research, including investment consumption structure, industrial structure, and financial structure, to form a set of theoretical systems. And on the basis of this system, policies for the solution of the imbalance can be more targeted and effective.

Finally, structural economics can offer a set of theoretical approaches to measure the degree of China's economic structure imbalance from a systematic perspective. Using the theory of structural economics, judgments of the degree of the imbalance can be made in the five structural areas: current investment and consumption, the industrial structure, financial structure, regional economic structure, and the international balance of payments. This enables us to see the annual variation magnitude of the imbalance in economic structure.

Guiding principles

Structural economics not only meets the urgent need for both theoretical and practical development, but also systemizes and methodizes the structuralist theory. It requires both the previous studies inherited from its predecessors and the need for more, bold innovation. From the point of view of the elements for scientific construction, the use of structural economics should follow these three guiding principles:

Marxist way of thinking

Marxist Dialectical Materialism and Historical Materialism are the common property of mankind and provide us with a psychology in the observation of the movement, change and regulation of things. The creation of structural economics is facilitated by employing the Marxist way of thinking. Unlike quantitative change, structural change is in the very nature of things, with self-improvement and negation as processes in structure transformation. Marxism emphasizes starting in reality and looking at new things with an eye for development. The structure of economics is new and it should develop alongside the development of the objective economic and social situation. At the same time, the interests and systems analysis of Marxist Economics emphasize the distribution of income and value the process of social reproduction, in such a way that the fundamental contradictions of the capitalist system are revealed. Changes in economic structure involve the interests and system adjustment of all aspects. Therefore if we ignore or avoid these fundamental contradictions, future problems will be more complicated rather than solved.

Theoretical innovation

Structural economics is not generated from naught. Its generation has close links with classical economics, development economics, institutional economics, and sustainable development. It does not piece together existing economics but creates a new discipline from inheriting, mining and criticizing previous ones and the innovation of a theory is a difficult process. First, it needs to standardize the structure and scope of the basic concepts of economics, which is the foundation of establishing a new discipline. Second, it must determine

STRUCTURAL ECONOMICS IN CHINA

theoretical assumptions and the assumptions within structural and neoclassical economics are different. For example, neoclassical economics holds the view that the main feature of economy is the constantly changing equilibrium price while structural economics believes, from a more practical perspective, that structure changes in a non-continuous way. Third, it is asked to construct core theories. Structural economics, in general, needs to answer two core questions: first, how does economic structure evolve and how does it continue to evolve? And second, why does imbalance occur in the process of economic structure evolution and how can this imbalance be corrected? Therefore, the two basic theories required for the establishment of structural economics are structure evolution theory and structure imbalance theory.

A global vision

Structural theory studies should not involve only developing countries. The economic structure problems in both developed and developing countries must be studied collectively, so the scope of structural economics will exceed that of development economics. The economic structure consists of two dimensions: one is the horizontal spatial structure, including a regional structure, the international structure, and urban and rural structure; the other the vertical production value chain with the industrial structure as core, this mainly refers to the investment and consumption structure, industrial structure and financial structure. The distribution structure and the circulation structure are reflected in both the horizontal and vertical economic structures. Influenced by the imbalanced development of different countries, global economic circulation often deviates significantly from normal in the long run, which leads to economic structural imbalance and complex economic relationships between different countries. Therefore, the creation of structural economics in the open economy cannot be limited to national or local interests, but must take into full account the mutual development and prosperity of all mankind and the common interests of both developed and developing countries in promoting the establishment of a reasonable and fair global economic and political order.

Chapter 2

The Theory of the Evolution of Economic Structure

STRUCTURAL ECONOMICS IN CHINA

The evolution of economic structure is a huge and complex dynamic process with its own law of evolution. The evolutionary theory of economic structure is an important theoretical foundation for structural economics and also one of its core components. The dynamic and the transmission mechanisms of the evolution of economic structure are systematically elaborated in this chapter, as based on existent research findings from development economics, institutional economics, innovative economics, and evolutionary economics, as well as other relevant disciplines.

Characteristics and Factors Affecting the Evolution of Economic Structure

With the increasing levels of social productive forces, economic structure is constantly evolving in accordance with certain rules. Thus, the evolution of economic structure has its own inherent logical stipulation, and that logical stipulation is related to the characteristics of economic development at different stages. This section focuses on the definition, features, and affecting factors of the evolution of economic structure.

What is the evolution of economic structure?

With ongoing social development, the internal relationship of the economic system becomes more and more complex and the behavior of various economic entities become more complicated, which results in many economic phenomena and decision-making behaviors not being reasonably explained within the framework of traditional economic theories. Evolutionary economics is a new discipline that has adapted to the needs evolving modern economics. Evolution, biologically speaking, is the process in which living beings develop gradually from low to high, from simple to complex, from few to many.[1] Therefore, evolutionary economics emphasizes the role of conventions, innovations, and imitations in the economic evolutionary process, and makes a comprehensive explanation of economic change and structural transformation.[2]

Change in economic structure is an evolutionary process reflecting the mutual adaptation between production relations and productivity. The so-called evolution of economic structure is a dynamic process, in which and under the influence of the technological progress and institutional innovation, etc., the economic structure of a country or a region transforms constantly from lower to higher while various internal elements grow constantly in terms of coordination and adaptability. It involves three aspects. First, with the improvement of productivity, evolution demonstrates a vertical escalation of economic structure. Second, from a long-term perspective, evolution is always a process of transformation from the uncoordinated to the coordinated, reflecting the coordination of the horizontal relationship of economic structure. Third, the evolution of economic structure in different countries or regions is open and inclusive, and there are differences in the course of development.

Characteristics

According to the rules of the social development, the evolution of economic structure generally features the path dependence, self-adjustment, non-continuity, and co-evolution.

Path dependence

Evolution, as a process, is essentially irreversible, one-way, unrepeatable, and thus it determines the path dependent feature of the evolution of economic structure. The concept of path dependence was initially put forward in the 1980s by American economists Paul David and Brian Arthur and was creatively applied to economic theories by the eminent fellow American and economist Douglass North. It refers to an institution which, once formed, whether effective or not, will continue to exist in a given period and wield an influence on the future selection of institutions, in that following a particular path, "previous choice-making determines current possible choices."[3] The evolution of economic structure can be interpreted as a complex process of transformation, which means the evolution of economic structure, once on a particular path, will show characteristics of coherence and interdependence, and this set direction will self-reinforce in future development.

Thus, the evolution of economic structure features self-reinforcing path dependence. This means that, in accordance with the established development path, the evolution of economic structure may shift to a coordinated track and promote economic and social development; or conversely, may be deteriorating along an unbalanced path towards economic stagnation and perhaps even economic and social crisis.

Self-adjustment

Self-adjustment of the evolution of economic structure is primarily manifested in the fact that numerous scattered individual economic activities integrate into

STRUCTURAL ECONOMICS IN CHINA

a unit of social economic activities.[4] With strong adaptability to the external environment, the system of economic structure operates as an organic whole. Households, businesses, governments, and other entities are engaged within it and experience mutual interaction, restraint and development under certain rules. It also has a great adaptability to the external environment, wherein a variety of mechanisms regulate, with different forces, the behavior of economic agents and contribute to strong self-adjustment within the economic structure. Of course, because this self-adjustment has boundaries, adjustment and transformation of the economic structure remains limited.

Non-continuity

The evolution of economic structure has distinctive differences from the change of economic aggregates. One fundamental difference is that the former is non-continuous, whereas the latter is continuous. The so-called non-continuity of the evolution of economic structure means that when a number of factors in the economic structure reach a certain critical level, the structure shifts to a new, steady state; however, when the evolution of economic structure is confined in an inefficient or unbalanced state, a number of external forces are needed to reverse the direction of evolution, and evolution at this time is no longer a gradual, smooth process of change, but sees a non-continuous and mutational leap.

Co-evolution

The word "co-evolution" is derived from biological theories. Biological studies have shown that individual creatures are part of the ecological environment, so biological individuals with mutual interaction feature "co-evolution." When one species evolves, it may pressure other species, thus causing those or other species to adapt and eventually leading to a series of changes in related species. Therefore, biological evolution does not occur unaccompanied or unaided, but is conducted on a basis of mutual influence between the environment and its dwellers.[5]

The evolution of the economic structure works the same way. In an open economic system, its various sub-systems are interrelated and interactive. When a subsystem evolves along a rational path, it will promote the efficiency and structural optimization of other subsystems, thus provoking a coordinated development of the entire economic system. Conversely, when a subsystem is disharmonious or unbalanced, it will prevent other subsystems from working as usual, thereby constraining the normal operation of the economic structural system.

Factors affecting the evolution of economic structure

As a complex open system, the economic structure has many factors affecting its evolution. Among them, technological progress and institutional innovation are the most fundamental and play a decisive role in its advancement and coordination. Technological progress improves the efficiency of factors of production, which causes the industrial structure to upgrade and the output boundary of the economic system to change; system innovation is represented as changes in terms of the allocation and incentive mechanism of production factors and the improvement of the flexibility and coordination of the economic structure, thereby causing the output boundary of the economic system shift in the optimal direction. Additionally, since industrialization, the relationship between the economic system and its external systems, particularly that of resource and environment, has been drawing closer. With the rapid economic growth, resource profligacy and environmental pollution are getting increasingly serious and the resource environment has gradually become an important external constraint on the evolution of economic structure.

Technological progress—the fundamental driving force

The evolution of economic structure is constrained by the development of productive forces. Technical progress, the core element of the productivity system, turns out to be the fundamental driving force in the promotion of the evolution of economic structure to a more rational optimization. Technological progress has the most direct impact on changes in industrial structure and exerts indirect influences on changes in other economic structures. In general, impacts placed by technological progress on the evolution of industrial structure are elaborated in the following three levels.

First, technological progress determines the rise and upgrade of industries. From the perspective of the history of industrial development, technological progress is the decisive force in the rise and development of industrial sectors. This is mainly reflected in the following: first, technological advances have created new products and industries, resulting in the continuous emergence of new industries; second, technological advances reduce production costs and increase productivity by improving existing industrial production processes and thereby expanding the industrial scale while boosting quality; third, technological advances expand the scope of available resources, import more resources into production, and increase the supply of resources, thereby introducing the possibility of resource transfer between industries; and lastly, technological advances expand the entire industrial chain; that is, when a department improves its production techniques, its downstream production departments will change their own demands as a direct result of changes in supply, and also stimulate structural changes in the production techniques of upstream sectors, that lead to changes both in the structure of supply and of demand, resulting in the upgrade of the entire economic structure.

Second, technological progress determines the orderly evolution of industries. Technological progress not only determines the rise and upgrade of industries, but also orderly industrial changes. According to their developing status, industrial sectors can be divided into three categories: low-growth industries, high-growth industries and potential high-growth industries, and the development and alterations of those three types determine industrial development and the shifts in focus. With the shift in focus of technological innovation, some high-growth industries slow down their expansion, which leads to a decline of their share in the economy and they will consequently being replaced by the potential high-growth industries. Any and every round of technological innovation inspires and establishes new potential high-growth industries, and a developing system of orderly change will be formed in such a cycle. Therefore, technological progress has an inherent regularity and the evolution of related industrial structures features orderly change accordingly.

Third, technological progress determines the direction of the evolution of economic structure. At a particular stage, clusters of technological innovations have polarization effects,[6] enabling those fast-growing industries to attract and stimulate the development of other industries, resulting in a country or region having multiple high-growth industrial sectors. Affected by market demand and the rate of return, some high-growth industries can only support economic growth in a specific period and therefore do not necessarily bring about the advancement of industrial structures. Only innovation-oriented industries, which accumulate rapidly within a particular sector and have strong diffusion effects, are able to become leading or key industries. And these key industries play a guiding role in economic development and the evolution of industrial structure, thus determining the evolutionary direction of economic structure.

Institutional innovation—a necessary approach

Development of productivity requires the proper adjustment of production relations, which is often achieved through institutional innovation. At the same time, institutional innovation is the "lubricant" for the adjustment and optimization of the economic structure and can stimulate or accelerate the process of its evolution. This is manifested in the following three aspects.

First, institutional innovation can provide an effective incentive mechanism for the evolution of economic structure. Each institution has its specific functions and values. Institutional innovation can create an effective incentive mechanism for economic entities, and accordingly promote economic growth and structural upgrades. The continuous optimization of the incentive structure can provoke constant human innovation and therefore continuously improve productivity. Institutional innovation, scientific and technological innovation, and theoretical innovation are interlinked and mutually constraining, thus constituting as a unit an important driving force for social development.

Second, effective institutional innovation can provide institutional basis and guarantee the adjustment and optimization of the economic structure. Institution is comprised of formal and non-formal constraints, aiming to create transaction order and to reduce uncertainties, thereby cutting transaction costs. Technical progress serves only as a potential source of modern economic growth. To make technology effectively and widely applied, there must also be institutional adjustment and innovation. If there is no supporting institutional innovation, it will be impossible to optimize the economic structure and technological progress will lose power or even stagnate.

Third, institutional innovation can offer an entry-exit mechanism of industrial alternation. Change in industrial structures is achieved by altering dominant industries. Through institutional innovation, industries can create appropriate access-withdrawal barriers that provide incentives and constraints for the access and withdrawal of market entities. This promotes a survival of the fittest theory among market entities and creates a competitive and dynamic market environment. Thus, institutional innovation can improve the efficiency of resource allocation, so that production factors are able to flow into those departments which yield more efficient output, guiding the alteration of old and new industries and thereby promoting the optimization and upgrade of industrial structures.

The Functional Mechanism of Technological Progress on the Evolution of Economic Structure

Technological progress directly promotes the optimization and upgrade of industrial structure and thus instigates an upgrade in economic structure and the co-evolution of the economic structure system. By elaborating on theories of technological progress, this section focuses on the theoretical model and the transmission path by which technological progress impacts on the evolution of economic structure and explains the functional mechanism of technological progress on the evolution of economic structure.

What is technological progress?

A definition

Technological progress can be interpreted from many perspectives. Currently, the popular view in the academic community and definition by the Organization for Economic Cooperation and Development (OECD) in their *Science, Technology Policy Outlook (1988)*, sees technological progress as "an integrated process consisting of three overlapping and interacting factors. The first element is the invention of new or improved technology in the realm of scientific research; the second is innovation, meaning the first commercial application of the invention; and the third element is diffusion, which refers to the widespread use of innovation."[7]

In the process of technological progress, technological innovation is crucial. This is because if science and technology want to become the main driving force in economic development, then it has to be transformed from an ideological form to a material form and from potential productivity to practical productivity and this transformation is achieved via technological innovation. From the perspective of the development of economic theory, the first person to propose the concept of this innovation and apply it to economic analysis is the Austrian-American economist Joseph Schumpeter. He believed that innovation was the transformation of a production function that creates a new combination of productive factors and conditions that never before existed in the production system. The new combination involves five aspects: the production of new products, the introduction of new production processes, the entry into a new markets, the control of the sources and supply of raw materials, and the establishment of a new organization.[8] The initial pair of aspects belongs to technological-based innovation and constitutes the main thrust of Schumpeter's innovation theory; while the latter three aspects are more dependent on or caused by these technological changes.

Technical innovation can save labor and capital and improve the efficiency of economic operations, thereby creating a technological gap between innovators and non-innovators. In order to eliminate this difference, a balanced power would encourage the diffusion of innovations and techniques from suppliers to the surrounding areas. The American economist J. Stanley Metcalf believed that the spread of technological innovation is a process of selection, which begins with the enterprises choosing different techniques at different levels. Successful companies tend to accept advanced techniques that are efficient, cost-effective and consumer-friendly and those companies who refuse innovative techniques will be eliminated. Through this interactive selection process, technological innovation has been widely disseminated in the market and thereby completes the diffusion process.[9]

When considering economic development, technological diffusion is more important than innovation itself. The economic benefits of new techniques derive from this diffusion process. And only when new techniques spread effectively can we achieve greater economic benefits. In an open economy, the channels of technological diffusion focus mainly on international trade, foreign direct investment (FDI), and the activities of research and development (R&D). In international trade, techniques will materialize into tangible goods and more advanced products can be produced directly through the import of key equipment, assembly lines and other capital goods, which generates technological diffusion. By absorbing FDI and introducing more advanced foreign techniques, then countries whose technology is relatively underdeveloped can promote diffusion. And finally, in the context of globalization and the continuous exchange of talent and knowledge, technological innovation will spread through multiple channels, which will positively facilitate R&Ds.

Review of the theory of technological progress

Driven by the new wave of technological revolution, research into the effects of technological progress have reached greater heights and have formed a number of theoretical schools but in general, the theory of technological progress has experienced three developing phases:

The exogenous study (the 1950s—the early 1960s)

In 1956, the American economist Robert Solow proposed the neoclassical production model through the introduction of exogenous technological progress.[10] This theory attempts to distinguish between the contributions to economic development from improved efficiency as opposed to other factors, emphasizing that technological progress is a process of spontaneous evolution with its own, inherent laws. This process, to the economic system, is non-controllable and exogenous. Studies of the theory of technological innovation developed rapidly during this phase and focused on changes to the organizational structure and risky decision-making behavior of the innovation subject and also involved the exchange of information and environmental innovation. The research methodology is primarily limited to case study and has no complete theoretical framework.[11]

The endogenous study (1960s—early 1980s)

The neoclassical growth theory has contributed much to the economic growth theory. There are serious flaws however, especially when considering exogenous technological progress cannot effectively explain disparities in the inter-regional economic growth. After the 1960s and the increasing contribution to economic growth made by advances in technology, more and more economists tried to create a model of endogenous technological progress. In 1962, the American economist Kenneth Arrow proposed the "learn-by-doing" model, using endogenous technological progress to explain economic growth for the first time. In 1965, Japanese economist Hirofumi Uzawa further proposed a two-sector model by inserting endogenous study into exogenous technological progress.[12] Furthermore, the theoretical study of technological innovation made considerable progress during this phase. For example, the British economist Christopher Freeman established a more systematic set of theories on innovation economics[13] and the American economist Edwin Mansfield founded the theory of technological imitation and innovation.[14] These studies primarily formed the theoretical system of the technological innovation.

The research of the endogenous growth theory (the late 1980s till now)

According to research conducted by American economists Paul Romer and Robert Lucas, technological progress is a determinant in the achievement of a country's sustainable growth. Human capital investment increases the efficiency of production and improves the productivity of other enterprises via the external effects of technological progress.[15] Technique and human capital have significant spillover effects that are essential to a sustainable economic growth.[16] Technical innovation studies became comprehensive during this period and its theoretical framework was sketched out.

How does technological progress promote the evolution of economic structure?

The evolution of the industrial structure and technological progress are closely related in the course of the evolution of the economic structure. Technical innovation is the root cause of both industrial development and the orderly

The Theory of the Evolution of Economic Structure

change in technological progress. The technological progress will inevitably lead to changes in the industrial structure and the industrial structure is the fundamental economic structure. Thus, changes in the industrial structure will definitely bring about changes in the economic structure.[17]

Fig. 2.1.   Technological diffusion and the logical time

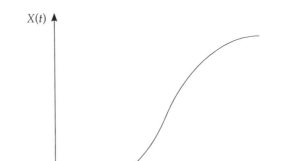

The mechanism of technological progress on promoting the evolution of industrial structure

Transformation in industrial structure is a disequilibrium and qualitative process which, with the influence of technological progress, features the constant destruction of old industries and the creation new ones. This process is known as the "industrial mutation." The mechanism of technological progress in promoting the evolution of industrial structure can be analyzed from three perspectives: intra-industrial, inter-industrial and inter-regional.

Technological innovation starts with intra-industrial spread, which enables its adoption by other corporations within the industry. The British scholar Rod Coombs proposed a technological infection model in the 1980s, arguing that the spread of technique is akin to the spread of an epidemic. In the early stages of technological diffusion, there are few adopters due to scant knowledge of the technique itself and the enterprise risks high uncertainties to introduce the technique. With gradual technological diffusion and information spread, the number of enterprises that have introduced this technique increases significantly and this process will continue until all manufacturers have adopted the "new" technology.[18] This process can be summarized in a diffusion curve composed of technological diffusion and the logical time, which is demonstrated in an S-shape (see Fig. 2.1).

In the technological infection model, the speed of technological diffusion and the trend of the diffusion curve are mainly determined by business scale, technological attributes, management, technological proficiency, and the costs and benefits of the innovation.[19] As demonstrated in Fig. 2.1, the speed of technological diffusion and the number of adopters increases rapidly as time (t-axis) goes by, then comes to a slowdown when reaching the inflection point and finally reaches the verge of saturation.

Technical innovation and diffusion are not merely intra-industrial, but also inter-industrial; thus promoting an orderly industrial transformation, i.e. the constant destruction of old industries and the creation of new ones. The birth of new industries will inevitably cause intra-industrial split and restructuring, thus facilitating the industrial structure's ongoing development. The three main variables affecting the process of industrial evolution are individual adoption, the market environment, and competition with other industries. Generally, for industries whose technological innovation efficiencies are higher than average, the output value will quickly stabilize due to its advanced techniques at the early stage of the evolution of the industrial structures. But, as technology advances, prompted by innovation and the positive effects of resource utilization, the industry gains more space for development and increased market demands are created thereafter. In addition, the expansion of market capacity will increase its output to a higher level, and gradually becomes the main promoter of the optimization and upgrade of the industrial structure.

Technological innovation and diffusion also spread around its surrounding areas from the region of innovation. In the early 1960s, Swedish scholar Torsten Hägerstrand was the first to discuss the theory of spatial diffusion in techniques and he took the distance factor into the research perspective, believing that the adoption of innovation was primarily a result of "learning" or "exchanging," within which the effective flow of information was crucial.[20] Furthermore, he compiled a detailed conclusion and summary of several important regulations in spatial diffusion, such as the infection mechanism, the neighborhood effect, the ranking effect, etc.

In the 1970s, Richard Morrill conducted further studies on the time and spatial diffusion tendency of technological innovation, analyzing the two factors' respectively influences on the process of technological innovation diffusion in terms of influential magnitude and the roles these the two factors themselves play. Morrill believed the influence of time on diffusion can be divided into two levels. First, potential adopters needed to spend time deciding whether to adopt the techniques and second, if there was a lack of enthusiasm and willingness to the diffusion, then such resistance curbed the innovation's diffusion. Because the dispersion of homes restricts the distance of diffusion, the ability for the innovation to diffuse will decrease gradually with the elongation of space.[21]

The mechanism of technological progress on the evolution of other industrial structures

Technological progress is the core strength of industrial restructuring, and the diffusion and transfer of technological progress continues to affect economic structures, such as the structure of investment and consumption, the financial structure, the regional economic structure, and the structure of the international balance of payments.

Technological progress promotes the upgrade of the investment and consumption structure

The promotion and application of technological achievements can promote the evolution of techniques, increase the return on investment in the industry, and improve the structure of the investment. At the same time, technological advances can effectively reduce the productive cost of high-tech products in order to expand their potential market, which induces and alters the upgrading of the consumption structure. Through effective diffusion, advances can promote economic development and lead to an increase in per capita income that would affect changes in consumption, which is bound to promote the adjustment of the industrial structure to accommodate this change.

Technological progress promotes complexity in the financial structure

Technological progress promotes the development of financial innovation, provides new financial instruments and methods of the transaction, and improves the quality of human and material resources and these greatly improve the trading efficiency of the financial industry. Generally speaking, the department with faster technological progress will reduce its transaction cost. Thus, the process of financial innovation also leads to continuously decreasing costs in financial transactions and improves the financial status of resource allocation. On the one hand, financial technological innovation eliminates technological obstacles in the segmentation of the financial market, enabling a more convenient and free circulation of financial resources between markets and also improves the ability to supply the financial products of financial institutes and promotes the variety within the financial structure to a high level.[22] On the other hand, with the cross-development of the financial operations within financial industries, the boundaries of division in the original function of the financial industry have become increasingly blurred. The appearances of the financial derivative markets, venture capital and growth enterprise market (GEM), and the market in asset-backed securities further increase the levels of financial markets and complicate their structure. The explosive growth of financial derivational tools especially leads to an inverted pyramid in the financial market, resulting in increasing complication and virtualization of the development of the financial market.

The spatial diffusion of technological progress improves the coordination of the regional economic structure

The spatial diffusion of technological progress promotes industrial gradient transfer. In other words, the transfer process of the industrial gradient is actually a transfer process of the element of production that focuses on the core of production technology. The inter-regional imbalances in economic development objectively form a gradient division pattern based on resource endowments and technological differences. In an open market, the industrial gradient transfer, driven by technological progress, can produce strong positive externality and as techniques advance, the industrial transfer will gradually speed up. The industrial structure of different regions within a country will continue to upgrade and adjust, showing the "flying geese paradigm" in industrial structural evolution, which contributes to the onward transformation of the regional economic structure.

Trade and technological transfer promote the international balance of payments

The domestic industrial structure determines its commodity structure, which accordingly determines its international supply structure. Technical advancement can dramatically accelerate the upgrade of industry and products and improve the international competitiveness of pillar industries and leading industries and upgrade the structure of products from low-value-added, labor-intensive products to high-tech ones with more techniques. Technical progress can also constantly enhance the country's ability to substitute import and lay the foundation to expand exports and maintain a long-term international balance of payments. In open conditions, developed countries transfer those industries, which do not have global competitiveness or certain value, to other countries so as to upgrade the industrial structure. Developing countries achieve actually substitute import and promote export by rationally undertaking industries with techniques higher than their own.

In summary, technological progress, which is the internal driving force of economic structural evolution, mainly influences this evolution by affecting industrial input-output conditions and the allocation efficiency of production factors. Technological progress initially promotes the optimization and upgrade of industrial structure, which in turn motivates the evolution of the structures of investment consumption, finance, regional economics, and the international balance of payments.

Impacts of Institutional Innovation on the Evolution of Economic Structure

Institutional innovation, which is important for the improvement of the approach and efficiency of resource allocation, is an important motivation for the evolution of economic structure. This section will discuss the impact of institutional innovation on the evolution of economic structure based on the institutional innovation theories.

The denotation and basic content of institutional innovation

What is institutional innovation?

Institutional innovation, which is often regarded as synonymous with institutional change and institutional development, is used to express the dynamic process in which "institution building and transformation change over time."[23] Early in the nineteenth century, the American economist Thorstein Veblen, a representative of institutional economics, pointed out that the analysis of economic theory should involve the study of the various institutions in the human beings' social and economic life. In his opinion, the institution was the conventional wisdom of an individual or a society, regarding some relation or function.[24] To a certain extent, institutional transformation is an unconscious activity and a result of adaptation to a new environment and not the product of consciousness. Another representative in institutional economics and fellow American, John Commons comprehended institution as "the control, expansion, and liberation of collective actions over individual actions."[25]

In the 1960s, American economist Douglass North inherited and developed Schumpeter's innovation theory and proposed a theory of transaction cost. He believed that "institution is a social rule and, normatively speaking, it was considered as an artificial constraint that determines the relationship between people."[26] Institutional innovation was institutional transformation, which allowed the innovator gain potential profits. When the potential profits achieved by means of institutional innovation were greater than the costs for gaining these profits, institutional innovation would take place.[27] North also emphasized the importance of clear property rights in the process of institutional innovation.

After the 1990s, the Japanese economist Masahiko Aoki and some others introduced the EGT[28] into research on institutional transformation and analyzed the evolution and diversity of the economic institution. Aoki regarded economic activity as a game process, believing that "the institution is a self-maintaining institution depending how the game is played."[29] Institutional transformation was the mental process that allowed a game participant to constantly change their beliefs. In this process, cultural, historical, political, and legal factors played important roles.

Dynamics of institutional innovation

In a market economy, the continuous interactions between institutions and organizations are of great significance to institutional innovation. Induced factors of institutional innovation lie in the fact that the subject hopes to maximize potential profits by means of institutional transformation. Potential profits are usually collected from four main sources: 1) from new techniques and the large-scale economy of increasing returns; 2) from internalizing the external economy; 3) from overcoming risk; and 4) from transferring and reducing trade costs.[30] When profits cannot be gained in the existing institutional arrangement, institutional innovation must occur, which internalizes profits currently divorced from the existing institutional arrangement structure.

Main types of institutional innovation

Generally, the main bodies of institutional transformation involve individuals, enterprises, or government organizations. According to different subjects of institutional innovation, it can be divided into induced institutional transformation and mandatory institutional transformation.[31]

Induced institutional transformation is when the change or substitution of an existing systematic arrangement is spontaneous and is organized and implemented by individuals or groups in response to the potential opportunity of gaining profits. This institutional transformation has the following characteristics. First, it is profitable. The dynamic of institutional innovation is to maximize personal interests and achieve expected profits, i.e. those that outweigh the expected costs. Second, it is spontaneous. Induced institutional transformation is the spontaneous reaction of certain groups to the institutional disequilibrium and the incentive of this spontaneous reaction is the prospect of the potential profits. Third, it is progressive, it is an ongoing process. The conversion, substitution, and diffusion of institutions need time and many complex processes take place in the journey from the discovery of the external profits to the internalization of those profits.

Mandatory institutional transformation is a radical top-down transformation and takes place within governments (including central and local governments). Mandatory institutional transformation is mainly determined by three aspects. First, the institutional supply is the basic function of a country. Second, the institution has the characteristics of public goods, which are generally produced by the country. And third, the institutional equilibrium is minimal; in fact the institution is often in disequilibrium. The country needs to implement mandatory institutional change to compensate for the lack of institutional supply.

In practical terms, it is difficult to definitively distinguish induced institutional transformation from the mandatory version. They are often interrelated and mutually restrained and together they promote institutional innovation. On the one hand, when induced institutional transformation cannot meet the needs of the social institution, the national implementation of mandatory institutional transformation can make up for the inadequacy of institutional supply. On the other hand, there are levels and differences between institutions. Some level of institutional transformation can be mandatory, such as the legal institution, while some institutional transformations can only be implemented by a specific group.

Stages and processes of institutional innovation

Institutional innovation is a long process and there is a certain time lag. Lance Davis and Douglass North divide the whole process of institutional innovation into five stages. The first stage is the formation of the primary action group, which is the group who can foresee potential economic interests and realize that these potential interests can be obtained if the institution is innovated. They are the decision-makers, pioneers, and promoters of institutional innovation, among whom, according to Schumpter's theory, the "entrepreneur." The primary action group plays a major role in institutional innovation. The second stage is the institutional innovation blueprint proposed by the primary action group. The primary action group proposes innovative system solutions in order to enter the next stage of institutional innovation. If there is no feasible solution, then the group will wait for innovations from other institutional aspects. The third stage occurs as the group compares and selects from the various innovative programs. This stage requires a certain value criterion in order to assess the various innovative programs and make trade-off decisions. The fourth stage sees the formation of the secondary action group, which refers to the organizations and individuals who help the primary action group in obtaining the economic interests required for the process of the institutional innovation. Without this secondary group, which can consist of government agencies, private organizations, and/or individuals, the primary action group may never achieve their chosen institutional innovation program. The fifth and final stage is the implementation and achievement of institutional innovation and is a stage requiring collaborative efforts from the primary and secondary action groups.

Davis and North believed that the process of institutional innovation was a result of fluctuations between institutional equilibrium and disequilibrium. Institutional equilibrium refers to the equilibrium state in which institution supply meets its demand. Under institutional equilibrium, if the reform of the existing institution does bring the reformers increased interests, then there is no motivation or strength for institutional innovation. However if external conditions, such as a change in market scale and a change in production technology, contribute to the emergence of new potential interests, institutional innovation may emerge. This in turn will topple the old system of institutional equilibrium to achieve a new equilibrium state via institutional evolution. Therefore, economists in the within the institutional school believe that perfecting the institution is a constant and dynamic process from institutional disequilibrium to institutional equilibrium.

Promoting economic structural evolution via institutional innovation

Institutional innovation is not isolated and the relationship between institutions are interrelated and mutually constrained. Every arrangement between institutions must be related to arrangements between other institutions and is consequently integrated in the institutional structure. Hence, the importance of innovations in the institutional structure cannot be stressed too much.[32] The institutional structure operates, obviously, in stages and the functions of the myriad institutional arrangements modify the entire institutional structure. In the various types of institutional innovation, the evolution of the economic structure is closely related to the institution of property rights, finance, and technology innovation. Among them, the system of property rights, which is the core to institutional structure, belongs at the macro-level, while finance and technological innovation belong at the micro-level.

The influence of institutional innovation in property rights

As the core of the entire institutional structure, the institution of property rights determines the operation and transformation of the other institutional arrangements. Its innovation plays an important role in the evolution of the economic structure of a country or region, which becomes even more evident in countries in transition. Although, when making the transition to a market economy, different countries vary greatly in their economic structures and the institutional innovation of property rights has led countries to significantly re-allocate production factors or adjust the economic structure. As North emphasized, "as with agricultural gains, industrial gains are attributed to the establishment of effective ownership in both the factor market and the product market."[33] With the introduction of property rights, since investors will assume all investment risks, decisions as to when and where to invest will be more cautiously made as per changes in market conditions. The conditions generated by institutional innovation make the correlation effect possible among leading departments, which spreads from the new division to the entire economic institution, thus achieving transformations in production methods and the basic economic structure.[34] Moreover, the investment structure also undergoes a significant improvement. Government investment gradually withdraws from competitive areas to focus on infrastructure and social undertakings, in order to avoid conflict with private investment. In addition and with economic globalization, the creation of an open market, as is represented by the institutional innovation of property rights, greatly reduces the upgrade of the industrial structure in transitional economies and provides a rare opportunity to foster its leading industries and achieve the rationalization and expansion of the industrial structure.[35]

The influence of institutional innovation in financing

As an arrangement for financial institutions, finance is an important channel to connect capital supply with capital demand. The motivation of its innovation to the economic structure is manifested in promoting the coordination of the real economic structure and the fictitious economic structure. Facilitated by the financial market, social resource allocation is achieved by the market economy and the adjustment of capital flow, to a certain extent, determines the evolution of the economic structure.[36] The innovation of the financing institution is achieved by the establishment of an efficient financial system, whereby financial resources are rationally allocated in the national economy and provide adequate financial support for industrial growth. This growth greatly enhances the extent of the socialization of production and the scale of capital integration, thus promoting the rapid development of dominant industrial groups. At the same time, it can nurture the growth of potentially advantageous industrial departments and motivate the subsequent evolution of that industry. Throughout the history of economic development in major industrial countries in the West, the innovation of the financial institution always accompanies an onward marching in industrial structure, which illustrates them as highly synchronized.

The innovation of the financial institution can also alter the finance structure between production and management. The interaction from reconfigurations between effective capital allocation and other elements makes profound changes in the investment and financial institution, which consequently contributes to the optimization of social resources under the changing financial structure of many production and management departments. As the financial structure transitions, so does the industrial structure, which enables the mutual promotion of the evolution of the fictitious and the real economic structures, and hence supports the effective operation of the national economy.

The influence of institutional innovation in technology

Technical innovation is an important institutional arrangement that will affect the evolution of economic structure, because there are spillover effects. If there is no system to protect innovation, the innovator will not gain the corresponding interests, which will severely dampen the enthusiasm of the innovator. In order to secure enthusiasm and prevent free-rider problems occurring in innovation diffusion, it is necessary for the government to plan the according institutional arrangements. Innovation protection is generally and initially secured by the arrangement of the property rights for technological innovation, of both the tangible and the intangible versions. Tangible property rights refer to property that the main body responsible for the technological innovation owns, including plants, equipment, and other fixed assets employed in the process of innovation; intangible property rights refer to intellectual property rights, including the patent, copyright and trademark institutions. On the one hand, the property rights of technological innovation can motivate further innovations and induce the innovators to monopolize their sole rights in the prescribed time limit. Generally speaking, profits are attractive and from the profits-driven perspective, this institution also motivates continuous innovation. On the other hand, the property rights of technological innovation can facilitate innovation diffusion to achieve industrial innovation and the innovation of the overall economy, which ultimately achieves the adjustment and upgrade of the economic structure.

Chapter 3

The Theory of the Imbalance of Economic Structure

STRUCTURAL ECONOMICS IN CHINA

The imbalance of economic structure is an off-normal state in the evolutionary process of economic structure. It has specific characteristics and is also associated with the various stages of global economic development. This section begins with a discussion on the definition and meaning of this imbalance then analyzes its formation mechanism.

What Is the Imbalance of Economic Structure?

Beginning with the concept of disequilibrium, this section clarifies the meaning and basic content of economic imbalance, the concept of imbalance in economic structure, and its main characteristics and classifications.

The general meaning of "imbalance"

Equilibrium, disequilibrium and imbalance are three basic economic concepts, which are internally related and strictly differentiated. Equilibrium originates in Physics and refers to the opposing forces that are balanced either in a stationary state or in a uniform linear motion. The concept of economic equilibrium refers to is a state where economic forces are balanced and there is an absence of external influences. Equilibrium is an ideal state, which requires the market to be perfect and prices flexible "enough." However, owing to the asymmetric distribution of information and other causes, this ideal state does not exist in the real economy. Since the Great Depression in the 1930s especially, people have begun to recognize that clearly equilibrium is a target that is far from reality and unable to be realized. And thus the idea of disequilibrium came into being. The Keynesian theory of disequilibrium holds that no matter the state of the market, because of changes wrought by the adjustment of variables, the economy will never exist in a steady state free from internal changes. This disequilibrium is also known as Non-Walrasian Equilibrium.[1] But disequilibrium can achieve equilibrium by the adjustment of variables in the economic system. The process of the entire economic operation is shown as "disequilibrium-equilibrium-disequilibrium," in which disequilibrium is the normal state and equilibrium is merely the target and therefore the direction of economic adjustments.

Economic imbalance is a special disequilibrium in the process of economic operation. It refers to the dynamic process in which a particular area of the economic system or the system as a whole constantly deviates from the state of equilibrium, and cannot return to it, whatever the self-adjustment. Economic imbalance has a serious negative impact on all the aspects of life, including the economy, society and the environment. Moreover, the meaning of economic imbalance can be further understood through the following three concepts. First, the degree of deviation from equilibrium; if the imbalance is created by a large deviation from equilibrium then the degree of deviation tends to increase. Second, the time span of the deviation from equilibrium; in that imbalance is caused by the constant accumulation of disequilibrium. Generally speaking, the economic system remains in disequilibrium for long periods of time, but when the accumulation of disequilibrium goes beyond the economic development capacity so disequilibrium becomes imbalance. Third, the consequences; because imbalance is basically worsening disequilibrium, this leads to economic system disorder and causes the rapid accumulation of risk. Imbalance seriously interferes with the normal operation of the social economy and may even trigger economic or social crisis.

The concept and characteristics of the imbalance of economic structure

The imbalance of economic structure and the imbalance of economic aggregate are intrinsically connected. They have similar provisions in their definitions, but they are different in nature and character.

Concept

The imbalance of economic structure is the root cause of economic imbalance and its basic meaning can be deduced from the definition of economic imbalance. The imbalance of economic structure is defined as a constant deviation from equilibrium within various elements of the economic system, and between the economic system itself and the resources and environment and social systems, in the process of economic growth, and hence leading the economic system toward a state of disorder. The imbalance of economic structure undermines the interdependent relationship between the economy, society and resources and the environment, which leads to unreasonable allocation of resources, low efficiency in economic operation, and the loss of social welfare. A serious imbalance of economic structure is likely to trigger an entire economic, social and environmental crisis, which will radically damage sustainable development of the economic system.

Characteristics

The imbalance of economic structure has the general properties of economic imbalance but also has its own unique characteristics. The imbalance of

STRUCTURAL ECONOMICS IN CHINA

economic structure has the following four basic characteristics.

First, the imbalance of economic structure is universal. Historically, before the breakdown of the Bretton Woods System, structural problems were often confined to a few specific countries and regions but currently, they have become commonplace and major issues across the globe. The evolution of a country's economic structure is affected not only by a variety of domestic factors, but also by many international factors. Changes in the international division of labor, comparative advantages, and opportunity costs cause the global industrial structure to transfer and aggravate the hollowing-out of traditional industries in developed countries as well as the relatively low level of industrial structure in developing countries. This leads to imbalance in the global industrial structure and the trade structure. In the global flow of capital, developed countries purchase equipment and raw materials and hire labor forces as a form of transnational production by transferring capital to developing countries. This creates a great deal of capital flow to developing countries but in return, developing countries tend to adopt the policy of controlling foreign exchange by accumulating foreign exchange reserves to buy the bonds of developed countries, thus making capital flow back to developed countries. Due to the inherent fragility of financial systems in developing countries, international hot money tends to speculate on a large-scale via the inflow and outflow of capital, thereby increasing the imbalance of global capital flow. It is clear then that, under the impact of the global industrial transfer gradient and the acceleration of economic and financial integration, problems in economic structure in one country can and usually do spread via international trade and capital flow. This inevitably causes economic structures around the world to experience varying degrees of imbalance and thus, structural problems are universal.

Second, the imbalance of economic structure is complex. As a complex evolutionary system, structure consists of many sub-systems, such as the economic, ecological, resources and environment and so on and its affecting variables include not only structural variables such as industries, investment and consumption, finance, and distribution of income, but also general economic variables such as resources, the environment, and ecology, as well as non-economic variables such as economic laws, regulations, institutions, and policies. Because variables interact with each other to form complex levels of intricate relations, because information is incomplete and uncertain, and because the ecological environment has external limits, the internal structure of the economic system becomes more and more complicated. In addition, sustainable economic development requires a large number of products and services to be provided by the ecological environment, and the research on structural problems cannot be separated from the analysis of the interaction between the ecological environment and the economic system. Both ecological and economic structures, as important parts of the structure, have very complex compositions. The complexity of interaction between the economic and the ecological systems is manifested not only in the complex nonlinear relationship of variables in their sub-systems, but also in the equilibrium of energy exchanges between the ecological, economic and social systems. This adds complexity to the imbalance of economic structure.

Third, the imbalance of economic structure is long-term. The imbalance of economic structure is comprised of a number of inter-related and interactive regional imbalances. As historical conditions change, the nature and extent of the imbalance of economic structure will change accordingly. Any form of economic structure will incur a major structural contradiction or problem in the process of evolution. As time moves on, that major structural contradiction or problem may mutate and evolve into a new imbalance. Therefore, the imbalance of economic structure features long-term complexity.

Fourth, the imbalance of economic structure is destructive. On the one hand, its destructiveness is reflected in the destruction of the normal operation of the national economy. From the perspective of the structural imbalance of aggregate supply and demand, structures of aggregate supply and demand are often mutually incompatible in the macro-economy, but that does not necessarily give rise to the imbalance of economic structure. Imbalance happens only when the structure of supply and the structure of demand are incompatible to the extent that the normal operation of the national economy is affected.[2] Therefore, the negative results of the imbalance of economic structure on a national economy are often the root cause of the current financial crisis or economic crisis. Moreover, the imbalance of economic structure also damages the resources and environment system and the social structure, which is mainly manifested in the undue exploitation of natural resources, the degradation of the environmental quality, increasingly serious social conflicts caused by unfair distribution, and so on.

Five major imbalances of economic structures

The imbalances of modern economic structure are summarized in five areas in Chapter One. The definitions of the five major imbalances of economic structure are analyzed respectively as follows.

The imbalance of investment and consumption structure

The investment and consumption structures reflect the proportional relationship

STRUCTURAL ECONOMICS IN CHINA

between investment and consumption and the adaptability of its internal structure. Consumption is the fundamental driving force and the ultimate goal of the cycle that is social reproduction. Investment and consumption, the basic variables in the national economy, are a unity of opposites. Their "oppositeness" is manifested in the fact that when investment rises, consumption falls; and consequently, consumption will rise due to investment's decline. Their "unity" refers to the internal connection that exists between investment and consumption. They will maintain a stable and rational proportional relationship for a certain period but if their internal connection breaks, imbalance will occur. Thus, the imbalance of the investment and consumption structures comes about when the proportion of investment to consumption constantly deviates from a reasonable range, so that the organic connection between the two is cut, leading to a serious gap between the aggregate social supply and demand, and hence causing unsustainable development of the national economy.

In general, the imbalance of the investment and consumption structures includes two basic situations. First, when the investment portion is too high, i.e. excessive investment. Excessive investment is associated with excessive saving, which inevitably curbs consumption. Unduly high investment leads to a substantial increase in aggregate supply, which is often the cause of excessive production capacity. In addition, an unduly high investment portion will risk excessive surplus in current accounts. Second, when the consumption portion is too high, i.e. over-consumption and the reduction in savings. An overly high consumption portion will curb supply and thus may trigger inflation and a substantial current account deficit.

The imbalance of industrial structure

The industrial structure refers to the qualitative connection formed between industries in their economic activities and the quantitative proportional relationship thereof. As the most basic part of economic structure, the industrial structure reflects the specific stage and level of the productive forces' development. Marxist economics argues that the industrial structure is the distributive proportion of aggregate social labors in various departments under certain economic conditions. The proportion implies a certain balance, that is, the balance between aggregate supply and aggregate demand.[3]

The market mechanism is imperfect and therefore markets can fail, so the competitive mechanism is often distorted and causes the imbalance in aggregate social supply and demand as well as an imbalance within the structure of supply and demand, which results in the imbalance of industrial structure.

The Theory of the Imbalance of Economic Structure

The so-called imbalance of industrial structure means that the qualitative relationship and the quantitative proportional relationship formed by various industries in economic activities are increasingly inharmonious and hinder the normal operation and sustainable development of the national economy.

Industrial imbalance manifests itself in the following three aspects. First, there is a mismatch among production factors in various industries. If the production factors in related industries cannot reach mutual adaptation and the input-output relationship among and/or within industries becomes hindered and social reproduction exacerbates the bottleneck, which seriously affects the normal operation of the national economy. Second, there is discord in the relative status among industries. In certain stages of economic development, industrial structure has a clear hierarchy wherein primary, secondary and tertiary industries, plus various industrial departments, should be a unity of mutual coordination and promotion. And if this hierarchy collapses, there will be imbalance between the different levels of the industrial structure. Third, the alternation of industrial development phases is not coordinated. Generally speaking, changes in industrial structure are characterized by the alternation of industrial phases. Human society and the industrial structure always evolve from the agricultural to the industrial economy and finally to the service economy. In these three major industrial development phases, many processes of specific industrial alternation occur, and if the structure reverses or the industrial phases alternate too fast, the proportion of industrial structure will deviate from its normal, operational state.

The imbalance of financial structure

The financial structure reflects a combination of all the various parts of finance. It reflects the overall economic structure from the perspective of fund and credit values, including the structure of the financial system, the structure of financial instruments, the structure of interest rates, and so on. Imbalance in the financial structure means that imbalances exist between financial departments, between financial factors, and between finance and the real economy. Imbalance exists when the organic connection among financial factors, financial industries, and the real economy becomes severed and some functions of the financial system become disordered, dislocated, and lost. Consequently finance can no longer play its effective, supporting role in the development of the real economy. As finance holds a very special status in economic growth, imbalance of the financial structure holds a very great danger to the healthy economy of a country.

Imbalance of the financial structure is defined and manifests itself at three

STRUCTURAL ECONOMICS IN CHINA

levels. The first is imbalance in the structure of financial factors. Namely, the relative scale of various financial factors, as well as the proportions of distribution and the growth rate in financial institutions and the financial market, becomes unreasonable or distorted. This leads to the destruction of the organic connection among these financial factors and a reduction in their aggregate quality. The second is imbalance of the structure of financial industries. Namely, unbalanced development in financial industries results in a decrease in the links between their various departments; imbalance of financial structure often leads to the overexpansion of certain functions and the decay or even loss of others within the financial system. The third is imbalance in the adaptability of the financial structure and the economic structure. When this occurs, the financial structure cannot meet the developing needs of the structure of the real economy and cannot adapt to changes in the economic structure.

The imbalance of regional economic structure

Any economic activity is inseparable from a given geographical space. Regardless of the level of its development, ultimately, it is able to find its "shadow" in a particular space. This combination of economic activities and its specific geographical space gives rise to the regional economy.[4] The structure of the regional economy represents economic relationships between countries, between regions, or between different regions in one country. The relationships are generally reflected in common distinctions of regional economic development. Many countries experience the processes of change inherent in gaps within regional economic development. In the global experience, there is disequilibrium in the regional economic development of any country. Distinctions in the distribution of production factors between regions lead to distinctions in productivity between regions and finally cause gaps in regional economic development. If these gaps exceed a "threshold," namely, a critical value that a society can bear, then economic development will be inhibited and social conflict will be exacerbated.

The imbalance of balance of payments structure

International payments are a comprehensive reflection of the internal and external relationships of the economic structure in a country or a region. They represent the contrasting relationship between the total income of monetary capital from abroad and the total payments of monetary capital going overseas of a country or region during a given period. If the total revenue is more than the total expenditure, there is an active balance of payments or a surplus balance of payments. If expenditure is more than income, then it is an adverse balance of payments, or a deficit balance of payments. The so-called imbalance of the structure of international payments refers to a constant and significant surplus or deficit in a country or a region. This will exacerbate the imbalance of domestic economic development.

To understand the imbalance of international balance of payments is to understand the following two levels. The first is the imbalance in its overall level, which corresponds with the general definition of the international balance of payments. The balance of international payments, in general, refers to any international trade that automatically generates two records of cancellation in international payment accounts, wherein the sum of the current account balance and capital account balance must equal zero.[5] The imbalance of international payments refers to a situation where a surplus or deficit exist in the overall international payments of a country (or region) in the long run. It matters not if it is a surplus or a deficit; it is a comprehensive reflection of imbalance of the domestic economic structure. The second is the imbalance of the internal structure, meaning a prolonged and wide imbalance in the relationship ratio between projects that directly generate international payments and sub-projects, for instance, the balance between the internal trade of goods and services and current transfers between accounts. An extreme mismatch between direct investment, portfolio investment, and other projects of investment all contribute to the internal structural imbalance.

The Formation Mechanism of the Imbalance of the Economic Structure

Imbalance in the economic structure is systematic and involves a number of specific areas in the economy. Every economic school has different perspectives and theoretical analyses of imbalance and its formation mechanism in various economic structures. This section focuses on analyzing the internal logic of the imbalance in economic structure and its five areas.

The internal logic of economic structure

From the perspective of social reproduction processes, a gap between investments and savings is often the source of imbalance in the modern economic structure. In a developing economy, the difference between domestic investment and domestic savings are always related to the balance of payments. The relationship is shown in the following equation (3–1):

STRUCTURAL ECONOMICS IN CHINA

$$I-[S+(T-G)]=M-X \qquad (3-1)$$

In this equation, I, S, T, G, M, X represent investment, savings, government taxation, government purchase, import, and export respectively. $(T-G)$ can be seen as government savings, which create domestic savings when added with private savings (S). And $(M-X)$ represents the difference between import and export. Therefore, the equation means: when domestic investment exceeds domestic savings, there must be a net inflow of foreign resources, i.e. the trade deficit; and when domestic investment is less than domestic savings, it will lead to a net outflow of national resources, i.e. the trade surplus.

In the real economy, investment and savings are difficult to balance and in general, the higher the savings rate, the higher the investment rate. In the case of fixed income, savings are the function of consumption therefore the ratio of savings depends on the preferences of consumers.[6] Insufficient consumption will cause an increase in savings while excessive consumption will result in reduced savings. Sustainable over- or under-consumption results in an inability to effectively run the national economy (economic overheating), which causes an imbalance in the structure of investment and consumption. Moreover, imbalance in the structure of investment and consumption generates internal disharmony within the structure of industrial production, resulting in reduced efficiency of the industrial structure and a structural imbalance. Meanwhile, in the operational processes of a national economy, real economic variables and financial variables are closely related. Imbalances in the real economy lead to dramatic changes in the financial structure and in turn, a number of important variables in the financial system will affect real economic variables; for example, the significant impact on consumption, savings, and investment from the interest rate. So, when variables within the financial system cannot truly reflect the supply and demand of the financial market, the system of the real economy and finance will be disconnected and when financial parameters cannot function well, financial structural imbalance occurs.

Due to imbalance in regional economic development, the effects of imbalances within the structures of investment and consumption, industry, and finance differ in various geographical spaces, which in turn cause an imbalance in regional economic structure. Within one country, this leads to a widening gap in regional economic development; while from a global perspective, the economic imbalance in one country (especially a major power) may have significant impact on the world economy and may instigate economic fluctuations in other nations and induce a structural imbalance in the international balance of payments.

In summary, in an opening economy like China's, the imbalance of economic structure includes imbalances in five primary structural areas: investment and consumption, industry, finance, regional, and international payments. These areas of economic structural imbalance are mutually affected, penetrated, and constrained. When a country or region is in serious imbalance, economic system disorder will occur locally or even globally. A delayed and ineffective correction of these imbalances will inevitably result in economic recession or even economic crisis.

The formation mechanism of the imbalance of investment and consumption structures

The formation of imbalance in the structure of investment and consumption is relatively complex and includes factors of economy, society, culture, etc. From an economic perspective, imbalance in the investment and consumption structures derives from disorder in the savings rate, purchasing power, the degree of social credit, and variables in the financial budget, which lead to an imbalance in the investment and consumption structure.

Over-saving and a lack of purchasing power are the main reasons for inadequate consumption, which is, in general, always related with excessive saving. The theory of over-saving, as early representatives Thomas Malthus and Jean Sismondi expounded, explains the causes of inadequate consumption. Malthus believed money is not only a medium of circulation, but also a means of savings. Supply will not equal demand if consumers save money and create inadequate consumption.[7] Sismondi discussed, in detail, the contradictions between investment and consumption under a capitalist society,[8] arguing that a balance between production and consumption cannot be maintained by a capitalist system, because of the conflict between the infinite and blind expansion of production with ever-diminishing consumption. The root of inadequate consumption is the widening gap between the rich and the poor brought by the unfair system of distribution. Thus Sismondi distilled the main source of economic crisis as this fundamental contradiction of capitalism, the contradiction between the infinite expansion of production and inadequate consumption (caused by capitalist production and its unreasonable system of distribution). American economists William Foster and Waddill Catchings together with the British economist John Hobson also reached the same conclusion,[9] believing that economic crisis and recession are not caused by insufficient purchasing power but by the high proportion of saving from current income, which disturbs the balance between production and consumption.

Another British economist, George Cole, put forward the theory that a lack

STRUCTURAL ECONOMICS IN CHINA

of purchasing power causes inadequate consumption and explains the causes of an unbalanced ratio between investment and consumption from the perspective of the distribution of income.[10] In this theory, the distribution of income consists of two aspects within the process of social reproduction: one is the payment of workers, including wages and bonuses, etc., and the other is the payment of enterprises, including the purchase of raw materials, machinery and payments of financial interests. Within the two payments, only the payment of workers can be directly converted into consumer purchasing power. If there is a gap between the current productive value and income of the consumer, it serves as the lack in purchasing power. In the real economy, this gap can be compensated for through bank credit but the repayment of the loan will create a new gap in purchasing power, which increases the investment and consumption gap and affects the normal conduct of social reproduction.

In the modern market economy, uncontrolled monetary credit and soft budget constraint (SBC) will lead to an expansion in investment or consumption and imbalance of the investment and consumption structures is closely related with monetary credit. Ludwig von Mises and Friedrich Hayek conducted systematical studies on this theory and represented of the Austrian school of economics, von Mises as the founder and Hayek as the synthesizer. The basic view of their theory was that the imbalance between the structures of production and consumption are rooted in a bank's monetary credit, and imbalances within this will cause irrationality both in the structures of production and of investment. In the modern financial system, finance is the hub of the entire economy. Monetary credit plays an important role in the regulation of balance in the structures of production and investment. If the financial system increases bank credit improperly, it can cause a rapid increase in investment demand, which in turn requires the increased support of bank credit. And with the money multiplier effect, investment accelerates and grows. When the growth rate of consumption lags behind that of investment, a structural imbalance will eventually form between investment and consumption, which will negatively affect the industrial structure, employment, the balance of payments, and so on. Meanwhile, the arbitrary expansion of consumer credit will create over-consumption. In developed countries, where financial innovation has accelerated and an overdraft has become very common (including formats such as deferred payment, subprime mortgages, credit cards, etc.) a serious deviation between the physical economy and virtual economy becomes increasingly apparent. And this tends to lead to financial or economic crisis due to weak financial supervision.

The SBC is seen mainly in a rational state-owned economy. The Hungarian academic and world-renowned economist, János Kornai produced a systematic exposition of this theory,[11] and argued that "shortage" is the most common economic characteristic in a highly centralized economy. In a shortage economy, corporate investment is inefficient and that necessitates an increase in the scale of the investment, making SBC the root cause of investment and the primary cause of the enterprises. SBC means a company's investments exceed the scope of its current benefits, or to put it another way, agencies offering funds do business by spending beyond their limit as determined by the present value of future income. Kornai's analysis focused on the relationship between government and state-owned enterprises and he believed SBC existed in socialist state-owned enterprises because central government implements paternalism in enterprises. In addition, due to the presence of SBC, companies underestimate the risk of investment even when the scale of investment is much larger than its paying ability. Then, once the company encounters financial difficulties, the state will use tax breaks, preferential loans, and loss funding, etc. to rescue the company. This leads to low efficiency of investment, labor productivity, and low wages. The latter forces an increase in savings and a curb in consumption, which then results in imbalance of the investment and consumption structures.

The formation mechanism of the imbalance of industrial structure

An incomplete, unsystematic market without an appropriate industrial development strategy may together or individually lead to imbalance in the industrial structure. An incomplete market induces inefficient industry and the lack of a system hinders any upgrade of the industrial structure, and therefore, an inappropriate industrial development strategy will lose any comparative advantage. The three factors mentioned above are not isolated, but are mutually affected. They determine imbalance in industrial structure as a united force.

The theory of industrial organization created by the American economists Edward S. Mason and Joe Bain pointed out that it is necessary to allow full play to the role of competition and to take advantage of the economic scale in industry within a market economy. On the one hand, only through competition will each company have enough power and impetus to improve operations and technology, while continuing to reduce cost of the service or product. On the other hand, the cost of an industrial unit can only reach its lowest point by taking advantage of the economic scale. Every enterprise pursues economic scale, but the market size of each industry is limited. In this way, the limited size of the market and the behavior of companies seeking economies of scale, push the market structure towards monopoly. Monopoly relaxes an enterprise's

STRUCTURAL ECONOMICS IN CHINA

internal management and its technological innovation because there is no restraint from the mechanism of market competition. This leads to inefficiency in production and operation because these companies control the market price, which results in the low efficiency of the industrial configuration of social resources. In addition, information asymmetry and the moral hazard, in addition to other reasons, can also generate distorted market signals, causing the disordered development of related industries. This creates a dysfunctional proportion in the relationship between the input and the output of the industry.

The lack of a system refers to the phenomenon in which a delayed or inadequate supply of a particular system or several systems in the process of industrial development emerges. There are two types of lack of a system: the first is an absence of a core system, a system which has critical impact on industrial development, such as a patent system. The second is the lack of a supporting system, a relevant system which ultimately ensures the implementation of a core system. The lack of a system may easily cause barriers to be erected within technological innovation, thereby potentially halting it. For example, the lack of a patent system and the safeguards it enables, disallows innovators the ability to protect their innovations, which leads to a diminished driving force behind technological innovation and blocks the upgrade of industrial structure. A long-term lack of a particular system will cause the industry to become a bottleneck in the economic development. And the long-term lack of an industrial development system will lead to lower levels in industrial development of a country or a region and a consequent loss of power for economic development, which will inevitably slide the economy into recession.

A defective strategy to industrial development will cause industrial structure to deviate from a reasonable direction. According to the basic theory of international trade, each country's industrial structure is influenced by the international division of labor. The international division of labor and trade is based on comparative advantage, meaning that a mutually beneficial international division of labor can only be formed when all countries produce their own products within a comparative cost advantage. The differences of comparative cost arise due to differences in the endowments of factor. A country will be in a more favorable position if it engages in specialized production and an international exchange of goods involving its own relatively abundant factor of production. The division of labor and trade based on this creates specialized production and continues the evolution of industrial structure. A country's foreign trade affects its industrial structure through the stimulation of increased domestic demand, i.e. increased exports and increased domestic supply via imports. If a country or region is always in the lower echelons of the division of international labor, then the industrial structure of this country or region will become distorted and will lead to imbalance in its balance of payments.

The formation mechanism of the imbalance of financial structure

Imbalance in the financial structure is not a static process but is a dynamic one as based on the economic history of development processes. Imbalance in the financial structure is the result of internal imbalance within the financial system and an incompatibility with the external system. Its formation mechanism differs for different types of countries. In general, financial inhibition or excessive financial innovation may distort the allocation of financial resources and this kind of irrational industrial structure would undermine economic and financial internal relations. Imperfections in a financial legal system can also lead to financial disorder and inefficiency, which results in financial structural imbalance.

For many developing countries, financial repression is the leading cause of imbalance in the financial structure. In the 1970s, renowned American scientists, Edward S. Shaw and Ronald I. McKinnon, stated in their analysis of the theories of the financial deepening[12] and financial repression[13] respectively, that developing countries tend to fall into a vicious cycle of financial repression and economic protraction due to excessive government intervention in financial development so it cannot play its role in promoting economic development. After McKinnon and Shaw, economists Professor Basant Kapur of the National University of Singapore, Troy D. Matheson from the International Monetary Fund, and Professor Michael J. Fry of the University of California, developed McKinnon and Shaw's static analysis into dynamic analysis using different research methods to further clarify the importance of alleviating financial repression and implementing financial deepening in order to improve economic development in developing countries.

The financial repression theory suggests that there is "financial duality" associated with the dual economic structure in the economies of developing countries, due to their low level of monetization and lack of sound financial markets. While achieving high reserve ratio policies through—among other methods—the establishment of special credit institutions, high reserve requirements, interest rate regulations, and non-convertibility of currency, the authorities also impose severe financial repression. In order to reduce the cost of capital and ensure that investment requirements for key national projects are met, deposit and lending rates are subject to different levels of government regulation in developing countries, while the interest rate is usually set lower than the market equilibrium interest rate. Moreover, real interest rates are often negative in developing countries due to high inflation and, as a direct result of interest rate regulation, structural imbalances in the financial market occurs, which leads to the phenomenon of credit rationing. In fact, excessive intervention and regulation over financial implementation is repeated in many developing countries in the course of economic development regardless of national conditions. Mere duplication of traditional monetary theory without any analysis causes a gap between financial development and economic development and severe imbalance in the financial structure. Therefore, one core issue of financial development in developing countries should be to abandon excessive government intervention and regulation so the market mechanism can play its role in resource allocation. But, based practices in developing countries, if the government completely abandons even moderate supervision and intervention over financial institutions and markets, fair competition would be lost, which could lead to financial crisis and would undermine the goal of macroeconomic equilibrium growth. In fact, the market mechanism is not a panacea. Market failures are likely to appear in sections of commodity production and consumption, including monetary and financial markets, so reasonable and appropriate government intervention is indispensable.

For some Western countries, financial innovation increases the system's instability and may cause financial crisis. Financial innovation creates a re-optimized combination of various elements and a re-allocation of a variety of resources in a financial sector, which, to a certain extent, serves to shift and spread risks. But this innovation can only serve to shift and spread individual risks; it is unable to reduce the overall risks of an entire financial system. Financial innovation activities based on financial derivatives are particularly prone to inflating a bubble economy and instigating a serious departure from innovations within reality-based economic development, which results in structural imbalance and the departure of financial development from the line of economic development. Hyman Minsky (1986) argued that the increase of financial levels and the continuous invention of new financial instruments (i.e. without analyzing financial data) are enough to prove the increasing vulnerability of a financial system.[14] Michael Carter (1989) also pointed out that financial innovation as a blocking policy in finance actually conceals growing financial fragility and will eventually stimulate speculative financing based on future revenue and expected asset prices, both of which are difficult to achieve.[15] Thus, financial innovation has a tendency to increase the overall vulnerability of the financial system. Moreover, the elasticity of the demand of money with respect to the interest rate declines and makes defining and measuring currency increasingly difficult, which leads to some failures in monetary policy instruments and a resultant weakening of the central bank's monetary regulation. Inevitably then, financial structural imbalance may occur and the structural imbalance as a national whole will be more difficult to tackle. Thus, it can be seen that financial innovation, on the one hand, conceals many traditional and additional, complex risks; while on the other hand, leads to a lack of market transparency, over-expansion of financial assets, intense fluctuations of interest rates, and other phenomena. In particular, innovation activities around financial derivatives centralize a variety of risks in the social economy. Derivative transactions also have a powerful and high leverage rate, so risks are constantly transferred to and accumulated in financial intermediaries. Thus, the instability of the global financial system is significantly increased and structural imbalance becomes more prominent. In fact, the U.S. subprime mortgage crises of 2007 bears witness to the fact that excessive financial innovation is an important cause of structural imbalance.

An irrational industrial structure in the long-term will increase the vulnerability of links between the real economy and the virtual economy and will damage macroeconomic efficiency. In general, a country's industrial structure depends on both factor endowments and central development strategies, with the financial structure is often dependent on the industrial structure. In other words, the optimal industrial structure is the one that can adapt to the factor endowment structure at the particular stage of economic development, while the optimal financial structure is the one that can adapt to this optimal industrial structure. If government development strategies deviate from the optimal industrial structure because of factor endowments, the financial structure will be affected and will deviate from its optimal path.[16] In fact, due to the relative scarcity of factor endowments, most developing countries tend to put their limited resources into a "preferred" industry, so the development of industrial structure deviates from its optimal path. As finance is an important channel for resource allocation, when the development of the industrial structure deviates from its optimal path, some functions of the financial system will be strengthened and others weakened, which may result in the disturbance of functions within the financial system and a decrease in the efficiency of resource allocation. This would eventually cause financial structural imbalance.

The integrity and efficiency of the financial legal system is the key in determining the level and quality of financial services. Various legal systems have been adopted in different countries around the world, so equity owners and creditors enjoy different degrees of protection depending on where they are. Countries that operate under the common law system dole out severe punitive measures against a company's internal actions; if they deprive equity owners and creditors their interests. This is conducive to the development of financial intermediaries and the capital market. Countries operating under the civil law system see the protection of investors vulnerable and capital markets underdeveloped, although the banking system is relatively more developed. In fact, Britain, America, and other countries using market-based financial structures, are indeed superior to other countries in terms of shareholder rights, law enforcement, and accounting standards. This reflects the important influence the integrity of the legal system has upon the formation of a country's financial structure.[17] Furthermore, in developing countries, if the market-based financial structure is established when the legal system is not qualified to establish such a market-based financial structure, it would lead to an inefficient financial system and make the financial architecture deviate from the requirements for national economic development. And again, structural imbalance would result.

The formation mechanism of the imbalance of regional economic structure

The imbalance of regional economic structure results from long historical precedence. In a market economy, an important element to this imbalance is the difference between institutions and factor endowments. The different economic growth modes of backward regions as opposed to developed regions would lead to non-equilibrium of factor mobility, would influence the marginal benefit and scale of economic development between regions, and would exacerbate the imbalance of economic development.

Market imperfections affect the free flow of products and factors between regions. In a market economy, the proliferation and flow of technology, knowledge, management, and other production factors can stimulate regional economic development. However, when market imperfections occur, these advanced factors of production cannot effectively or orderly flow from developed to backward regions. Market imperfections are characterized by asymmetric information, an imperfect trading system, etc. In addition, in many developing countries, regional protectionism is widespread. Thus, serious economic as well as non-economic barriers remain between regions, thus impeding the efficient flow of trade and factors and further enlarging the economic development gap.

Regional differences in factor endowments will strengthen imbalances in regional economic development and due to a scarcity of resources, it will be almost impossible for a country or region to fully develop all sectors. Instead, the limited resources can only focus on certain industries or certain regions, so the resources, limited as they are, can achieve some comparative advantage. In this way, investment in backward regions is often ignored. The Swedish economist Gunnar Myrdal proposed the cumulative causation model theory, which argues that all factors are interlinked and therefore reinforce each other to present a development trend of circular accumulation in a dynamic socio-economic development process.[18] In developing countries, poverty would further deteriorate in backward regions as a result of low per capita income and education, as well as cultural backwardness and low labor quality and productivity. Consequently, the gap between developed and backward regions increases in terms of per capita income and economic development levels, and backward regions become helplessly trapped in the vicious cycle of low income and poverty.

The passive attachment of backward regions to developed regions seriously weakens the competitiveness of the former. In the 1950s, Raúl Prebisch proposed the center-periphery theory, in which developed European countries were taken as central regions and backward Latin American countries were taken as peripheral regions. He discovered that the central regions, the developed countries, imported cheap raw materials and primary products from the backward countries, while simultaneously dumping industrial products on them. The backward regions were confronted with deteriorating terms of trade in the international market, which also inhibited the improvement and upgrade of their present and future industrial structure.[19] In the 1960s, the American economist John Friedman extended the center-periphery theory into the realm of a country's regional economic research. He argued that a country's regional economic system consists of central and peripheral sub-space systems, wherein resource, market, technology, environment, and other regional distribution differences exist. When certain regions gather together to form an accumulated development trend, these regions will acquire a much more powerful economic competitiveness to their outlying regions and will develop into the core or center of the regional economic system. Relative to the center (these developed regions), the periphery (the under-developed regions) adopts a dependent status, which can easily lead to the emergence of imbalances in the dual structure of the country/district. The periphery would be weakened over time and therefore imbalance in regional economic development would result.

The center-periphery imbalance would systematically be aggravated by the advantages gained from increasing returns in the developed regions. Since the 1990s, regional economic disparity theory has made new developments within the framework of imperfect competition and increasing returns of scale.

STRUCTURAL ECONOMICS IN CHINA

In 1991, the center-periphery theory was further improved by Paul Krugman, who revealed the internal operating mechanism of economic geography aggregation. He argued that the role of increasing returns was to make each product profitable only when produced at a certain location, the result being the production of different products at different places. Due to links traveling to and fro, some kind of self-sustained and concentrated trend will occur in a region of large economic scale. And of course, the lower the transaction cost, the more obvious the economy of scale is for micro-firms. Thus, Krugman believed that the level of regional economic development is determined by economies of scale, transportation costs, and the share manufacturing has in regional income.[20] The American economist Anthony Venables argued that, when factors of production are freely mobile, regional economic differentiation, as caused by the production process, is bound to occur, if the intermediate goods are affected by both economies of scale and freight costs. In this case, regions with a large manufacturing sector can provide a relatively broad market for intermediate goods, making these countries and regions move towards regional integration, and downstream production can enjoy this advantage in costs, and further strengthen the advantage.[21] The American economist P. Martine, key proponent of New Economic Geography, analyzes the causes of increasing regional economic disparities from the perspective of regional competition. He argues that the regions that initially win the regional competition appeal greatly to enterprise, which obtain benefits from the external economy, as formed by the industrial accumulation in the region. Therefore, the number of manufacturers in the same region would increase in line with the increasing advantages of exogenous relative costs and endogenous aggregation. Obviously, when the phenomenon of increasing returns exists, the inter-regional yield gap of the factors of production remain stable; the yield of well-developed regions continues to be higher than that of less-developed regions, while the share of gains in the less-developed regions continues to decrease, and the regional economic structure again comes up against a growing gap.

The formation mechanism of the imbalance of international balance of payments structure

The imbalance of international payments structure reflects conflict and constraints in the internal and external economic structures of a country or region. As the imbalance is related to the country or region's business cycle, international division of labor, currency changes, capital flows, and other factors, the country or region will be put at a disadvantage in international trade if production cannot fully exploit its comparative advantages. At the same time, money regulation, capital regulation, and other factors will affect imbalances in the capital account. Long-term imbalance between current and capital accounts will inevitably lead to the structural imbalance of international payments.

The business cycle can lead to the structural imbalance in international payments. When the economy is in boom phase, the country's national income will show rapid growth and employment remains at a high level, which leads to vigorous social demand and rising prices. When not in a boom phase, the country's imports will increase while exports decline, which will cause a deficit in the balance of payments, and vice versa.

Imbalance in the international division of labor will lead to imbalance of the trade structure. Due to geographical environment, natural resources, labor productivity differences, and other economic conditions, different countries set their own economic pattern, industrial structure, and import and export structure. However, global demand for a country's export products, or supply of its import requirements constantly change, so countries must constantly change their economic structure in order to adapt. If a country's economic structure is not flexible enough to adapt to changes in the structure of the international division of labor, it will face a structural imbalance of international payments. The structural imbalance of international payments includes two aspects. First, the imbalance caused by changes in the structure of commodity supply and demand and second, the imbalance caused by the failure of a country's factor prices to reflect changes in ratios within factors of production.

Fluctuations in the value of a country's currency will cause changes in domestic price levels, thus other countries effect changes in that country's general price level, which leads to the structural imbalance of international payments. For example, when a country suffers serious inflation, its export commodities manifest the rising trend of production costs. When exchange rate changes are not considered, the country's foreign currency denominated export prices will rise, resulting in its decreasing competitiveness in international markets, and therefore inhibiting the exports. At the same time, due to the relatively cheap price of imported commodities, imports will increase, which will finally create a deficit on the international balance of payments. In addition to inflation, high or low exchange rates resulting from inappropriate adjustments by monetary authorities will also lead to the disequilibrium in the balance of payments.

International speculative capital can also cause the structural imbalance of international payments. Since the 1990s and in the pursuit of high profits, international hot money has often flowed in to and out of different countries and different markets. The fact that large-scale international capital frequently flows in to and out of a country will change its supply of, and demand for, foreign currency and this influences enormously upon the activities of microeconomic agents as well as on macroeconomic variables, and thus causes tremendous impact on the international balance of payments. Moreover, short-term capital inflows or outflows can lead to a supply and demand imbalance in a country's financial markets, and result in drastic fluctuations of interest rates, and financial asset prices, thereby increasing the structural imbalance of international payments.

Abovementioned five factors may not apply to all countries due to different historical stages of economic structural imbalances of different countries or regions, as well as their different political, economic, and cultural backgrounds. In the present condition of deepening economic globalization, the countries' economic structural imbalances are inter-related, interacting, and inter-transformable and therefore, both the laws of globalization and of locality should be valued when the laws of economic structural imbalances are examined. Only then can the root causes of the economic structural imbalances of a country or region be scientifically identified and practical corrective measures be proposed.

Chapter 4

The Interaction of the Evolution of Economic Structure and the Resource Environment

STRUCTURAL ECONOMICS IN CHINA

The resource environment is the basis for human survival and development. Since the industrial revolution, problems within resource environment have become the greatest challenge for the continued development of human society as well as the most important constraint on the evolution of economic structure. These problems have eventually come to determine the size and mode of economic development. Therefore, the interaction between the evolution of the economic structure and the resource environment becomes an indispensable and integral part of structural economics. Under the constraints of resource environment and from the perspective of sustainable development, this chapter aims at discussing the impact the evolution of economic structure has on resource environment in order to analyze the interactive mechanism of interdependence and mutual restraint between them.

A Theoretical Review of the Relationship between Economic Development and the Resource Environment

There are complex relationships between the economic system and the resource environment; they interact with and interrelate to each other to form an interdependent whole via the exchange of materials, energy, and information. With the development of the global economy and accompanying acceleration of industrialization, economic development heaps great pressure on resources and the environment while contributing enormous material wealth to humans. The patterns and laws of inter-relationships between economic development and the resource environment have long been the focus of studies and the literature relating to different historical periods of research is summarized as follows.

The theory of resource constraints in classical economics

Studies on the relationship between economic development and resource environment can be traced back to before the middle of the nineteenth century when classical economics emerged. Classical economics focuses on the analysis of agricultural production and emphasizes research on the output efficiency of natural resources such as land. For example, William Petty, the founder of classical economics, realized that natural conditions impose constraints on wealth and expounded his well-known assertion; "Nature is the mother of wealth and the father of labor."

The Evolution of Economic Structure and the Resource Environment

After Petty, famous British economists Thomas Malthus, David Ricardo and John Mill all discussed the relationship between economic development and the resource environment, thus launching breakthrough research on problems of economic development and resource environment. In his monographs *The Principle of Population and Principles of Political Economy*, Malthus elaborated that a rise in population will result in land resources becoming increasingly scarce while conflict between humans and resources will become increasingly prominent and social and economic conditions will become increasingly poor as well.[1] Malthus calculated the demand for natural resources on the basis of the growth of population and income indexes, and the supply of resources and a means of livelihood on the basis of arithmetic progression. Therefore, as time goes by, human demands for resources will definitely exceed supplies of resources. If population growth cannot be effectively controlled, the growing population will undoubtedly deplete all means of production and livelihood on earth. It is thus clear that Malthus was pessimistic about human economic development and the resource environment.

In his book *On the Principles of Political Economy and Taxation*, Ricardo pointed out that with population growth, society will constantly increase its demand for agricultural products. However, in the usual condition that the amount of land available is fixed, two trends will emerge. First, people will have to cultivate inferior land with low productivity and second, people will keep investing in their original land, and the law of decreasing returns will develop.[2] This will lead to the increasing price of agricultural products, constantly rising rent and wages, and a gradual slowing of economic growth, perhaps even economic stagnation. Ricardo emphasized that scarcity in the natural environment will impose an important constraint on economic growth. However, in opposition to Malthus's point of view, he believed there is no absolute scarcity of natural resources, only the relative scarcity of natural resources with higher productivity. His theory on resources constraint is described as the relative scarcity of natural resources."

Mill inherited ideas from Malthus and Ricardo in terms of studies on the relationship between economic development and resource environment. In his masterpiece *Principles of Political Economy*,[3] Mill holds that economic growth will definitely be influenced by diminishing scale and returns of agriculture in the long term, causing rents and wages to rise and profits to decline and thus inevitably leading to economic stagnation. However, Mill notices that technological progress slows the trend of stagnation. Mill believed in the absolute scarcity of resources, but he claimed that social advance and technological innovation could delay its arrival. At the same time, Mill put forward a conception of the static economy"[4] and believed that humans had the ability to overcome a relative scarcity of resources. He did not, however, agree to conquer nature by applying this ability to explore and utilize all resources for human consumption. Mill claimed that the environment, the population, and wealth should stay in static and stable, meaning far from the limits of natural resources such as a lack of food and the loss of many natural resources.

The theory of resource regulation in neoclassical economics

After the rise of the marginal revolution in the 1870s, neoclassical economists, represented by Brits Alfred Marshall and Arthur Pigou, began to research the optimal allocation of resources when they are scarce or limited. Overall, neoclassical economists were optimistic about sustainable economic development and they believed that scientific and technological progress could improve the productivity of production factors, such as land, and slow the decreasing trend of returns to scale. The basis being that prices respond to the extent of the scarcity of resources, so the more scarce a resource is, the higher the price and cost, which will become the internal driving force behind technological innovation. Meanwhile, with economic development and the improvement of living standards, people tend to choose a reduction in family size, which relieves the contradiction between population growth and resource consumption.

Neoclassical economists claimed that relatively scarce resources are allocated through the price mechanism and will not restrain economic growth for quite a long period of time. This view was worshiped as a classical theory until the 1960s when instead of the decreasing returns to scale of land emphasized by classical economics, Marshall stressed that humans could place the fertility of land under their own control using science and technology.

From the early twentieth century to the 1960s, mainstream Western economics focused on economic growth, leaving the scarcity of natural resources and environmental degradation without widespread concern. In the early 1960s, Harold Barnett and Chandler Morse put forward the theory of scarcity in environmental resources, holding that, as the supplier of raw materials and energy in the process of production, resources and the environment are scarce. Generally speaking, scholars in this period were optimistic about economic growth and the problems regarding resources and the environment. As D. William pointed out, technological innovation and an increase in productivity can reduce people's reliance on natural resources in the long term, so there will be no long-term problems in resources and the environment and therefore no constraints on economic growth.

The Evolution of Economic Structure and the Resource Environment

The modern theory of constraints on the resource environment

Since the 1960s, the rapid development of industrialization has resulted in the increasingly serious problem of environmental pollution. The decline in environmental quality has seriously threatened the ecological balance and human life, and has changed people's widespread views about the relationship between economic growth and the resource environment. Economic growth has instigated many problems into the development of human society. And at this time, theories show that people have acquired a more pessimistic attitude towards economic growth and environmental issues. In 1962, American scientist Rachel Carson in her book *Silent Spring* condemned sharply the acts of destruction on nature and the harm to human life caused by the use of the pesticide DDT and posed a question about how humans could possibly live in harmony with nature. In 1966 American scholar Kenneth Boulding put forward his theory, spaceship economy that claimed that the earth, the eco-system that humans rely on, is like a small spaceship in the universe and if the population and the economy keep increasing, humans will eventually pollute the entire spaceship and become extinct by losing the very object they depend on to exist.[5] Spaceship economics expounds the view that the resource environment does impose constraints on economic activities and has a profound impact on the understanding of the relationship between resources, the environment, and economic development.

In 1972, in their book *The Limits to Growth*, Donella Meadows and the other members of the Club of Rome pointed out that the main factors affecting economic growth are population growth, food supply, capital investment, resource consumption, and environmental pollution; and because some important environmental resources are exhaustible and the natural environment has a limited ability to absorb waste from the economic system, economic growth is not sustainable. *The Limits to Growth* is the representative work of the pessimistic school. It, from a brand new perspective, inspires humans to understand the relationship between man and nature, and reminds humans not to be blindly intoxicated by the fruits of economic growth, and the book undoubtedly plays a cautionary role.

The theory of sustainable development

Academic debates on whether economic growth has limits and on how to understand the relationship between economic growth and resource environment continued into the 1980s, when two opposing theoretical views had been basically formed. First, the market mechanism and technological progress

STRUCTURAL ECONOMICS IN CHINA

can spontaneously solve the environmental problems confronting human beings. Second, the market mechanism and technological progress is incapable of solving environmental problems. Then, after the 1980s, people's understanding of the relationship between economic growth and the environment became more rational. They realized the destruction of the environment had a negative impact on economic development and environmental protection could promote sustainable economic development. Because environmental protection and economic development are uniform, countries around the world devoted themselves to exploring new methods and models for sustainable development in order to promote the harmonious development of economic growth and the resource environment.

In 1987, the World Commission on Environment and Development put forward the systematic strategy of sustainable development in the report *Our Common Future*, holding that economic development must be confined within what the environment can bear, or else it will suffer the consequences of environmental degradation. In 1992, United Nations Conference on Environment and Development passed two programmatic documents *The Rio Declaration and Agenda 21*, which expressed the consensus of countries around the world on development under the guidance of sustainable development and from many perspectives such as environmental protection, political equality, and the eradication of poverty. In September 2000, the second World Summit, held in Johannesburg, summed up the implementation of sustainable development across the world since the Rio conference and created *The Johannesburg Plan of Implementation* and *The Johannesburg Commitment*, which is considered to be the catalyst for the world to move toward the road of sustainable development. *The World Report 2005* written by the World Watch Institute drew the latest trends of global environmental and social development, and explained the underlying causes of threats against global security from the perspective of the global energy crisis, ecological crisis, and demographic crisis. This report pointed out that poverty, infectious diseases, environmental degradation, and the increasingly fierce competition for oil and other finite resources are the root cause of global turmoil.

In February 2008, during the tenth special session of the Governing Council/Global Ministerial Environment Forum of the UNEP in Monaco, UNEP officially released the *UNEP Yearbook 2008*, which said that emerging green economy exists, albeit in infancy, but challenges remain to a future and feasible to accelerate our the pace towards a global low-carbon economy."[6] Thus, it is clear that the concept of sustainable development won unanimous endorsement around the world once it was put forward. Sustainable development, as the idea for the harmonious development of the economy, the environment, and society, indicates the direction human development should take and countries across the planet are beginning to adopt this idea as a guide to economic development.

A Theoretical Analysis of the Evolution of Economic Structure Affecting the Resource Environment

The impact that economic development exerts on the resource environment is ultimately reflected in whether the ecological environment is balanced. With their growing understanding of sustainable development, scholars began to explore what impact economic growth and structural change have on the environment, and established a number of theoretical models to study the relationship between the two. According to the characteristics of these analysis models, they can be divided into four categories: the neoclassical growth model with environmental factors, the neoclassical growth model with the environment as a factor of production, the environment and the endogenous economic growth model, and the environment and other economic growth models.[7] In all these studies, Environmental Kuznets Curve (EKC) is one of the most important and most widespread tools.

Explanation of the Environmental Kuznets Curve (EKC)

In his studies on the income gap, American economist Simon Kuznets, found that the income gap initially increases with economic growth and then gradually shrinks during the process of economic development. If the income gap is set as the vertical coordinate and income per capita as the horizontal coordinate, the two then show the relationship of the inverted U-shaped curve, which is called Kuznets Curve. Later, scholars studying economic development and environmental pollution found similarly that environmental conditions initially deteriorate and then improve during the process of economic development. In their study of the environmental impact from the North American Free Trade Agreement, Gene Grossman and Alan Krueger[8] found that the relationship between the movement trends of most pollutants and income per capita adopts the inverted U-shaped curve. Namely, the degree of pollution first rises and then drops with income per capita, and the peak degree of pollution resides at around the middle-income stage. Grossman and Krueger later[9] further confirmed the existence of this relationship, and this inverted U-shaped curve relationship between environmental pollution and income per capita is known as the EKC.

Fig. 4.1.   The Environmental Kuznets Curve (EKC)

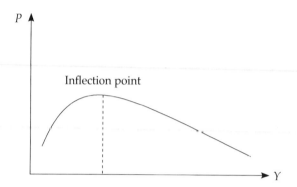

The EKC shows that in the lower income level, environmental pollution rises with the growth of income; then as the economy develops to a certain stage, environmental pollution reaches its maximum; and as the economy continues to develop, environmental pollution falls. This shows that the growth of income per capita will eventually lead to the improvement of the environment. P represents environmental pollution and Y represents income per capita.

If the EKC does exist, it indicates that when economic development reaches a certain turning point, the growth in income contributes to the improvement of the environment; namely, solutions to environmental problems still rely on economic growth, which means economic growth should remain the primary objective of policies. On the basis of the EKC, many empirical studies have shown that there is indeed an inverted U-shaped relationship between environmental quality and income per capita. Shafik (1994)[10] found that with the growth of income per capita, Suspended Particulate Matter (SPM) and sulfur dioxide (SO_2) first deteriorate and then improve; Selden and Song (1994)[11] examined emissions of four important air pollutants SO_2, carbon dioxide (CO_2), nitrogen dioxide (NO_2), and SPM to find there is an inverted U-shaped relationship between each of them and income; Xepapadeas and Amri (1995)[12] confirmed that there is also the same conclusion for the concentration of SO_2 in the atmosphere; Grossman and Krueger (1995)[13] made a cross-country analysis using wider data of environmental quality indicators than they had in 1993 and found that there was no evidence to show that environmental quality keeps deteriorating with economic growth; on the contrary in fact, most indicators deteriorate in the initial stage of economic growth and then show a process of steady improvement. Xepapadeas and Amri (1995)[14] proved that concentrations in the atmosphere also have the same conclusion. Chinese scholars including Chen Wenhua (2004)[15] also examined the relationship between air quality and environmental quality and found that there is an inverted U-shaped relationship between environmental quality and income, therefore verifying the Environmental Kuznets Hypothesis

There are however many scholars who dispute the EKC and who have been recognized by the academic community. The EKC is a simple model which does not propose that economic growth will spontaneously resolve environmental problems and besides, various countries have greatly differing points of inflection and shape of the curve. Therefore, the theory only provides a guideline for the interpretation of complex problems, namely economic development and environmental pollution. Empirical research still requires specific analysis.

As stated before, the EKC studies the relationship between per capita income and environmental pollution indicators and shows the degree of impact economic development has upon environmental pollution. But it is only a simple functional form of per capita income and environmental pollution; it only shows the net effect of changes from per capita income on environmental pollution and fails to take into account what impact individual factors may have on environmental pollution. Therefore, economists began to conduct a factor analysis of economic development on environmental pollution, including scale effects, structural effects, and removal effects.[16]

Scale effects

With the growth of per capita income and the expansion of economic scale, more resources are required; a positive correlation remains between the two. Meanwhile, increasing economic output means an increase in waste and pollutants, hence the decline in environmental quality standards. This is the so-called "scale effects" (see Fig. 4.2a). Andreoni and Levinson (2001)[17] argue that the existence of scale effects is key to the establishment of the EKC. Clearly, for scale effect, environmental pollution is a monotonically increasing function of per capita income.

Structural effects

With increasing levels of productivity, economic structure continues to evolve. As Panayotou (1993)[18] states, when a country's agrarian economy is transformed into an industrial one, the rate of resource consumption begins to exceed that of resource regeneration, the amount of waste generated will increase significantly, and the degree of environmental pollution will also be deepened and the level of environmental quality declines. As economic development mounts to a higher level however, the industrial structure further escalates and shifts from resource-intensive heavy industry to services and technology-intensive industries and environmental pollution will then be reduced. This is known as "structural effects" (see Fig. 4.2b). The structural effects of environmental improvement has also been proved by research from Stern (2004).[19] In fact, structural effects implies technology effects; the upgrade of industrial structure requires technological support; advances in technology improve the utilization of resources in the production process and outdated technologies are replaced by advanced ones; and emissions of pollutants tend to be reduced, all of which contribute to the improvement of environmental quality.

Removal effects

In the early stages of economic development, per capita income remains low, and the focus of attention is how to get rid of poverty and achieve rapid economic growth. Consequently, environmental protection is ignored and environmental deterioration follows. As income levels rise, the consumption of these richer people change and the demand for environmental quality increases as people become concerned about environmental protection. When government revenue is limited, government regulation of environmental pollution remains poor and environmental pollution continues with economic growth. As the economy develops to a certain level, the government's financial capabilities strengthen and its management capabilities improve and environmental laws and policies to protect the environment are also strengthened and the degree of environmental pollution is gradually improved. Therefore, solely for the government's capacity of treatment of environmental pollution, the relationship between environmental pollution and income level is monotonically decreasing, and this is called "removal effects" (see Fig. 4.2c).

To summarize, the EKC can be explained by the following facts: when per capita income is relatively low, its impact on environmental pollution is mainly negative scale effect; when per capita income reaches a certain threshold, structural effects and removal effects come into play and the sum of them will exceed the scale effects. In this case, environmental pollution presents itself as an inverted U-shaped curve in relation to increasing income levels.

Fig. 4.2. The impact of per capita income on environmental pollution

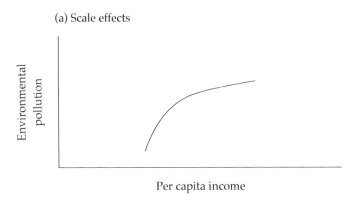

(a) Scale effects

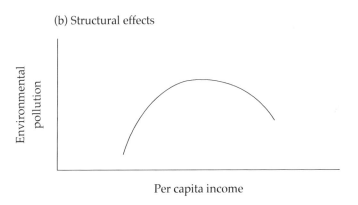

(b) Structural effects

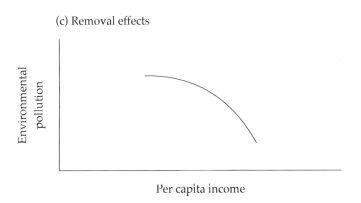

(c) Removal effects

Model analysis of the impact of evolution of economic structure on the environment

Because of different resource consumption in different sectors, different impacts are caused on environmental quality. Of the three industries, secondary industry is more likely to be a pollution-intensive industry than either first or tertiary. With economic development, the structures of the three industries will go through a corresponding adjustment and the effects of structural adjustment on environmental pollution will also change. If the proportion of industrial added value of GDP is used to represent economic structure, it can be seen from the history of economic development that the proportion of industrial added value initially increases with economic growth and then begins to decline as the economy develops from the pre-industrial to the post-industrial stage. Thus, when other factors remain unchanged, the impact of economic structure upon environmental pollution is also an inverted U-shaped curve.

From the perspective of the EKC, changes in the economic structure are a key factor to environmental pollution. This structural effect has caused great concern to many scholars, all of whom have conducted in-depth studies. de Bruyn (1997)[20], Panayotou (1997)[21], López (1994)[22], Jean and Duane (1999)[23], David (2002)[24], Markus (2002)[25], Antonio (2003)[26] and others who explain the EKC from economic structural changes and argue that the EKC is the result of both scale effect and the natural evolution of economic structure. From the studies on the impact of economic structural changes on environmental pollution, the studies are all achieved via the decomposition of polluting emissions. The basic decomposition model decomposes the changes in pollution into the scale effects, which is caused by the expanding economic scale; the structural effects, which is caused by economic structural changes; and the technological effects, which is caused by the changes in the pollution intensity of various sectors. And the extended model can further deconstruct the technology effect into energy composition, energy efficiency, and other technological effects. There are many decomposition models in this respect, but the basic idea is the same. This chapter briefly describes two types of decomposition models.

The three-factor decomposition model

This model divides the impact of economic growth on the environment into three factors, which are intrinsically similar and generally include scale effects, structural effects, technology or policy effects, etc. The following two typical examples are used for an analysis.

The Evolution of Economic Structure and the Resource Environment

The de Bruyn decomposition model[27]

de Bruyn (1997) decomposes the impact of economic growth on environmental quality into three effects, and gives the decomposition model of pollution emissions as follows:

$$\frac{\dot{E}}{E} = \frac{\dot{Y}}{Y} + \sum_{j=1}^{n} e_j \frac{\dot{S}_j}{S_j} + \sum_{j=1}^{n} e_j \frac{\dot{I}_j}{I_j} \qquad (4-1)$$

In the formula, E refers to the country's pollution emissions during the period of t; Y is GDP during period t; e_j is the share of pollution emissions in sector j of total emissions; S_j is the proportion of added value of sector j in GDP during period t; I_j is the intensity of pollution emissions in sector j during period t, that is, E_j/Y_j. In addition, the fractions in the formula represent the rate of change of the variables.

In the above formula, the left item indicates the growth rate of pollution emissions. The first item on the right reflects the scale effects, that is, the growth rate of output, meaning that an increase in output will lead to more pollution; the second item reflects the structural effects, that is, higher contributions to economic growth by a low polluting industry, the lower growth rate of total pollution emissions, and the higher when the opposite is true; the third item is the technology effects, which means that the faster the technological progress in a high pollution emissions sector, the lower the total pollution emissions. The relative importance of various effects can be determined by the above decompositions, in particular, the contribution of structural changes to the environmental pollution reduction.

The Panayotou decomposition model[28]

Panayotou (1997) and Islam, Vincent and Panayotou (1999) pointed out three factors affect the quality of the environment. They are first, the scale of economic activity; second, the structure or composition of economic activity; and third, the income effect on the demand and supply of efforts to reduce pollution. Their environmental effects can be defined as: scale effects, structural effects, and removal effects. The corresponding mathematical expression is:

Pollution level = Per unit area GDP × GDP composition × Efforts of pollution reduction

The model shows that the scale effects of pollution are monotonically increasing functions of income, because the larger the scale of the economic activity per unit area, the higher the level of pollution. With the process of economic growth, economic structure will change. In the low income level stage, changes in economic structure are dominated by the shift from agriculture to industry, with a corresponding increase in the intensity of pollution emissions. In the high income level stage, changes in economic structure are dominated by the shift from industry to services, with its corresponding reduction in emissions intensity. Therefore, the changes in economic structure can be presented by the proportion of industrial added value of GDP, and as a non-monotonic function (an inverted U-shape). After the removal of scale effects and structural effects, the rest is the pure income effect representing the demand and supply of environmental quality.

Four-factor decomposition model

de Groot (2000)[29] also divides the economy into three sectors: the first sector being agricultural, which is in the middle position in respect of the intensity of pollutant emissions in production; the second sector is manufacturing, which holds the largest intensity of emissions; and the third sector is the service sector, which enjoys the lowest emissions intensity. The products of the three sectors are poorly alternative. On the basis of classification of sectors, the decomposition formula of the growth rate of pollution emissions comes into being. The decomposition formula of pollution emissions by de Groot can be expressed as:

$$\frac{\dot{E}}{E} = \frac{\dot{C}}{C} + \sum e_i \frac{\dot{p}_i}{p_i} + \sum e_i \frac{\dot{l}_i}{l_i} + \sum e_i \frac{\dot{s}_i}{s_i} \qquad (4\text{--}2)$$

In the formula, E refers to the amount of pollution emissions; C, the actual total output based on the constant price, and $C = C_1 + C_2 + C_3$; the unit labor emissions $\frac{E_{it}}{L_{it}}$ is expressed as p_i; the reciprocal of labor productivity $\frac{L_{it}}{C_{it}}$, l_{it}; the share of total output $\frac{C_i}{C}$, s_i; the share of pollution emissions $\frac{\dot{E}}{E}$, e_i.

In the above formula, the changes in pollution emissions consist of four parts: changes in output, changes in the unit labor, changes in labor productivity, and changes in the output structure. The latter three changes go through the weighted calculation of the sector's share of total emissions. The combination of the changes in rate of labor emission and labor productivity can be taken as the technological effects, which is related to the technological change and supply, while structural changes are driven by the demand.

de Groot argues that, as a result of the interaction of supply and demand, the changes in industry structure arise from both the technological differences of various sectors, which is a factor of supply, and the different income elasticity of demand for different products, which is also a factor of supply. Changes in the structure of demand resulting from rising incomes would make production and consumption less polluting. With concerns about environmental pollution, the structure of demand would be subject to change and governmental protection of the environment would follow. However, in de Groot's decomposition model, it is difficult to find corresponding cases in practice for the division of the three sectors, let alone corresponding emissions data. Of course, structural changes must meet the following two pre-requisites when imposing an impact on environmental quality: First, industries have different pollution intensities; second, there is a mechanism of change in the structure of industry. When these two conditions are met, changes in economic structure will inevitably have a major impact on environmental pollution, and the degree of impact can be measured and analyzed by the corresponding decomposition model.

A Theoretical Analysis of Constraints of the Resource Environment on Economic Development

Due to its limited carrying capacity, the resource environment is bound to impose strong constraints on the evolution of economic structure. At present, many countries in the world are faced with varying degrees of the excessive consumption of resources, worsening environmental pollution, and other problems. Therefore, human society needs to adjust its economic structure under this constraint in the development process, in order to meet the internal needs of the development of society.

The intrinsic link between the resource environment and economic development

For the existence of scale effects and structural effects, economic development will inevitably have a significant impact on the resource environment. At the same time, the resource environment imposes constraints on the direction and pattern of the evolution of economic structure. The core economic activity is human production and consumption. Production refers to the human involvement in the transformation of the material resource environment. The range of both resource consumption and environmental changes are limited, as excessive consumption of resources will cause the destruction of the human living environment and make social reproduction unsustainable. In order to understand the inherent relationship, factors in the resource environment should be divided into resource factors and environmental factors. The binding relation between the factors and economic growth are analyzed in Fig. 4.3.[30]

Fig. 4.3 can be divided into four quadrants, in which quadrant I refers to

Fig. 4.3. **The binding relationship between output and pollutant emissions**

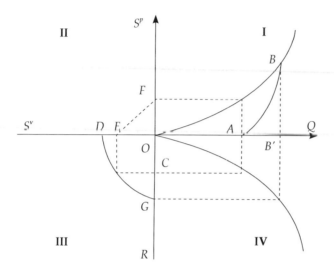

the relationship between output Q and pollutant emissions S^p; quadrant II, the relationship between pollutant emissions S^p and pollutant reduction S^v; quadrant III, the relationship between resources R and pollutant reduction S^v; quadrant IV, the relationship between the resources put into production R and its output Q.

The OB in quadrant I refers to the pollution emission curve. In the case of constant techniques, the emission function has the potential to increase marginal emissions, and the emission function of pollutant production is convex. The curve of quadrant IV is the yield curve, which is concave, as the production function has the characteristic of diminishing marginal productivity. If pollution regulation or reduction is not taken into account, the maximum output of the fixed amount of resources OG is OB', while the pollution emission is OF. When net pollution emissions are 0, there must be a reduction OE equivalent to OF, while the economic resources of the amount of OC are consumed when the pollution of the amount of OE is controlled. The corresponding output is OA, that is, the production reduction is AB'. Therefore, the curve BA shows the binding relation between pollution regulation and production reduction, and reflects the conflicts between environmental quality and the goals of economic growth. At the same time, as a result of technological advances, the production curve moves to the right (quadrant IV), the emissions function decreases (quadrant I), and ultimately the curve BA moves to the right. Sustainable economic development is a dynamic process of economic growth to find the optimal path under the constraints of resource consumption and environmental degradation, in which economic growth proceeds at moderate resource consumption and has environmentally friendly conditions. Economic growth cannot be realized at the expense of resource depletion and environmental degradation. Instead, it must be gained under the guidance of the concept of sustainable development, to coordinate the relationships between economic growth, resource consumption, and environmental protection.

Analysis of the influencing factors of the environmental capacity

A suitable environment is not only the basic condition for human survival and development, but is also the basis for the expansion of social reproduction. In the process of material exchange between humans and the environment, the capacity of the environment is limited, i.e. there are constraints on environmental capacity. Environmental capacity is decided by natural conditions and production technology, as well as other factors. When the level of economic development is well below the limits of environmental capacity, there is great potential in economic development due to weak constraints on economic development by the resource environment. With sustainable development of economy and natural resources, the constraints on economic development by the environment continues to increase. Overall, the factors which can have an impact on environmental capacity in a certain period of time include the following three aspects:

Scale factors

Environmental capacity has a close inner contact with population size and economic scale. The production scale and the consumption scale of human beings have a positive correlation with pollution, which means the larger the population scale, the greater the economic scale and the greater the pollution scale.

The population scale

At present, the issues concerning population and the environment are focused on whether the increase in population will lead to an acceleration in environmental pollution. The neo-Malthusian population pressure hypothesis points out that population growth increases the needs for farmland, which results in deforestation from transforming forests into farms. The population growth also increases the pressure of the environmental absorption of pollutants and waste generated by human activities, which increases environmental pollution and reduces environmental carrying capacities.[31] Grossman and Krueger (1995) studied the effect of population size on environmental quality and pollution emissions, pointing out that population size has a positive scale effect on pollution emissions. In contrast, opponents of the population pressure hypothesis argued that although population growth alone does lead to the environmental degradation, economic development and technological progress will offset or even surpass its negative impact on the environment. In fact, the increasing scarcity of arable land resources will lead to the occurrence of induced technological change in agricultural production, which will offset environmental damage, such as deforestation, caused by population growth. Moreover, with economic development and increasing per capita income, the ability to treat sewage will be improved correspondingly and environmental conditions will eventually also be improved.

The economic scale

Effects on the environment instigated by economic scale include both positive and negative effects, within which, the ultimate result depends on the size of two effects. Negative effects of economic scale mean that economic expansion will increase the level of natural resource usage when the intensity of emission per unit and the economic structure remain unchanged, resulting in increased pollution. This negative effect will be significantly enlarged especially when property rights cannot be clearly identified, the environmental pollution cannot internalize externalities, and government is out of control. Positive effects of economic of scale mean that the expansion of economic scale and increased income will stimulate demand for a clean environment. People are more willing to buy products manufactured within strict environmental standards that reduce pollution on the environment. Thus, when negative effects exceed positive effects, the economic scale will lead to environmental degradation but when negative effects are less than the positive effects, the economic scale will improve the quality of the environment. In general however, the negative is often greater than the positive, which means expansion of economic scale tends to bring the deterioration of the environmental quality. Shafik and Bandyopadhyay (1992)[32] discovered, after studying the environmental factors and per capita incomes of 149 countries, that urban proportions of people who lack sanitation facilities and clean water decline with economic growth, while municipal waste and urban sulfur dioxide emissions increase as income increases.

One economic scale that is a factor affecting the environment and is

The Evolution of Economic Structure and the Resource Environment

increasingly being drawn to the world's attention is international trade. Western scholars have conducted many studies on international trade and environmental issues, believing multi-dimensional links exist between trade and the environment. One view is that free trade and economic growth will lead to increased pollution, threaten the environment, and increase the incidence of market failure. The higher the environmental standards implemented by countries to protect the environment will form export barriers against other countries and will hinder the development of free trade. Another point of view is free trade based on comparative advantage. If a comparative advantage is obtained by the relaxation of international standards, then developing the trade in those goods with that comparative advantage will bring negative impact to the environment and will damage the environmental interests of the country, which will lead to the deterioration of international terms of trade. The polluted haven hypothesis states that under comparative advantage and the international division of labor, there is a vast difference between the effects international trade development has on the environment of developed and developing countries. Lopez (1994)[33], Suri and Chapman (1998)[34] and Copeland and Taylor (1994)[35] argued that because of international trade and direct investment, a situation has arisen whereby high-pollutant products are produced in low-income countries and are consumed in high-income countries. This environmental dumping ameliorates environmental quality in developed countries but deepens environmental degradation in developing countries.

Structural factors

Structural factors often determine the density of pollution. Distinctive differences exist in the industrial structure and technological progress between different countries or regions. In general, the higher the level of industrial structure, the faster technological progress is implemented and the lower relative level of emissions. Conversely, if no attention is paid to the potential pollution control from technological innovation during the industrialization process, then the destruction of nature will become increasingly serious, and will seriously affect the survival and development of human society.

The industrial structure

Industrial structure determines the level and type of resource consumption and environmental pollution and generally has a close relationship with economic development. Because the intensity of emissions differs in different industries, changes in the industrial structure will have a significant impact on environmental capacity. When the proportion of pollution-intensive industries reduces or their development pace decreases, the levels of economic growth that the environment can bear will improve. When the proportion of pollution-intensive industries increases or their development pace accelerates, the limits of economic growth that the environment can bear will decline. Historically, in the development of global economy, a country's level of environmental pollution is closely related to its stage of economic development. When a country's economic development is based primarily on agricultural development, then deforestation and soil erosion are more serious but industrial pollution is less so. When a country enters the industrialized stage, natural resources will be over-harvested and waste emissions will rapidly increase leading to a sharp deterioration in the ecological environment. When a country's economy of one country enters the high-tech and service oriented industries, then proportion of the manufacturing will reduce. An increase in high-tech industries and services enables economic development to no longer over-depend on resource extraction and energy consumption; it is now based on technological innovation, productivity increase, and the innovation of management and organizational forms. This significantly reduces industrial pollution in the production process and the limits of economic growth that the environment can bear will be significantly enhanced.

The technological innovation

A relatively complex relationship exists between environmental capacity and technological progress, and it can both expand and reduce environmental capacity. Most scholars (for example Selden and Song [1994][36] and Magnus [2002][37]) argued that scientific and technological improvements have increased energy and resource efficiency, while reducing resource consumption and pollution emissions. Thus technological progress can significantly expand environmental capacity. Take energy consumption for example. The energy density peak in the U.S. during its period of industrialization in 1920 was lower than that of British industrialization around 1880 and of Japan's energy density peak in its industrialization during the 1960s and 1970s. This means that technological progress plays an important role in improving energy efficiency. Other scholars believed that technological progress was a double-edged sword, in that some technological progresses benefit the improvement of the environmental quality while others may increase pollution emissions. Kristrom (2000)[38] believed that the impact on the environment by technological progress could be divided into the income effect, which has a positive effect on environmental quality, and the substitution effect, which has a negative effect on environmental quality. When the income level is low, the substitution effect is the dominant status and technological progress at this time will cause degradation of the environmental quality as the economic scale expands.

The environmental protection policy

Government supervision and control of environmental protection are important factors affecting environmental capacity. New institutional economics believes that the environmental problems within economic and social development result from externalities whose root cause lies in defects within the property rights system. For instance, who owns the ozone layer? Clean air is difficult to define and the costs of definition are often too high and in the absence of property rights everyone enjoy the free and uncontrolled exploration the resources and the environment with no charge and no responsibility, which causes excessive waste and even the potential depletion of the resource environment. The solution to this problem requires government to draw up relevant policies in order to protect the resource environment.

Any economic activity is carried out using certain resources in certain geographical locations, and relies on certain external environments. The supply of resources is limited and so is environmental capacity. Economic growth, its structure and its methods will be subject to these constraints in environmental capacity. It has been shown that the environment is the very foundation of economic development and it determines the pattern and speed of economic development, which should optimize its internal structure and industrial distribution. Economic development transforms the mode of economic growth and promotes development according to environmental capacity and economic carrying capacity.

The Green Solow Model

With the continuous advance of industrialization, it is ever increasingly significant that the economic development is affected by the constraints of the resource environment. Some economists introduced the factors of resources and the environment into the study of impact on the economic growth by the environmental pollution based on the Solow Model that is the most basic model in the studies of the modern economic growth, giving a good explanation to this problem. Among them, William A. Brock and M. Scott Taylor (2004)[39] gave a systematic exposition of the Green Solow Model, offering basic evidence to the study of the relationship between the economic development and the environmental constraints.

STRUCTURAL ECONOMICS IN CHINA

The Solow Model and its economic implication

The Solow Model, commonly known as the Neoclassical Growth Model, was proposed by the American economist Robert Solow in the 1950s, to describe the source of economic growth and the mechanism by which its growth rate by the growth of the various elements within it. The model has made an important contribution to the study of economics.

In the classic Solow Model, without taking technological progress into account and assuming first, social saving is a function of total social income with s as the saving rate; and second, the labor force grows at a constant rate of n; and third, the production scale and returns remain unchanged. Using a method of factor decomposition, the following core formula (4–3) is reached[40]:

$$\Delta k = sf(k) - (\delta + n)k \qquad (4-3)$$

In this formula, Δk is the effective labor growth per capita, which is a process where the per capita capital grows over time, i.e. capital deepening. Effective labor refers to labor where technological progress exists; $f(k)$ is the per capita output; s is the savings rate; δ is the depreciation rate of capital; and n is the rate of labor growth. Because $sf(k)$ is saving per capita, $(\delta+n)k$ represents the depreciation and increase of the amount of capital needed by the population growth, i.e. capital widening. Therefore, the above formula can be expressed as:

Capital deepening = savings per capita – capital widening

The neoclassic growth model is derived by inserting technological progress (as represented by g), which is an externality:

$$\Delta k = sf(k) - (\delta + n + g)k \qquad (4-4)$$

The Solow Model has profound economic implications: economic growth will converge as a balanced path of growth, on which total output, consumption, and capital grow at the rate of $g+n$ while the corresponding output per capita, consumption per capita, and capital per capita are only determined by technological progress. An increase by the rate of g, that is when technological progress is taken into account, will lead to sustainable growth in output per capita. Once the economy is stable, the increasing rate of output per capita only depends on the growing pace of technological progress, which results from changes in the economic structure, especially industrial structure. Therefore, it can be seen that changes in economic structure cause growth in output per capita. The Solow Model, as a basic model of economic growth, also has limitations. It assumes that technological progress is exogenous but it cannot explain the source of technological progress.

The Solow Model and the constraint of structural revolution

Human economic activities, especially industrial production, will cause environmental pollution. When environmental pollution has accumulated to a certain degree, a serious imbalance in the ecological environment will trigger a global environmental crisis. This will directly harm the survival of human society and sustainable development. Therefore, upon becoming an industrialized society, environmental management and the reduction of pollution becomes an essential part of human social development.

This Green Solow Model improved the traditional Solow Model. It introduced environmental factors into the model and took the reduction of environmental pollution via technological progress into consideration. If we suppose that during a period of time, a country or region has a certain scale of economic activity, it will produce some pollution. But, if measures for reducing environmental pollution are adopted, then the actual amount of pollution spreading into the natural environment will be less than the amount of pollution generated in the economic activities. Meanwhile, the reduction of the environmental pollutants requires some consumption of economic resources, and in this situation, the actual production from human economic activities will be reduced. We assume the proportion of economic activities which aim at the reduction of the environmental pollution is θ of total economic output and the actual ratio of effective output is $1-\theta$. According to the above ideas, the Green Solow Model can be obtained on the basis of the classical Solow Model and be represented as the following equation:

$$\Delta k = sf(k)(1-\theta)-(\delta+n+g)k \qquad (4\ 5)$$

The economic implications of the equation are: first, there is a balanced path of growth in the Green Solow Model, as in the classic Solow Model. However, because some activities that can reduce environmental pollution exist in the Green Solow Model, i.e. some parts of the models are used to manage the environmental pollution, then the convergence value in the Green Solow Model is less than that of the standard Solow model, and so is the value of final output. Second, when environmental pollution does not reduce technological progress, the equilibrium path of growth of the Solow model under environmental constraints is unsustainable. Only when technological progress to reduce environmental pollution exceeds the growth rate of total output can a balanced path of growth be achieved. Third, there is a relationship, as described in

STRUCTURAL ECONOMICS IN CHINA

the Kuznets curve, between the environmental pollution and the level of per capita income. It can be seen that environmental pollution and its control are important in constraining the adjustment of the industrial structure one of a country. At the same time, a country needs to improve its ability to purify the environment via the technological progress, reduce the constraints to economic growth of environmental pollution, and promote the harmonious development of both economic growth and the environment.

Chapter 5

Evolution and Imbalance of China's Investment and Consumption Structures

STRUCTURAL ECONOMICS IN CHINA

Since reform and opening up, both China's investment structure and consumption structure have upgraded and the proportion of the two has experienced great changes. Especially since the 1990s, investment rates have kept hiking, while the growth of consumption stayed crawling; at the same time, over-investment has exerted more pressures on the resource environment, and economic and financial risks have been amplified, thus undermining the sustainable development of the economy. This chapter focuses on analyzing main characteristics of China's investment and consumption structures, and the degrees and causes of the imbalance of these structures.

Main Characteristics of China's Investment and Consumption Structures

With the increasing per capita income, the structure of China's demand has been constantly optimized, so has the investment structure.

Dramatic changes in the investment and consumption structures

The rapid economic development contributes to a rapidly expanding fixed assets investment (see Fig. 5.1). During the Eighth Five-Year Plan, the investment of fixed assets amounted to RMB6.38 trillion with an average annual clip at 36.9%.[1] During this period, investment in pillar industries such as machinery and electronics, automobile, and petro-chemistry increased dramatically. During the Ninth Five-Year Plan, investment continued to grow yet at a slower average annual rate of 12.4%. Investment in this five-year period was mainly devoted in large-scale infrastructure such as railways, highways, power plants and communicative facilities; and constructions in processing industries were drastically reduced. Since the Tenth Five-Year Plan, the investment of fixed assets has rebounded rapidly. The rapid growth of industries including residences, automobiles, telecommunications and infrastructure directly brings about the development of heavy chemical industries such as iron and steel, nonferrous metals, machinery and chemical industry. It is thus clear that, since the 1990s, China's heavy industry–oriented investment structure has a significant impact on industrial development and economic operation.

Besides, with the rapid increase in per capita income, the consumption structure has been optimizing. The consumption expenditure per capita of urban households increased by 6.82 times from RMB1,278.89 in 1990 to RMB9,997.47 in 2007; while that of the rural households increased by 4.51

Evolution and Imbalance of China's Investment and Consumption Structures

times from RMB584.63 in 1990 to RMB3,223.85 in 2007. Engel's coefficient of urban residents decreased year on year, from 54.2% in 1990 to 36.3% in 2007; Engel's coefficient of rural residents was as high as 58.8% in 1990 and reduced to lower than 50% in 2000 and to 43.1% in 2007.[2] Developmental and enjoyment consumption, such as transportation, communications, culture, education and entertainment, and medical care increased substantially and the proportion increased steadily. For example, the per capita expenditure on transportation and communication of urban households was RMB40.51 in 1990 and increased by 32.5 times to RMB1,357.41 in 2007; the per capita expenditure on culture, entertainment and education increased from RMB112.26 in 1990 by 10.8 times to RMB1,329.16 in 2007.

Fig. 5.1.   Changes in China's fixed assets investment, 1980–2007

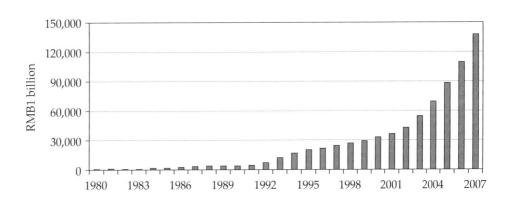

The overall rise of the investment-to-consumption ratio

The ratio of investment to consumption is an important indicator to measure the investment and consumption structures. Investment rate and consumption rate can be calculated by expenditure-based GDP;[3] and then dividing the investment rate by the consumption rate to obtain the investment-to-consumption ratio.[4] Table 5.1 shows that the investment rate generally demonstrated an ongoing trend from 1978 to 2007 while the consumption rate went the opposite direction.

Specifically, China's consumption rate declined from 62.1% in 1978 to 49% in 2007, whereas the investment rate rose from 38.2% in 1978 to 42.1% in 2007. In this process, there were two major changes. The first one happened in 1993, during which China's economic growth accelerated, and investment in the whole society, especially investment in infrastructure, increased rapidly.

STRUCTURAL ECONOMICS IN CHINA

Investment rate rose from 36.6% to 42.6% and consumption rate declined from 61.7% to 59.3% in 1992. The second change occurred during 2001 to 2003, when investment rate rose from 36.5% to 41.0% and consumption rate declined from 61.4% to 56.8%. Investment-led economy has become increasingly dominant, and the development of heavy industries is more prominent (see Fig. 5.2).

Table 5.1. Changes in the investment-to-consumption ratio, 1978–2007

Year	Consumption Rate (%)	Investment Rate (%)	Ratio of Investment to Consumption
1978	62.1	38.2	0.62
1980	65.5	34.8	0.53
1985	66.0	38.1	0.58
1990	62.0	35.2	0.57
1995	58.1	40.3	0.69
1998	59.6	36.2	0.61
2000	62.3	35.3	0.57
2001	61.4	36.5	0.59
2002	59.6	37.9	0.64
2003	56.8	41.0	0.72
2004	54.3	43.2	0.80
2005	51.8	42.7	0.82
2006	49.9	42.7	0.86
2007	49.0	42.1	0.86

Source: *China Statistical Yearbook (2008)*.

Fig. 5.2. Changes in China's fixed assets investment, 1980–2007

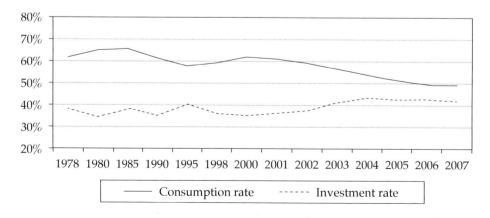

Evolution and Imbalance of China's Investment and Consumption Structures

It can be seen from Fig. 5.3 that the overall proportion of investment to consumption shows a ladder-like upward trend. The ratio of investment to consumption was between 0.5 and 0.6 in 1978–1992, between 0.6 and 0.7 in 1993–2003, and between 0.7 and 0.9 in 2003–2007. These three changes were accompanied by small fluctuations, but the rising trend of the investment-to-consumption ratio did not change.

Fig. 5.3. Changes in China's fixed assets investment, 1980–2007

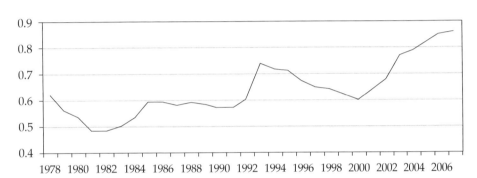

The widening gap between urban and rural consumption

Urban income has long been higher than rural income, and the rural consumers' demands keep weak, which triggers an ever-enlarging gap between rural and urban areas. It can be seen from Fig. 5.4 that the year 1990 is the turning point. Before 1990, the portion of urban residents' consumption was less than that of rural residents' consumption; the year 1990 saw the urban residents' initial overtaking, and this outscoring has been maintained and enlarged ever since. The proportion of urban residents' consumption in the total consumption reached 74.4% in 2007, which implies that the increase of China's consumption in recent years mainly came from urban residents. In fact, rural people accounting for 60% of the national population only had 40% consumption, while urban people accounting for 40% had 60% consumption, which reflected China had an inverted "dual-structure" phenomenon of urban-rural income and consumption.

STRUCTURAL ECONOMICS IN CHINA

Fig. 5.4. Changes in consumption of China's rural and urban residents, 1978–2007

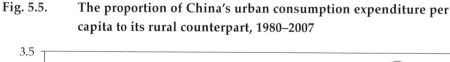

From the perspective of per capita consumption, the per capita consumption expenditure of urban residents in 1980 was RMB412.44 and exceeded RMB5,000 in 2000, and then it reached RMB9,997.47 in 2007, an increase of 23.24 times compared with 1980; the per capita consumption expenditure of rural residents was RMB162.21 in 1980 and exceeded RMB1,000 in 1994, and it reached RMB3,223.85 in 2007, an increase of 18.87 times compared with 1980. From the proportion of the urban consumption expenditure per capita to the rural one, the figure always remained at more than 2 times and this proportion was 2.63 from 1980 to 2007, which fully demonstrates that there is always a considerable gap between China's urban and rural consumption levels. Specifically, this gap declined in the early stage of the reform and opening up and expanded in the mid-late 1980s. This gap has expanded to over 3 times since 2000, and especially, the gap reached the maximum 3.5 times in 2003 (see Fig. 5.5).

Fig. 5.5. The proportion of China's urban consumption expenditure per capita to its rural counterpart, 1980–2007

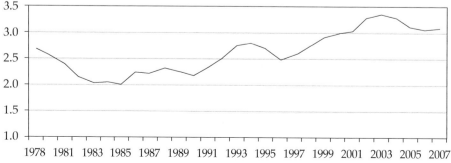

Evolution and Imbalance of China's Investment and Consumption Structures

There are gaps of consumption levels between consumer groups of different income levels in the two main groups of urban residents and rural residents. The gap between the high-income group and the low-income group, in particular, is quite big. The per capita consumption expenditure of the urban high-income group (accounting for 10% of the total urban population) was RMB9,250.63 in 2000, while that of the urban low-income group (accounting for 10% of the total urban population) was RMB2,540.13. The gap between the two was 3.64 times. However, the figures were RMB23,337 and RMB4,036 respectively in 2007 and the gap expanded to 5.8 times. Meanwhile, the per capita consumption expenditure of the rural high-income group (accounting for 20% of the total rural population) and the rural low-income group was RMB5,994.43 (accounting for 20% of the total rural population) and RMB1,850.59 respectively in 2007. The gap expanded to 3.2 times, smaller than its urban counterpart.

The significant increase in the proportion of the government investment

The government's investment is an important means of macroeconomic control. The main object of investment is public goods such as public facilities and public utilities. Since the 1990s, the absolute amount of Chinese government's investment and its proportion in GDP has been on the rise. Especially since 2003, the growth of governmental investment has accelerated noticeably. From the perspective of the absolute figures, the government invested RMB59.6 billion in 1992 and over RMB1,000 billion in 2006, 15 times more than in 1992. Since the Asian financial crisis in 1997, the Chinese government, in order to expand the domestic demand, has adopted an active fiscal policy by issuing a large number of treasury bonds to increase investment. In August, 1998, China first issued long-term treasury bonds of RMB100 billion which were invested in transportation, energy, raw materials and other infrastructure. China then issued more treasury bonds year by year. During 2001 to 2007, China issued treasury bonds worth a total of RMB5.96 trillion. Active fiscal policies lead to investment of many sources such as counterpart fund of local governments, departments, and corporations, and bank loans.

In addition, since 1992, the proportion of governmental investment in GDP has also shown a ring trend (see Fig. 5.6). Governmental investment accounted for 2.21% in GDP in 1992, and this figure kept increasing to 3.59% in 2002 despite of minor fluctuation, and to 7% in 2003 and then remained stable at around 5%. The reason why governmental investment increased rapidly is that the government increased investment in public infrastructure such as transportation, construction, energy and raw materials, and in public service facilities such as health care.

STRUCTURAL ECONOMICS IN CHINA

Fig. 5.6.   Changes in the proportion of the Chinese government investment in GDP, 1992–2006

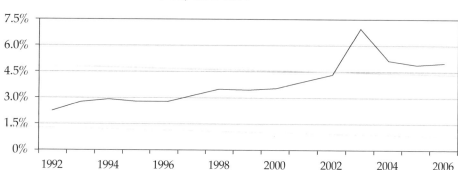

The dramatic increase in real estate investment

As the basis of urban construction, real estate is an important part of the national economy. In August 2003, the State Council Document No. 18 clearly placed the real estate industry as a pillar industry of China's national economy. Real estate has become an important part of economic development and a new growth point of the national economy.

Since the 1990s, China's investment in real estate has constantly expanded. Investment in the development of real estate was only RMB25.33 billion in 1990, and it exceeded RMB100 billion in 1993 and RMB1,000 billion in 2003. The national investment in real estate development was up to RMB 2,530 billion, 99.8 times compared in 1990. Moreover, the growth rate of investment in real estate was generally faster than that of gross capital formation (GCF). As shown in Fig. 5.7, apart from 1995 to 1997, the growth rate of investment in real estate during other years was higher than that of GCF. During 1991 to 1994, both growth rates experienced a fluctuation of a rapid increase and then decrease; the volatility of the growth rate of real estate development was obviously greater than that of gross capital formation. After 1998, both the growth rate began to recover yet in a slow clip, but the growth rate of investment in real estate was significantly higher than that of the GCF.

The rapid development of real estate can be reflected in the changes of the proportion of investment in real estate in GCF. As shown in Table 5.2, during 1990 to 1994, the proportion of investment in real estate in GCF increased rapidly from 3.75% to 12.56%, and then declined slightly from 1995 to 1997. After 1997, this proportion rebounded to 10.61% in 1997 and to 22.93% in 2007, which displayed the great potential of the development of this industry.

Evolution and Imbalance of China's Investment and Consumption Structures

Fig. 5.7. The comparison between the growth rate of real estate investment and that of the total investment

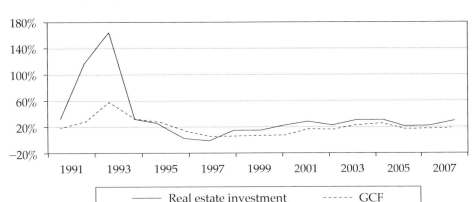

Table 5.2. The proportion of China's real estate investment of GCF, 1990–2007

Year	Investment in Real Estate (RMB100 million)	GCF (RMB100 million)	Proportion of Investment in Real Estate of GCF (%)
1990	25.33	674.70	3.75
1995	314.90	2,547.01	12.36
1996	321.64	2,878.49	11.17
1997	317.84	2,996.80	10.61
1998	361.42	3,131.42	11.54
1999	410.32	3,295.15	12.45
2000	498.41	3,484.28	14.30
2001	634.41	3,976.94	15.95
2002	779.09	4,556.50	17.10
2003	1,015.38	5,596.30	18.14
2004	1,315.83	6,916.84	19.02
2005	1,590.92	7,955.98	20.00
2006	1,942.29	9,440.20	20.57
2007	2,527.97	11,025.08	22.93

Source: *China Statistical Yearbook.*

The rise in income of residents and the growing demand for real estate bring about the continuous increase in real estate prices, in which prices of commercial housing and prices of residences are the most representative. Fig. 5.8 shows that the average price of commercial housing was only RMB786/m² in 1991. It increased slowly from 1997 to 2002 and suddenly accelerated in 2003. It reached the peak in 2005 and amounted to RMB3,112/m² in 2006. Meanwhile, the increase trend of residence prices was basically consistent with that of commercial housing prices. The prices of residences were just slightly below prices of commercial housing. Because locations and economic development of various regions around the country were quite different, local housing prices varied widely. The increase of housing prices in large and medium-sized cities, in particular, was far above the national average. For example, real estate prices of big cities like Beijing, Shanghai and Guangzhou always stayed ahead in the country.

Fig. 5.8.   The average price of China's commercial and residential housing, 1991–2006

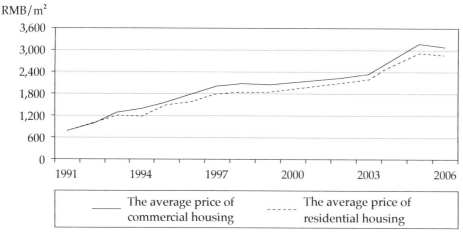

Judgment of China's Unbalanced Investment and Consumption Structures

Modest investment-to-consumption ratio is an important condition for the normal economic growth, while the unbalanced structure of investment and consumption will lead to an inefficient and unsustainable macroeconomic cycle. This section focuses on the national economic operation, comparison of international experience, investment efficiency and real estate prices, to determine the degree of unbalanced structure of China's investment and consumption.

Evolution and Imbalance of China's Investment and Consumption Structures

Judgment of the degree of the unbalanced investment and consumption structures

It is difficult to measure an unbalanced investment and consumption structures, because it is hard to determine a recognized evaluation standard. According to the domestic and foreign research results, plus the actual situation of economic operation, the extent of unbalanced structure of investment and consumption can be determined from the following four perspectives.

First, it is the determination based on the economic operation indicators. In Western countries, the Phillips curve is usually used in measuring the relationship between potential output and actual output, so as to determine whether the investment and consumption are reasonable. In the case of a high rate of inflation corresponding to the Phillips curve, the investment will be overheated, and the unemployment rate relatively low; while in the case of a low rate of inflation corresponding to the Phillips curve, the investment will be too rigid, and the unemployment rate relatively high. Western countries usually develop discretionary fiscal and monetary policies based on this relationship, to keep the inflation rate and unemployment rate within a socially acceptable level. However, due to China's developing market economy, it would go awry when these two indicators are alone used to determine whether the investment and consumption structure is reasonable. A number of indicators of the national economy must be integrated to the determination.

Second, it is the determination based on the investment efficiency. The investment efficiency is an important evaluation criterion in determining whether the investment is overheating. It consists of two levels: the macro-yield of investment, namely, how much the total fixed asset investment promotes the economic growth; the profitability of micro-enterprise capital, which determines the level of return on investment. Herein we mainly analyze the macro-investment-output ratio, in order to judge whether the structure of China's investment and consumption is balanced and reasonable.

Third, it is the determination based on the housing price earnings ratio. When industrialization and urbanization develop to a certain stage, there would be a rapid escalation of demand for the real estate development, and the proportion of real estate investment of the total investment will continue to increase. But, as a high risk industry, the rapid development of the real estate development will lead to a rapid expansion of housing credit of the financial institutions, driving up a virtual rise of asset prices, and thus may lead to a bubble economy. Thus, when a country's economy develops to a certain level, the extent of unbalanced structure of investment and consumption can be determined by the comparison between the real estate prices and income levels.

Fourth, it is the determination based on the international comparison. Although the structure of investment and consumption is closely related to the cultural traditions, habits and many other special factors of the countries, some universal laws still remain in the evolution of the structure of investment and consumption, hence a good reference for the after-coming national economic development. Especially in the case of a failure to find a specific optimal ratio of the structure of investment and consumption, the experience of the development and changes of different countries in different historical stages, the structure of investment and consumption of similar countries or countries in the same stage of development can serve as a reference for the reasonable range of China's structure of investment and consumption. It is worth emphasizing that the international comparison of the structure of investment and consumption includes two levels of analysis: the summary of general laws of the investment and consumption structures; the investment and consumption structure of the countries in the same stage of economic development.

Judgment based on economic operation indicators

The main indicators of national economic operations include the GDP growth rate, inflation rate, unemployment rate and balance of payments. In the analysis of indicators, the resident consumer price index is used to represent the rate of inflation, the registered urban unemployment rate to represent the rate of unemployment,[5] and the foreign trade surplus ratio to reflect the balance of payments. Since the reform and opening-up, China's GDP continued to show a rapid growth, and the average annual GDP growth rates during 1979–2007, 1991–2007, and 2001–2007 were respectively 9.8%, 10.4% and 10.5%; the price levels suffered drastic fluctuations before the Reform, while basically remain stable at a low level in the 21st century; the foreign trade steps from deficit to surplus, with an increasing size of surplus; the unemployment rate dropped to a lower level in the early period of the Reform, but slowly rises in the 1990s and later periods, as shown in Table 5.3.

The varying relationships of China's four major economic target variables after the Reformation and Opening are shown by Fig. 5.9. All the macroeconomic indicators were in a good condition during 1981–1987, which was characterized by the rapid economic growth, stable price level, decreasing unemployment rate, and the basic balance of international payments. During this period, the average consumption rate was 65%, and the average investment rate 35%. From the late 1980s to the late 1990s, the national economy shifted from inflation to deflation, the total supply and demand seriously in imbalance.

Evolution and Imbalance of China's Investment and Consumption Structures

The national economy stepped out of the shadow of deflation in 2003, but there remained two major problems: First, as a result of the development model of rapid development of heavy chemical industry and the slow development of service industry, the employment elasticity remained low and the unemployment rate increased; second, with China's entry to the WTO, the export surplus increased dramatically. In 2006, the trade surplus accounted for nearly 7% of GDP, while in 2007 this proportion rose to 10.8%. According to the basic principles of macroeconomics, the surplus is a result of the high domestic savings rate, high investment rate and low consumption rate. Thus it can be seen that the main indicators of China's national economy since the late 1980s suffered a certain degree of skewness, and the proportion of investment and consumption remained in a relatively reasonable range.

Table 5.3. Changes in China's main macroeconomic indicators, 1978–2007 (%)

Year	GDP Growth Rate	Consumer Price Index	Surplus Rate (Deficit Rate) of Foreign Trade	Registered Urban Unemployment Rate
1978	11.7	100.7	−0.5	5.3
1980	7.8	107.5	−0.6	4.9
1985	13.5	109.3	−5.0	1.8
1990	3.8	103.1	2.2	2.5
1995	10.9	117.1	2.3	2.9
1996	10.0	108.3	1.4	3.0
1997	9.3	102.8	4.2	3.1
1998	7.8	99.2	4.3	3.1
1999	7.6	98.6	2.7	3.1
2000	8.4	100.4	2.0	3.1
2001	8.3	100.7	1.7	3.6
2002	9.1	99.2	2.1	4.0
2003	10.0	101.2	1.5	4.3
2004	10.1	103.9	1.7	4.2
2005	10.4	101.8	4.6	4.2
2006	11.6	101.5	6.8	4.1
2007	11.9	104.8	10.8	4.0

Source: *China Statistical Yearbook (2008)*.
Note: The surplus rate (deficit rate) of foreign trade is obtained when the surplus (deficit) is divided by the value of GDP.

Fig. 5.9. Changes in China's major economic indicators, 1978–2007

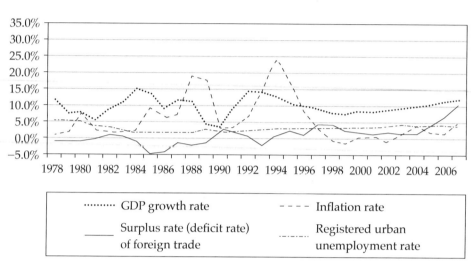

Fig. 5.10. Changes in China's ICOR, 1981–2007

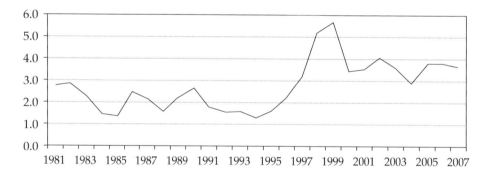

Judgment based on the investment efficiency

The increment capital output ratio (ICOR)[6] is an internationally accepted core indicator of the evaluation of investment efficiency. In the case of constant economic growth, the high investment rate is associated with the relatively low macroeconomic efficiency.

It can be seen from Fig. 5.10 that the ICOR changes are significantly divided into two phases: the first phase is from the early 1980s to 1996.

ICOR has been fluctuating around 2, and the investment efficiency is relatively high; the second phase begins from 1997, when ICOR gradually increased, while the investment efficiency declined. After the Asian Financial

Evolution and Imbalance of China's Investment and Consumption Structures

Crisis, the central government implemented a proactive fiscal policy, so that the investment rose sharply in terms of both scale and speed, and the economic growth increased, but there were a lot of repeated construction and blind construction, resulting in decreasing investment efficiency. China's ICOR in 2007 was 3.65; the macro-investment efficiency was increased, but the overall trend was still downward.

Japan experienced the period of rapid economic growth in the 1960s and South Korea 1980s, in a certain degree, comparable to China's current economic development. It can be seen from Fig. 5.10 and Table 5.4 that the investment efficiency during 1983–1996 was relatively high, and ICOR remained below 2.5. The ratio investment to consumption in this phase should be relatively reasonable. The average investment rate during this period was 37.7%, while the average consumption rate 62.2%. The average ICOR from 1997 to 2006 was 4, higher than the level of Japan and South Korea during the rapid economic growth periods, indicating that the investment efficiency was low. It is clearly unsustainable that high economic growth relies on high investment. On the one hand, this model will increase the economic and financial risks. As Krugman put after the East Asian financial crisis, as of 1997, Malaysia had to use 40 percent of GDP for investment and Singapore 40% to 45%, in order to maintain high growth rates; in the entire East Asian region, the ICOR mounted up to 5 times.[7] As the capital and other resources are limited, this model created a huge economic bubble, and eventually led to the Asian financial crisis. On the other hand, this extensive model of economic development of high input led to excessive use of the resource environment. According to the calculations of Lin Yifu, China's GDP accounted for 5.5% of the global total in 2006, while the energy consumption accounted for 15% of the world's total, the steel consumption 30%, and the cement consumption 54%.[8] China has been paying for the high environmental costs; according to statistics, the economic loss due to the environmental pollution in 2004 was RMB511.8 billion, accounting for 3.05% of GDP.[9] Thus, the high investment rates in recent years are inefficient and unbalanced.

Table 5.4. ICOR comparison of China, Japan and South Korea during their rapid economic growth periods

Country	Year	GDP Growth Rate (%)	ICOR
Japan	1961–1970	10.2	3.2
South Korea	1981–1990	9.2	3.2
China	1997–2006	9.2	4.0

Sources: Based on the relevant years of *International Statistical Yearbook* and *China Statistical Yearbook (2007)*.

Judgment based on the housing price earnings ratio

Housing price earnings ratio is an international composite indicator commonly used to measure the urban housing purchasing power and the housing price level, as well as a basis to determine whether the real estate investment is overheated or there are economic bubbles. There has not been a uniform definition of the housing price earnings ratio in China. It is generally defined as "the ratio between the housing price level and income," while based on the *Urban Indicators Toolkit Guide*[10] published by the Human Settlements Center of the United Nations, the housing price earnings ratio refers to the "ratio between the median free-market price and median household income of the dwelling unit," and the housing price refers to the median housing price of various types of houses in the market.[11]

We use the ratio between the average housing sales price and the disposable income per urban household to reflect the housing price earnings ratio, and do not use the assumption of "80m² (or 60m²) per household and the family of three (or two)," so the impacts of the changes in family size, urban per capita living area upon the housing price earnings ratio can be objectively reflected. This indicator reflects the average level of housing ability to pay and, to some extent, can measure whether the housing prices are relatively high to the buyers, and whether there exist bubbles. As can be seen from Table 5.5, the housing prices income ratio during 1992–1993 was relatively high, more than 6. The housing prices income ratio remained stable from 1994 to 2003, of which the rise of housing prices during 1995–1998 was slightly higher than that of the income, and the housing prices income ratio steadily increased; the rise of residential income during 1999–2003 was slightly higher than that of the housing prices, and the housing prices income ratio steadily declined. Since 2004, the housing prices increased faster than the income growth; the housing prices income ratio rose fast, over 6 in 2004 and up to 7.12 in 2007.

The housing prices income ratio of developed countries is generally 3 to 4 times higher than the international standard, that is, a middle-level family can buy a medium-grade house equivalent to their three to four years' total incomes. The current U.S. housing price earnings ratio is about three times above the standard, Japan is five to six times. It is reasonable for the ratio to maintain in a three-to-six-time range; while the housing prices are relatively "unaffordable" when it exceeds six. In 1998, the State Council of China made it clear in relevant documents on housing reform that housing subsidies should be offered when the housing price earnings ratio is more than 4 times.[12] With reference to the standard, China's housing price earnings ratio has been significantly high, especially in some major cities. For example, the housing price earnings ratios in Shenzhen were 6.52 times and 9.83 times respectively in 2004 and 2005, and even soared to 15.7 times in 2006; while the housing price earnings ratios of Shanghai, Beijing, Guangzhou and other cities have all hit double digits.

Table 5.5. The average housing price earnings ratio of China, 1992–2007

Year	Per Capita Housing Area	Average Population Per Household	Average Housing Area Per Household	Unilateral Housing Price	Total Housing Price Per Household	Average Per Capita Total Annual Income	Total Annual Income Per Household	Housing Price Earnings Ratio
	(1)	(2)	(3)=(1)×(2)	(4)	(5)=(3)×(4)	(6)	(7)=(2)×(6)	(8)=(5)/(7)
	m²/one person	person/household	m²/one person	RMB/m²	RMB/household	RMB/person	RMB/household	—
1992	14.8	3.37	49.88	996	49,676	2,032	6,848	7.26
1995	16.3	3.23	52.65	1,509	79,447	4,288	13,850	5.74
1998	18.7	3.16	59.09	1,854	109,557	5,458	17,247	6.35
1999	19.4	3.14	60.92	1,857	113,121	5,888	18,488	6.12
2000	20.3	3.13	63.54	1,948	123,774	6,296	19,706	6.28
2001	20.8	3.10	64.48	2,017	130,056	6,869	21,294	6.11
2002	22.8	3.04	69.31	2,092	145,001	8,177	24,858	5.83
2003	23.7	3.01	71.34	2,197	156,727	9,061	27,274	5.75
2004	25.0	2.98	74.50	2,608	194,296	10,129	30,184	6.44
2005	26.1	2.96	77.26	2,937	226,901	11,321	33,510	6.77
2006	30.7	2.95	90.57	3,119	282,472	12,719	37,522	7.53
2007	31.6	2.91	92.00	3,356	308,604	14,909	43,385	7.12

Source: National Bureau of Statistics. The housing prices therein referred to are obtained from *Macro China* (available online at www.macrochina.com.cn).

Judgment based on the international comparisons

Due to the different models of industrialization, economic structures, the investment rates vary greatly from country to country. In the industrial period, the investment rate increases with the increasing degrees of industrialization, while the consumption rate shows an opposite trend. But both the investment rate and consumption rate remain stable after the process of industrialization. According to the studies of Chenery and others, the average investment rate in the initial stage of industrialization is 15%; the middle stage, 20%; the last

STRUCTURAL ECONOMICS IN CHINA

stage, 23%.[13] As the economic system, industrial structure, consumption habits and traditions are different from country to country, the investment rates and consumption rates will be different too, even in the same stage of development, but the comparison between countries help us understand the general laws of international investment rates and consumption rates.

Comparisons of the investment rate and the consumption rate

From the developing trend, in the process of the industrialization at the early and mid-term stages, as the level of the income per capita increases and the industrial structure upgrades, the investment rate is improved in fluctuation, corresponding to the gradual decline in the consumption rate. This trend will remain for a longer period. The fluctuation range of the investment rate and consumption rate will decrease gradually and eventually comes to a relatively stable state.

From the trend of the world development, there is a trend of gradual decline of the average investment rate of the world but a slow upward trend of the consumption rate, as shown in the Table 5.6. The world's average investment rate was 23.4% in 1990, 22.4% in 2000 and reduced to 20.7% in 2003. Since the 1990s, the investment and consumption rates in China have turns an opposite trend to the global trend. From 1990 to 2007, the investment rate rose from 35.2% to 42.1% with an increase of 6.9% while the consumption rate decreased significantly from 62% in 1990 to 49% in 2005 with a decline of 13%.

Analyzed from the relationship between the income level and the ration of the investment and consumption, the level of income goes in the opposite trend with the investment rate but in the same direction with the consumption rate, excluding in the low-income countries. That means, with the improvement of the level of income, the investment rate decreases constantly but the consumption rate increases continuously. China belongs to the ranks of middle-income countries, but the direction of changes is on the contrary with the universal law since the 1990s.

Compared with in developed countries as Japan and the U.S., the investment rate in China exceeds nearly 20%. South Korea is one of the countries with relatively high investment rate in the world with 37.5% in 1990 and a stable level of 30% currently. But China's investment rate was 43.2% in 2004, higher than that of South Korea. Compared with in other developing countries and transforming courtiers, the investment rate in China is significantly high. It was about twice than that of Mexico, Brazil and Russia in 2005. The international comparison shows that the investment rate is high since the 1990, which exceeds not only the global average level, but also the level of high investment rate in the world. However, the consumption rate is far below the world average.

Table 5.6. The International comparison of the investment rate and consumption rate in different periods (%)

Country	Investment Rate					Consumption Rate				
	1990	2000	2003	2004	2005	1990	2000	2003	2004	2005
World Average	23.4	22.4	20.7	—	—	76.8	77.7	—	—	—
Low Income Countries	21.1	22.2	24.8	26.6	29.0	82.4	80.3	79.7	79.1	78.0
Middle Income Countries	25.9	24.2	24.6	25.9	26.0	73.4	73.5	71.7	78.2	—
Low-and-middle Income Countries	25.2	23.9	24.6	26.0	34.0	74.7	74.5	72.8	71.2	—
High Income Countries	22.9	22.0	19.9	20.0	34.0	77.3	78.4	71.0	71.0	—
The U.S.	17.7	20.5	18.0	—	—	83.7	83.4	86.5	—	—
Japan	32.9	26.3	23.9	23.0	—	66.2	72.3	74.5	75.4	—
South Korea	37.5	31.0	30.0	30.0	30.0	63.6	65.8	67.7	65.4	67.6
Mexico	23.1	23.9	20.5	22.1	21.8	78.0	78.1	81.1	80.0	79.8
India	24.2	27.2	31.0	33.0	77.4	76.8	74.0	71.9	69.6	24.1
Brazil	20.2	21.5	19.8	21.3	19.3	78.6	80.0	76.6	74.2	71.9
Russia	30.1	18.7	20.8	20.8	20.9	69.7	61.3	67.9	66.8	65.3

Source: *International Statistic Yearbook (2007)*.

The international comparison of the investment rate

It is generally considered to be an important period of economic and social transformation of a country or region when the per capita GDP reaches USD1,000. During this period, the industrialization transforms from the primary stage to the mid-term stage where the urbanization of population accelerates and the level of the investment rate is relatively high.

It can be concluded from Table 5.7 that the other nine countries apart from China, the highest investment rate was 33.5% in Japan (1966) when the per capita GDP reached USD1,000 while the lowest was 22.8% in both Mexico (1974) and Malaysia (1977). China's investment rate was 42.9% when China's per capita GDP reached USD1,000, but the average investment rate of the other nine countries was only 27.2%. This shows that when the per capita GDP hits USD1,000, China's investment rate was much higher than that of the other nine countries, which proves China's unduly high rate of investment.

Table 5.7. The comparison of investment rate when the per capita reached USD1,000

Countries	Year when per Capita GDP Reached USD1,000	Investment Rate (%)
Japan	1966	33.5
Thailand	1988	31.8
Indonesia	1995	31.3
South Korea	1977	29.6
Brazil	1975	25.1
Argentina	1961	24.3
The Philippines	1995	23.5
Mexico	1974	22.8
Malaysia	1977	22.8
China	2003	42.9

Sources: *International Statistic Yearbook* (various years).

Note: In order to reduce the effect of the fluctuation and precisely reflect the investment rate when the per capita GDP reached 1,000 U.S. dollars, the average amount of three years in all the countries other than China was adopted instead of the actual number of the specific year.

Generally, in the 1980s, the relationship of China's investment-to-consumption ratio struggled an overall balance, but since the 1990s, the overall level of investment rate has been increasing while the consumption rate has been declining, showing a changing trend running on the contrary with the change of the relationship of the rate between the global investment and consumption. Particularly in recent years, the investment rate has always been high yet the consumption rate has continuously declined. There is a trend that the imbalance between the investment and consumption structures will be exacerbated, which will seriously affect the sustainable development of the national economy and the improvement of people's living standard.

Analysis of the Imbalance of the Investment and Consumption Structures

The reasons for the imbalance between the structure of investment and consumption in China are vary. There are internal factors including the industrialization and the rapid development of the urbanization, as well as the external factors involving the institutional and the macroeconomic policies.

Evolution and Imbalance of China's Investment and Consumption Structures

Generally, reasons for the imbalance of the investment and consumption structures involve: the underdeveloped investment system, the irrational development of the element market, the low labor wages, the large distribution gap of income and the imperfect system of the social security.

The underdeveloped investment system

Along the process of China's economic transformation, the imperfect investment system has always been the main reason for the investment inflation and the economic instability. First, the orientation of the tax system is unreasonable. The implementation of the tax distribution system since 1994 has played an active role in increasing the government's income, raising the proportion of the central government's revenue and enhancing the function of the financial regulation, which fuels the asymmetric distribution of the authority of office and the authority of finance in central and local governments. To meet the requirement of expenditure, all levels of local governments put efforts to expand the income resources both budgetary and non-budgetary. The local government turns to direct investment for high returns when fails to meet the financial target through tax. In the value-added tax–based system, a way to achieve a short-term return of the government is to set up the projects of the simple processing industries and the heavy industry which enjoy a high productivity and large tax in a large scale. But the expenditure used to cover the "absence of some functions" in the public service is still insufficient, which determines the high investment rate. The second is the orientation of the GDP-based assessment. Affected by the extensive mode of economic development, the GDP-bound assessment has always been favored by central government. For this reason, most local governments are keen to follow suit in a new round of investment frenzy by setting up the projects, conducting business, or even assign some mandatory targets to their sub-departments. This new "Great Leap Forward" potentially undermines the environmental system, technological innovation, and most importantly, the optimization of the industrial structure. The third is the export-oriented industrial policy. Since reform and opening, China has successfully implemented the strategy of the export-oriented economic development and drawn up the basic policies of import replacement and export replacement, enabling export to be the main engine of rapid economic development. The rapid increase in export will substantially increase the domestic investment. But the investing accelerator will, in turn, results in an insufficient investment of consumption demands. The excessive productive capacity resulted from over investment can only be released through the export of cheap manufactured goods, forming a vicious cycle of the imbalance of the structure of investment and consumption.

STRUCTURAL ECONOMICS IN CHINA

The irrational development of the element market

The elements market in China has made significant progress, but has not yet reached the point of full market. The reasons include both the intervention of the government, and also the imperfect of the market mechanism. In general, the price of the element of resource has always been suppressed or underestimated, resulting in a low capital of investment. This further brings about an investing impulse by the microeconomic subjects. As released by the International Energy Agency, the level of China's industrial tariff is 5.1 cents/kWh, which is 62.5% of the level in Japan, Italy and other developed countries, 83.3% of the level in Argentina, Korea and other developing countries and 76.9% of the level in the resource-based countries as Canada, Australia, etc. The ratio of the prices of the land expropriation, leasing and dealing, in some developed areas, has reached 1:10:50. Some local governments treat the difference between the prices of the expropriation and leasing as the "second property," racing to drive down the price of the land and the compensational standard of land expropriation and default the compensation fee of the land withheld.[14] These data show that investment in China has a significant advantage in comparative cost. It's reasonable to say the low investing cost is the inter incentives of the investors' blind investments.

Moreover, government's actions that are not standard indulge the unfair allowance of the invested projects. It is the market behavior that the corporations invest on their earning surprise and are responsible for their results of investment. The government should not interfere. But the failure of the market signals due to the uncompleted marketization of the elements and the lack of the social control of the government makes the enterprises underestimate the costs of investment, leading to the blind options of the projects in the market by the enterprises. Many local governments adopt a lot of preferential policies, lower the cost of investment, expand the profit margin of the investment and increase the attractiveness of foreign or domestic capital, in order to attract investment. In addition, due to the lack of the social control, many enterprises invest inadequately in the environmental protection, the productive security, social security and other aspects. Although the companies save a lot of costs of input, huge external costs are generated, resulting in great environmental costs and social risks.

Low labor wages

Low wage in the initial distribution in general is the important reason for the imbalance of the structure of investment and consumption. Low rate of wage, on the one hand, contributes to the impulse of the company's investment; and on the other hand, suppresses the consumption level of the residents. According to the studies, the overall costs of the Chinese labor are low, being equivalent to 2.89% of that in Japan, 6.54% of that in South Korea. Even within the countries in transition, the maximum is only 65.87% in Romania. The per capita costs of the manufacturing labor per year in Malaysia, Indonesia, Thailand and the Philippines are between USD2,000–6,000. The costs in China are less than 50% when compared with the costs in these neighboring Asian countries, and equal to 95.6% of that in the neighboring country India.[15]

There are two groups with the lowest income: the first is the group of the rural migrant workers in the cities. The group of the migrant workers is enlarging in the process of urbanization, but their reasonable remuneration and other benefits have long been squeezed. Their income is less. The second is the group of the ordinary workers in the urban private companies. Currently, due to the imperfect protection mechanism of the market and the system of the government protection, the system of a large number of the workers in the urban private companies is unreasonable. The labors are completely in a weak position. Because the supply of labor exceeds the demand, their wages are lower and grow slowly. The over-low wages of the ordinary workers in the urban private companies reluctant and even unable to spend money. The level and structure of consumption are still stuck in meeting the basic survival needs.

Low remuneration of the labor, on the one hand, constitutes the China's comparative advantage in low labor costs, attracting the direct foreign investments to improve the competitiveness of export; on the other hand, it also restricts the increase of income of the ordinary workers, especially workers at the bottom level. It suppresses their consumption demand, which is against to the optimization of the structure of investment and consumption.

The large income distribution gap

The level of income determines the consumption and purchasing power of the citizens. In general, the marginal propensity to consume for the earners with high income is low and high for the earners with low income. Thus, too large gap of the division of income will reduce the overall trend of consumption, restricts the increase of the consumption demand and the upgrading of the structure of consumption, increases the injustice of consumption and leads to unstable social sentiment.

STRUCTURAL ECONOMICS IN CHINA

At present, China's over-large distribution gap of the income is mainly in two aspects: firstly, the gap of income between different industries expands rapidly. *The Annual Report of the Distribution of the Residents' Income in China (2007)*[16] reported that the increase of income is significantly quicker in finance and insurance, telecommunications, electricity, gas and other industries than in extractive industries, construction, agriculture, forestry, animal husbandry and fishery etc. What forms a great contrast with the rapid growth of the income of the workers from the monopoly industries is the slow increase of the income of the rural migrant workers in the cities and the ordinary workers from the non-state-owned and the collective enterprises. Secondly, the gap between the incomes of the urban-rural residents is too large. According to the data released by the National Bureau of Statistics, the average growth of income in the rural per capita was only 4.5% from 1990 to 2006, far below the 7.7% of the growth of the urban disposable income and the growth rate of GDP in the same term. The income of the urban residents has remained 3.2 times than the income of the rural residents. The actual gap will be widened if we add the variety of subsidies and welfare enjoyed by the urban residents.

In fact, the widening gap of income has become a structural factor that affects the decline of the overall residents' trend of spending and a weak growth in the demand of consumption. The empirical research[17] proves that there is a strong and significant negative relationship between the gap of the urban residents' income and division in China and their demand of consumption. On the one hand, the lagging rural income seriously restrains the rural consumption. On the other hand, the ever-increasing gap between incomes brings about a fault in consumption—the consumption of food and high-end durables consumer goods comes to saturation at the low level while the higher level of consumption demand is still in accumulation.

This difference in the levels of consumption makes the demands of market diversified. The market is in a period where the structure is transforming. During this period, the demands at the low level are excessive while the demands at the high lever are inadequate. This inhibits the consumption potential of consumers at different levels of consumption.[18]

The imperfect social security system

The system of social security is one of the self-regulators in the system of economic operation, directly affecting the residents' behaviors of savings and consumption. It is also an important external factor affecting the structure of investment and consumption. The sound system of social security plays a counter-cyclical role in the regulation. During the economic prosperity, it can reduce the current consumption and increase savings through the accumulation of payment; during the economic recession, it can protect the basic life of the people and maintain the basic social needs through relief and social insurance. In this way can it improves the basic imbalance between consumption and accumulation in the economic cycle. Moreover, the income can be increased through the transfer payments and redistribution in the system of social security. This is beneficial to the narrowing of the gap between incomes and the improvement of the overall social marginal propensity to consume. On the contrary, the lack of social security will result in the deteriorating consumption conditions and the unstable consumption environment, affect most residents' consuming confident. This will bring about the increase of the uncertainty of expectation and the increase of the propensity to save, and thereby inhibits the effective increase in the consumption demands.

At present, there is still a wide gap between China's level of social security and people's growing demands. The expenditure of social security in 2005 accounted for only 5.5% of GDP, which is not only much lower than developed countries, but lower than some developing countries. For example, the level of social security is more than 20% of GNP in Germany, France, Sweden and other countries; about 12% in the liberal countries as UK, the U.S.; 15% to 20% in the Czech Republic, Hungary and other countries who are under the economic transition; and more than 7% of GDP in India. At the same time, due to delayed construction of system of the rural old-age security, there is a lack of basic security for 130 million employees of township enterprises, 120 million rural migrant workers in the cities and 45 million farmers whose land has been in acquisition.[19] This results their strong uncertainty of the future income and expenditure, high rate of the savings and a fluctuation between low and high of the consumption rate.

Chapter 6

Evolution and Imbalance of China's Industrial Structure

STRUCTURAL ECONOMICS IN CHINA

As the core of the economic structure, industrial structure is technologically economic ties forged between industries, within industries and in the process of social reproduction. This chapter elaborates on the characteristics of the evolution of China's industrial structure since the reform and opening-up. The extent and causes of the imbalance of industrial structure is demonstrated from three perspectives—the coordination of proportional relations within and between industries, the operative efficiency of the industrial structure, and the consistency of the changing trend of both domestic and international industrial structures.

Main Characteristics of the Evolution of China's Industrial Structure

The evolution of industrial structure is manifested in the dynamic process, escalating from simple to complex. As the ongoing economic development and technological advances, industrial structure has undergone major changes. This section analyzes the basic characteristics of the evolution of industrial structure since China opened its door to the world.

A rational development of the primary industries

Since the reform and opening-up, the agricultural economy is experiencing dramatic changes, and conditions for agricultural production have been greatly enhanced. Agricultural production has increased steadily and the rural infrastructure has been strengthened; farmers' living standards have constantly improved; and at the same time, the industrial structure has been continuously optimized. These economic fruits are mainly manifested in specific areas.

A substantial decline of the proportion of the primary industries' added value

At the beginning of the reform and opening-up, as the rural "household contract responsibility system" (*lianchan chengbao zeren zhi*) was widely implemented, agricultural productivity was released, which promoted the rapid development of the primary industries. The proportion of the increase in the primary industries relative to the GDP increased significantly, from 28.2% in 1978 to 32.1% in 1984. After 1984, as the focus of economic reform was switched from the rural area to the urban area, the urban economy began to develop rapidly. Accordingly, the proportion of increase in the primary industries to the GDP decreased from 32.1% in 1984 to 11.3% in 2007 (see Table 6.1), which indicates that the sharp decline in the proportion of the primary industries was the most typical feature of the industrial structure's transformation as China entered the accelerated phase of industrialization. Despite the primary industries' declining proportion, the structure of the secondary industries generally remained stable, and the proportion of the increase to the GDP in the tertiary industries showed a rapid growth.

Table 6.1. Changes in the proportion of increase relative to the GDP in China's primary, secondary and tertiary industries (%)

Year	Primary Industries	Secondary Industries	Tertiary Industries
1978	28.2	47.9	23.9
1980	30.2	48.2	21.6
1985	28.4	42.9	28.7
1990	27.1	41.3	31.6
1995	19.9	47.2	32.9
1996	19.7	47.5	32.8
1997	18.3	47.5	34.2
1998	17.6	46.2	36.2
1999	16.5	45.8	37.7
2000	15.1	45.9	39.0
2001	14.4	45.1	40.5
2002	13.7	44.8	41.5
2003	12.8	46.0	41.2
2004	13.4	46.2	40.4
2005	12.2	47.7	40.1
2006	11.3	48.7	40.0
2007	11.3	48.6	40.1

Source: *China Statistical Yearbook (2008)*.

An optimizing internal structure of the primary industries

Before Deng Xiaoping's reform, the structure of the primary industries persisted that "agriculture focuses on crop farming, and crop farming focuses on grain production." The subsequent adjustment of central economic policies and the implementation of policies lifted farmers' outlook of production. In addition, the diversified primary industries collectively decreased the proportion of agriculture and increased the proportions of forestry, animal husbandry, fisheries. In 2007, agriculture, forestry, animal husbandry, fisheries accounted for 50.4%, 3.8%, 33% and 9.1%, respectively, in the primary industries. Compared with 1978, the share of agriculture fell by 29.6%, and the shares of forestry, animal husbandry and fisheries rose by 0.4%, 18.0% and 7.5%, respectively (see Table 6.2). In terms of the internal structure of the primary industries, grain production underwent a stable development with the expansion of the planting areas of cash crops, the constant optimization of the agricultural products' structure, and the obvious adjustment effect of the crop farming structure. In terms of the composition of animal products, the proportion of pork in the total meat production was 62.5% in 2007 and declined by 31.7% since 1978, whereas the proportion of beef and mutton rose to 14.5%, and the proportions of animal products such as eggs and milk, for example, increased significantly. It is thus clear that the long-standing agricultural-based economy is gradually being diversified and the structure is being optimized.

Table 6.2. Changes in the internal structure of the primary industries, 1978–2007 (%)

Year	Agriculture	Forestry	Animal Husbandry	Fisheries
1978	80.0	3.4	15.0	1.6
1980	75.6	4.2	18.4	1.7
1985	69.2	5.2	22.1	3.5
1990	64.7	4.3	25.7	5.4
1995	58.4	3.5	29.7	8.4
1996	60.6	3.5	26.9	9.0
1997	58.2	3.4	28.7	9.6
1998	58.0	3.5	28.6	9.9
1999	57.5	3.6	28.5	10.3
2000	55.7	3.8	29.7	10.9
2001	55.2	3.6	30.4	10.8
2002	54.5	3.8	30.9	10.8
2003	50.1	4.2	32.1	10.6
2004	50.1	3.7	33.6	9.9
2005	49.7	3.6	33.7	10.2
2006	52.7	3.9	29.6	9.7
2007	50.4	3.8	33.0	9.1

Source: *China Statistical Yearbook (2008)*.

Evolution and Imbalance of China's Industrial Structure

An accelerating labor transfer in the primary industries

Since the household contract responsibility system was implemented in rural areas, the rural labor productivity continued to increase, creating excessive workforces for the agricultural sector. With the development of non-agricultural industries, the surplus rural labor continuously transferred from the primary industries to the secondary and tertiary industries. These noticeable changes can be seen in the employment structure of the three industries: the proportion of employment in the primary industries fell 29.7%, from 70.5% in 1978 to 40.8% in 2007—a remarkable rural labor transfer. The proportion of labor in the secondary industries rose 9.5%, from 17.3% in 1978 to 26.8% in 2007. Due to the rapid development of the tertiary industries, the proportion of its labor forces increased significantly by 20.2%, from 12.2% in 1978 to 32.4% in 2007 (see Table 6.3). It is clear that with the further deepening of the reform and opening-up, and the rapid development of the economy, labor forces continue to transfer from agriculture to the secondary and tertiary industries. This change is consistent with the general law of the world's employment structure's evolution.

Table 6.3. Changes in proportions of labor forces in China's primary, secondary and tertiary industries, 1978–2007 (%)

Year	Primary Industries	Secondary Industries	Tertiary Industries
1978	70.5	17.3	12.2
1980	68.7	18.2	13.1
1985	62.4	20.8	16.8
1990	60.1	21.4	18.5
1995	52.2	23.0	24.8
1996	50.5	23.5	26.0
1997	49.9	23.7	26.4
1998	49.8	23.5	26.7
1999	50.1	23.0	26.9
2000	50.0	22.5	27.5
2001	50.0	22.3	27.7
2002	50.0	21.4	28.6
2003	49.1	21.6	29.3
2004	46.9	22.5	30.6
2005	44.8	23.8	31.4
2006	42.6	25.2	32.2
2007	40.8	26.8	32.4

Source: *China Statistical Yearbook (2008)*.

STRUCTURAL ECONOMICS IN CHINA

The volatile development of the secondary industries

In the process of industrialization, as a major supporting role in the development of the national economy, the secondary industries developed rapidly, further enhancing and their dominance in the national economy. In the secondary industries, the contribution rate[1] and the pulling rate[2] of industry to the national economy ranked first among the three industries and industrialization of the national economy significantly improved.

Domination of the secondary industries

In terms of the proportion of the increase in the secondary industries to the GDP, it increased a mere 0.7%, from 47.9% in 1978 to 48.6% in 2007, but the overall trend showed a steady increase. Specifically, the proportion had short-term fluctuations in the early 1980s, and had a downward trend from 1982 until 1990 when it reached its lowest point of 41.3%. Afterwards, it continued a volatile rise and reached almost 50% in 2007. This demonstrates how the secondary industries came to play a dominant role in the national economy.

The contribution rate of the secondary industries declined but was still surpassing 50% and the pulling rate of the secondary industries; was significantly higher than those of the primary and tertiary industries (see Table 6.4).

Table 6.4. Contribution rates and pulling rates of China's primary, secondary and tertiary industries, 1991–2007 (%)

Year	Contribution Rates			Growth Rate of GDP	Pulling Rates		
	Primary Industries	Secondary Industries	Tertiary Industries		Primary Industries	Secondary Industries	Tertiary Industries
1991	7.1	62.8	30.1	9.2	0.6	5.8	2.8
1992	8.4	64.5	27.1	14.2	1.2	9.2	3.8
1993	7.9	65.5	26.6	14.0	1.1	9.2	3.7
1994	6.6	67.9	25.5	13.1	0.9	8.9	3.3
1995	9.1	64.3	26.6	10.9	1.0	7.0	2.9
1996	9.6	62.9	27.5	10.0	1.0	6.3	2.7
1997	6.8	59.7	33.5	9.3	0.6	5.6	3.1
1998	7.6	60.9	31.5	7.8	0.6	4.8	2.4
1999	6.0	57.8	36.2	7.6	0.4	4.4	2.8
2000	4.4	60.8	34.8	8.4	0.4	5.1	2.9
2001	5.1	46.7	48.2	8.3	0.4	3.9	4.0
2002	4.6	49.7	45.7	9.1	0.4	4.5	4.2
2003	3.4	58.5	38.1	10.0	0.3	5.9	3.8
2004	7.8	52.2	40.0	10.1	0.8	5.3	4.0
2005	6.1	53.6	40.3	10.4	0.6	5.6	4.2
2006	5.3	53.1	41.7	11.6	0.6	6.2	4.9
2007	3.6	54.1	42.3	11.9	0.4	6.5	5.1

Source: *China Statistical Yearbook (2008)*.

Evolution and Imbalance of China's Industrial Structure

Significant changes of the internal structure

In the process of industrialization, changes in industrial structure were an important factor affecting economic development.

As shown in Table 6.5,[3] the agro-food processing industry, the textile industry, and the general equipment manufacturing industry decreased dramatically. Of these, the textile industry had the steepest decline of 11.7%, from 16.3% in 1985 to 4.6% in 2007. At the same time, industries including oil processing and coking, ferrous metal smelting and rolling processing, transportation and equipment manufacturing, electrical machinery and equipment manufacturing, electronic equipment manufacturing (such as communications equipment and computers), and production and supply (of electricity, steam and hot water) collectively accounted for a remarkable portion in the gross industrial output. The proportions of the electronic equipment manufacturing industry, which included communications equipment and computers, had the biggest increase from 3.5% in 1985 to 10.2% in 2004. It dropped slightly to 9.7% in 2007, but overall, rose by 6.2% compared to 1985. In addition to the significant changes in proportions of these industries, the proportions of other industries generally kept steady, with only slight fluctuations.

The proportion of the general processing and manufacturing industry remained relatively stable or declined slightly, whereas technology-intensive industries and high-tech industries, which were mainly supported by the electronics and communications manufacturing industry, grew rapidly. Industrial structure entered a stage of a high degree of processing, backed by the processing and assembly industry. It transformed and upgraded from labor-intensive and capital-intensive industries to capital- and technology-intensive industries. Since 1998 in particular, industrialization oriented toward heavy industry. The growth rate of heavy industry has always been higher than light industry. In the new round of rapid economic growth since the second half of 2003, the development of the heavy chemical industry has played a more evident leading role.

The moderate development of the tertiary industries

The development of the tertiary industries has entered a new period of development with great internal structure changes.

Table 6.5. Changes in the internal structure of China's industries (%)

Industries	1985	1990	1994	2000	2004	2007
Coal Mining Industry	2.3	2.4	2.0	1.5	2.1	2.3
Oil and Gas Mining Industry	1.9	2.3	2.6	3.7	2.1	2.0
Agro-food Processing Industry	11.3	11.6	10.4	4.4	1.5	4.3
Textile Industry	16.3	12.3	12.4	6.0	2.1	4.6
Textile and Garment, Shoes, Hat Manufacturing Industry	2.4	2.2	2.6	2.7	1.4	1.9
Petroleum Processing, Coking and Nuclear Fuel Processing Industry	2.5	2.7	3.7	5.2	2.1	4.4
Chemicals and Chemical Products Manufacturing Industry	6.6	8.0	6.2	6.7	6.3	6.6
Non-metallic Mineral Products Industry	4.5	4.8	5.8	4.3	4.5	3.8
Ferrous Metal Smelting and Rolling Processing Industry	5.2	6.9	8.1	5.5	7.8	8.3
Non-ferrous Metal Smelting and Rolling Processing Industry	2.2	2.7	2.3	2.5	2.8	4.5
Fabricated Metal Products Industry	2.8	2.8	3.3	3.0	2.9	2.8
General Equipment Manufacturing Industry	11.0	9.0	4.7	3.6	4.6	4.5
Special Equipment Manufacturing Industry	—	—	3.5	2.6	2.6	2.6
Transportation Equipment Manufacturing Industry	4.3	3.8	6.2	6.3	6.5	6.7
Electrical Machinery and Equipment Manufacturing Industry	4.4	4.3	4.5	5.6	5.4	5.9
Manufacturing Industry of Communications Equipment, Computers and Other Electronic Equipment	3.5	3.1	3.9	8.8	10.2	9.7
Industry of the Production and Supply of Electricity and Heat	3.3	3.6	3.9	5.4	6.7	6.5

Sources: *China Statistical Yearbook* (various years).

The stable rise of the proportion of the tertiary industries relative to the GDP

With the expansion of urbanization, the proportion of the tertiary industries in GDP showed a rapidly upward trend and rose by 10% in the 1980s. Despite the slow rise in the early 1990s, it later showed a trend of rapid increase. Specifically, during the period of steady development of the tertiary industries, the proportion of its incremental value rose from 23.9% in 1978 to 24.8% in 1984. At that point, the proportion of the tertiary industries began to increase rapidly and exceeded the primary industries in 1985. During the period from 1990 to 1996, the proportion of its incremental value was generally steady, fluctuating within the range of 31% to 35%. Afterwards, with the continuous improvement of the market economy, this proportion showed a steadily upward trend, rising by 5.9%, from 34.2% in 1997 to 40.1% in 2007 (see Table 6.1).

The tertiary industries play a more significant role in economic growth

The industrial contribution rate of the tertiary industries fluctuated. From 30.1% in 1991, declined, and then rose again in to its maximum of 48.2%. After 2001, the contribution rate showed a downward trend again until 2004, when it turned upward, reaching 42.3% in 2007. Compared to other industries, the contribution rate of the tertiary industries maintained a stable rise, whereas contribution rates of the primary and secondary industries showed a downward trend, indicating that the tertiary industries contributed more to the economic growth (see Table 6.4). In addition, the pulling rate of the tertiary industries was 2.8% in 1991 and increased to 3.8% in 1992. It then declined to 2.4% in 1998. This indicator began to rise in fluctuations from 1999 and reached 5.1% in 2007. Compared to other industries, the gap between pulling rates of the tertiary industries and the secondary industries tended to be narrow. The gap was 3% in 1991, whereas the gap was only 1.4% in 2007. The tertiary industries have become major driving forces to promote economic growth, consistent with the direction of the evolution of the international industrial structure.

The optimization of the internal structure of the tertiary industries

While the proportion of the tertiary industries relative to GDP gradually increased, its internal structure underwent profound changes. At the beginning of the reform and opening-up, the tertiary industries concentrated on traditional industries such as commerce, catering, residential services, transportation and telecommunications. However, emerging industries, including information, consulting, finance and insurance, real estate, science, education, culture, and health developed rapidly over 30 years. From 1979 to 2007, the incremental value of the transportation, storage and postal industry increased by 14.4 times, and the proportion to GDP rose from 5.0% to 5.9%; the incremental value of the wholesale and retail industry increased by 12.6 times, and the proportion in GDP rose from 6.6% to 7.3%; the incremental value of the accommodation and catering industry increased by 30.2 times, and the proportion in GDP rose from 1.2% to 2.3%.[4] Since the 1990s, proportions of wholesale, retail, trade, catering, transportation and warehousing in the tertiary industries have all declined, whereas new service industries such as telecommunications and science, education, culture, and health have developed rapidly and their proportions in the tertiary industries have shown an upward trend. In addition, the development of real estate continues to increase; its proportion rose by 2.6%, from 2.2% in 1979 to 4.8% in 2007.

The widening gap of labor productivity between the primary, secondary and tertiary industries

From the perspective of labor productivity, per capita labor productivity of the whole society continued to rise by 34.7 times, from RMB907.9 in 1978 to RMB32,410 in 2007. The per capita labor productivity of the primary industries increased by 23.6 times from RMB363 to RMB8,935; the per capita labor productivity of the secondary industries increased by 22.4 times from RMB2,513 to RMB58,840; that of the tertiary industries increased by 21.5 times from RMB1,784.2 to RMB40,155 (see Table 6.6). After the 1990s in particular, labor productivity of the secondary and tertiary industries improved quickly, and labor productivity of the primary industries increased slightly. At the same time, the gap of labor productivity among the primary, secondary and tertiary industries widened. Before 1992, the gap between the secondary industries and the tertiary industries was small, reaching a minimum of 1.1 times in 1991. Afterward, the gap between the three industries continued to expand, which was reflected in the widening gap between the primary and secondary industries, and the widening gap between the secondary and tertiary industries.

The gap of the comparative productive labor was still large. According to the research conducted by Kuznets,[5] the general changing trend of the comparative productive labor[6] was that the comparative productive labor in the primary industries maintained stable when the per capita income was low, but increased significantly when the per capita income reached a certain level. The comparative productive labor in the second and tertiary industries, in general, declined rapidly with the increase of the per capita income.

Table 6.6. Comparison of per capita labor productivity between the primary, secondary and tertiary industries (RMB)

Year	Aggregate Labor Productivity	Primary Industries	Secondary Industries	Tertiary Industries
1978	907.9	362.9	2,512.9	1,784.2
1980	1,073.1	471.0	2,844.2	1,775.2
1985	1,807.8	823.8	3,723.6	3,092.5
1986	2,003.7	892.3	4,005.6	3397.8
1990	2,883.1	1,300.8	5,569.7	4,915.6
1995	8,931.7	3,415.7	18,319.7	11,835.6
1996	10,322.9	4,025.1	20,881.9	13,011.8
1997	11,311.0	4,145.2	22,688.7	14,642.0
1998	11,948.7	4,212.3	23,496.5	16,214.5
1999	12,560.9	4,129.4	24,988.5	17,637.8
2000	13,763.6	4,146.4	28,088.0	19,529.8
2001	15,016.1	4,322.1	30,405.5	21,930.8
2002	16,318.5	4,485.2	34,155.1	23,660.0
2003	18,247.9	4,756.1	38,835.8	25,679.6
2004	21,260.4	6,071.3	43,678.7	28,056.7
2005	24,163.2	6,599.9	48,310.4	30,891.8
2006	27,738.7	7,383.1	53,660.3	34,420.0
2007	32,410.7	8,934.9	58,840.1	40,154.7

Source: *China Statistical Yearbook (2008)*.

The comparative labor productivity in China's primary industries is relatively low when compared to that of the international changing trend, but in China's secondary industries, it is high (see Fig. 6.1). According to the general trend of the comparative productivity of all three industries at the international level, with the increase of the per capita income and the variation of the industrial structure, the gap of the comparative labor productivity between industries tends to shrink, especially in the secondary and tertiary industries where the comparative labor productivity drops by a large margin and tends to converge. But a large gap still exists in the comparative labor productivity of China's three industries, which has been reflected by the gap of the comparative labor productivity between the secondary and tertiary industries since the 1990s. The gap was 0.17 in 1991 and grew to 0.58 in 2007. The comparative labor productivity of the tertiary industries only accounted for 68.3% of the secondary industries. The ratio of the comparative labor productivity in the tertiary and secondary industries declined from 0.91 in 1991 to 0.68 in 2007.

STRUCTURAL ECONOMICS IN CHINA

A substantial increase in the proportion of the energy consumption in the industrial sectors

Changes of the GDP per unit of energy use[7] indicated a steady decrease in the overall energy consumption per unit of GDP between 1978 and 2007. The volume totaled 15.68 tons of standard coal in 1978, sharply decreased to 5.29 tons of standard coal equivalent (TCE) in 1990, continually dropped to 1.4 TCE in 2000, and mildly declined to 1.06 tons of standard coal in 2007 (see Table 6.7).

Energy consumption per unit of GDP is a comprehensive calculation based on the energy consumption of the industrial and residential sectors. The energy consumption of the two sectors has various impacts on per unit GDP of energy use. For example, the proportion of the energy consumption is high in the residential sectors in developed regions due to their high living standards. China is a developing country, thus the proportion of the energy consumption in the poorer residential sectors is low. Consequently, the energy consumption per unit of GDP in China is largely determined by the energy use in the industrial sector (see Table 6.8).

Structures of China's three industries have undergone significant transformations since its opening-up. The proportion of the output value of the secondary industries has increased steadily and has become the leading force driving economic growth. This economic structure, with the secondary industries as its main subject, demonstrates that the industrial sector contributed to most of the energy consumption. Between 1978 and 2007, despite the added value of the industrial sector occupying a mere 40% of GDP in China, it accounted for roughly 70% of China's total energy consumption.

Fig. 6.1. Changes in the comparative labor productivity of China's three industries

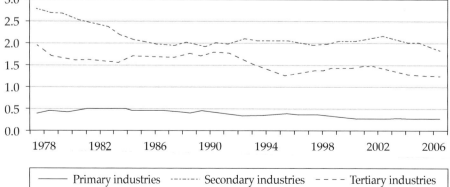

Table 6.7. Energy consumption per unit of GDP in China, 1987–2007 (tons of standard coal equivalents)

Year	The Energy Consumption Per Unit of GDP	Year	The Energy Consumption Per Unit of GDP
1978	15.68	2000	1.40
1980	13.26	2001	1.31
1985	8.51	2002	1.26
1990	5.29	2003	1.29
1995	2.16	2004	1.27
1996	1.95	2005	1.22
1997	1.74	2006	1.16
1998	1.57	2007	1.06
1999	1.49	—	—

Sources: calculated from *China Statistic Yearbook (1999) (2006)* and *(2008)*.

Table 6.8. Added value and the proportion of the energy consumption in China's industrial sectors, 1978–2007 (%)

Year	Proportion of the Industrial Added Value	Proportion of the Industrial Energy Consumption
1978	44.1	—
1980	43.9	68.04
1985	38.3	66.60
1990	36.7	68.47
1995	41.1	73.33
2000	40.3	68.89
2001	39.7	64.49
2002	39.4	67.31
2003	40.5	69.59
2004	40.8	70.48
2005	42.0	70.99
2006	43.1	71.12
2007	43.0	—

Sources: *China Statistic Yearbook* (various years).

STRUCTURAL ECONOMICS IN CHINA

Judgment of the Degree of the Imbalance of China's Industrial Structure

The industrial structure is an important factor affecting economic development. Its evolution is a continuous process. Despite an apparent ongoing process, there were still some outstanding structural contradictions. This section sheds lights on the judgment of the imbalance of the economic structure from three aspects.

Standards for judging the imbalance of the industrial structure

Backed up by existing theories on the industrial structure and the practical situation of China's economic structure, the judgment of the imbalance generally follows three standards: the coordination of the proportional relationship between and within the industries, the operational efficiency of the industrial structure, and the consistency of the changing trend of domestic and overseas industrial structures.

Coordination of the proportional relationship between and within the industries

The national economy is a complex system where different sectors and industries are closely related. However, disequilibrium may emerge due to differing development paces of various industries. Additionally, when the development of industries meets as a bottleneck, the overall development capability of the national economy will be restrained. In an ideal industrial structure, inputs required by each industry can always be fully satisfied, i.e., no "bottleneck industry" exists; Furthermore, the output of each industry can suitably meet the input of other industries and the consumption demands, i.e., no "surplus industry" exists, thus fostering an appropriate proportional relationship between industries. If either bottleneck industry or surplus industry exists in one industrial system for an extended period of time, this natural relationship will be ruptured; consequently the proportional relationship of the equilibrium in one industry will be destroyed, adversely affecting the normal operation of the national economy. Thus, the proportional relationship between and within industries is an important standard for judging the imbalance of the industrial structure.

Operational efficiency of the industrial structure

Production resources are limited. The inappropriate resource allocation will produce idle resources in some sectors and inadequate resources in others, affecting the operational efficiency of the industry. A rational industrial structure is able to fully and effectively utilize various resources by effectively allocating and using them in various departments, generating a high production efficiency. In the evolution of the industrial structure, the operation of the economic structure is of low efficiency or totally ineffective if pursuing an extensive growth pattern of "high investment, high energy consumption and high pollution." If this low efficiency cannot be reversed, then the industry cannot effectively allocate its resources. This will eventually result in the imbalance of industrial structure.

Consistency of the changing trends of domestic and overseas industrial structures

Although the changes in each country's industrial structure have their own particularities, the evolutions of the national industrial structure still have some common features. Because the common feature of the evolution of this industrial structure reflects certain regularity, the general trend of the evolution of the international industrial structure can be made as a reference to the imbalance. It is worth noting that it is difficult to the judge the imbalance of the industrial structures with the common standards of the industrial structure in different countries within different periods of time. In this case, the changing trends of the international industrial structure can, to some extent, be used as a reference for the judgment of the imbalance of the industrial structure.

Judgment based on the coordination of the proportional relationship between industries

The imbalance of the structures of the primary, secondary and tertiary industries' output value

The industrial structure improved as human society evolved from an agricultural economy to an industrial economy, and then to a service economy. It can be seen from the proportion of the added value in the three industries of countries with different incomes, there has been a continuously decreasing trend of that proportion in the global primary and secondary industries, but an ongoing bias in the tertiary industries. The world's average proportion in the primary industries has remained below 4% since 2000 with less than 2% in the high-income countries, less than 10% in the middle-income countries, and less than 25% in overall low-income countries. The world's average proportion of the secondary industries has been 30% or less, whereas the proportion in the high-income countries has been below 30%; the proportion has fluctuated between 35% and 38% in the middle-income countries, and has been between 26% and 29% in the low-income countries. The world's average proportion of the tertiary industries has been over 67%, with high-income surpassing that proportion, while both the middle-income and low-income countries reached just over 50% (see Table 6.9).

Table 6.9.   Added-value structures of primary, secondary and tertiary industries (%)

Country	Industry	1980	1990	1995	2000	2002	2003	2004	2005	2006
World	Primary Industries	7.0	5.0	5.4	3.7	3.8	3.5	3.4	—	—
	Secondary Industries	37.0	33.0	33.1	29.2	28.3	28.0	27.6	—	—
	Tertiary Industries	56.0	61.0	61.5	67.1	67.9	68.5	69.0	—	—
High-income Countries	Primary Industries	3.9	2.8	2.3	1.8	1.7	1.7	1.7	1.5	—
	Secondary Industries	37.1	32.4	29.7	28.0	26.3	26.0	25.7	26.2	—
	Tertiary Industries	59.0	64.8	68.0	70.2	72.0	72.3	72.6	72.3	—
Middle-income Countries	Primary Industries	18.0	15.6	12.1	9.7	9.6	9.5	9.4	8.9	8.4
	Secondary Industries	41.0	38.4	35.6	36.2	35.6	36.0	36.5	36.8	37.3
	Tertiary Industries	41.0	46.0	52.3	54.1	54.8	54.5	54.1	54.3	54.3
Low-income Counties	Primary Industries	34.6	31.2	28.9	26.4	24.2	24.0	21.8	21.5	20.4
	Secondary Industries	24.4	25.9	26.6	26.4	26.5	26.7	28.3	28.5	27.7
	Tertiary Industries	41.0	42.9	44.5	47.2	49.3	49.3	49.9	50.0	51.9

Source: Database of the International Bank.

Evolution and Imbalance of China's Industrial Structure

China is a middle-income country. Compared with the world average and other middle-income countries, China's industrial structure still needs further development. This is prominently shown in the situation where the proportion of the increased value in the secondary industries is high but low in the tertiary industries. China has recently been at the mid-stage of the development of industrialization, where the development of the heavy industry is faster than the development of the service industry. This has resulted in a lagging development of the tertiary industries. The proportion of the primary industries in China in 2007 accounted for 11.3%, equivalent to the level of the middle-income countries in the mid-1990s; the proportion of the secondary industries in China in 2007 accounted for 48.6%, which was 11.3% higher than the average level of the mid-income countries in 2006; the proportion of the tertiary industries was only 40.1%, which was 14.2% lower than the average number of the mid-income countries, equivalent to their average level in the mid-1990s. Thus, there is a large and obvious imbalance existing in the structure of China's three industries.

The industrial structural over-deviation

The industrial structural deviation is the difference between the proportion of employment and the industrial added value. If the proportion of employment is greater than that of the added value, it indicates low labor productivity and risks labor emigration. Theoretically, if each industry were perfectly competitive and the labor flowing were free, then labor would immigrate to the industries with higher labor productivity; it would ultimately reach the state where the labor productivity in all industries would become the same. The more asymmetric the structures of employment and the output value are, the more divisive these two factors are, and the less efficient the industrial structure of employment is, showing a more obvious imbalance between the employment structure and the industrial structure.

Considering the industrial structural deviations of the world's major countries (see Table 6.10), the industrial structural deviations are small for most countries, and especially so for developing countries. For example, the deviation indexes of Japan's primary, secondary and tertiary industries in 2000 were 3.4%, −1.1% and −2.3%, respectively. In 2005, the index changed without much fluctuation to 3.0%, −1.6% and −1.4%, respectively. Compared with those of developed countries, developing countries present a higher deviation. For instance, the deviation indexes of Mexico's primary and tertiary industries are over 10%, well above the developed nations' average level.

Table 6.10. Industrial structure deviations, 2000–2005 (%)

Country	Industry	2000	2001	2002	2003	2004	2005
UK	Primary Industries	0.5	0.4	0.4	0.3	0.3	0.5
	Secondary Industries	−2.8	−2.3	−1.6	−1.4	−1.8	−2.2
	Tertiary Industries	2.3	1.9	1.2	1.1	1.5	1.7
Germany	Primary Industries	1.4	1.2	1.4	1.4	1.1	1.4
	Secondary Industries	3.0	2.8	2.8	2.3	1.9	0.5
	Tertiary Industries	−4.4	−4.0	−4.2	−3.7	−3.0	−1.9
Japan	Primary Industries	3.4	3.2	3.0	3.0	2.9	3.0
	Secondary Industries	−1.1	−0.3	−0.5	−0.8	−1.7	−1.6
	Tertiary Industries	−2.3	−2.9	−2.5	−2.2	−1.2	−1.4
The U.S.	Primary Industries	1.4	1.2	1.5	0.5	0.3	0.4
	Secondary Industries	−1.0	−0.4	−0.6	−1.1	−1.4	−2.2
	Tertiary Industries	−0.4	−0.8	−0.9	0.6	1.1	1.8
South Korea	Primary Industries	5.7	5.5	5.2	5.0	4.3	4.5
	Secondary Industries	−12.5	−11.7	−11.0	−11.3	−13.0	−13.3
	Tertiary Industries	6.8	6.2	5.8	6.3	8.7	8.8
Mexico	Primary Industries	20.6	13.5	13.7	12.6	12.3	11.4
	Secondary Industries	−3.3	−1.2	−1.5	−0.8	−1.3	−0.3
	Tertiary Industries	−17.3	−12.3	−12.2	−11.8	−11.0	−11.1
Brazil	Primary Industries	—	14.6	14.2	13.5	14.2	—
	Secondary Industries	—	−6.9	−5.7	−6.9	−9.1	—
	Tertiary Industries	—	−7.7	−8.5	−6.6	−5.1	—

Source: The Database of the International Bank.

Although the labor structures in China's three industries have improved significantly, the employment structures in each industry are unreasonable, as demonstrated through the high proportion of employment in the primary industries and low proportion in the secondary and tertiary industries. If the structure of output value in the three industries becomes irrational, it will result in serious asymmetry between the compositions of the employment and output value in the three industries, essentially causing a large industrial structural deviation. As shown in Table 6.11, the industrial deviation has always been more

Table 6.11. Structure derivations of China's primary, secondary and tertiary industries, 1978–2007 (%)

Year	Primary Industries	Secondary Industries	Tertiary Industries
1978	42.3	−30.3	−12.0
1980	38.5	−30.0	−8.5
1985	34.0	−22.1	−11.9
1990	33.0	−19.9	−13.1
1995	32.3	−24.2	−8.1
2000	34.9	−23.4	−11.5
2001	35.7	−22.9	−12.8
2002	36.3	−23.4	−12.9
2003	36.3	−24.4	−11.9
2004	33.5	−23.7	−9.8
2005	32.6	−23.9	−8.7
2006	31.3	−23.5	−7.8
2007	29.5	−21.8	−7.7

Source: calculated from *China Statistical Yearbook (2008)*.

than 30% (except in 2007) in the primary industries, about 20% in the secondary industries, and about 10% in the tertiary industries, which is comparatively small. In fact, the large structural derivation of the primary industries implies low labor productivity and a comparatively higher probability of labor emigration.

Thus, a serious imbalance of industrial structure exists in China, both in the structure of the added value of the three industries and the industrial structure deviation.

Judgment based on the coordination of the proportional relationship within the industries

The irrational proportions of the light and heavy industries

The development of secondary industries, obviously influenced by the country's macroeconomic situation, shows great volatility. This reflects not only in its proportion in GDP, but also in its internal proportional relationship with the secondary industries. In terms of the light industry and the heavy industry, China's industrialization features periodicity. Since the 20th century, the industrialization has gradually become biased toward the heavy industry and the highly-processed industry (see Table 6.12).

STRUCTURAL ECONOMICS IN CHINA

Table 6.12.   Changes in China's light and heavy industries (%)

Year	Light Industry	Heavy Industry
1978	43.1	56.9
1980	47.2	52.8
1985	47.4	52.6
1990	47.0	53.0
1995	42.8	57.2
1996	43.0	57.0
1997	42.7	57.3
1998	42.9	57.1
1999	42.0	58.0
2000	39.8	60.2
2001	39.4	60.6
2002	39.1	60.9
2003	35.5	64.5
2004	31.6	68.4
2005	31.1	68.9
2006	30.0	70.0
2007	29.5	70.5

Sources: *China Statistical Yearbook* (various years).

After its founding, China had implemented the "heavy industry oriented" strategy which achieved significant results, but the lack of mechanism to coordinate the development of the light and heavy industries caused a structural deficiency—"too many heavy industries but few light industries." Since the reform and opening-up, policies to support the development of the light industry began to highlight the unbalanced situation of the light and heavy industries. In the early 1980s, policies to promote the development of the light industry were implemented, and the share of the light industry started to increase. It exceeded 50% for the first time in 1981; since then, it declined slightly but still accounted for nearly 50%. The pattern which "the light industry equals to the heavy industry" was formed. Since 1992, the gradual increase in the demand for durable consumer goods by the residents boosted the rapid development of the mechanical and electrical industry, with home appliances as the core. Meanwhile, the investment in infrastructure has promoted the development of basic industry. There was an increasing trend of heavy industrialization, but the proportions of the light and heavy industries were stable overall. After the Asian financial crisis in 1997, China adopted a positive fiscal policy, increasing its investments on the basic industry and infrastructure. The heavy industry began to grow rapidly, playing a leading role in the process of industrialization. The proportion of the heavy industry in the increased growth of industry increased 13.4% from 57.1% in 1998. After 2002, the proportion rose dramatically, from 60.9% in 2002 to 70.5% in 2007. The proportion of the light industry dropped from 39.1% to 29.5% in 2007. The gap in the proportions between the light and heavy industries became significantly larger. The current trend of the heavy industrialization has been obvious and closely related with the stage of industrialization. The changes in the structure of demand have improved the adjustment and upgrading of the industrial structure. The heavy industrialization and highly-processed industry have become the trend of the development of the industry. Even though heavy industrialization has been strengthened, the continuation of this situation will lead to the imbalance in the proportion of the structure of light and heavy industries, resulting in an unbalanced state of the industrial structure.

The low proportion of modern service industry

The internal output structure of the tertiary industries shows the following trend: when the level of per capita GDP is low, rapid development happens in the industries of commerce, hotel and catering, transportation and warehousing, and post and telecommunications, and the added value accounts for a high proportion in the tertiary industries. When the per capita GDP increases to a certain extent, the proportion of the output value of financial insurance and other "producer service industries"[8] will rise rapidly.

Based on the structural changes of the tertiary industries' internal output value, the structural changes between 1990 and 1978 remain the same with the general international trend, yet demonstrate a great deviation from the general international trend between 1991 and 2007. With the rapid increase of per capita income, the proportion of transportation, warehousing, post and telecommunications sectors in the tertiary industries decreased from 20.9% in 1978 to 14.9% in 1989—a decrease of 6%. Finance insurance and real estate maintained a rapid increase momentum, from 17.0% in 1978 to 28.5% in 1990, an increase of 11.5%; the commerce, hotel and catering industry also maintained a rising trend, but there was also a large degree of volatility. Between 1991 and 2007, the proportion of the added value of commerce, hotel and catering Industry maintained a downward trend, from 31.0% in 1991 to 23.9% in 2007, a decrease of 7.1%; the proportion of the added value of transportation, warehousing, and post and telecommunications sectors also maintained a downward trend, decreasing 4.8% from 19.4% in 1991 to 14.6% in 2007. The proportion of the added value of finance insurance and real estate shifted from the rapid increase to the evident decrease, rising from 24.8% in 1991 to 25.8% in 1995 and then decreasing to 22.9% in 2007.

STRUCTURAL ECONOMICS IN CHINA

From the perspective of the proportion of industrial added value in GDP, the proportion of added value of the sectors within the tertiary industries has been lower than the world average. The biggest gaps were in the commerce, hotel and catering industry, as well as in the financial insurance and real estate sectors. This is because China's tertiary industries are mainly composed of traditional services, while tertiary industries in developed countries mainly focus on the emerging service-oriented sectors. It can be seen from Fig. 6.2 that, since the 1990s, the internal structural imbalance of the tertiary industries is chiefly characterized by the decreasing proportion of the financial insurance industry, in both the tertiary industries and the GDP. This violates the general development rules of the world's tertiary industries and does not follow the general trend of structural optimization and the changes of the world's tertiary industries. Based on China's current stage of economic development, the internal output structure of the tertiary industries should be at the third stage of the international development of tertiary industries. This structure is chiefly characterized by the increase in the proportion of producer services in the tertiary industries, while the development of China's tertiary industries is mainly based on the traditional businesses and transportation sectors. Financial insurance, real estate, consultancy, information and other industries have not experienced effective development. The fact that these industries lag behind fully shows the internal proportion imbalance within the tertiary industries.

Fig. 6.2.   Internal structural changes of China's tertiary industries, 1978–2007

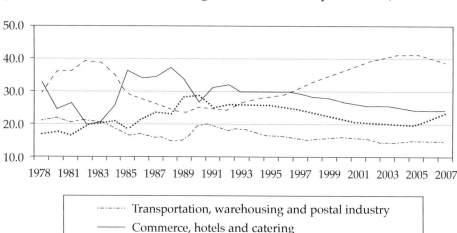

Judgment based on the operational efficiency of the industrial structure

In the evolution of industrial structure, rational industrial structure must fully take advantage of various resources, so that resources can be appropriately allocated and used by various departments, creating high output efficiency. Therefore, the level of industrial operational efficiency is an important basis to determine whether an industrial structure has been optimized.

As an important indicator to reflect the relationship between all the industrial inputs and outputs, the whole social labor productivity shows the development stage of social productivity and serves as an important indicator of the industrial resource allocation efficiency. Table 6.13 demonstrates the trend of China's whole social labor productivity in China: it increased from USD590/person in 1990 to USD3,505/person in 2006—an average growth rate of 11.8%. However, compared with developed countries or even some developing countries, China's social labor productivity is still relatively low. In 2006, the labor productivity in the United States and Japan were USD92,270/person and USD68,145/person, respectively, 26.3 times and 19.4 times greater than that in China. Compared with a number of new industrial and developing countries, China's social labor productivity is still not high. In 2006, Mexico was USD20,224/person, Russia was USD14,408/person, and Thailand was USD5,678/person, respectively; this is 5.8 times, 4.1 times and 1.6 times greater than that of China. Thus, when compared with both developed countries and some developing countries, China's whole social labor productivity is relatively low, reflecting China's low level of productivity and low efficiency of industrial resource allocation, both of which mirror China's industrial structure imbalance.

In addition, the operational efficiency of the industrial structure can also be reflected by the level of energy consumption per unit of GDP. Under the influence of technological progress, industrial structural adjustment and other factors, China's energy consumption factor per unit of GDP shows a continuous downward trend, while the energy consumption factor per unit of GDP is still high when compared with the international level. In 1978, China's energy consumption per unit of GDP was 21.3 TCE/ten thousand U.S. dollars (after conversion of GDP denominated by dollars); respectively this is, 2 times and 5.4 times that of the U.S. and Japan, which were 10.7 TCE/ten thousand U.S. dollars and 3.9 TCE/ten thousand U.S. dollars in the same period, This number dropped to 9.3 TCE/ten thousand U.S. dollars in 2004, while the gap between China and the U.S. and Japan reached respectively 3.7 times and 6.8 times. In comparison with developing countries, China's energy consumption per unit of

GDP was respectively 9 times and 2.3 times that of Brazil and India in 1993. The relative gap between China and Brazil and India decreased to 2.9 and 1.2 times in 2004, but the absolute energy consumption level was still higher than those two countries (see Table 6.14).

The energy consumption factor per unit of GDP in world's major countries will continue to decline with the increasing levels of the economy. Compared to India, China's per capita GDP was about USD1,700 in 2005, about 3 times that of India, which was USD640.[9] However, China's energy consumption per unit of GDP was just under twice that of India, which is not in line with the trend that the energy consumption per unit of GDP decreases with the level of economic development. This indicates that China's industrial growth is still relatively extensive and backward, and the energy use remains inefficient. The high-energy-consumption industrial structure will inevitably lead to a low operational efficiency of the industrial structure—a serious imbalance between the structure of industrial input and output, thus undermining an otherwise healthy and sustainable development of the national economy.

To sum up, from either the coordination of proportional relationships between or within industries, or the operational efficiency of industrial structure, there is a certain degree of industrial structural imbalance.

Cause Analysis of China's Industrial Structural Imbalance

Different countries have different industrial structures, and within a country, industrial structure varies in different stages. As the external manifestations of the economic development progress, the industrial structural changes in correspondence with the changes of technological advances, consumer attitudes, international economic environment, industrial policies, et cetera. When the industrial structure adapts to changes of relevant factors, the industrial structure is in a rational state, otherwise there will be imbalance. In the process of economic growth, structure imbalance may be caused by many factors. The factors that play a leading role include technological advances, efficiency of production factor utilizations, investment structure, industrial policies and the international division of labor.

Irrational investment structure

There is a close relationship between industrial structure and investment structure. The current industrial structure is the realistic result of past investment structure, while the current investment structure determines the

Table 6.13. Comparison of the social labor productivity (USD/person)

Country	1990	2000	2003	2004	2005	2006
China	590	1,671	2,215	2,582	2,971	3,505
Japan	48,770	72,042	66,918	72,517	71,485	68,145
The U.S.	48,762	72,683	79,633	84,330	88,379	92,270
South Korea	14,800	24,696	27,451	30,450	34,855	38,604
Russia	—	4,057	6,484	8,851	11,289	14,408
Brazil	7,528	—	6,944	8,057	—	—
Mexico	—	15,340	16,247	16,986	18,777	20,224
Thailand	2,777	3,771	4,138	4,585	4,894	5,678

Source: *International Statistical Yearbook (2007)*.

Table 6.14. Comparison of energy consumption per unit of GDP, 1993–2004 (TCE/ten thousand U.S. dollars)

Year	China	The U.S.	Japan	South Korea	Brazil	India
1993	26.86	4.20	1.36	4.24	2.97	11.61
1994	22.62	4.23	1.30	3.97	2.52	10.70
1995	18.73	3.98	1.21	3.58	2.07	10.14
1996	17.02	3.84	1.40	3.61	2.01	10.40
1997	15.34	3.60	1.53	4.08	1.98	9.86
1998	13.79	3.46	1.68	5.43	2.10	10.13
1999	13.50	3.35	1.49	4.65	3.07	9.43
2000	12.82	3.24	1.43	4.33	2.95	9.88
2001	12.18	3.08	1.63	4.72	3.55	9.57
2002	11.94	3.04	1.71	4.36	3.97	9.39
2003	12.35	2.86	1.55	4.01	3.56	8.24
2004	9.32	2.51	1.38	3.26	3.19	7.49

Sources: Relevant years of *International Statistical Yearbook*.

future industrial structure. Investment can create new productive capacities; its distribution in various industrial sectors is the direct cause of changes in the industrial structure and one important reason for industrial structural imbalance. Since the reform and opening-up, China's investment has maintained a high growth, but the irrational structure is rather prominent. This is mainly manifested in the secondary industries—particularly the manufacturing sectors, which enjoy a large scale of investment—while investment in the primary industries and tertiary industries remain relatively insufficient. The urban fixed asset investment grows rapidly, but the growth of rural fixed assets investment is relatively slow; the investment in real estate is sufficient, but relatively insufficient investment was seen in health care, education and other public sectors. Based on China's situation, the macro-control was once trapped by lack of guidance on the overall balance, regulation deficiency on repeated construction and unfair competition, and absence of regulation on environmental pollution. Additionally, the formulation of industrial policies did not thoroughly consider future consequences, resulting in a disorderly industrial development and an irrational investment structure. The direct consequence was the excessive growth of iron and steel, cement, and other heavy industries, as well as the increasing pressure exerted by high energy consumption and environmental pollution. With regard to the game theory, this irrational investment structure was caused by the gaming actions between the local governments and the central government, including the central government's ambition of realizing economic development, and the local governments' individual pursuits. In terms of the arrangement of the investment emphasis, the local governments favor the heavy industry, infrastructure, and large-and-medium-sized projects in order to meet the requirements of "performance evaluation indicators." It is a game between the central government and the local governments that make the implementation of industrial policies relatively weak and maintain the investment structure in an extended irrational state. Irrational investment structure often means high input, high consumption, high pollution, repeated construction, and unhealthy competition. The process of upgrading the industrial structure and slowly transforming the growth pattern will result in an unbalanced industrial structure.

Low distribution efficiency of the production factors

With the acceleration of industrialization and urbanization, the Chinese government increased its intervention in the land, capital, labor, finance, and other production factor markets. This lead to the structural imbalance of production factor distributions and was an important reason behind the industrial structural imbalance. At present, China's economic development is dependent on the land and other natural resources, but due to repeated construction, disorderly development and extensive exploitation, the waste of land has become rather serious, and the conflict between people and the land has become fairly prominent. Further fueled by the undersupply of land provisions, real estate prices inflated in some cities, and the real estate industry became one of the industries to suffer a serious supply-demand imbalance. Due to low technological level and high energy consumption, a great gap remains between China and developed nations in terms of the comprehensive utilization of energy. China's energy consumption coefficient is not only much higher than the developed countries', but also higher than the general level of the developing countries. The result is ever-increasing emissions of pollutants and increasingly serious environmental pollution. In terms of the labor factor, there remain prominent structural contradictions. On the one hand, highly skilled workers are in short supply; on the other hand, there is a serious surplus of low-skilled and unskilled labors, resulting in a low level of labor productivity. Thus, a variety of production factors in economic activities have suffered different degrees of low efficiency. This problem not only leads to industrial structural imbalance, but also affects sustainable economic and social development.

Lagged technological upgrading

China's industrial operation characteristics—"high input, high consumption"—are directly linked to technological upgrading. Since the reform and opening-up period, the upgrading of industrial structure has been backed up by the introduction of foreign capital, rather than by the independent intellectual property rights developed by the enterprises. The enterprises' lack of core techniques resulted in the serious heavy industry of manufacturing and the insufficient intrinsic motivation of industrial upgrading. As can be seen from the international division of labor, China, as the world's important manufacturing factory, is the low value-added link in the production chain—that is, the middle part of the "Smile Curve."[10] And both ends of the value chain (research and development, material sourcing, product design, brand marketing, logistics management, financial services, et cetera) remain relatively low (see Fig. 6.3). Most of China's core techniques and key equipment are basically dependent on foreign imports. With inadequate R&D funding and limited R&D capabilities, upgrading industrial technologies remains slow. Additionally, some industries are correspondingly characterized by high investment, high consumption, and hence, an imbalance in the industrial input-output structure emerges.

STRUCTURAL ECONOMICS IN CHINA

China's technological upgrading, to a large extent, was achieved through the use of foreign capital. Admittedly, the use of foreign capital for technological upgrading helped to narrow down the technological gap among developed countries. However, with the introduction of new techniques, the continuous expansion of the industrial scale, and the improved standardization of production, existing technologies stagnated at a certain level; when failing to increase the absorption capacity for the second development and t own their independent technologies, these companies would always lag behind the level of technological innovation of developed countries. In the long run, the situation wherein technological advances depend on "introduction" can only be changed by strategic technology absorption, enhancement of independent innovation capability, and the industry's ownership of the dynamic and powerful technological progress.

Fig. 6.3. The Smile Curve

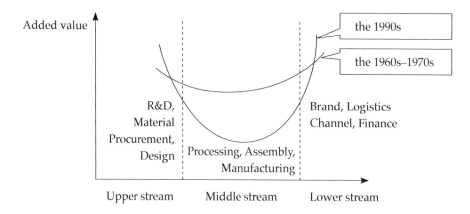

The international division of labor

The industrial structural imbalance is influenced by a variety of domestic factors, and is related to the international division of labor, international trade, international investment, international transfer of industry, and other external factors. Since the 1990s, economic globalization has been accelerating, strengthening the cross-national flow of production factors. The traditional international division of labor has changed the cross-national flow of production factors, resulting in a concentration of production factors in certain countries and the formation of a new pattern of world production. Driven by economic globalization, developed countries, largely represented by the United States, began to speed up industrial restructuring and transfer the manufacturing sectors of their traditional manufacturing and, industries, among others, to the emerging market regions, which have low-labor-cost advantages, relatively broad markets, and the capacity to support industry on a large scale. In this irrational system of division of labor, China actively participates in this international division of labor by taking the comparative advantage of labor. However, due to the less developed high-tech industries, modern service industry, and financial markets, for example, and because of the distortion of production factor prices, investment decisions are disproportionately influenced, and are coupled with the excessive flow of resources over the manufacturing sector, unnecessary manufacturing capacity and expanding trade surplus, and growing industrial structural imbalance.

Chapter 7

Evolution and Imbalance of China's Financial Structure

China's financial development sees dramatic progress since the 1970s, which is directly reflected in the expansion of financial assets and the increasing number of financial institutions. Compared with the expansion of financial scale, the financial structure has also undergone a lot of changes and its contribution rate to economic growth has improved remarkably. However, structural imbalance is still the main obstacle to financial development as well as economic growth. This chapter focuses on analyzing main characteristics of the evolution of financial structure since the reform and opening up, and judging the degree of imbalance of financial structure from three perspectives: the coordination of the structure of financial elements, the efficiency of financial structure, and the adaptability between the financial structure and the real economy, based on which main causes for the financial structure imbalance is further discussed.

Main Characteristics of China's Financial Structural Evolution

During the past 30 years of development, China's financial structure has undergone significant changes. The most prominent changes include diversification in the composition of financial institutions, in financial assets, and in financing methods of corporations. This section focuses on analyzing the basic characteristics of changes in the financial structure since the reform and opening-up.

The financial service system has been priliminarily established

At the beginning of the reform and opening-up, the composition of China's financial institutions was very distinct. It was typically exemplified by a large number of banking institutions, with the majority being state-owned banks, with very few non-bank financial institutions. After 30 years of the reform, China established a fully-fledged, efficient, safe, and modern financial service system with a wide range and reasonably distributed division of labor.

In terms of banking institutions, China is steadily advancing the reform of state-owned banks, new financial institutions are constantly expanding. By the end of 2007, there were 12 additional national joint-equity commercial banks and 3 additional policy banks. There were also 124 new city commercial banks, 113 additional rural cooperative banks and 17 rural commercial banks, through reorganizing and transforming the urban credit cooperatives and rural credit cooperatives. Moreover, China also formed a system of non-bank financial institutions including 4 financial asset management companies, 54 investment trust companies, 73 financial companies, 10 financial leasing companies, 9 auto financing companies, and 2 money brokerage companies. In addition, the introduction of foreign financial institutions has rapidly increased; 29 foreign banks have restructured their branches in China as foreign corporative banks, and foreign banks' operating agencies have reached 440. Securities institutions have shown a rapid development in recent years. By the end of 2007, China had 106 securities companies, 59 fund management companies, 346 securities investment funds and 177 futures companies. At the beginning of the reform and opening-up, China had only one insurance agency: China People's Insurance Company; China has now formed a relatively complete system of insurance institutions. By the end of 2007, insurance institutions included 8 insurance group companies, 9 insurance asset management companies, and 102 insurance companies, of which 59 were Chinese-funded insurance companies and 43 were foreign-funded insurance companies (see Table 7.1).

Table 7.1. Composition of China's financial institutions by the end of 2007

Industry	Name	Number	Name	Number
Banking	Policy Bank	3	Finance House	4
	State-owned Commercial Bank	5	Rural Mutual Cooperative	8
	Joint-equity Commercial Bank	12	Foreign Corporative Bank	29
	Postal Savings Bank	1	Foreign Bank's Operating Agency	440
	City Commercial Bank	124	Financial Asset Management Company	4
	Urban Credit Cooperative	42	Trust & Investment Companies	54
	Rural Credit Cooperative	8,348	Financial Company	73
	Rural Cooperative Bank	113	Financial Leasing Company	10
	Rural Commercial Bank	17	Auto Financing Company	9
	Village and Town Bank	19	Money Brokerage Company	2
Securities	Securities Company	106	Securities Investment Fund	346
	Fund Management Company	59	Futures Company	177
Insurance	Insurance Group	8	Foreign-funded Insurance Company	43
	Chinese-funded Insurance Company	59	Insurance Asset Management Company	9

Sources: Compiled from documents in *China Banking Regulatory Commission Annual Report (2007)*, *China Financial Stability Report (2007)*, and *China Financial Market Development Report (2007)*.

STRUCTURAL ECONOMICS IN CHINA

With the increasing diversification of financial institutions, the financial industry developed from a single banking industry to a comprehensive financial system consisting of many industries. However, constrained by many factors, the development of its industries is relatively unbalanced, which is prominently reflected in the dominance of the banking industry and the small scale of other financial industries, including insurance, trust and leasing industries. By the end of 2007, assets in the banking sector had reached RMB52.6 trillion and accounted for 92% in the total assets of the financial industry; assets of the securities sector amounted to RMB1.7 trillion and accounted for 3%; assets of insurance totalled RMB2.9 trillion and accounted for 5%.[1]

It is evident that the establishment and development of China's modern financial service system is still in the early phase, and the development of various financial institutions is relatively unbalanced, particularly with the small- and medium-sized financial institutions and non-bank financial institutions lagging behind in their development. The system of financial institutions still needs to be constantly improved in order to adapt to the sustainable and healthy development of the national economy.

Diversification of the financial assets structure

China's total financial assets have soared by 133.8 times in 23 years, from RMB623 billion in 1985 to RMB84 trillion in 2007. At the same time, these financial assets have tended to lean toward greater diversification, developing from the dominance of monetary financial assets at the beginning of the reform to the coexistence of various financial assets, including monetary financial assets, securities financial assets, and insurance financial assets. As shown in Table 7.2, changes in the structure of financial assets have the following three features.

Proportion of monetary financial assets declines

From 1985 to 2007, the total number of monetary financial assets increased 69.2 times from RMB597.8 billion to RMB42 trillion, in which the flow of cash increased 29.7 times from RMB98.8 billion to RMB3 trillion, and the total deposits increased 77 times from RMB499 billion to RMB38.9 trillion. The proportion of monetary financial assets in the total financial assets declined from 96% in 1985 to 50% in 2007. At the same time, proportions of both cash in circulation and deposits also experienced rapid downturns, dropping from 15.9% and 80.1% to 3.6% and 46.4%, respectively.

Meanwhile, the size of non-monetary financial assets increased from RMB25.2 billion in 1985 to RMB42 trillion in 2007, and the proportion in the

Evolution and Imbalance of China's Financial Structure

total financial assets rose from 4% to 50%. Although non-monetary financial assets became noticeably more important in the composition of financial assets, monetary financial assets still remained dominant.

Table 7.2. Changes in the structure of China's financial assets (%)

Item	1985	1990	1995	2000	2003	2005	2006	2007
Monetary Assets	96.0	93.3	87.4	66.5	73.7	77.6	70.1	50
Cash in Circulation	15.9	14.8	11.2	7.0	6.4	6.0	5.2	3.6
Total Deposits	80.1	78.5	76.2	59.5	67.3	71.6	64.9	46.4
Securities Assets	3.9	6.5	12.5	32.9	25.4	21.2	28.8	49.2
Bonds	3.9	6.5	7.6	9.8	11.6	13.1	11.5	10.2
Government Bonds	3.8	4.9	4.7	6.3	7.3	7.2	5.6	5.5
Corporate Bonds	0	1.1	0.5	0	0.6	1	1.1	0.9
Financial Bonds	0.1	0.5	2.4	3.5	3.8	4.9	4.9	3.8
Market Value of Shares	0	0	4.9	23.1	13.7	8.1	17.3	38.9
Insurance Assets	0.2	0.2	0.1	0.6	1.0	1.2	1.1	0.8
Premium	0.2	0.2	0.1	0.6	1.0	1.2	1.1	0.8
Total Domestic Financial Assets	100	100	100	100	100	100	100	100

Sources: calculated by the data from *China's Financial Market Development Report (2007)* and *China Statistical Yearbook (2008)*.

Dramatic changes of the internal structure of non-monetary financial assets

As shown in Table 7.2, there is a dramatic change in the internal structure of non-monetary financial assets, prominently reflected in the significant increase of the proportion of securities financial assets, which rose from 3.9% in 1985 to 49.2% in 2007 with an average annual increase of 2%. Specifically, the significant rise in stock assets is the main cause for the rise of the proportion of securities financial assets. At the beginning of the establishment of China's stock market in 1991, stock accounted for a mere 2% in financial assets, but the proportion reached 38.9% at the end of 2007 and rose by 21.6%, compared with the end of 2006. During this same period, bonds become more important in the composition of financial assets, and their proportion rose by 6.3% from 1985 to 2007. It is worth noting that the insurance sector, especially the life insurance business, has grown quite significantly in recent years.

STRUCTURAL ECONOMICS IN CHINA

Scale of bond assets remains small

Before the establishment of the stock market, bonds were the only negotiable securities in China. Although the bond market, particularly the corporate bond market, is growing rapidly and the scale of bond assets is expanding, the total number of China's bond assets still remains low compared to the mature market economies. Compared internationally, the scale of the global bond assets accounts for 95% relative to GDP; the U.S. 143%; Japan 136%; EU 82%; and Asian market economies 85%.[2] However, China's bond scale had only accounted for 34.9% relative to GDP by the end of 2007, equal to almost 1/3 of the global average.

Diversified financing methods

Since the reform and opening-up, companies' financing methods have undergone tremendous changes. Bank credit financing has gradually replaced fiscal financing, and the capital market is now used to carry out stock and bond financing. Financing methods of corporations are increasingly diversified.

Fig. 7.1. Changes in the asset-liability ratio of China's enterprises

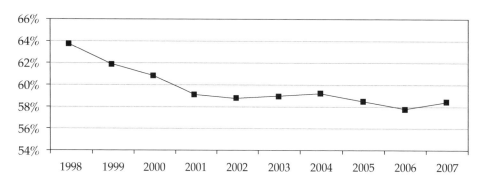

Proportion of internal financing increased, yet still low

The proportions of corporate internal financing in the U.S., UK and Germany all stand at more than 70% in their total financing. Moreover, the proportion of corporate financing of developed countries in their total financing also showed a rising trend during the period of 1962-1989. The U.S. rose from 76% to 85.4%; Germany rose from 66.5% to 78.6%; Japan rose from 39.4% to 52.3%.[3] Compared with these countries, Chinese enterprises' capabilities to accumulate internal funds proved to be weak, leading to a very low proportion of internal financing. The direct consequence was that the corporate asset-liability ratio was not only much higher than some developed countries, but also higher than many developing countries. In recent years, despite a declining trend, the asset-liability ratio of industrial enterprises above the designated size was still as high as 58.3% at the end of 2007 (see Fig. 7.1).

Indirect financing based on bank credit is the main source of corporate external financing

In the initial stage of China's economic transition, the responsibilities previously taken by the relevant fiscal authorities in the planned economy period were transferred to the reign of state-owned banks, leading to the financing of state-owned enterprises highly dependent on bank loans. With the gradual rise of the bond market and the stock market, the monopoly of bank credit in corporate external financing has been eroded. Direct financing methods such as stocks and corporate bonds have gradually taken the place; yet the highest proportion of corporate direct financing remained below 20% and the indirect financing has still kept its dominant position in corporate external financing.

Table 7.3. Changes in financing structure of Chinese enterprises, 1997–2007 (RMB1 billion)

Year	Loan		Equity		Corporate Bond		Financing Aggregate
	Amount of Financing	Proportion (%)	Amount of Financing	Proportion (%)	Amount of Financing	Proportion (%)	
1997	11,339	92.1	934	7.6	35	0.3	12,308
1998	11,846	93.3	804	6.3	42	0.3	12,692
1999	10,721	91.0	897	7.6	167	1.4	11,785
2000	12,499	85.1	2,103	14.3	83	0.6	14,685
2001	12,558	90.0	1,252	9.0	147	1.1	13,957
2002	19,228	93.7	962	4.7	325	1.6	20,515
2003	29,936	94.6	1,357	4.3	336	1.1	31,629
2004	24,066	92.9	1,504	5.8	327	1.3	25,897
2005	24,617	86.3	1,884	6.6	2,010	7.0	28,511
2006	32,687	87.9	2,246	6.0	2,266	6.1	37,199
2007	39,205	81.8	6,532	13.6	2,178	4.5	47,915

Source: Calculated with reference to the data obtained from *China's Financial Market Development Report (2007)*. The amount of loans and corporate bond financing is the net increase in that year; equity financing does not include the amount of public financing for financial institutions.

STRUCTURAL ECONOMICS IN CHINA

Direct financing fluctuates

As can be seen from Table 7.3, the proportion of direct financing in the corporate financing aggregate has always been in cyclical fluctuations. The scale of corporate equity financing tended to increase in the boom of the stock market and tended to decrease in the downturn of the stock market. For example, when China's stock market reached cyclical highs in 1997, 2000 and 2007, the scale and the proportion of corporate equity financing also respectively reached its cyclical highs, thus leading the scale and the proportion of direct financing to cyclical highs. In terms of corporate bond financing, the proportion of bond financing in corporate bond financing has always been low. In May 2005, China began to allow corporations to issue short-term financing bills. Because China adhered to being market-oriented in the process of releasing, corporations have been very positive in issuing the bills, thereby driving a significant increase in the size of corporate bond financing.

A more open financial sector

Since the introduction of the first foreign bank in 1981, China has always adhered to a safe and orderly expansion of its financial openness. Since China's entry into the WTO, financial openness has been significantly accelerated. By the end of 2007, 193 foreign banks in 47 countries and regions had set up 242 representative offices in 24 cities; 71 foreign banks in 23 countries and regions have set up 117 branches in China, and there were 26 foreign-owned and joint venture banking institutions registered in China. There had been 57 foreign bank branches and 25 foreign banks allowed to conduct RMB business, and 50 foreign banking institutions allowed to engage in the trading of financial derivatives. Assets of foreign financial institutions reached RMB1.25 trillion, accounting for 2.3% in the total banking assets (see Table 7.4). China also accelerated the introduction of foreign investors into Chinese banks. By the end of 2007, a total of 25 Chinese-funded commercial banks had introduced 33 foreign institutional investors and introduced foreign investment of 21.25 billion dollars. In addition, the banking industry significantly sped up the pace of "going out." By the end of 2007, Chinese banks had held or participated in shares of 9 foreign financial institutions, and had set up 60 branches in the U.S., Japan, UK, and Singapore, in addition to29 other countries and regions, with total overseas assets reaching USD267.4 billion.[4]

In order to improve the openness of the securities industry, China has promulgated some related regulations such as Foreign-Invested Securities Companies and Fund Management Companies, and has started mechanisms of Qualified Foreign Institutional Investors (QFII) and Qualified Domestic Institutional Investors (QDII). By the end of 2007, 7 joint venture securities companies and 28 joint venture fund management companies had been approved, and 52 foreign institutions had received QFII qualification. Additionally, 23 banks, 20 insurance companies, 12 securities investment fund management companies and 4 securities companies had gained QDII qualification.[5]

Compared to the banking and securities industries, the insurance industry is becoming significantly more open. The insurance industry fully opened in December 2004, and foreign insurance companies are encouraged to provide insurance service in any region of China. Foreign insurance companies in business increased from 18 before the entry into WTO to 43 at the end of 2007, while 128 foreign insurance institutions from 19 countries and regions set up 192 representative offices in China. In addition, the "going out" strategy of the insurance industry has made significant progress. By the end of 2007, China's insurance companies had established 42 business organizations and 9 representative offices or liaison offices in Hong Kong and Macau, Southeast Asia, Europe, North America, and other regions.[6]

Although China's financial sector has made significant progress in its opening-up development, its openness is still low and has a large space for development, compared with most emerging and transitional markets.

Table 7.4. Development of foreign banks in China, 2000–2007

Item/Year	2000	2001	2002	2003	2004	2005	2006	2007
Number of Business Institutions	191.00	190.00	180.00	192.00	211.00	254.00	312.00	440.00
Assets (USD1 billion)	34.43	45.05	39.15	48.80	69.41	87.66	103.30	171.46
Proportion in Total Assets of Banking Institutions (%)	2.10	2.30	1.40	1.50	1.80	1.90	2.10	2.30

Source. *International Statistical Yearbook* (2007).

Judgment of the Degree of Imbalance of China's Financial Structure

Although China's financial reform has made great progress and the financial development plays an increasingly significant role in promoting economic growth, structural problems remain the main obstacle to financial development and economic growth. This section focuses on judging the degree of the imbalance of China's financial structure in three aspects: the coordination of the constituent elements of the financial system, the efficiency of the financial system, and the adaptability between financial structure and economic structure.

Criteria judging the degree of imbalance of the financial structure

The imbalance of the financial structure is reflected in the structural imbalance of financial elements, structural imbalance of the financial industry, and imbalance of the adaptability between financial structure and economic structure.[7] Corresponding to these three levels, there are three criteria for judging the degree of imbalance of financial structure.

The first is coordination. This criterion corresponds to structural imbalance of financial elements, namely, whether a country's financial structure is unbalanced depends on the internal coordination of the financial system. If the proportional relationship among various elements within the financial system is unbalanced, the financial structure is unbalanced.

The second is efficiency. Coordination is the criterion for the internal value of financial structural imbalance, whereas efficiency is the criterion for its external value. In fact, whether it is a financial-market-oriented financial structure or a financial-intermediaries-oriented one, if it cannot effectively carry out basic functions of the financial system such as savings mobilization, resource allocation, risk management, or facilitating goods and service trade, it is an unbalanced financial structure.

The third is adaptability. Adaptability is the organic unity of the criteria of both the internal value and the external value of the financial structural imbalance. As a part of the socio-economic structure, the financial structure must adapt to the development of the real economy, which is the most basic requirement the market economy imposes on the financial structure. Only by adapting to the development of the real economy under certain historical conditions can the financial structure promote the stable and long-term growth of the economy, ensuring it can be optimized and upgraded in the changing structure of the real economy. If the financial structure does not adapt to the development of the real economy, the financial structure is unbalanced.

Judgment based on the coordination of the structure of the financial elements

The degree of financial structural imbalance can be judged in three aspects: the coordination of the structure of financial instruments, the coordination of the structure of financial institutions, and the coordination of the structure of financial market participants.

Imbalance of the structure of financial instruments

Disproportionality between equity-based financing instruments and bond-based financing instruments

As a major debt-based financial instrument, the issuance cost of corporate bonds is lower than that of stocks, and bond financing can increase returns on equity through the financial leverage effects. While bond financing increases corporate capital, it does not lead to stock dispersion, which helps protect the benefits of existing shareholders. Therefore, bond financing is favored by large international companies. With regard to corporate financing in UK, the U.S., and other countries, it seems that corporations definitely prefer to raise funds by issuing bonds. For example, in the 1980s, few American companies issued new shares, and during some years, companies repurchased stock by borrowing.

Fig. 7.2. Proportion of China's bond financing in enterprises' direct financing, 1997–2007

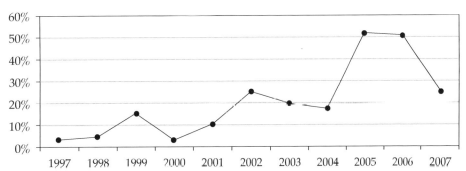

STRUCTURAL ECONOMICS IN CHINA

The phenomenon of "focusing more on stocks but less on bonds" became prominent when enterprises conducted the direct financing. The proportion of bond financing accounted for no more than 30% of the total direct financing before 2004. Since 2005, corporate bonds, especially the volume of short-term financing bonds issued, have increased significantly, resulting in a rapid increase of the proportions in 2005 and 2006 (see Fig. 7.2). Despite a large bond financing scale in 2007, the proportion of the bond financing scale in the enterprises' direct financing declined significantly due to the rapid increase of the equity financing.

An international comparison between the size of the bond market and the stock market demonstrates that China's size of the bond market is a mere 27% relative to the size of its stock market, which is far below the percentage in the United States and other developed countries, and also lower than in South Korea, India and other emerging countries (see Fig. 7.3).[8]

Fig. 7.3.   International comparison of the size between the bond market and the stock market

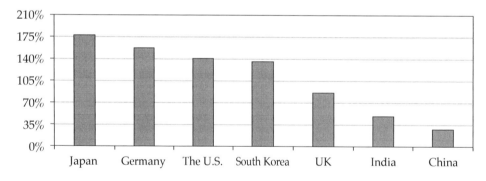

Internal imbalance of the debt-based financial instruments

Bonds in China are mainly dominated by government bonds and financial bonds, and in particular the treasury bonds, which occupy a large share. In fact, after a rapid, short-term growth in the early 1990s, the corporate bonds began to grow at a slow pace. In the wake of developing institutions of the size and method the corporate bonds issue, the market of the corporate bond has recovered to an accelerated growth. Especially after the issue of the new short-term corporate bond, financed by the People's Bank of China in 2005, the issue size of corporate bonds expanded rapidly. In 2007, the total amount of the bonds issued in

Evolution and Imbalance of China's Financial Structure

China reached RMB2.48 trillion (excluding RMB1.55 trillion of the central bank bonds and the special treasury bonds). Among those, the treasury bonds were RMB763.7 billion, i.e., 30.8% of the total size of issue; the corporate bonds were RMB505.9 billion i.e., 20.4% of the total size of issue (including RMB334.9 billion of the short-term corporate financing bonds); the financial bonds were RMB1.2 trillion, i.e., 48.1% of the total size of issue (including RMB1.1 trillion of the financial policy bonds, RMB37.7 billion of the financial institutions' subordinated debt, and RMB44.6 billion of the general financial bonds); and RMB17.8 billion of the asset-backed securities which accounted for 0.7% of the total issue size. The overwhelming issue sizes of both the treasury bonds and the financing bonds largely oppress the corporate bonds. For instance, the total debt balance was comprised of 53.3%, 37% and a mere 9.3% of the aggregate balance of the treasury bonds, financial bonds, and corporate bonds, respectively.

Highly-intensive banking market monopolized by the state-owned commercial banks

The structure of China's banking market experienced the monopolization by the People's Bank of China, and was then domination by the "Big Four" state-owned banks. Now, it has developed to a stage which sees competition among the Big Four, joint-stock commercial banks and other financial institutions. However, the monopolistic position of the state-owned commercial banks in terms of the total assets, deposits, loans and other aspects of the market has not changed.

The state-owned commercial banks still hold a large portion of the assets. At the end of 2007, total assets of the state-owned commercial banks were RMB27.3 trillion, accounting for 50.5% of the total banking assets (see Fig. 7.4).[9]

Fig. 7.4. Distribution of banking assets at the end of 2007

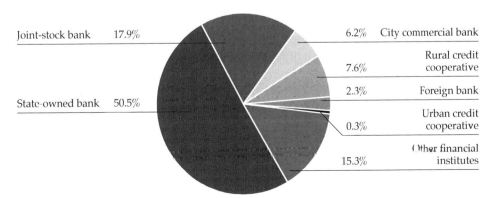

STRUCTURAL ECONOMICS IN CHINA

In terms of the shares in deposit and loan markets, compared with 1996, there was a decrease of 9.4% in the deposit market share and a slash of 24% in the loan market share of the four major state-owned commercial banks at the end of 2007; in particular, the loan market share declined to less than 50% in 2007 (see Table 7.5). This implies an increasingly intensive competition in the banking market, but state-owned banks remained in a monopolized position despite a descending trend in recent years.

Table 7.5. Changes of the concentration of China's banking market $(CR_4)^{10}$ (%)

Year	1996	1998	2000	2002	2004	2006	2007
Loan	72.7	72.0	76.5	62.1	58.2	50.8	48.7
Deposit	61.8	62.2	62.6	64.5	59.1	54.6	52.4

Source: Calculated from *the People's Bank of China Statistics Quarterly Reports*.

Imbalance of the structure of financial market participants

First, problems exist among the currency market participants, including insufficient involvement, narrow coverage, low level of participation, and lack of standards restraining trading behaviors. The banking institutions have been dominating China's currency market for a long time, but the business and commercial enterprises with the largest short-term financing needs have not been the participating subjects. Moreover, the currency market lacks the agencies such as currency market brokers and agencies, credit rating agencies, et cetera.

Second, there is an imbalance of structure between the institutional investors and individual investors. Compared with individual investors, the institutional investors have strong research capabilities and a wealth of investment experience, a strong ability to avoid risk, and relatively stable investment behavior. Therefore, the financial market with higher proportion of institutional investors enjoys better stability. With the stock market continuing to develop, the market will be transformed to one in which the institutional investors and the individual investors jointly participate. For example, the New York Stock Exchange denoted that the proportion of the household direct holdings increased to 90% in 1950 but fell to 41.1% in 1998; and the proportion was only 4.5% for the annuity funds (the mutual funds investors held in 1950), but increased to 24.2% in 1998.[11] The participants in China's securities market have long been composed of small and medium investors, and the proportion of the institutional investors has been low. The unbalanced structure of the investors is still prominent. At the end of 2007, the total number of accounts for investors in the stock market had reached 140 million, more than 95% of which were individual investors. Regarding the scale of holdings, even though China had initially formed an institutional investment team composed mainly of securities investment funds, individual investors in the stock market still increased by 51.3% by the end of 2007 (see Fig. 7.5).[12] In fact, the investment structure with individual investors as the main subjects deteriorated the volatility of the security market, leading to the inaccurate and lagged reaction of the stock price to reflect relevant information. As a result, the investors were unable to effectively impose external oversight on the listed companies.

Fig. 7.5. Market shares of the different types of investors in the stock market at the end of 2007

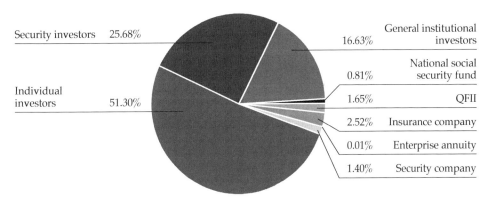

There has been an internal structure imbalance within the institutional investors. With the rapid development of institutional investors, the securities investment funds, especially the open-end funds, have become the largest institutional investors in the stock market. The institutional investors in the social security funds, insurance companies, enterprise annuities and other types of investment are relatively small. At the end of 2007, the stock market value of the securities investment funds occupied 25.6% of the aggregate market capitalization. This number accounted for 55% of the stock market capitalization by the institutional investors. The proportion of the insurance companies and the social security funds was a mere 6.4%—a remarkable contrast with the structure in developed countries where the main institutional investors in the stock market are the pension funds and insurance companies (see Fig. 7.6).[13]

Fig. 7.6. Constitution of the institutional investors in the stock market of developed countries

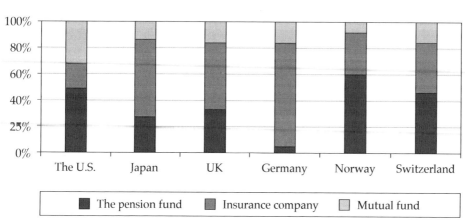

In summary, the imbalance of the internal structure of the financial systems is reflected in three areas. In terms of the financial instruments, imbalances exist in the proportional relationship between the direct and indirect financial instruments, between the equity-based and debt-based instruments and within the internal structure of securities. In terms of the constitution of the financial institution, imbalances are manifested in the unbalanced development of both the banking and non-bank financial institutions, and the monopolized position of the state-owned commercial banks. In terms of the structure of the financial market participants, imbalances are demonstrated in the irrational constitution of the currency market participants and the unbalanced proportional relationship between the institutional and individual investors in the security market.

Comprehensive judgment based on the efficiency of the financial structure

The direct consequence of the imbalance of the financial structure is that a variety of elements cannot be given full play to their proper functions, thus resulting in functional conflicts and inefficiency within the financial system. From the perspective of China's unique situation, the degree of the unbalanced financial structure can be judged from three aspects: financial macro-efficiency, efficiency of financial institutions, and efficiency of the financial market.

Evolution and Imbalance of China's Financial Structure

The financial macro-efficiency

In the market economy, the deposit subjects tend to be separate from the main investment subjects, making the deposit mobilization and the resource allocation important in the financial system. China and India are the world's largest developing countries with the fastest economic growth. The comparison of the capital distribution efficiency between China's and India's financial systems can indirectly reflect the operational efficiency of China's financial system.

As shown in Table 7.6, China's average annual deposit rate maintained at 42.2% between 1995 and 2006, which was much higher than India's 26.9%. This indicates a stronger capacity of China's deposit mobilization than that of India. Although both China and India have imposed strict controls on mobilizing deposit resources, China has more advantages in mobilizing deposit than India, due to its financial system in which the state-owned banks take the leading roles.

Table 7.6. Changes of the deposit rates and savings supporting rate of economic growth in China and India (%)

Year	Total Savings Rate		Economic Growth Rate		Saving Supporting Rate of Economic Growth	
	China	India	China	India	China	India
1995	41.9	24.4	10.9	7.3	3.8	3.3
1996	40.8	22.7	10.0	8.0	4.1	2.8
1997	41.0	23.8	9.3	4.3	4.4	5.5
1998	40.4	22.3	7.8	6.7	5.2	3.3
1999	38.8	24.8	7.6	6.4	5.1	3.9
2000	37.7	23.7	8.4	4.4	4.5	5.4
2001	38.6	23.5	8.3	5.8	4.7	4.1
2002	40.4	26.4	9.1	3.8	4.4	6.9
2003	43.2	29.8	10.0	8.5	4.3	3.5
2004	45.7	31.8	10.1	7.5	4.5	4.2
2005	48.2	34.3	10.4	9.4	4.6	3.6
2006	50.1	34.8	11.1	9.6	4.5	3.6
Average	42.2	26.9	9.4	6.8	4.5	4.2

Sources: *China Statistical Yearbook (2007), Economic Survey (2007–2008)*, also available at http://indiabudget.nic.in.
Note: Data of India were obtained from its Financial Year Database (2007).

STRUCTURAL ECONOMICS IN CHINA

The efficiency of the deposit resource allocation can be measured by the savings supporting rate of the economic growth. The so-called savings supporting rate of the economic growth refers to the deposit rate needed for a 1% economic growth in a period of time, i.e., the ratio between the savings rate and the rate of the economic growth in one country. Obviously, the higher the savings supporting rate of the economic growth, the more deposit resources are needed for the unit economic growth and the lower efficiency in the deposit resource allocation. From 1995 to 2006, China's average economic growth rate was 9.4%, far overweighing India's 6.8%, and so was the savings supporting rate of the economic growth. During 1995–2006, the average savings supporting rate of the economic growth was 4.5% in China, and 4.2% in India. This indicates the deposit resources consumed for the unit economic growth in China were more than in India, which indirectly implies that the efficiency of the capital distribution in the Indian financial system is higher than in that of China.

Efficiency of financial institution

Because China's financial institutions are dominated by the commercial banks, changes in the efficiency of financial institutions can be reflected by analyzing the profitability of the commercial banks, the asset quality, and the capital adequacy.

The asset profitability of the commercial banks is relatively low

Since the 1990s, the pre-tax asset profitability of the state-owned commercial banks has experienced a U-turn. From 1985 to 1992, the pre-tax profit of the four state-owned commercial banks maintained a rapid growth from RMB130 billion to RMB32 billion, with an average annual growth rate of up to 21%. But since the mid-1990s, due to the prolonged stagnation of the financial reform, the return on assets of the commercial banks dropped dramatically (see Table 7.7). However, in the wake of the reform of the joint-stock system, the profitability of the state-owned commercial banks has been significantly improved,[14] but there is still a large gap between domestic and international banks. In 2007, the capital profit margin of China's major commercial banks was 16.7%, with 16.1% of the Industrial and Commercial Bank of China (ICBC), 14.2% of the Bank of China (BOC), and 19.5% of the China Construction Bank (CCB), respectively.[15] Comparatively, the average margin of the world's top 1000 banks were 22.7% in 2006, reaching 29.1% in 197 U.S. banks.[16]

Evolution and Imbalance of China's Financial Structure

Table 7.7. Pre-tax asset profit margin of the state-owned commercial banks, 1991–2007 (%)

Year	ICBC	Agricultural Bank of China (ABC)	BOC	CCB
1991	1.35	0.23	0.75	0.28
1993	0.42	0.26	0.57	0.24
1995	0.15	0.35	0.52	0.36
1997	0.08	0.05	0.26	0.11
1999	0.12	−0.02	0.17	0.33
2000	0.13	0.01	0.22	0.34
2001	0.34	0.05	0.12	0.19
2002	0.14	0.10	0.38	0.15
2003	0.05	0.06	0.26	0.01
2004	1.13	0.21	0.84	1.37
2005	1.09	0.17	1.22	1.30
2006	1.02	0.78	1.33	1.31
2007	1.01	0.81	1.09	1.15

Sources: Calculated from the data obtained from *China's Financial Yearbook (1992-2007)* and *China Banking Regulatory Commission Annual Report (2007)*.

Fig. 7.7. Non-performing loan ratio of China's state-owned commercial banks (%)

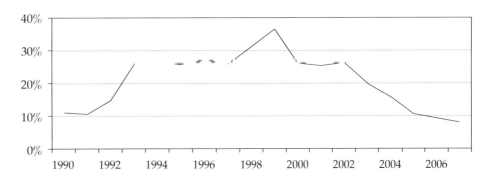

The quality of the asset of the commercial banks is relatively low

The bad loan ratio of China's state-owned commercial banks peaked in 1999 and has retreated ever since (see Fig. 7.7). A study done by the Moody's Investors Service in 1999 shows that the bad loan ratio in some Chinese state-owned banks

STRUCTURAL ECONOMICS IN CHINA

was as high as 50%, and the restructuring costs may reach 18% of GDP.[17] After 2000, with the strengthening of the financial system reform and the reform of the joint-stock system of the state-owned commercial banks, the non-performing loans of the state-owned commercial banks achieved continuous "double decreases" through state capital injection, asset stripping, and self write-offs.

Since 2004, the bad loans of commercial banks have continued to decline. The bad loan ratio in major commercial banks dropped from 13.2% in late 2004 to 6.7% in late 2007; from 15.6% in 2004 to 8.1% in 2007 for the state-owned commercial banks; and from 1.1% in 2005 to 0.5% in 2007 for the foreign banks. However, that ratio was still higher than the international leading banks.

Efficiency of China's financial market

The two major components of the financial market are the currency market and the capital market. These are complementary in order to make a reasonable cost of capital and to guide an efficient resource allocation. We primarily analyze the features of the efficiency of both the currency market and the stock market to reflect the changes of the efficiency in China's financial market.[18]

Low efficiency of the currency market

At present, China has established a relatively complete currency market, including the interbank market, the repo market, the commercial paper market and other sub-markets. The currency market has become not only the main site for various financial institutions to adjust the fund position, manage liquidity and invest on assets, but also an important platform for the central bank's macro-control. However, the overall efficiency of the currency market still remains low, manifested in three aspects.

First, the unbalanced development between the currency market and its sub-markets exposes serious market segmentation. Of the three major sub-markets of China's currency market, the trading scale in the repo market occupies a disproportionately large portion, leaving only a small share to the interbank market and paper market. In 2007, the total turnover of the interbank and bond repo markets[19] reached RMB10.7 trillion and RMB48.1 trillion, respectively, whilethe total volume of commercial bills issued in the paper market reached RMB5.9 trillion. The sum of the transactions of the three sub-markets accounted for 16.5%, 74.4% and 9.1%, respectively, of the total transactions of the currency market. In contrast, the development of the various sub-markets in developed countries is relatively balanced, with a few individual sub-markets occupying more than 50% of the aggregate market share. In addition to the unbalanced development of the sub-markets, there is also a serious segmentation in China's currency sub-market. For example, there are two repo markets in China: the exchange repo market and the interbank repo market. Because of the different market participants, transaction price formation mechanisms, and trusteeship and fund-clearing systems, there is clear market segmentation between the exchange repo market and the inter-bank repo market, resulting in a relatively larger sized inter-bank repo market. In 2007, the transaction volume of the inter-bank bond repo market was up to RMB46.3 trillion, accounting for 96.2% of the total transactions conducted in the repo market (see Table 7.8).

Table 7.8. Transactions of China's inter-bank repo market and the exchange repo market, 2000–2007

Year	Transaction Volume (RMB100 million)		Market Share (%)	
	Inter-bank Repo Market	Exchange Repo Market	Inter-bank Repo Market	Exchange Repo Market
2000	15,715	14,734	51.6	48.4
2001	40,186	15,487	72.2	27.8
2002	101,978	24,419	80.7	19.3
2003	119,758	53,000	69.3	30.7
2004	99,652	44,087	69.3	30.7
2005	165,078	23,261	87.6	12.4
2006	273,512	15,413	94.7	5.3
2007	462,872	18,345	96.2	3.8

Source: *China Banking Regulatory Commission Annual Report (2007).*

Second, transactions in the currency market are highly intensive. The shares of the transaction of the national commercial banks and city commercial banks are significantly large, while the non-banking financial institutions take up the small portion. Considering the pledged-style repo businesses in the inter-bank repo market as an example, in 2007, the size of the transactions of the reverse repo in the national commercial banks accounted for up to 75.1% of the total, and the city commercial banks accounted for 9.4%. These two amounted to 84.5% of the market share. In the total buy-back operations of the market, the size of the buy-back operations of the national commercial banks accounted for 25.2%, and the city national commercial banks accounted for 31.9%. They

STRUCTURAL ECONOMICS IN CHINA

Fig. 7.8. Proportions of the various traders in the inter-bank pledged-style repo market, 2007

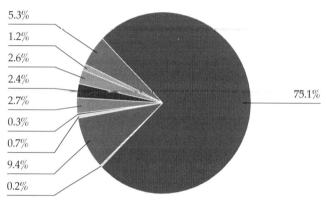

Reverse Repo

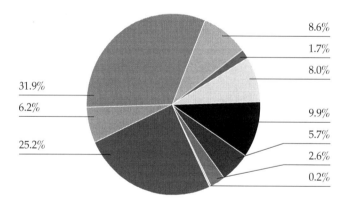

Buy-back Operation

amounted to 57.1% of the market share (see Fig. 7.8).[20] In terms of the variety of the transactions, the proportion of the short-term varieties was higher. For instance, in the total volume of the transactions of the bank lending market in 2007, the turnover of the overnight lending was RMB8 billion, accounting for 75.4%; the 7-day trading accounted for more than 20.5%; and the over-three-month lending transactions accounted for only 0.1% (see Fig. 7.9). The buy-back volume for the within-seven-day period was RMB39.9 trillion, accounting for 84.1% of the total pledged-style repo business.

Fig. 7.9.   Term structure of the transactional instruments in the inter-bank market

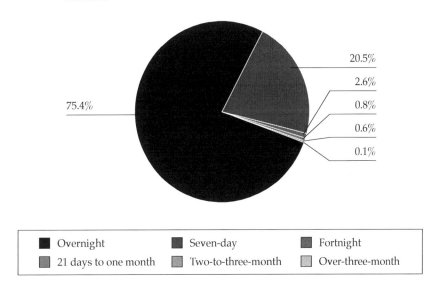

Finally, the formation mechanism of benchmark interest rate is imperfect. The benchmark interest rate plays a leading role in the overall financial market and interest system. Its establishment has been beneficial in promoting financial institutions to improve their ability in autonomous pricing, to provide pricing guidance for the currency market, to perfect the monetary policy transmission mechanism, and to promote the marketization of the interest rate. At present, China has established the position of the benchmark interest rate of the Shanghai Interbank Offered Rate (Shibor). Since coming into effect in January 2007, the standardization of Shibor has continuously risen. Its guiding function of product pricing has been increasingly prominent. A pricing mechanism pegged at Shibor has already been adopted in the short-term financing bonds, the corporate bonds, the floating-rate policy financial bonds, note discounts and transfer discounts, interest rate swaps and other financial products. However, there is still a considerable gap between Shibor and the real interest rate. In terms of the quotation quality, the postal savings banks and the Provincial Rural Credit Union are not involved in the quotation process and some transaction prices contain some non-market factors, undermining the representativeness and authority of Shibor. In reality, the price difference between Shibor (within three months) and the transaction price is small, but the interest margin between Shibor (over three months) and the transaction price is much larger. This indicates that the Shibor's quotation quality still requires improvement. In terms of the application range, Shibor is confined in the pricing of commercialized products. The pricing of deposit and lending rates, and the pricing of the internal capital transfer in the banking industry—especially in the local corporate financial institutions—has not yet been pegged on Shibor.

Low efficiency of the stock market

Deng Xiaoping's axe-wielding reform has greatly contributed to China's burgeoning stock market. Particularly because of the continuous basic institutional improvement of the market in recent years, the stock market efficiency has been greatly enhanced. However, compared with those established ones, the efficiency of China's stock market is still low. The stock market efficiency is examined mainly from the market liquidity and the risk characteristics.

First, the stock market liquidity is relatively low. Theoretically, strong stock market liquidity signifies low transaction costs and efficient resource allocation. Therefore, the market liquidity is not only an important indicator of the level of development of a country's stock market, but a key indicator to measure a country's financial market efficiency. In fact, the low market liquidity will not only stimulate speculation and market manipulation, but will also increase the market volatility and investors' transaction costs, thereby affecting a healthy and stable development of financial market. The price impact index and transaction costs are selected here as indicators to describe the liquidity in China's stock market.

In general, the greater the price impact index,[21] the higher the transaction costs, and the worse the market liquidity. In recent years, although the price impact index of China's stock market generally declined and the costs of liquidity have seen a substantial reduction, there still remains a big gap when

Evolution and Imbalance of China's Financial Structure

compared with the major international stock markets. As shown in Fig. 7.10, the price impact index in both Shanghai Stock Exchange and Shenzhen Stock Exchange is not only much higher than that in the U.S., UK, Germany, Japan and other fully-established markets, but also higher than that in India, South Korea and other emerging markets. The stock market transaction costs generally include transaction tax and commissions. Recently, China's stock market transaction costs were averaging at 30 basis points, consisting of about 10 basis points of stamp duty and about 20 basis points of commissions. Compared with the established markets, these transaction costs are relatively high. For example, the average transaction cost of the U.S. stock market is only 13 basis points, made up of 0.4 basis points of transaction cost and 12.6 basis points of commission.[22]

Fig. 7.10. International comparison of the price impact index of the stock market transactions

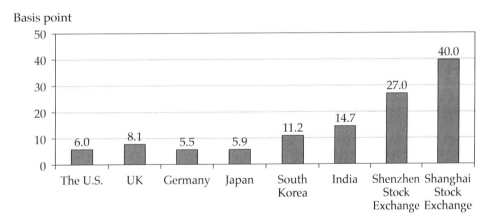

Second, the stock market is prominently risky. China has an emerging stock market where small investors are the major players, hence breeding the short-term shareholdings, excessive speculation, and other behaviors which may, in all likelihood, undermine the whole stock system. Due to the lack of sophisticated value investors, the stock market may risk massive short-term speculation, which is mainly reflected in the high turnover rate[23] and high price-earnings ratio.

With further development of the stock market, the increasing number of institutional investors, the increasing investment in share dealing, and decreasing speculation, the transactions will be biased toward more rational behavior, and thus the stock turnover rate will correspondingly decline. However, based on China's reality, the turnover rate in China's stock market has been climbing in recent years. In 2007, the turnover rate in Shanghai Stock Exchange and Shenzhen Stock Exchange were as high as 936% and 1,062%, seriously mirroring a lack of authentic long-term stock market investors. The fact that the market investment is mainly composed of short-term speculations makes the stock market turnover significantly but naturally higher than that of other fully-fledged stock markets (see Fig. 7.11).

Fig. 7.11. International comparison of turnover rate in the stock market

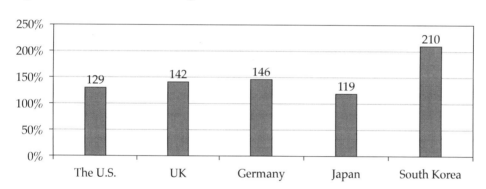

Currently, the price-earnings ratios in the U.S., UK, Hong Kong, and other established markets has fluctuated in the range of 10 to 20 times the price; the average price-earnings ratio in the Japanese market has remained in the range of 23 to 25 times. Except for Taiwan where the fluctuating range of the price-earnings ratio is larger, the price-earnings ratio in most markets remains in a relatively stable range. In China's stock market, the price-earnings ratio rose from 16 times at the end of 2005 to 59 times at the end of 2007 in the Shanghai stock market, and rose from 16 times at the end of 2005 to 72 times at the end of 2007 in the Shenzhen stock market. A high level of the price-earnings ratio denotes a high level of investment risks and low investment values, a thick atmosphere of market speculation, and a large portion of bubbles, so the overall high level of price-earnings ratio was not expected to last for long. In 2008, dramatic changes occurred in the stock market. In late October, the weighted average price-earnings ratio of Shanghai Stock Market and Shenzhen Stock Market, respectively, dropped to 14.07 times and 13.95 times, the risks partly released. The drastic fluctuations of price-earnings ratio reflected the characteristics of high risks in the stock market.

The overall financial efficiency of China's financial system is still not high. A summary can be made from three aspects: first, from a macro-perspective, both the allocation and use of resources are not efficient; second, with regard to the financial institutions, there is a big gap between China's commercial banks and the advanced international banks in terms of profitability and asset quality; third, in terms of the financial markets, market segmentation, and overdue trade concentration, imperfect benchmark interest rate exists in the currency market; while problems like the low liquidity and risk features throw wrinkles in the stock market. In fact, the relatively low financial efficiency is an important indicator of financial structural imbalance.

Judgment based on the adaptability of financial structure to the real economy

The financial system needs to ensure that its internal factors are mutually compatible and coordinating, and more importantly, it needs to adapt to the real economy. Only when the financial structure is consistent with the economic structure, can it actually facilitate economic development. In the wake of the reform and opening-up, China's financial structure has undergone substantial adjustment, but its adaptability to the economic structure remains low.

Insufficient support of the financial system to the financing of the private economy

Based on the changes of the entire ownership structure of the national economy, an important result of the gradual reform is a declining proportion of the state-owned economy in the national economy, and rising proportions of the collective economy, private economy and other economic sectors. After developing into the capital-intensive stage, the non-state-owned economy, represented by the private economy, is in urgent need for the financial system to provide appropriate financial support. But the financial system, mainly based on the state-owned property, is still primarily providing financial support to the state-owned economy. In fact, neither the state-owned banks nor the business market or stock market are able to provide effective financial or financing support to the private economy. For example, in 2007, the state-owned and state-holding industrial enterprises accounted for 32.8% of the industrial added value, and the private-sector-based non-state-owned economy occupied 67.2%, while the total short-term loans of the township enterprises, individual and private enterprises, and foreign investment enterprises over the same period took up only 11.1% of all short-term loans of the financial institutions.[24]

STRUCTURAL ECONOMICS IN CHINA

Rural finance is the weakest link in the financial system

Currently, China's economy has entered a new period in which industry nurtures agriculture, cities support rural areas. So a key link in constructing the harmonious socialist society is to solve the "three rural issues" (*san nong wen ti*), namely, agriculture, rural areas, and farmers. The targets of agricultural development, rural prosperity, and increased rural incomes cannot be achieved without effective financial support. After years of reform and development, the framework of financial services with the division of labor of commercial finance, policy-based finance, cooperative finance, and other financial organizations has taken an initial shape. The number and types of rural financial services and business are increasing, the rural financial infrastructure has been further improved, and the supporting role of finance to the rural economic development has become increasingly prominent. By the end of 2007, the banking financial institutions in rural areas covered all the counties (cities) in China, a total of 108,173 outlets; there were 88.1 million rural households supported by loans, accounting for 34.6% of the total number of rural households.[25] Meanwhile, the sustainability of rural financial institutions has been significantly improved. In June 2003, the State Council officially launched the pilot reform in the rural credit cooperatives. With the implementation of state financial support, policies like tax relief, and supporting policies introduced by the local authorities, some historical burdens of the rural credit cooperatives were resolved. The operating conditions were significantly improved and the capital adequacy rate substantially increased. At the end of 2007, the non-performing loans ratio and capital adequacy ratio of rural credit cooperatives (including rural cooperative banks and rural commercial banks) were 9.3% and 11.2%, respectively, falling by 28% and increasing by 20%, compared with the beginning of the pilot reform.[26]

Great achievements have been made in the rural financial reform and development. However, it is still the weakest link in the entire financial system, prominently reflected in four areas.

First, based on the distribution of financial resources, the gap between rural and urban areas tends to expand in terms of the possession of financial resources. At the end of 2007, the total balance of deposits in the rural areas at and below the county level was RMB10.2 trillion, accounting for 23% of the deposit balance in China's banking financial institutions; the total outstanding balance was RMB5.7 trillion, accounting for 22% of China's outstanding balance; the per capita loan amount in rural areas at and below the county level was RMB7,700, while the urban per capita loan amount was RMB35,000.

Second, based on the coverage of financial services, there are still many blind spots in the rural financial services. There are still 2,868 towns where there is not any branch of any financial institution, and there are 8,901 towns where there is only one branch of a financial institution being set up.[27] A rural survey shows that, in the western mountainous areas, farmers have to travel tens of kilometers to reach the nearest bank branch.[28]

Third, based on the availability of the financial services, the great demand for financial services in rural areas cannot be met. In the bank branches at and below the county level, less than 20% of the banks are able to offer services except for saving, loaning, and remittance. The bank outlets in most administrative villages cannot provide basic loans, so the problem of a "hard to get loan" for both farmers and small rural enterprises has not yet been fundamentally alleviated. Although the state has increased efforts to support the development of agricultural insurance in recent years, there is still a wide gap between agricultural insurance and the actual needs of rural economic development. In 2007, the agricultural insurance premium income was only RMB5.18 billion, covering 231 million *mu* (Chinese acres) of crops, 57 million livestock of several varieties, and 325 million poultry birds, only able to provide RMB112.6 billion of risk protection to the agricultural production.[29]

Fourth, based on the sustainability of financial institutions compared with urban financial institutions, there are large differences in rural financial institutions in the aspects of business environment, customer objects, risk management, et cetera. Thus, the asset quality of rural financial institutions is generally poorer than that of urban financial institutions. At the end of 2007, the average non-performing loans of financial institutions in counties accounted for 13.4%, much higher than the average level of 6.2% of all commercial banks.[30]

In summary, the imbalance is a normal state in the changes of China's financial structure, but varies to different degrees in different periods. In recent years, with the steady progress of the financial market-oriented reforms and the deepening reform of state-owned commercial banks, the financial structural imbalance has been slightly alleviated, but is still worthy of our serious attention.

Cause Analysis of China's Financial Structural Imbalance

Financial structure varies in different countries or in a country's different periods. Its evolution depends on the economic and financial development, and the behavior selection of economic agents, is governed by economic and financial systems, technological conditions, and degree of innovation, and is influenced by social psychology, historical and cultural backgrounds, including openness and other factors. The formation of China's financial structure imbalance is closely related to the top-down progress of the economic reforms. Furthermore, China's financial structure imbalance in the early stages of the reform and opening was not simply rooted in the structure imbalances in the real economy, but also was confined to government-led changes in the financial system. In addition, the delayed financial market reforms and imperfect legal system toward the protection of investors were closely related to the financial structural imbalance.

Imbalance of the real economic structure

A country's financial structure derives mainly from the country's factor endowment structure and industrial technological structure. When the factor endowment structure and industrial technological structure undergo changes, the financial structure must also be subject to the corresponding changes in order to meet the financing requirements of different industries and businesses. The factor endowment structure and industrial technological structure directly determine the level of a country's economic development, which determines the country's financial structure. According to the theory of endogenous financial development, because of the low level of per capita income, people cannot afford to pay the initial transaction costs required by the involvement in the financial system in the early stages of economic development. It does not make sense, even if they could afford to pay, because the trading volume would be too small and the unit transaction costs would be too high. Thus, due to the lack of demand for financial services, there can be no supply of financial services; therefore, the financial intermediaries and financial markets would not exist. When the economic development reaches a certain level, the income of those who get rich first would reach the threshold of the financial intermediation system, and then an intrinsic motivation to establish financial intermediaries would be triggered in the economies. In addition, with the advance of time and further economic development, the income level of an increasing number of people would reach the threshold of access to financial markets, and then the

Evolution and Imbalance of China's Financial Structure

financial markets would be established. It can be seen from this that the most fundamental factor to determine a country's financial structure is the level of economic development.

Due to the low level of economic development in the early stages of the reform and opening-up, the requirements of the real economy for financial services focused on the deposit mobilization. As banks were at comparative advantages in the deposit mobilization, and people's income levels could only meet the transaction costs required for the participation in banks and other intermediaries, the financial intermediaries (based mainly on the state-owned banks) were able to experience rapid expansion. In this stage, the state-owned economy served as the main driving force of China's economic development, and the state-owned enterprises became a major client of the state-owned banks. Under the influence of low efficiency of enterprises and other factors, a large number of financial risks were accumulated in the banking system that had been based mainly on the state-owned banks during this period, making the financial structure imbalance quite conspicuous. With an increasing level of economic development and significant changes in the factor endowment structure, the private economy has become an important force in China's economic growth. At the same time, the overall income level of the people significantly increased, and the income level of some people reached and even exceeded the initial transaction costs required for participating in the stock market, which led to the gradual establishment of the stock markets. However, as the state-owned economy was still the early client of the stock market, and the state-owned shares that cannot circulate account for a large proportion of the total share capital of listed companies, the stock market resource allocation remains inefficient. Thus, the financial development is still incompatible with real economic growth, and the risks of financial structural imbalance still exist. In recent years, as the financial market system improved and the reform of banks is further advanced, the resource allocation efficiency of both the banking system and the stock market, to some extent, has been improved, and the level of financial structure imbalance, to a certain degree, has also been alleviated.

Transition of the government-led financial institutions

Similar to the economic reform, the reform in China's financial sector has also

STRUCTURAL ECONOMICS IN CHINA

taken a gradual approach. The financial reform has always been subordinate to the overall objectives of government-led economic reform. In fact, based on the past 30 years of financial reform, China's financial system has seen a gradual deepening process from outside sectors to inside sectors, from the increment to the stock, and from government-led to market-oriented. The reform in the financial system was initiated when the "grand unified" financial system in the traditional planned economic system was broken. The establishment of ICBC in 1984 was taken as a symbol that China had entered into the professional banking system from the "grand unified" banking system. In the professional banking system, the relationship between the banks and finance, between banks themselves, between banks and enterprises, between banks and all levels of governments could not really be solved. The result was the severe dependence of finance on the banks, causing the lack of competition between banks, the extremely high debt ratio of enterprises, and the competition between local governments for credit schemes. Accordingly, a banking system which was monopolized by the state-owned specialized banks was created in China. In the late 1980s, China set out to change this situation by establishing 11 new commercial banks and numerous urban credit cooperatives, and started to establish securities markets in the early 1990s. The level of competition in the financial system increased through the incremental reform, but because the monopoly of the state-owned banks in the entire financial system was not fundamentally changed, the structure imbalance in the financial system was still very prominent, and the financial structure and economic structure remained incompatible with each other. In 1999, China initiated the reform of financial stocks by means of elimination of bad loans. After 2003, through additional capital, introduction of strategic investors, equity division reform, and initial public offerings (IPO), the market-oriented reform of the state-owned commercial banks became significantly accelerated. The overall efficiency of the banking industry was also greatly improved. At the same time, the institutional development of the money market significantly accelerated the capital market, and rapid development was seen in the financial market. In this case, the level of structure imbalance in the financial system was alleviated, and the adaptability of financial development to the economic development, to some extent, was also improved.

Lagged reforms in the financial market

Remarkable achievements have been made in China's financial reform and financial development. The process of financial marketization is significantly quickened, especially in the past 10 years. But the level of marketization in the financial sector is still low, when compared with that of other economic sectors. Since the 1990s, China has taken a series of measures to promote the marketization of interest rates. However, there has not been a market interest rate system of a high level of association and sharp response, which resulted in the failure of interest rates to fully reflect the supply-demand relations of market funds. At the same time, the marketization of financial property rights lagged behind, so the financial credit is still in the hands of the government. The financial resources are still mainly controlled by the state-owned financial institutions, and the private financial strength remains very weak. In addition, the development of capital markets is under the excessive impact of macroeconomic policies and administrative power, resulting in dislocation of functions of the capital markets. Based on the experience of developed countries, the primary function of the capital market is not fund-raising, but spreading risks and optimizing the resource allocation. But the financing function of China's stock market is over-emphasized, causing the inefficient operation of the market. It can be seen from this that a direct consequence of the low level of financial markets is that the various elements of the financial system cannot be allocated in accordance with the market principles, which may exacerbate the imbalance of the financial structure, and ultimately lead to the inadaptability of the financial structure to the economic structure.

Imperfect financial and legal systems

The quality of financial operation depends on the normative behaviors of all relevant subjects. While the financial and legal systems are institutional arrangements to standardize and adjust the legal relationship involved with the financial institutions and their financial businesses, they are also institutional arrangements to standardize and constrain the administrative decisions of the financial supervision managers. The financial and legal systems are tools which adjust the various trading relations between the supervisors, financial institutions, and parties of financial products. In addition to the function of regulating the legal relations, the financial and legal systems are responsible for the punishment, encouragement or prohibition, guidance, and other functions, which, in an economic sense, is aiming at reducing transaction costs so that the parties can accurately measure the expected profit or losses.

After the reform and opening-up, China's legal system saw significant progress, particularly in the financial and legal systems. Nevertheless, it should be noted that, with the deepening of China's financial institutional reform, the openness of the financial sector, and the accelerating pace of financial innovations, a large gap still remains between the current financial and legal systems and the actual needs of financial development. Due to lack of coordination, credit risks, operational risks, and cross-market, cross-industry financial risks hidden in the financial system have always been rather prominent, which threaten to worsen the imbalance of the financial structure. For example, the existing legal system for the cross-market, cross-industry financial risks lacks not only the relevant legal requirements for the financial holding company, but also the strict legal definition for the new business of financial institutions, so that the cross-market, cross-industry financial risks have become new hidden dangers set in China's seemingly stable financial system. On the one hand, in the existing legal framework, *Law of the People's Republic of China on the People's Bank of China*, *Law of the People's Republic of China on Banking Regulation and Supervision*, *Law of the People's Republic of China on Commercial Banks* and other laws are all relevant to the financial holding company, but none of them can completely resolve the regulatory problems. On the other hand, the banks, securities, and insurance regulatory authorities conduct supervisions of the most active cross-market financial products (namely, the commissioned financing products) in accordance with their respective criteria, so a unified regulatory legal system is lacking.

Chapter 8

Evolution and Imbalance of China's Regional Economic Structure

STRUCTURAL ECONOMICS IN CHINA

Regional economic disparities and urban-rural development gap have long been curbing China from greater prosperity. This chapter, based on those two urgent problems, sheds lights on China's regional economic structure from the sectional level and the urban-rural level, focusing on the main features, levels of imbalance and the reasons for the evolution of the regional economic structure.

Evolution and Imbalance of the Inter-regional Economic Structure

The analysis of the sectional economic structure can be made from two levels: the inter-province and the areas. On the one hand, China's basic administrative divisions are provinces, autonomous regions, and municipalities. This division tactics has already been widely used in the analysis of the regional economy. On the other hand, although China's regional divisions adopt "trichotomy," "quartering," "sixing," "octave," et cetera, the more acknowledged method is "quartering," which divides China into four geographic zones: eastern, central, western and northeastern.[1] This chapter analyzes China's regional economic structure from the levels of inter-province and the areas, focusing on the main features, levels of imbalance, and the reasons for the evolution of the regional economic structure.

Main features of the inter-regional economic structure

Since the 1990s, great changes have taken place in the inter-regional economic structure. The main features are as follows.

A coordinative development of the regional economies

Developing scientific and rational development strategies and policies for regional economies is vital in promoting sustainable regional and national economic development. Since the reform and opening-up, China has drawn up and implemented the strategy of gradient regional development. China set up special economic zones, opened coastal cities, developed the Yangtze River Delta, Pearl River Delta and Bohai Economic Rim, later developed the west, and revitalized the northeast and central China. The potential of the regional economy has continued to inspire, and the coordinative development of the regional economy has achieved some success.

Relying on the policy and regional advantages, the eastern region has achieved sustainable and rapid economic development by developing an export-oriented economy. The Yangtze River Delta, Pearl River Delta and the Bohai region have become important areas of promoting the economic development, demonstrated by its leading position and radiating effects. In 2007, the GDP of the eastern part accounted for 55.2% of the total GDP—significantly more than the 11.8% in 1978. The total industry output accounted for 65.9% of the total national amount, increasing from 17.2% in 1978. Driven by the strategies of western development, and the revitalization of northeastern and central China, the economies in central and western China have experienced an unprecedented strong momentum of development; in recent years especially, the growth of the main economic indicators have increased more rapidly than in the eastern region. The gap between the growth of the GDP in central and east decreased from 2% in 1999 to 1% in 2007; the gap between the growth of the GDP in eastern and northeastern regions narrowed from 1.9% to 0.2%, and the gap between the growth of the GDP in west and east had changed from 2.6% slower to 0.2 % faster.[2]

Significant differences of inter-regional industrial structures

In the evolution of economic structure, there has been an advanced changing trend in the sectional industrial structures: the ratio of the primary industries continued to decline, and the ratios of the secondary and the tertiary industries increased gradually. However, there exist some significant differences in the changing speed and magnitude of the ratio of non-agricultural output, especially in some central and western provinces, where the shares of non-agricultural output have increased rapidly. For example, proportions of the non-agriculture industry in Tibet, Jiangxi and Guizhou were 84%, 83.6% and 83.7%, respectively, up by 34.8%, 23% and 22.8% in 1991, as shown in Fig. 8.1.[3]

Despite the significant upgrading of the industrial structure in the four main areas, the speed of industrial upgrading in eastern areas was faster than in western and northeast areas. Specifically, between 1991 and 2007, the proportion of the growth in the primary industries in GDP dropped quickly from 21.1% to 7.1%; while the proportion of the secondary industries increased from 45.6% to 51.8%. The ratio of the tertiary increased from 33.3% to 41.1% due to the rapid development of new service industries supported by finance, insurance, information consultation, and the real estate sectors. Even though the starting level of the secondary industries was low, it maintained a rapid-growing momentum. The proportions of the secondary industries in central and western areas in 2007 stood at 49.7% and 45.9%, respectively, increased by 10.9% and 11% in 1991; the proportion of the tertiary industries of the GDP in

STRUCTURAL ECONOMICS IN CHINA

central and western areas also rose, yet in a fluctuating manner. In 2007, the proportion of the tertiary industries output reached 35.2% and 37.6%, increasing by 4.9% and 4.7% compared with 1991. Driven by the strategy of revitalizing the old northeastern industrial bases, the proportion of the output of the secondary industries began to rise again from its lowest point of 47.2% in 2002 to 51.4% in 2007, and the output of the proportion of the tertiary industries rose from 33.4% in 1991 to 36.2% in 2007 (see Table 8.1).

Fig. 8.1. Changes of proportions of the non-agricultural industry in different regions, 1991-2007

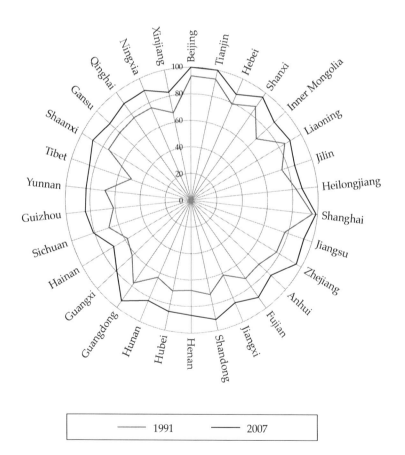

Evolution and Imbalance of China's Regional Economic Structure

Table 8.1. Changes of the proportions of the inter-regional industrial structures, 1991–2007 (%)

Year	East China			Northeast China			Central China			West China		
	Primary Industries	Secondary Industries	Tertiary Industries	Primary Industries	Secondary Industries	Tertiary Industries	Primary Industries	Secondary Industries	Tertiary Industries	Primary Industries	Secondary Industries	Tertiary Industries
1991	21.1	45.6	33.3	18.1	48.5	33.4	30.9	38.8	30.3	32.2	34.9	32.9
1992	18.3	48.0	33.8	16.6	49.8	33.6	28.2	40.8	31.0	29.6	36.4	34.0
1993	15.8	50.3	33.8	15.7	51.9	32.4	26.2	42.5	31.3	26.9	40.0	33.1
1994	15.8	50.2	34.0	17.7	50.1	32.3	27.2	41.4	31.4	27.3	40.1	32.7
1995	15.8	49.2	35.0	18.0	49.2	32.8	28.3	39.9	31.8	27.0	39.5	33.5
1996	15.1	48.7	36.2	18.8	48.7	32.5	27.9	39.7	32.4	26.9	39.1	34.0
1997	13.9	48.6	37.5	16.9	48.5	34.6	26.6	39.9	33.5	26.3	39.1	35.0
1998	13.1	48.1	38.8	16.9	47.7	35.5	25.0	40.1	34.9	24.9	38.7	36.4
1999	12.2	47.7	40.1	15.2	48.4	36.5	22.8	40.1	37.1	23.2	38.4	38.4
2000	11.0	47.8	41.1	13.2	49.6	37.3	21.2	40.4	38.3	21.6	38.6	39.8
2001	10.4	47.2	42.4	13.2	48.1	38.8	20.2	41.0	38.7	20.3	38.4	41.3
2002	9.6	47.2	43.2	13.2	47.2	39.6	19.2	41.5	39.3	19.4	38.5	42.1
2003	8.7	49.3	42.0	12.6	47.8	39.5	17.0	43.5	39.5	18.7	39.8	41.5
2004	8.5	50.8	40.8	13.5	47.3	39.2	18.1	44.4	37.6	18.7	41.1	40.2
2005	7.9	51.6	40.5	12.8	49.6	37.6	16.7	46.8	36.6	17.7	42.8	39.5
2006	7.3	52.2	40.5	12.2	50.7	37.1	15.4	48.8	35.8	16.3	45.1	38.6
2007	7.1	51.8	41.1	12.4	51.4	36.2	15.1	49.7	35.2	16.5	45.9	37.6

Sources: Sorted from *China Statistical Yearbook* (various years).

STRUCTURAL ECONOMICS IN CHINA

Alleviation of the imbalance of the inter-regional public service expenditures

China's current financial transfer payments, based on the tax distribution system reform of 1994, mainly include: tax rebates, general transfer payments, and special transfer payments.[4] The general government transfer payments are an important means to achieve the inter-governmental financial balance and the equalization of basic public services. Since 1995, China adopted the general transfer payment system, putting more efforts on the development of the central and western areas, particularly the reform of income tax revenue sharing in 2002. The central government committed all the income of the tax reform into the general transfer payments, enabling transfer payments continue to grow rapidly. In 2006, the general transfer payments reached RMB152.7 billion, or 72 times the payments in 1995. The rapid growth of the general transfer payments effectively eased the financial situation in the areas with financial difficulties, and promoted the inter-regional equalization of basic public services. This offered financial support to the realization of the inter-regional coordinative development.

Fig. 8.2. The coefficient of variation of the per capita expenditure in education, science, culture and health of different provinces, 1991–2007

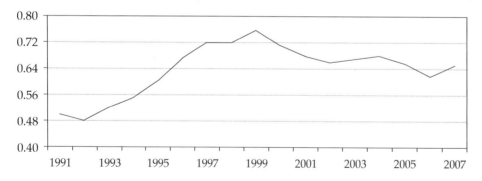

Since the 1990s, the imbalance of inter-regional public spending has increased; however, with the government's dedication on the transfer payments in the central and western areas and the increase of the fiscal solvency in the central and western areas, the situation has been eased to a certain degree in recent years. Through the analysis of the coefficient of variation[5] of the per capita expenditure in education, science, culture, and health in different provinces, there has been an "inverted U-shape" trend of the regional differences of basic public service in different provinces since 1991. As shown in

Fig. 8.2, the coefficient of variation of the per capita expenditure in education, science, culture, and health in different provinces in 1991 was 0.5, which rose significantly after a slight decline in 1992, peaked at 0.76 in 1999, then decreased to 0.65 in 2007. In general, differences in the per capita expenditure in education, science, culture, and health of different provinces are still greater than the level in the early 1990s. There is enough room for decrease.

Table 8.2. Distribution and concentration of the production capacity of the basic industries, 1991–2007

Industry	1991		2007	
	Concentrating Degree	Top Five Provinces	Concentrating Degree	Top Five Provinces
Crude Coal	0.55	Shanxi, Henan, Heilongjiang, Sichuan, Shandong	0.60	Shanxi, Inner Mongolia, Shaanxi, Henan, Shandong
Crude Oil	0.85	Heilongjiang, Shandong, Liaoning, Henan, Xinjiang	0.74	Heilongjiang, Shandong, Xinjiang, Shaanxi, Tianjin
Natural Gas	0.90	Sichuan, Heilongjiang, Liaoning, Shandong, Henan	0.86	Xinjiang, Sichuan, Shaanxi, Guangdong, Qinghai
Electricity	0.32	Hebei, Liaoning, Jiangsu, Shandong, Guangdong	0.36	Guangdong, Shandong, Jiangsu, Inner Mongolia, Henan
Cement	0.41	Guangdong, Shandong, Jiangsu, Sichuan, Zhejiang	0.42	Shandong, Jiangsu, Zhejiang, Guangdong, Hebei
Steel	0.54	Liaoning, Shanghai, Hubei, Beijing, Sichuan	0.53	Hebei, Jiangsu, Shandong, Liaoning, Tianjin

Sources: sorted from *China Statistical Yearbook* (1992) and (2007).

STRUCTURAL ECONOMICS IN CHINA

Dispersed distribution of the production capacity of basic industries

The spatial layout and the changes of the production capacity of basic industries embody the regional economic structure and its evolutionary trend. Since the 1990s, the regional distribution of the production capacity of coal, oil, gas, electricity, cement, steel, and other basic industries has undergone important changes. In 1991, these six industries concentrated in 14 provinces (autonomous regions and municipalities). Of these, Shandong was the important national production base of crude oil, cement, electricity, natural gas, and coal; Liaoning and Sichuan were the important production places for the four major industries as well as natural gas and the steel industry; Henan and Heilongjiang were the important sources for crude coal and oil as well as natural gas. In 2007, the spatial distribution of the six industries was dispersedly located in 16 provinces (autonomous regions and municipalities). Although Shandong was still the main place of cement, crude oil, electricity, and coal production, its output of natural gas was listed below the top five. At the same time, provinces including Jiangsu, Shaanxi, Guangdong, Xinjiang and Zhejiang emerged as pillars with multiple industries, and Qinghai became a "New World" of profound natural gas (see Table 8.2).

Compared to 1991, within the six basic industries, the concentration degree increased slightly in crude coal and electricity, remained stable in cement and steel; but the crude oil and natural gas industries was biased toward dispersion in 2007. The decrease of the traditional energy production bases and the fast-track of the emerging energy bases are the important factors triggering the decline of the concentration degree in the above industries.

Enlarging gap of the inter-regional energy storage distribution

As an important financial resource, the distribution of household deposits differs greatly in geographical terms, demonstrated in a gradient manner in Table 8.3. The size of deposit in the eastern region is the largest, followed by the mid-western area, with the smallest share found in the northeastern region (see Table 8.3).

In the eastern region from 1991 to 2007, the deposits increased from RMB445.8 billion to RMB9.5 trillion, while the proportion rose from 48.9% to 54.1%. The household deposits decreased from 19.4% to 18.2% in central region, and from 18.3% to 18.1% in the west region. The proportion of the household deposits decreased from 13.4% in 1991 to 9.1% in 2007.

Table 8.3. The inter-regional distribution of the household deposits, 1991–2007

Year	Absolute Amount (RMB100 million)				Relative Amount (%)			
	East	Northeast	Midwest	West	East	Northeast	Midwest	West
1991	4,457.7	1,218.2	1,764.7	1,666.4	48.9	13.4	19.4	18.3
1995	15,425.0	3,566.4	5,492.6	5,176.4	52.0	12.0	18.5	17.5
2000	33,933.1	7,588.6	11,403.1	11,385.1	52.7	11.8	17.7	17.7
2001	39,074.7	8,386.1	13,215.4	13,086.3	53.0	11.4	17.9	17.7
2002	46,595.5	9,459.1	15,588.4	15,265.0	53.6	10.9	17.9	17.6
2003	56,071.0	10,938.6	18,524.9	18,076.1	54.1	10.6	17.9	17.4
2004	64,642.8	12,039.6	21,613.6	20,900.0	54.1	10.1	18.1	17.5
2005	76,703.2	13,826.9	25,427.7	24,683.2	54.4	9.8	18.0	17.5
2006	88,126.2	15,182.5	29,258.9	28,462.0	54.5	9.4	18.1	17.6
2007	95,246.7	16,080.0	32,145.6	31,836.3	54.1	9.1	18.2	18.1

Sources: Data from 1991 to 2006 were sorted from *China Financial Yearbook (1992–2007)* and data from 2007 were from *China Regional Financial Operation Report*.

Note: Some deposits were not divided according to the regions, so the relative amounts cannot be added to 100%.

Judgment of imbalance of the inter-regional economic structure

The imbalance of China's inter-regional economic structure can be analyzed from the changing trend of the inter-regional economic difference and the international comparison.

Criteria

There are two criteria judging the imbalance of the inter-regional economic structure: the first is the changing trends of the inter-regional economic development disparities. The second is the international comparison of the inter-regional economic disparities. Many countries have experienced some fluctuating economic disparities, and there is a general range of such disparities. Therefore, the degree of the imbalance of the inter-regional economic structure can be illustrated through the comparison of the range in China and that in other countries.

STRUCTURAL ECONOMICS IN CHINA

Judgment based on the trend of the economic disparities

The trend of the inter-provincial economic development disparities

The inter-provincial economic development disparity can be measured by the ratio of GDP per capita between the richest and poorest provinces. We use the extreme value ratios of GDP per capita of three provinces (autonomous regions or municipalities) which obtain the highest or lowest GDP per capita, and another three which obtain the lowest GDP per capita, to reflect the changes in China's inter-regional economic development disparities. Since the 1990s, the three municipalities of Shanghai, Beijing and Tianjin have remained the regions where the GDP per capita is the highest in China, while the three regions where the GDP per capita was the lowest were subject to changes. In 1991, the GDP per capita was RMB5,490 in the three municipalities, but only RMB1,103 in Guangxi, Anhui and Guizhou provinces, where the GDP per capita was the lowest. In 2007, the GDP per capita mounted to RMB56,504 in the three municipalities (Shanghai, Beijing and Tianjin) and RMB9,263 in Yunnan, Gansu and Guizhou provinces, where the GDP per capita was the lowest. In this case, the extreme value ratio of GDP per capita between the three provinces (autonomous regions or municipalities) where the GDP per capita was the highest, and the three provinces where the GDP per capita was the lowest, was 4.98 times in 1991. In the next several years, the extreme value ratio of the GDP per capita between regions increased rapidly to a record high of 7.2 times in 1998; between 1999 and 2004, the extreme value ratio of GDP per capita between regions fluctuated at a high level. Since 2005, the extreme value ratio of GDP per capita between regions has shown a significant declining trend and dropped to 6.1 times in 2007 (see Fig. 8.3).

Fig. 8.3. The ratio of the extreme value ratio GDP per capita between top three provinces (municipalities) and bottom three provinces (municipalities)

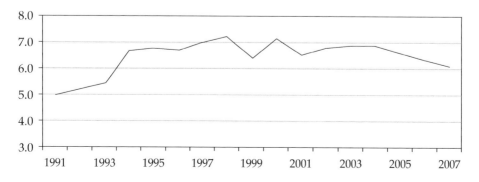

Evolution and Imbalance of China's Regional Economic Structure

Based on the absolute disparity of GDP per capita, in 2007, the GDP per capita of Shanghai, Beijing, and Tianjin was respectively USD8,981, USD7,841 and USD6,201,[6] attaining the level of middle-income countries[7] and moving closer to that of high-income countries. The GDP per capita was respectively USD998, USD1,414 and USD1,438 in Guizhou, Gansu and Yunnan, the lowest in the country; these three provinces had just entered the lower-middle income economies level. Thus, the inter-provincial economic disparities, including both relative disparity and absolute disparity, appear to cause an immediate concern.

The trend of the economic development disparities of the top four economic regions

In geographical terms, the regional economic development is evidently characterized by the distribution of "a downshift from east to west." In 1991, the GDP per capita of the eastern regions was close to that of the north-eastern regions, respectively, RMB2,521 and RMB2,470; the GDP per capita of the central regions is close to that of the western regions, respectively, RMB1,328 and RMB1,316. Since the 1990s, as a result of the uneven economic development, the inter-regional disparity of GDP per capita has been significantly expanding. In 2007, the GDP per capita of the eastern regions reached RMB27,190—1.5 times, 2.2 times and 2.4 times that of the northeast, central and western regions, respectively (see Fig. 8.4). In general, China's inter-regional economic disparity shows a trend of gradual expansion.

Fig. 8.4.   Changes in inter-regional GDP per capita, 1991–2007

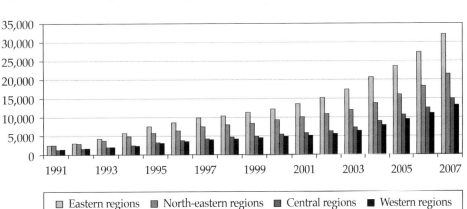

STRUCTURAL ECONOMICS IN CHINA

Judgment based on the international comparison

According to international experience, the warning level of the interregional GDP per capita disparity is generally 5 to 6 times.[8] If the extreme value ratio of GDP per capita exceeds the warning level, a country's economic development may be slow and the social conflicts will be more intensive, which will affect the political stability and may even induce the inter-regional and inter-ethnic conflicts. As China and India have similar conditions, a comparison is made on the interregional economic development disparity between the two countries.

Since the 1990s, unbalanced economic development and disparity increased between regions in India, as a result of the export-oriented development strategies, like economic liberalization and globalization. Between 1980 and 2000, the absolute disparity of GDP per capita continued to expand in 16 regions of India, while the relative disparity narrowed in the 1980s and expanded in the 1990s. Between 1990 and 2000, the disparity of GDP per capita was between 3.8 to 5.6 times in 16 states; the largest disparity of GDP per capita was not more than 6 times between wealthy regions and poor regions.[9] The extreme value ratio of China's inter-regional GDP per capita since 1994 has remained above 6 times, and even more than 7 times in some years—higher than the inter-regional disparities in India. As we all know, interregional disparities are very serious in India, so we can see that a serious imbalance remains in China's economic structure between regions.

In summary, since the 1990s, the imbalance of China's interregional economic structure has increased significantly. Although the level of imbalance has been reduced in recent years, a serious imbalance still remains in the overall economic structure, which brings great negative impacts on the coordinated development of the economy and society.

Cause analysis of imbalance of the inter-regional economic structure

A serious imbalance remains in the evolution of inter-regional economic structure. There are many specific causes, including the following four aspects.

Disparities in the initial resource endowment

The resource endowment is the basis and the initial conditions of the regional economic development, including natural resources and geographical environment. Both the central and western regions are at an absolute advantage of natural resources, but the resource utilization remains at the primary level due to the lack of funds and technological support. In addition, the geographical environment, in particular, the geographic location, is also an important contribution to the interregional economic disparities. Since the 1990s, China has developed an export-oriented economy on a large scale. By taking full advantage of their superior geographical location, the southeastern coastal provinces received the transfer of both technological and economic resources from developed countries, and promoted economic development with the investment of the compatriots returning home from Hong Kong, Macau, Taiwan and foreign countries. It can be seen from this, that with the differences in such initial resource endowments as natural resources, geographical environments are an important reason for the formation of interregional economic disparities.

Disparities in the pattern of economic growth

Physical capital and human capital are the basic elements necessary to promote modern economic growth, which is especially prominent in the initial stage of industrialization. With the development of industrialization, technological progress is increasingly a key driver of modern economic growth. As the technological progress is quite different in different regions, the efficiency of resource allocation is directly affected. For example, the efficiency of resource allocation that remains low in underdeveloped regions mainly relies on the land, raw materials, initial labor and other traditional elements to promote the economic growth, while the technological progress and promotion of productivity are valued in the developed regions, so that the interregional economic disparity is further widened. With the examination of the major factors affecting China's interregional disparities since the 1990s, the contribution rate of the total inputs differences to the interregional disparities was 37%, of which the physical capital was approximately 12%, the human capital about 25%, and the average contribution rate of the total factor productivity affecting the interregional disparities reached 63%.[10]

Disparities between the market development levels

The interregional economic structural imbalance is primarily due to different regional economic maturity. In recent years, despite the rising market index in various regions, the regional processes of marketization are evidently different, especially between the eastern and western regions. In 2005, the average score of marketization of the eastern regions was 8.2 points—a full 1.7 points higher than the national average, which was 6.5 points. The other regions are all below the national average: 6.3 points in the northeast regions, 6 points in the central regions, and only 4.9 points in the western regions.[11] In fact, as a result of the lagging market economic reform, the economic development in the central, western, north-eastern regions were subjected to institutional constraints. On the one hand, the restructuring of ownership in these regions remained slow and the non-public economy accounted for a small proportion, so that the market failed to fully play its role in the process of resource allocation. On the other hand, the changes in governmental functions and management were relatively lagging behind in the central and western regions, which exacerbate the economic structural imbalance between regions. The local governments have taken many initiatives in the aspects of function changes and improvement of administrative efficiency in recent years however, problems such as poor transparency of implementation of policies, poor continuity, conservative ideas, and irregular market environment still remain in many regions, especially in the central and western provinces.

Enforcement of unbalanced inter-regional development strategies

Since the reform and opening-up, in order to encourage some people and regions to become wealthy first, China employed an interregional development strategy that progressively moves from the coastal regions to the inland regions. A series of special preferential policies on finance, taxation, investment, credit, and others were also introduced in the eastern coastal regions, which took the lead in economic reform and opening-up. Relative to the geographical factors, the policy factors imposed powerful and direct impacts on the regional economic growth and structural upgrading. With the national preferential policies and investment, significant improvements were witnessed in the ports, airports, roads and other infrastructure constructions in the eastern regions, and a number of world-class special economic zones like Shenzhen Special Economic Zone, Shanghai Pudong New District, Tianjin Binhai New District suddenly appeared on the horizon. The result was that the eastern regions obtained a long-term sustainable economic momentum and the level of industrial structure was much higher than that in the central and western regions.

Evolution and Imbalance of Urban and Rural Economic Structures

The acute structural imbalance between urban and rural economies reflects the dual structure in China's modernization process. This section will explore the main features of interregional economic structural evolution and the extent of

Evolution and Imbalance of China's Regional Economic Structure

imbalance and causes, from both the urban and rural levels.

Main features of the evolution of the urban and rural economic structures

Since the reform and opening-up, the urban and rural economic structures have changed dramatically. The following characteristics are shown in financial support for agriculture, urban and rural residents' consumption structure, the investment structure of urban and rural regions, and other aspects.

Growing financial support in the agricultural sector

Since the 1990s, the state's financial investment and protection in the field of agriculture has steadily increased. The ratio of agricultural expenditure against the added value of the first industry remains a generally upward trend, which provides important financial support to the rural economic restructuring, improvement of agricultural productivity, and the increase of rural income.

The agricultural expenditure accounted for only 6.1% of the agricultural GDP in 1990, and the proportion remained between 4.7% and 6.5% from 1991 to 1997 (see Fig. 8.5). With the proposal of the establishment of the framework of public finance compatible with the market economic development in 1998, China continually adjusted and optimized the output of fiscal expenditures, so that the

Fig. 8.5. 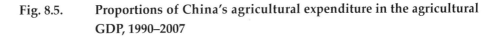Proportions of China's agricultural expenditure in the agricultural GDP, 1990–2007

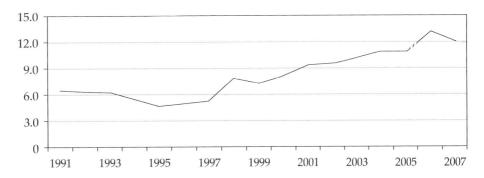

agricultural expenditure accounted for a rising proportion of agricultural GDP. That proportion reached a record high of 13.2% in 2006.

Synchronous upgrading of the consumption structure of urban and rural residents

With the rapid economic development, the consumption structure continued escalating and the living standards continued rising. For both urban and rural residents, the Engel coefficient[12] demonstrated a steady downward trend, dropping from 53.8% in 1991 to 36.3% in 2007, while the Engel coefficient of rural residents dropped from 57.6% in 1991 to 43.1% in 2007 (see Fig. 8.6). In recent years, the Engel coefficient of rural residents dropped significantly more than that of urban residents. For example, compared to 2004, the Engel coefficient of rural households fell by 4.1% in 2007—2.7% higher than that in urban regions.

In addition, the per capita consumption expenditure of urban and rural residents showed a growth in 2006, by 71% and 61.4% respectively, than that

Fig. 8.6. Changes in the Engel coefficient between urban and rural residents, 1991–2007

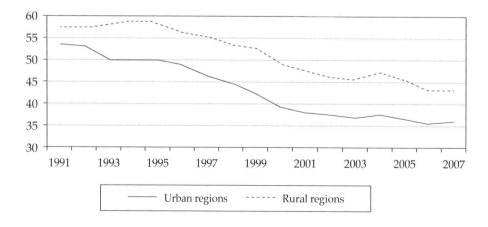

in 1991. This reflected a growing trend of social services of the urban and rural households, a rising demand for consumer services, and a bypass flow of consumption expenditures to consumer services.

Growing disparities between urban and rural investment

Urban and rural structure of investment is the ratio between the amount of the total national investment in urban and rural regions. In the 1980s, China strengthened the construction of agricultural infrastructure, so that the proportion of the rural investment in fixed assets slightly increased from 26%

Table 8.4. Changes in the ratio of investment between China's urban and rural regions, 1981–2007

Year	Investment in Fixed Assets (RMB100 million)	Proportion of Urban Areas (%)	Proportion of Rural Areas (%)
1981	961.0	74.00	26.00
1985	2,543.2	73.35	26.65
1990	4,517.0	72.49	27.51
1995	20,019.3	78.14	21.86
2000	32,917.7	79.66	20.34
2001	37,213.5	80.62	19.38
2002	43,499.9	81.58	18.42
2003	55,566.6	82.44	17.56
2004	70,477.4	83.75	16.25
2005	88,773.6	84.59	15.41
2006	109,998.2	84.88	15.12
2007	137,239.0	85.55	14.45

Source: *China Statistical Yearbook (2008)*.

in 1981 to 27.5% in 1990. Since the 1990s, the urban development has remained rapid, but a serious shortage of investment was seen in fixed assets in rural regions. The proportion of rural investment in fixed assets decreased from 27.5% in 1990 to 14.5% in 2007 (see Table 8.4).

The disparity of the investment between rural and urban fixed assets has led to the growing disparity between urban and rural development and the growing conflicts of interests, which would not only affect the regional economic development, but would also threaten the sustainable, stable and coordinated macroeconomic development. In particular, the investment in public goods in rural regions was seriously insufficient, resulting in a huge disparity between the urban and rural public services.

Judgment of the degree of imbalance between urban and rural economic structures

The dual economic structure of urban and rural areas is the concentrated reflection of disequilibrium of social and economic development in developing countries, and is the outstanding problem to solve in the evolution of economic structure. The degree of imbalance between China's urban and rural economic structures is examined mainly from the following perspectives: the changing trend of differences between urban and rural economic development, economic impacts, and international comparisons.

Criteria

First, judge the degree of imbalance according to the changing trends in differences between urban and rural economic development. From the dynamic point of view, the changing trend of differences in urban and rural economic development in different periods should have a certain critical value. If the gap can fluctuate in a relatively small and reasonable range, the gap between urban and rural areas is normal; if the gap continues to expand and breaks through the threshold of a reasonable range, there is structural imbalance between the urban and rural economy.

Second, judge the degree of imbalance according to the impacts that differences between urban and rural development exert on the domestic economic development. In the early stages of industrialization, it is necessary to achieve rapid industrial development at the cost of slow development of the rural economy. However, the gap between urban and rural economic development may be both a catalyst to promote economic structure evolving toward rationalization and advancement, and a trigger to push a country's economy toward danger. As a part of the whole macroeconomic structure, differences in urban and rural economic development will have an impact on other economic variables and social objectives. An appropriate gap can effectively promote the transfer of surplus labor and the improvement of the entire social labor productivity. On the contrary, a large gap is bound to bring a series of negative problems and have a negative impact on economic and social development. Moreover, the more serious the imbalance in urban and rural economic structures, the greater harm it will do to economic operation and social development.

Finally, judge the degree of imbalance according to international comparisons of differences between urban and rural economic development. Historical experience shows that modernization of any country starts from the primitive accumulation of agriculture and achieves industrialization by the transfer of agricultural resources to urban areas and industrial sectors. Therefore, using international experience to examine gaps between the urban and rural economies of different countries at different stages of development, the degree of reasonability of change in the gap between China's urban and rural structures can be roughly determined, based on which whether the structural imbalance in China's urban and rural economic development can be judged.

Judgment based on the changing trend of the gap between urban and

Table 8.5. Comparison of the per capita net income of China's urban and rural residents

Year	Per Capita Disposable Income of Urban Residents (RMB)	Growth Rate Year-on-year (%)	Per Capita Net Income of Rural Residents (RMB)	Growth Rate Year-on-year (%)	Ratio of the Per Capita Income of Urban Residents to Rural Residents
1991	1,700.6	7.1	708.6	2.0	2.40
1995	4,283.0	4.9	1,577.7	5.3	2.71
1996	4,838.9	3.8	1,926.1	9.0	2.51
1997	5,160.3	3.4	2,090.1	4.6	2.47
1998	5,425.1	5.8	2,162.0	4.3	2.51
1999	5,854.0	9.3	2,210.3	3.8	2.65
2000	6,280.0	6.4	2,253.4	2.1	2.79
2001	6,859.6	8.5	2,366.4	4.2	2.90
2002	7,702.8	3.4	2,475.6	4.8	3.11
2003	8,472.2	9.0	2,622.2	4.3	3.23
2004	9,421.6	7.7	2,936.4	6.8	3.21
2005	10,493.0	9.6	3,254.9	6.2	3.22
2006	11,759.5	10.4	3,587.0	7.4	3.28
2007	13,785.8	12.2	4,140.4	9.5	3.33

Source: Compiled with reference to *China Statistical Yearbook (2008)*.

STRUCTURAL ECONOMICS IN CHINA

rural economic development

Since the 1990s, due to the changing patterns of residents' income distribution and their widening income sources, the changing trend of the income gap between urban and rural residents generally continued to expand, despite repeated setbacks.

From 1991 to 2007, the per capita disposable income of urban households increased from RMB1,700.6 to RMB13,785.8, and the per capita net income of rural households increased from RMB708.6 to RMB4140.4. The ratio of the per capita income of urban residents to rural residents was 2.4 in 1991, and the ratio rose to 2.86 in 1994. Later, under the influence of "downsize staff to improve efficiency" of state-owned enterprises, there were a large number of laid-off workers, leading to a relative reduction in income of urban residents. In addition, the government adopted a series of policies and measures to reform the social security system, which also contributed to the narrowing of the urban-rural income gap, and the ratio dropped to 2.47 in 1997. However, since the 21st century, the ratio of the per capita income of urban residents to rural residents has shown the trend of rapid expansion. It historically broke through 3 and reached 3.11 in 2002, and reached a peak of 3.33 in 2007 (see Table 8.5). It is thus clear that the urban-rural income gap has not been curbed effectively, but instead has been growing in recent years. It is noteworthy that because the government implemented farmer-beneficial policies of agricultural tax reduction, and exemption and direct subsidies for growing grain in 2004, coupled with the rising market prices of major agricultural products, the increase in the per capita net income of rural residents improves more than the past, but there is still a large gap compared with the annual growth of the per capita disposable income of urban residents.

According to the change in the intensity of dual economic structure,[13] the feature of urban-rural dual economic structure remained prominent in China. Table 8.6 shows that 1991–1996 was the period when a shortage economy transformed to a surplus economy, farmers worked in urban areas and began to make up for labor shortages in informal sectors of urban areas, and the substantial reduction in rural surplus labor forces promoted the weakening of the intensity of dual economic structure (which fell to 4.15 in 1996). However, from 1997 to 2003, the intensity of dual economic structure tended to expand and even reached 6.58 in 2003. Township enterprises had a weakened ability to absorb the rural surplus labor force, and the reform of state-owned enterprises brought a lot of urban laid-off workers; re-employment had a "crowd-out effect" on the transfer of the rural surplus labor force. Since 2003, under the

Table 8.6. Intensity of China's urban and rural dual economic structure, 1991–2007

Year	Agricultural Comparative Labor Productivity	Non-agricultural Comparative Labor Productivity	Intensity of Dual Economic Structure
1991	0.41	1.87	4.56
1992	0.37	1.88	5.08
1993	0.35	1.84	5.26
1994	0.36	1.75	4.86
1995	0.38	1.68	4.42
1996	0.39	1.62	4.15
1997	0.37	1.63	4.41
1998	0.35	1.64	4.69
1999	0.33	1.67	5.06
2000	0.30	1.70	5.67
2001	0.29	1.71	5.90
2002	0.27	1.73	6.41
2003	0.26	1.71	6.58
2004	0.29	1.63	5.62
2005	0.27	1.59	5.89
2006	0.27	1.55	5.74
2007	0.28	1.50	5.36

Source: *China Statistical Yearbook (2008)*.

concept of adhering to the scientific development, the country made balancing urban and rural development and eliminating the dual economy an important measure to establish both a socialist harmonious society and a moderately prosperous society, and implemented a series of policies and measures to lay a solid foundation for the adjustment of rural economic structure and economic development. Thus, the intensity of the dual economic structure of this stage tended to decrease, and fell to 5.36 in 2007.

Judgment based on differences in urban and rural public services

With economic and social development, urban residents enjoy more and more social and public goods, but public goods related to agriculture, rural areas and farmers increase slowly, which leads to increasing inequity of public goods and services among urban and rural residents. Owing to the extended shortage of investment funds, the supply of public goods in rural areas was in a serious shortage; it was difficult to adapt to the growing demand of farmers for public goods, typically exemplified by the extremely low standards of health care rural to which residents have access. According to data released by the World Health Organization, the fairness of China's distribution of health care ranks No.188—the last but three in the world. At present, Chinese urban residents accounting for 30% of the total population enjoy 80% of health resources, whereas rural residents accounting for 70% of the total population enjoy only 20% of health resources. In fact, although some economically developed rural areas initially established the rural minimum living security system, the social pension insurance system and the social health care system, a considerable number of farmers in rural areas have almost no institutionalized, stable social insurance.

Fig. 8.7. Changes in the Gini coefficient, 1991–2006

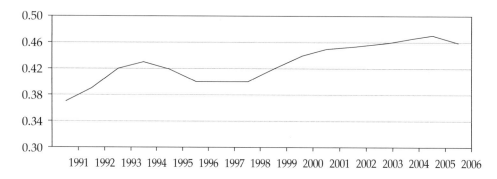

Table 8.7. Variations of the Gini coefficient among several Asian countries

Country (Region)	Period	Starting Year	Ending Year	Variation
India	1993–2004	32.89	36.22	3.33
Indonesia	1993–2002	34.37	34.30	−0.07
South Korea	1993–2004	28.68	31.55	2.87
Malaysia	1993–2004	41.22	40.33	−0.89
Mongolia	1995–2002	33.20	32.84	−0.36
Pakistan	1992–2004	30.31	31.18	0.87
The Philippines	1994–2003	42.89	43.97	1.08
Thailand	1992–2002	46.22	41.96	−4.26
Vietnam	1993–2004	34.91	37.08	2.17

Source: Asian Development Bank, *Key Indicators 2007. Inequality in Asia*.

Judgment based on international experience

According to changes in the Gini coefficient,[14] since 1991, China's Gini coefficient has shown a fluctuating upward trend. It was 0.37 in 1991 and gradually increased; it declined slightly from 1995 to 1998. In the 21st century, the Gini Coefficient increased year by year, rising from 0.44 in 2000 to its peak of 0.47 in 2005, and falling slightly to 0.46 in 2006 (see Fig. 8.7).[15]

Data released by the Asian Development Bank shows that China's Gini coefficient is the highest in major Asian countries—higher than India, the Philippines, and many other developing countries (see Table 8.7). Moreover, China's Gini coefficient is close to that of Latin American countries and has reached the warning state.

In summary, there is a serious structural imbalance in the urban and rural economic structure, whether in terms of the changing trend of the urban-rural income gap, in international comparisons of the Gini coefficient, or in economic impacts of the urban-rural gap.

Cause analysis of the imbalance between urban and rural economic structures

There are many causes for the worsening imbalance of urban and rural economic structure, including the urban-rural dual management system, the weak economic foundation of agriculture, the imperfect traditional rural land system and the delayed supply of rural public goods.

The urban-rural dual management system

The urban-rural dual management system, which originated in the 1950s and continues to this day, is an important trigger to the imbalance of China's urban and rural economic structure. This institutional arrangement artificially divides urban and rural residents into social groups with unequal social statuses, concluding that population movements between urban and rural areas are obstructed and the agriculture has to endure the heavy pressure of employment with little output. Therefore, productivity remains low for a long time. In addition, since registered permanent residence is the fundamental criterion for determining residential identity, status and welfare of urban and rural residents, residents with a registered urban permanent residence enjoy superior treatments to residents with registered rural permanent residence in employment, income, pension, social welfare, children's schooling, and other aspects.

The weak economic foundation of agriculture

Because agriculture is significantly constrained by the natural environment, the uncertainty of the external natural environment directly determines the efficiency of agricultural production and management. In a market economy, due to the low income elasticity of agricultural products, farmers often face unavoidable market risks in production and management. Meanwhile, the agricultural production in China has long been following the traditional production mode. Central and western rural areas in particular are lacking modern means of agricultural production, and their productive technology is relatively backward; other agricultural industries, such as the agricultural processing industry and agricultural insurance, lack development. Therefore, under the poorly-controlled conditions that science and technology and productivity exert over external natural forces, coupled with the underdeveloped insurance market, the high risk of agriculture has been fully borne by the farmers themselves. The weak nature of agriculture and the high risk of the market increase the difference between agricultural production and industrial production, thus leading to the imbalance between urban and rural economic structures.

The underdeveloped rural land system

With the accelerated pace of the new rural development and the coordinated urban-rural development, the rural economic construction is also developing innovation. However, the traditional rural land system is not perfect, which, to a certain extent, affects the development of the rural economy. First, farmers cannot protect their own land rights. Because the complementary mechanism of the rural land is not perfect, farmers' rights to use, derive benefits from and dispose of land are often restricted or violated. There are, in some places, serious phenomena such as forcibly seizing and occupying land contracted by farmers at low prices, retaining and withholding farmers' settlement allowance, forcing farmers to transfer their contracted land, and illegally changing the agricultural purpose of land. Second, land is still the most important or even the only wealth to farmers in the relatively backward rural areas. However, the rural land contracting ownership has many restrictions on farmers' use of land rights, which leads to farmers' lack of necessary collaterals for loans.

The deviation of economic development policies in the practical implementation

Since the 1990s, China has been pursuing a policy orientation of "giving priority to efficiency with due consideration to fairness"; however, in the specific formulation and implementation of policies, the tendency of giving priority to efficiency has often been unconsciously amplified. This, accordingly, triggered the formation and strengthening of uncoordinated issues of urban and rural development in the process of marketization. Firstly, local governments attached importance to the growth of GDP and fiscal revenue, and favored the development of industrialization and urbanization which could have boosted agricultural development. Secondly, the social development and supply of public goods in rural areas were strong in externalities and were easy to cause market failure. The optimal allocation of resources could not be achieved by relying on the market mechanism and the absence of governments for many years, and lead to the lagging of social development and supply of public goods in rural areas, and aggravated the vicious cycle of rural economic and social development. Therefore, the imbalance between urban and rural economic structures became more serious.

Chapter 9

Evolution and Imbalance of China's Balance of Payments Structure

STRUCTURAL ECONOMICS IN CHINA

China's balance of payments has gone through a bumpy journey, in terms of both overall situation and internally proportional relations. This chapter makes judgments of the evolutionary imbalance of the structure of the balance of payments from the two aspects: the coordination of internal structure of the balance of payments, and the adaption of the structure of the balance of payments and economic development, clarifying the major causes of the structural imbalance of payments.

Main Features of China's Balance of Payments Structure

Through 30 years of economic development, China's balance of payments has experienced an evolution from the basic balance to the "double surplus." This section surveys the main features of the evolution of the balance book in terms of the formation of the "double surplus," the internal structure of the current account, the internal structures of the capital and financial account, and the structure of the growth of the sources of the foreign exchange reverses.

The swelling of the "double surplus"

From the publication of the balance of payments in 1982, the overall pattern of the balance of payments has transformed from a basic balance to the "double surplus" and rapid expansion. As shown in Table 9.1, this process can be divided into four stages.

The first stage was from 1982 to 1984 when the current account of the balance of payments surplus and the capital and financial account deficit occurred. At this stage, there was a surplus of the current account which accumulated to USD11.94 billion. At the same time, there was a small deficit of the capital and financial account which accumulated to USD890 million. Because the current account played a leading role in the balance of payments at this stage, the overall performance of the balance of payments was a surplus which led to a continuous increase in foreign exchange reserves.

The second stage was from 1985 to 1993 when the current account deficit and the capital and financial account surplus occurred. The fluctuation of the current account was relatively large. In 1987, 1990, 1991 and 1992, there was a surplus, but a deficit for the rest of the years. It showed a deficit during the nine years and the accumulated amount reached to USD6.5 billion. There was an overall surplus of the capital and financial account, and with the exception of a small deficit in 1992, the accumulated amount for these nine years hit USD66.3 billion. Dominated by the capital and financial account in the balance

Evolution and Imbalance of China's Balance of Payments Structure

of payments at this stage, the overall performance of the balance book was marked a surplus due to the great growth of the current account. This led to a rapid increase in foreign exchange reserves. During these nine years, the foreign exchange reverses increased by USD28.8 billion. It is worth mentioning that there was a "double surplus" in both the current account and the capital and financial account in 1990 and 1991.

The third stage was from 1994 to 2001 when the pattern of the "double surplus" initially formed. China implemented the system reform of foreign

Table 9.1. An review of China's balance of payments accounts 1982–2007 (USD100 million)

Year	Current Account	Capital and Financial Account	Reverse Assets	Net Error and Omissions
1982	56.7	3.4	−62.9	2.8
1983	42.4	−2.3	−41.3	1.2
1984	20.3	−10.0	−1.0	−9.3
1985	−114.2	89.7	23.5	0.9
1986	−70.3	59.4	19.5	−8.6
1987	3.0	60.0	−49.3	−13.7
1988	−38.0	71.3	−23.2	−10.1
1989	−43.2	37.2	5.0	0.9
1990	120.0	32.6	−121.2	−31.3
1991	132.7	80.3	−145.5	−67.5
1992	64.0	−2.5	21.0	−82.5
1993	−119.0	234.7	−17.7	−98.0
1994	76.6	326.4	−305.3	−97.7
1995	16.2	386.8	−224.8	−178.1
1996	72.4	399.7	−316.4	−155.7
1997	369.6	210.2	−357.2	−222.5
1998	314.7	−63.2	−64.3	−187.2
1999	211.1	51.8	−85.1	−177.9
2000	205.2	19.2	−105.5	−118.9
2001	174.1	347.8	−473.3	−48.6
2002	354.2	322.9	−755.1	77.9
2003	458.8	527.3	−1,170.2	184.2
2004	686.6	1,106.6	−2,063.6	270.5
2005	1,608.2	629.6	−2,070.2	−167.7
2006	2,498.7	100.4	−2,470.3	−128.8
2007	3,718.3	735.1	−4,617.4	164.0

Sources: Various years' international balance of payments tables released by SAFE.
Note: " " in the current account and the capital and financial account means deficit and "−" in reverse assets means increase of reverses.

exchange management, achieving the unity of the official exchange rate and the market exchange rate, and formed a manageable, market-based, one-way floating rate management system. The stability of the RMB exchange rate had greatly contributed to the inflows of the export growth and the foreign direct investments. Specifically, the current account surplus had maintained its surplus, as had the capital and financial account (except for a deficit during the 1998Asian financial crisis). The surplus of the current account and the capital and financial account accumulated to USD144 billion and USD167.9 billion in the eight years, respectively. Affected by this, the foreign exchange reverses increased rapidly and the annual growth was significantly higher than the level before 1993. Thus, the pattern of the "double surplus" of the current and the capital accounts was fostered.[1]

The fourth stage began in 2002, when the pattern of "double surplus" continued to strengthen. At this stage, China began to accelerate the speed of integration into the world economy, opening up further, and driving both the current account and the capital and financial account surplus to expand rapidly. The pattern of the "double surplus" of the balance of payments became significant. The current account surplus increased rapidly, from USD17.4 billion at the end of 2001 to USD371.8 billion at the end of 2007, with an increase of 20.4 times; despite the large fluctuation of the capital and financial account surplus, it still reached USD73.5 billion in 2007, with its maximum at USD110.7 billion in 2004. It was because of continuous strengthening of the "double surplus" that the foreign exchange reserves reached USD1.5 trillion at the end of 2007.

A substantial increase in the goods trading

Regarding the constitution[2] of the current account surplus, goods trade has long been taking a large portion in the current account. Thus the surplus of the current account is mainly fed by the surplus in goods trade.

The long-term, ever-enlarging surplus in goods trading

The total imports and exports of goods from 1994 to 2007 increased from USD236.6 billion to USD2,174 billion,[3] with an increase of 8.2 times. Specifically, the import and export of the goods had always been rapid before 1997, but the total amount decreased by USD1.2 billion due to the impact of the 1998 Asian financial crisis. The trade in goods entered a new round of rapid growth since 1999. The total amount of import and export increased annually with its maximum at USD2,173.8 billion in 2007 (see Fig. 9.1).

The growth rate of export is more rapid than of import overall in the comparison of the growth of the total amount of the import and export. From

Evolution and Imbalance of China's Balance of Payments Structure

Fig. 9.1.   Changes of the total amount of China's goods trading, 1994–2007

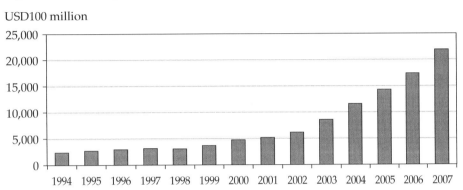

1994 to 2007, the total amount of export increased from USD121 billion to USD1,218 billion, with an increase of 9.1 times; while the total amount of import increased from USD115.6 billion to USD955.8 billion, with an increase of 7.3 times (see Fig. 9.2). Since 2004 in particular, the amount of export has dramatically increased, with an ever-enlarging gap of the amount of import, which makes the goods trade surplus expand annually. The trade surplus in goods increased from USD7.9 billion to USD315.4 billion from 1994 to 2007, with an increase of 42.3 times.

Fig. 9.2.   Variations of the total amount of China's import and export, 1994–2007

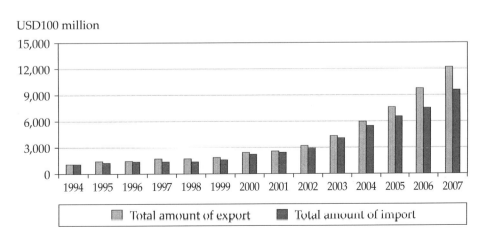

STRUCTURAL ECONOMICS IN CHINA

Table 9.2.   Changes of China's trade in services, 1994–2007 (USD100 million)

Year	Export	Import	Total Amount	Balance	Year	Export	Import	Total Amount	Balance
1994	163.7	163.0	326.7	0.7	2001	333.4	392.7	726.0	−59.3
1995	191.3	252.2	443.5	−60.9	2002	397.4	465.3	862.7	−67.8
1996	206.0	225.9	431.9	−19.9	2003	467.3	553.1	1,020.4	−85.7
1997	245.8	303.1	548.9	−57.3	2004	624.3	721.3	1,345.7	−97.0
1998	240.6	289.8	530.4	−49.2	2005	744.0	838.0	1,582.0	−93.9
1999	237.8	312.9	550.7	−75.1	2006	920.0	1,008.3	1,928.3	−88.3
2000	304.3	360.3	664.6	−56.0	2007	1,222.1	1,301.1	2,523.2	−79.1

Source: The table of the international balance of payments released by the State Administration of Foreign Exchange (SAFE).
Note: "−" in the balance means deficit.

A mild deficit of the trade in services

Trade in services kept an ongoing trend from 1994 to 2007. The total amount of trade increased from USD32.7 billion to USD252.3 billion with an increase of 6.7 times.; Of this total, the total amount of services export increased from USD16.4 billion to USD122.2 billion with an increase of 6.5 times, and the total amount of import increased from USD16.3 billion to USD130.1 billion with an increase of 7times. When comparing the balance between the import and export of the trade of services, it maintained a small deficit with the exception of a USD70 million surplus in 1994.

Regarding the constitution of the trade in services, transportation and tourism play the leading roles, while the ratios of the trades of finance, insurance, communication, and computer information remain relatively low. In 2007, the amount of the accounts of transport and tourism accounted for 56% of the total scale of trade in services. The largest surplus existed in the tourism trade while the largest deficit existed in the transport account. The export amount of tourism accounted for 30.5% of the total export amount, and the import amount of tourism accounted for 33.3% of the total import amount.

The goods trading–led current account balance variations

The surplus of the current account expanded continuously from USD7.66 billion to USD371.8 billion with an increase of 47.6 times from 1994 to 2007. Under three sub-accounts of China's current accounts, the trades in goods and services played leading roles, while the profits and current transfer account were

Evolution and Imbalance of China's Balance of Payments Structure

subordinate. Therefore, the direction and size of the balance in the profits and current transfer account is determined by the direction and size of the balance of the trades in goods and services. In the constitution of the goods and services accounts, despite the trade deficit of the services, its deficit balance was much smaller than the trade surplus of the goods; thus, the deficit of the services accounts did not affect the direction of the surplus of the goods and services. As demonstrated in Fig. 9.3, the trade deficit in services accounted for less than 25% of the trade surplus of the goods, with the exception of an over 30% performance in 1995. In recent years, the trade surplus of the goods expanded rapidly, and the proportion of the trade balance of the goods to the trade balance of the services has shown a rapid decrease. The proportion was only 2.5% in 2007. In this case, the increase of the trade surplus of the goods naturally led to a corresponding surplus increase in the current account.

Fig. 9.3. The proportion of the balance of trade in services in the total balance of goods trade, 1994–2007

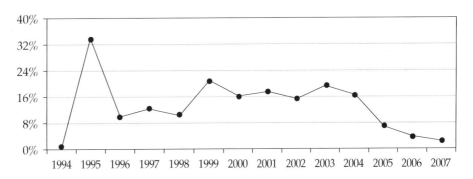

Increased volatility in the balance of the capital account

The structural changes of the capital account[4] are mainly in three aspects: the first is the changes of the balance of the financial and capital accounts; the second is the changes of the balances of the financial and capital accounts respectively; the third is the changes of the ratio of the relationship of the sub-accounts in the financial account. Through the analysis of these three aspects, it can be found that the structural changes of China's capital and financial accounts are volatility.

STRUCTURAL ECONOMICS IN CHINA

Balance between the capital and financial accounts fluctuates

Before 1992, the size of the capital and financial accounts was relatively small. The highest surplus was USD8.97 billion in 1985, and the highest deficit was only USD1 billion in 1984. The fluctuation amplitude of the balance of the capital and financial accounts were confined within a small range at this stage (see Fig. 9.4). Since Deng Xiaoping's tour to South China in 1992, the accelerated pace of China's reform and opening-up led to the rapid increase in FDI. The surplus of the capital and financial accounts soared to USD23.47 billion in 1993 and continued increasing until 1996. Hit by the Asian financial crisis, there was a significant decrease of the surplus of the capital and finance accounts, with 1998 having the largest deficit at USD6.32 billion since the reform and opening-up. The surplus of the capital and finance accounts increased with volatility during 2001 to 2007. The surplus was USD34.78 billion in 2001, reached its peak of USD110.66 billion in 2004, dramatically decreased to USD10.04 billion in 2006, and bounced back to UDS73.51 billion in 2007. Within 20 years of the changes of the capital and financial accounts, the fluctuations of the balance are frequent and more intensive.

Fig. 9.4. Fluctuations of the balance between China's capital and financial accounts

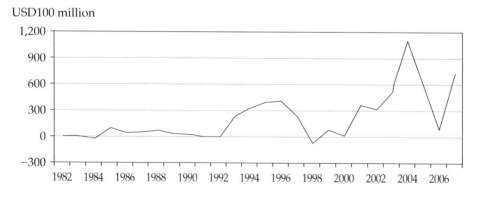

Since the balance of the financial account is the main source of the balance of the capital and financial accounts, the fluctuant situation of the former determines the fluctuant range and size of the latter. There has been a surplus in China's financial accounts since 1994, except a deficit in 1998 of USD6.27 billion, but the fluctuant range was large. The maximum fluctuation was

USD110.73 billion in 2004, while the minimum was USD1.96 billion in 2000, with a balance of over USD100 billion. Particularly since 2003, there has been a dramatic fluctuation of surplus from year to year. For example, the surplus of the financial account decreased USD52.84 billion in 2006 from 2005, and had an increase of USD64.39 billion in 2007 over 2006 (see Table 9.3).

Table 9.3. Changes of the balance of China's capital and financial accounts, 1994–2007 (USD100 million)

Year	The Capital Account	The Financial Account	Year	The Capital Account	The Financial Account
1994	—	326.4	2001	−0.5	348.3
1995	—	386.8	2002	−0.5	323.4
1996	—	399.7	2003	−0.5	527.7
1997	−0.2	229.8	2004	−0.7	1,107.3
1998	−0.5	−62.7	2005	41.0	588.6
1999	−0.3	76.7	2006	40.2	60.2
2000	−0.4	19.6	2007	31.0	704.1

Sources: Sorted from the table of China's balance of payments from 1997 to 2007, released by the SAFE.

It is in contrast with the dramatic fluctuation of the balance of the financial account that the balance of the capital account has remained stable. From 1997 to 2004, there has always been a small deficit of less than USD100 million of the capital account. Since 2005, significant changes in the balance of the capital account occurred, from a slight deficit to a small surplus. In 2007, however, the size of the surplus was USD31million. The capital account mainly recorded the capital transfers and trades of the non-productive and non-financial assets. China's economic scale is not large; therefore, the income and expenses of the capital account take up very little in the total capital and financial accounts.

Significant changes in the balance of and proportional relationship between the items within the financial projects

Based on the internal structure of the financial projects, and the balance of and proportional relationship between direct investments, portfolio investment and other investments have undergone changes in recent years. First, the size of the surplus of direct investment has shown a steady increase, while the balance of portfolio investment and other investments underwent drastic fluctuations (see

Table 9.4). Between 1994 and 2007, the direct investment account maintained an ever-increasing surplus, from USD31.79 billion in 1994 to USD121.42 billion in 2007, an increase of 2.8 times. At the same time, the portfolio investment balance and other investments went through drastic fluctuations. These took on certain cyclical characteristics, that is, the alternate appearance of deficit and surplus. The surplus increased to USD19.69 billion in 2004 and the deficit up to USD67.56 billion in 2006. The huge deficit of portfolio investment in 2006 was mainly due to the rapid growth of foreign portfolio investments (which were mainly based on the banks, insurance companies and other institutions). The changes in the absolute size of other investment projects showed a trend of "decrease first, increase second," that is, the size of the deficit decreased before 2004 but expanded after 2005. Notably, the deficit reached USD69.68 billion in 2007.

Table 9.4. Changes in the internal balance of China's financial projects, 1994–2007 (USD100 million)

Year	Direct Investment Balance	Portfolio Investment Balance	Other Investment Balance
1994	317.9	35.4	−26.9
1995	338.5	7.9	40.4
1996	380.7	17.4	1.6
1997	416.7	68.0	−255.0
1998	411.2	−37.3	−436.6
1999	369.8	−112.3	−180.8
2000	374.8	−39.9	−315.3
2001	373.6	−194.1	168.8
2002	467.9	−103.4	−41.1
2003	472.3	114.3	−58.8
2004	531.3	196.9	379.1
2005	678.2	−49.3	−40.3
2006	602.7	−675.6	133.1
2007	1,214.2	186.7	−696.8

Source: Based on the Table of China's Balance of Payments Between 1997 and 2007 published by the SAFE.

Second, the financial project balance was determined by the direct investment balance (which was basically the financial project balance), as the portfolio investment balance and other investment balance were very small before 1996. After 1997, as a result of the growing proportion of portfolio investment and other investments in the financial projects, the financial project balance was less determined by the direct investment balance, although it was still the most important decision factor of the financial project balance. In fact, after Deng Xiaoping's speech in Shenzhen in 1992, the FDI inflows increased every year. In addition, due to the limited size, the large-size inflows of FDI naturally led to the long-term surplus in China's FDI projects as well as the financial projects. What is noticeable is that Chinese enterprises significantly accelerated the pace of "going out." The FDI increased from USD11.87 billion to USD18.93 billion in 2007.

Finally, as the direct investment project surplus maintained a steady growth, and while the portfolio investment and other investment projects balance underwent drastic fluctuations, the proportional relationship among the three account balances within the financial projects was very unstable. In 1994, the financial project showed a surplus of USD32.64 billion, of which both direct investment and portfolio investment showed a surplus, while other investments showed a deficit of USD2.69 billion; in 1998, the financial project showed a deficit of USD6.27 billion, mainly due to the emergence of a deficit of USD43.66 billion in other investments. In the following years, due to the increasing size of the direct investment surplus, the financial projects were able to maintain a surplus, even if the portfolio investment and other investments showed a deficit. What is noteworthy is that a deficit of USD67.56 billion emerged in the portfolio investment in 2006, which caused the financial project surplus to be USD6.02 billion that year. A deficit of USD69.68 billion emerged in other investments in 2007; the financial project surplus was still confronted with a large disparity from its high point in 2004, although the direct investment surplus hit a record of USD121.42 billion in 2007.

Rapid growth of foreign exchange reserves

Between 1994 and 2007, China's foreign exchange reserves maintained a momentum of rapid growth, from USD51.6 billion to USD1.5 trillion, an increase of 28.6 times, which meant that China owned the world's largest foreign exchange reserves (see Table 9.5). The rapid growth of foreign exchange reserves is closely related to the pattern of "double surplus" of the balance of payments. In 1994, China's foreign exchange system reform established the system of mandatory exchange, settlement and sales, and a managed floating exchange rate system, after which the foreign exchange reserves began to steadily increase. With China's entry into the WTO and the increasingly established pattern of "double surplus" of the balance of payments, the foreign exchange reserves grew markedly, and the balance showed a trend of stable increases (see Fig. 9.5).

STRUCTURAL ECONOMICS IN CHINA

Table 9.5. Size and growth of foreign exchange reserves of some Asian countries at the end of 2007

Country	Size (USD100 million)	Growth (%)	Country	Size (USD100 million)	Growth (%)
China	15,302.8	43.2	Singapore	1,629.6	19.6
Japan	9,527.8	8.3	Malaysia	1,010.2	23.0
South Korea	2,621.5	9.7	Thailand	852.2	30.5
India	2,669.9	56.4	Indonesia	549.8	33.8

Source: The database of World Bank.

Fig. 9.5. Changes in China's foreign exchange reserves, 1994–2007

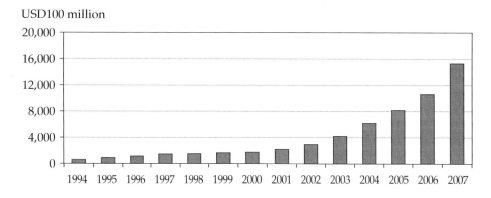

In fact, the growth of the foreign exchange reserve is an inevitable result of continued expansion of "double surplus" of the balance of payments. Between 1994 and 2007, the accumulated surplus of current account and capital account of the balance of payments was USD1.59 trillion, of which only 5% was absorbed by the projects of "net errors and omissions," and the remaining 95% was all transformed into incremental reserve assets through the system of mandatory exchange, settlement and sales.

Evolution and Imbalance of China's Balance of Payments Structure

The major source of the increase in foreign exchange reserves was the direct investment surplus, before China's accession to the WTO, which was followed by the commodity trade surplus. From 1994 to 2001, the accumulated surplus of direct investment accounted for 156.2% of the accumulated addition of foreign exchange reserves, and the accumulated surplus of commodity trade accounted for 126.9%, while the accumulated deficit of other projects accounted for −183.1%.[5] After China's entry into the WTO, the commodity trade surplus became the largest source of the increase in foreign exchange reserves, while the direct investment surplus took the second place. Between 2002 and 2007, the commodity trade surplus accounted for 61.9% of the accumulated increase in foreign exchange reserves, while the proportion of accumulated surplus of direct investment was 30.1% and the proportion of the accumulated surplus of other projects was 8.0%. Significantly, the proportion of trade surplus of the increase in foreign exchange reserves increased during 2005, while the proportion of direct investment surplus decreased. As displayed in Fig. 9.6, the proportion of trade surplus of the increase in foreign exchange reserves was 64% in 2005 and increased rapidly to 88% in 2006, an increase of 4%, with a slight decline in 2007; the proportion of direct investment surplus dropped from 32% in 2005 to 26% in 2007. It can be seen from this that the trade surplus has currently become the largest source of the increase in foreign exchange reserves.

Fig. 9.6.   Contribution rate of commodity trade surplus and direct investment surplus to the increase in foreign exchange reserves

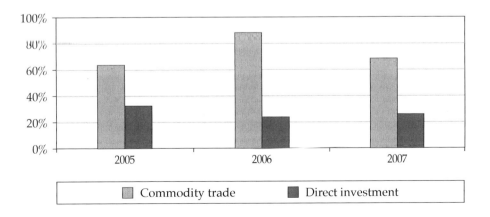

The Degree of Imbalance of China's Balance of Payments Structure

The imbalance of China's balance of payments structure includes not only the overall imbalance of the book, but the surplus or deficit of the items within the book. This section focuses on the coordination of the internal structure of balance of payments and the adaptation of the balance of payments to the economic development, to judge the degree of the imbalance of China's balance of payments.

Criteria

In general, there are two aspects to judge the degree of structural imbalance of balance of payments: First, an analysis of whether the overall balance of payments and the internal structure keep a long-term deviation from the equilibrium (which is based on China's actual situation); second, an analysis of whether the structure of balance of payments imposes long-term negative effects upon the economy (which is based on the impacts of balance of payments on the macroeconomic operation). Thus, the degree of imbalance is judged by a system rather than some single indicator.

Based on this, the following two criteria can be used to measure the degree of imbalance. 1) An analysis of the proportional relationships between the current account and capital account, between the sub-accounts of the current account and the capital account within China's balance of payments, which is based on the structural coordination of the balance of payments. 2) An analysis of the impacts of the overall balance of China's balance of payments on the macro-economy, which is based on the adaptability of the structure of balance of payments to the macro-economy.

Three methods above can be used for the analysis of the imbalance either from the perspective of the coordination of the internal structure of balance of payments or from the perspective of the adaptability of the structure of balance of payments to the macro-economy. 1) An analysis on the representative indicators. For example, when judging whether the proportion of current account is too large, the historical data of the proportion of current account can be employed. 2) International comparison on the indicators. In the internationally comparable conditions, if the value of an indicator exceeds the internationally recognized level or the average level, the indicator is more likely in an unbalanced state. 3) The development trend of indicators. If the value of an indicator shows an ongoing bias, the indicator can be judged by its future tendency.

Judgment based on the coordination of the balance of payments structure

From the perspective of the internal coordination of the structure of balance of payments, the level of structural imbalance of China's balance of payments can be judged from the size and composition of current account surplus, the internal structure of the capital account and financial project, the structural relationship between the current account and capital account, and other aspects.

The proportion of the current account balance in the GDP exceeds the internationally-recognized normal level

Prior to 2004, the proportion of the current account balance of GDP remained below 5% and peaked at only 3.1% in 1997. However, the proportion increased significantly from 2005 and was as high as 10.9% in 2007. IMF believes that the proportion of the current account balance of GDP should be less than 5%. In fact, the highest value of the proportion of the U.S. current account balance of GDP was only 5.8% in 2005; this value does not exceed 5% in most countries. Thus, the proportion of the current account balance of GDP has far exceeded the internationally-recognized normal level (see Fig. 9.7).

Fig. 9.7.   Changes of the proportion of China's current account balance in the GDP, 1992–2007

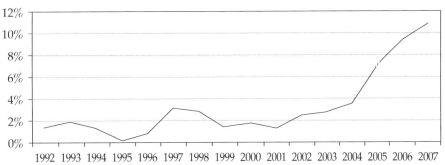

Moreover, based on the trend of the changes of the current account surplus, the surplus will continue to expand. In fact, as long as the domestic savings exceed the domestic investment, the trade surplus will last for a long time. International experience shows that, with the increase of GDP per capita, the saving rate in developing countries presents an evident upward trend. China's saving rate was

STRUCTURAL ECONOMICS IN CHINA

only 27% between 1965 and 1970, but remained at 35% between 1981 and 1990 and at 40.5% from 1991 to 2000. From 2001 to 2007, the average domestic saving rate increased to 45.3%. Therefore, the current account surplus is unlikely to be reversed in the short term, but the U.S. subprime mortgage financial crisis might help to ameliorate the unduly large current account surplus.

The internal structure of the current account is unbalanced

The current account of balance of payments is not only manifested in a large surplus, but also the imbalances in its internal structure, which is mainly denoted as the structural imbalance between the commodity trade, service trade and income account, as well as the serious imbalance in the commodity trade.

The imbalance of commodity trade, service trade and income account structures

The commodity trade surplus is the main source of the surplus of current account of balance of payments, while the service trade has maintained a deficit since 1997, and the income account shifted from a slight deficit to a surplus in 2005. First, the service trade maintained a long-term deficit. Although the small amount of deficit is not sufficient enough to affect China's current account surplus situation, the long-term deficit of the service trade marks the lagged development of the third industry. It also reflects the irrational domestic industrial structure as well as the considerable room for adjustment, because the level of development of the service trade represents the level of development of the national industrial structure. Second, the income account remained in a state of modest deficit before 2004, mainly due to the remittance of foreign direct investment earnings. Between 2005 and 2007, the income account showed a surplus, partly because China increased its foreign direct investment, which increased the repatriation of investment earnings, and partly because a large number of foreign investment income remained in China for reinvestment, as a result of appreciation of the RMB, the rising asset prices and other factors, so that the "double surplus" further increased (see Fig. 9.8).

The commodity trade has been dominated by the processing trade for a long time, which reflects the imbalance of China's commodity trade pattern. In general, the commodity trade can be divided into general trade, processing trade, and other trades, of which the general trade and processing trade are the most important trade patterns. Prior to 1994, the general trade and processing trade went through both surplus and deficit, but the total amount was not great. After the exchange rate reform in 1994, the structure of the general trade and processing trade underwent significant changes, and the large proportion of processing trade became an acute problem (see Fig. 9.9).

Evolution and Imbalance of China's Balance of Payments Structure

Fig. 9.8. Changes in the balance of trade in services and the balance of income account, 1994–2007

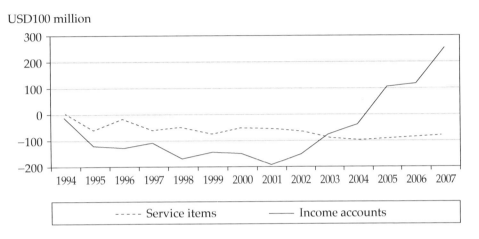

Fig. 9.9. Changes in the general trade balance and the balance of processing trade, 1994–2007

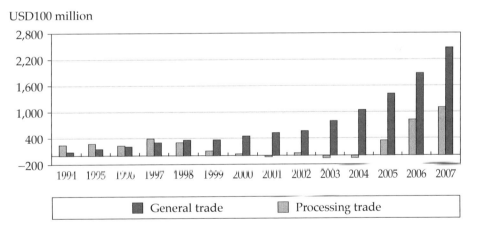

As shown in Fig. 9.9, both the general trade balance and processing trade balance in commodity trade showed a surplus from 1994 to 1997, and the general trade balance was greater than the processing trade balance. This situation was reversed in 1998. The general trade balance showed a decreasing surplus year by year, and even showed a deficit in 2001, 2003 and 2004; the surplus increased rapidly in the processing trade over the same period. The general trade surplus kept a rapid growth between 2005 and 2007, and peaked at USD109.93 billion in 2007, but was only 44.1% of the surplus of the processing trade, which was USD249.26 billion. As a large country with abundant labor resources, China took advantage of the labor cost and prepared preferential policies to attract international capital to invest in the processing trade, which made up for the lack of funds in the rapid development of the domestic economy, and helped help solve the employment problem of a surplus labor force in the urbanization process. However, excessive dependence on the processing trade for economic development will fundamentally impede the upgrading of the industrial structure and improvement of technological innovation capacity, thus exacerbating the imbalance in the domestic economic structure.

Fig. 9.10.   Changes in China's short-term external debt ratio, 1994–2007

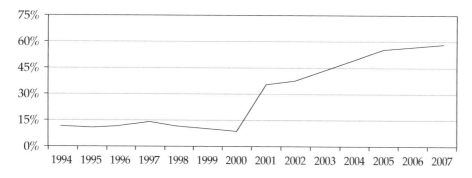

Fig. 9.11.   International comparison of short-term external debt ratio

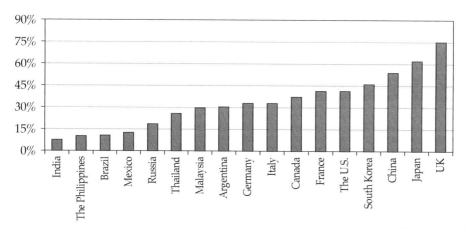

Evolution and Imbalance of China's Balance of Payments Structure

Risks of the internal structural imbalance of the capital and financial accounts

The uncoordinated internal structure of capital and financial account is reflected not only in the instability of the proportional relationship of direct investment, portfolio investment, and other investment balance, but also in the too-high short-term debt ratio.

As mentioned above, since 1997, the direct investment account balance has remained relatively stable with foreign direct investment always greater than China's foreign direct investment, enabling this account to sustain a surplus for a decade. Meanwhile, portfolio investment and other investment account balances are unstable and volatile, directly leading to the unstable proportional relationship among direct investment, portfolio investment and other investment. In fact, the volatility of portfolio investment and other investment reflects the frequent in-and-out short-term capital flows. International experience shows that large-scale, short-term capital flows tend to be a threat to national financial security. Take the Southeast Asian financial crisis as an example. Financial crisis occurred in Thailand, Indonesia, the Philippines, Malaysia, and South Korea and is, to a large extent, related to the huge short-term international capital outflows. At present, although China maintains a huge surplus in its current account, the potential risk of a large-scale flow of short-term capital cannot be ignored. In addition, the unduly high, short-term external debt ratio[6] indicates imbalance in the internal structure of China's capital and financial account. According to international standards, the international warning line of the proportion of short-term external debt in external debt balance is 25%. Before 2000, China's short-term external debt ratio remained below 20%, lower than the international warning line. However, since 2001, this ratio has recovered, and hit 58.9% in 2007 (see Fig. 9.10), suggesting that the risk of short-term external debt is currently in a very serious condition. China's short-term external debt ratio was much higher than that in Germany, India, the United States and other countries—just below UK and Japan (see Fig. 9.11).[7] The high short-term external debt ratio in UK and Japan is mainly due to their status as international financial centers; however, China's high short-term external debt ratio is mainly due to the expectations of RMB appreciation, debt management and other factors. In circumstances of strong appreciation of the RMB and the positive carry between domestic and foreign currencies, enterprises' motivation to increase foreign exchange debt is particularly strong. Foreign enterprises, in particular, enjoy more preferential policies than Chinese-funded enterprises in borrowing and in settlement of exchange, so their external short-term borrowing (mainly in the form of shareholder loans) grows rapidly. Moreover, although China has adopted the quantity control over the short-term external debt and medium- and long-term external debt, the medium- and long-term external debt can only be used once, whereas short-term external debt can be recycled. In this case, in order to make maximized use of the amount of external debt, foreign enterprises and foreign banks in general tend to borrow short-term external debt.

In summary, China's internal structure of international balance of payments has developed from a general balance to a deteriorating imbalance. The trade surplus has increased dramatically since entering the WTO; the capital and financial account has maintained a surplus which is mainly from foreign direct investment, and the major factors to attract FDI are low prices of elements and the expected appreciation of the RMB. At the same time, there is a great degree of imbalance in the structure of the capital and financial account. Large-scale, short-term capital inflows give rise to the increase of a short-term external debt ratio which far exceeds the international warning level, and its risks have been initially apparent.

Judgment based on the structure of balance of payments and the adaptability of economic development

From the perspective of the structure of international balance of payments and the adaptability of economic development, the structural imbalance of international balance of payments is prominently reflected in being unbeneficial to the sustainable economic development, undermining the autonomy and effectiveness of domestic monetary policies, and causing degradation of the international environment, based on which the economy develops.

Large surplus of goods trading and direct investment worsen the imbalance of the industrial structure

In a relatively short period of foreign exchange reserves, "double surplus" played a positive role in China's economic development. However, if the huge surplus of goods trade and direct investment lasts for a long time, it will have negative impacts on economic development.

The surplus in China's goods trading mainly comes from the surplus in processing trade; substantial long-term surplus in processing trade is not conducive to sustainable economic development, and is mainly reflected in three aspects. First, the excessive development of processing trade will make China's economic structure become more dependent on labor-intensive industries, most of which are eliminated in the upgrading process of industrial structure by developed countries, and are low-value-added sunset industries at the low end of the industrial chain. Relying on the processing trade for a long time is bound to affect the upgrading of industrial structure and will put China in a disadvantaged position in the international division of labor. Second, the processing trade is over-dependent on low labor costs and reduces consumptive power of domestic residents, thereby aggravating the insufficient domestic demand and causing an increasing dependence of economic growth on external demand. Accordingly, it increases the uncertainty of economic development. Third, the processing trade relies on the excessive consumption of resources and causes too much damage to the environment, which makes the current society almost unbearable and the future development unsustainable.

The emergence of the huge surplus of China's direct investment account is closely related to transfer of industries caused by the international division of labor. Undeniably, foreign direct investment plays a very important role in promoting economic growth, increasing employment opportunities, and stimulating market competition. While affirming the positive role of foreign direct investment, we should also note its negative impact on China's economic development. China has always supplied foreign enterprises with many preferential policies in investment, finance, taxation and other aspects. The unfair competition caused by these treatments has negative impacts on domestic enterprises. It causes crowd-out effects on domestic capital and undermines the developing ability of national industries, which induces market monopoly, and to some extent threatens China's economic security. A research report published by the State Council Research and Development Center in June, 2006 pointed out that the top five companies in each of the open industries in China are almost exclusively controlled by foreign funds; foreign funds own the majority of assets in 21 of China's 28 major industries.[8] Moreover, some local governments blindly offer foreign investors excessive preferential policies, and their examination and approval of the project are not strict, leading to the excessive consumption of resources and serious environmental pollution in foreign-invested enterprises. High-consumption and high-pollution industries such as tanning, dyeing, electroplating, papermaking, rubber and plastic became hot spots of foreign investment in coastal areas.[9]

Large balance of payments surplus undermines the autonomy and effectiveness of monetary policies

The continued large balance of payments surplus will not only lead to the excessive growth of foreign exchange reserves, but will also erode the autonomy of domestic monetary policies. In China's current regime of exchange rate and system of exchange settlement and sales, the increase in foreign exchange

STRUCTURAL ECONOMICS IN CHINA

reserves directly gives rise to the rapid growth of foreign exchange, and thereby the passive growth of the monetary base. In order to control domestic supply of money and suppress inflation, the central bank has to offset the passive increase in supply of money caused by the "double surplus" of international balance of payments by issuing central bank bills, raising the deposit reserve ratio, and other means. When the double surplus of international balance of payments still remains and may even further expand, the central bank's sterilization operations will be increasingly difficult, and will also be unable to completely offset the monetary base putting by the increase in foreign exchange. Due to the increasing impact of foreign exchange, the exogenous nature of putting in a monetary base becomes more and more obvious, and seriously erodes the independence of monetary policies. Moreover, the surge in foreign exchange reserves also increases the expectation of appreciation of RMB and thus limits the role of the control means of the interest rate.

Large balance of payment surplus causes a deteriorating international environment of economic development

In recent years, influenced by the continued increase in balance of payments surplus, and the rising trend of protectionism in international trade, incidents of trade friction between China and some western developed countries are increasing, and the U.S.-led Western countries continue to impose pressure on China in terms of trade surplus and the exchange rate of the RMB, causing the international environment of China's economic development to worsen. In 2007, the U.S. Congress introduced 50 bills of trade protection against China. Although most of these bills were not passed due to the objection of the U.S. government, they still had many adverse effects on economic and trade relations between the two countries. In 2007, the European Union repeatedly indicated that it required China to speed up the pace of RMB appreciation to reduce the trade surplus between China and Europe. At present, China has experienced more anti-dumping investigations than any other country in the world. About one-sixth of anti-dumping cases filed by WTO members are against China. At the same time, trade friction has gradually extended from goods trade to many other areas such as trade in services, investment, intellectual properties, and from the micro-level of enterprises to the macro-level of the whole system. The exchange rate of RMB, intellectual property and other fields, in particular, are confronted with significantly intensive pressure. In addition, trade friction between China and developing countries also tends to expand. Anti-dumping investigations into China launched by India, Turkey, South Africa and other developing countries are also increasing in number.

Cause Analysis of the Imbalance of China's Balance of Payments Structure

Causes of the imbalance of international balance of payments are both domestic and foreign factors, are both factors of demand and supply, and are both factors of endowments of resources and the institution and system. Intertwined with many factors, causes for the imbalance of international balance of payments are quite complex.

Imbalance of the industrial structure

Since the reform and opening-up, China has taken combined policies of encouraging the development of domestic manufacturing and actively promoting export trade of goods to stimulate the development of the national economy. With the worldwide industrial restructuring, the transfer of the international manufacturing to China is accelerated, which further promotes the development of the secondary industries. There is noticeable disequilibrium between the development of the secondary and tertiary industries. At present, the proportion of China's tertiary industries in GDP is even lower than many developing countries. Most of its service fields (such as telecommunications, transport, finance, and insurance) are dominated by a small number of state-owned enterprises whose competitive ability in the market is not enough, thereby slowing the pace of development of the tertiary industries. For example, because rapidly-developed manufacturing products generally lack high technology, their added value is difficult to improve. In the circumstance of a structural imbalance of two main industries, the problem of domestic economic structure is reflected in the external economy. Enterprises do everything possible to expand export in order to absorb the excessive domestic production capacity, leading to a sharp rise in foreign trade surplus.

Furthermore, the processing trade has always been playing an important role in foreign trade, which, under normal circumstances, definitely leads to export exceeds import. In 2007, the export of China's processing trade reached USD617.66 billion, almost USD80 billion more than normal trade exports. In fact, it is because China's industrial structure lags behind developed countries that its technology is low, and because the processing trade has occupied an important position, that balance of payments surplus remains.

STRUCTURAL ECONOMICS IN CHINA

Imbalance of the investment-consumption proportion

For a long time, a prominent contradiction in China's economic development was that the investment rate was high, while the consumption rate was always low. China's savings rate is among the highest in the world, not only higher than the domestic savings rate of Japan in its economic take-off period, but much higher than Latin America and other developing countries. The proportion of China's final consumption in GDP declined from 62.1% in 1978 to 49.0% in 2007, in which even the residential consumption rate dropped from 48.8% to 35.3%, whereas China's savings rate rose from 37.9% to 51%. High savings and low consumption is bound to translate into high investment. Because the domestic consumption cannot digest the production capacity formed by high investment, the excess capacity necessarily requires external demand to make a balance, and the substantial increase in international balance of payments surplus is inevitable. Thus, insufficient consumption brings about high savings and high savings bring about high investment. During weak domestic consumption, the excess production capacity produced by high investment can only be released by export, which leads to the widening trade surplus.

Preference for export-oriented development

In order to solve the contradiction between the shortage of capital and foreign exchange and economic development, China has adopted a series of preferential policies of encouraging export and foreign direct investment. In terms of foreign trade, China takes the traditional trade strategy based on the principle of "accumulating foreign exchange through export." "Awarding export and limiting import" results in the growth rate of export always being higher than the growth rate of GDP. As China is located in the low-end position of the international division of labor in the world, a considerable part of the trade surplus comes from the medium-end and low-end processing and assembly and export of products of "high pollution, high energy, and resources." In terms of direct investment, China observes the basic idea of "encouraging capital inflows and limiting capital outflows." China implements economic policies of "Super-national Treatment" to foreign capital, whereas it imposes stringent policies of control on capital outflows, which gives rise to a large surplus in a capital account. In order to expand the scale of foreign investment, some local governments take over-preferential policies of slashing transfer prices of land use rights and lowering environmental standards, so that foreign companies easily obtain excess profits, which to a large extent stimulates the influx of global capital to China.

Expectation of the RMB appreciation

With the constant depreciation of the U.S. dollar, there is an increasing degree of deviation between the nominal exchange rate and the real effective exchange rate of RMB. Meanwhile, the constant increase in China's trade in goods causes trade friction to deteriorate, causing the international community to have an increasing demand for the appreciation of RMB. On July 21, 2005, the formation mechanism of RMB was reformed, and at the same time, the exchange rate of RMB against USD rose to 8.11:1. On April 10, 2008, the middle price of the exchange rate of the RMB against the USD entered the "time of six" with the rate of 6.992:1, rising 18%, compared with the reform of exchange rate. However, in the process of the steady, slight appreciation of the RMB, the surplus in the current account does not decline but stimulates the expectation of appreciation and the increase of surplus. In terms of general trade, its export is very sensitive to change in the exchange rate, and the appreciation of the RMB will cause the export of general trade to decline. However, as for the processing trade, its export's sensitivity to change in exchange rate is relatively weak. Especially since joining the WTO, China's trade in goods has been subject to a number of non-exchange factors; the adjustment of exchange rate alone is difficult to alleviate the excessive growth of the surplus of trade in goods.

At the same time, the exchange rate of RMB has maintained a small but steady appreciation since July 2005, which also has had a great impact on the surplus in the capital and financial account. Stimulated by the appreciation of RMB, foreign direct investment has been increasing in recent years, and the reinvestment of profits of foreign-invested enterprises has also shown a sharp increase. In addition, because the appreciation of RMB provides foreign capital with the opportunity of having excess capital gains, and international hot money tries to seek arbitrage in China, the surplus in China's capital and financial account has tended to rapidly increase.

Chapter 10

Integrated Analysis of the Imbalance of China's Economic Structure

STRUCTURAL ECONOMICS IN CHINA

Based on the in-depth analysis of the evolution and imbalance of China's investment-consumption structure, industrial structure, financial structure, regional economic structure, and structure of international balance of payments, this chapter makes a comprehensive evaluation of the positive effect of China's economic structural evolution, and measures and analyzes the degree of imbalance in the economic structure since 1992 by building an indicator system of measuring the imbalance of economic structure, and explains the overall performance and potential risks of "imbalances and growth."

Positive Effects of the Evolution of China's Economic Structure

After 30 years of development, China has actively engaged into the global economic activities; its industrialization and urbanization has accelerated significantly; and the overall evolution of the economic structure has made significant progress, strongly fuelling the national economy to sustain rapid growth.

The improvement of the comprehensive economic strength

With the rapid development of China's economy, its comprehensive economic strength has improved constantly. In 1978, GDP was only RMB364.5 billion, accounting for 1.8% of the global aggregate economy; in 2007, GDP exceeded RMB20 trillion, reaching RMB24.95 trillion and accounting for 6.0% of the total world economy. The average annual GDP growth rate from 1978 to 2007 was 9.8%. Since 2003, China's GDP maintained a 10%-odd growth rate for five consecutive years and the average rate was 10.6%, which was 6.8% higher than the world's average growth in the same period. From the point of view of the world rankings in economic scale, China ranked 10th in 1978, moved up to No. 6 in 2000, and ranked No. 4 both in 2006 and 2007. Compared with the world's top three—the U.S., Japan and Germany—China's GDP accounted for 6.5%, 15.2% and 20.6%, respectively, in their GDPs in 1978, and the figures rose to 23.7%, 74.9% and 99.5 % in 2007 (see Table 10.1).

With the rapid development of the national economy, China's revenue has constantly improved. Its revenue was RMB113.2 billion in 1978 and increased by 44.3 times to RMB5,130 billion in 2007. During this time, the central fiscal revenue increased by 156.8 times from RMB17.58 billion to RMB2.77 trillion and the local fiscal revenue increased by 23.6 times from RMB95.65 billion to RMB2.36 trillion. The growth of the national financial strength improved the government's capacity to resist risks and provided a financial guarantee for the governments to better fulfil functions of social management and public service. In addition, there has been rapid increase in foreign exchange reserves. The foreign exchange reserve was only USD167 million in 1978, grew to USD1.53 trillion in 2007, and ranked the first around the world after exceeding USD1 trillion in 2006. Adequate foreign exchange reserves mean that China has a strong capability of international payment and demonstrates China's growing comprehensive economic strength from another perspective.

Table 10.1. Comparison of countries with high GDP rankings in the world (USD100 million)

Country	1978		2000		2006		2007	
	GDP	Ranking	GDP	Ranking	GDP	Ranking	GDP	Ranking
The U.S.	2,276.9	1	9,764.8	1	13,244.6	1	13,811.2	1
Japan	967.6	2	4,746.1	2	4,367.5	2	4,376.7	2
Germany	716.6	3	1,900.2	3	2,897.0	3	3,297.2	3
China	147.3	10	1,198.5	6	2,645.2	4	3,280.1	4
UK	322.0	5	1,438.3	4	2,373.7	5	2,727.8	5

Source: Database of the World Bank and *World Economic Outlook (2008)*.

With the rapid development of the national economy, China's revenue has constantly improved. Its revenue was RMB113.2 billion in 1978 and increased by 44.3 times to RMB5,130 billion in 2007. During this time, the central fiscal revenue increased by 156.8 times from RMB17.58 billion to RMB2.77 trillion and the local fiscal revenue increased by 23.6 times from RMB95.65 billion to RMB2.36 trillion. The growth of the national financial strength improved the government's capacity to resist risks and provided a financial guarantee for the governments to better fulfil functions of social management and public service. In addition, there has been rapid increase in foreign exchange reserves. The foreign exchange reserve was only USD167 million in 1978, grew to USD1.53 trillion in 2007, and ranked the first around the world after exceeding USD1 trillion in 2006. Adequate foreign exchange reserves mean that China has a strong capability of international payment and demonstrates China's growing comprehensive economic strength from another perspective.

STRUCTURAL ECONOMICS IN CHINA

The gradient development of regional economy

With the gradient implementation of strategies of regional economic development, the potential of regional economic growth has been constantly enhanced. The strategy of developing the eastern region first has led the Yangtze River Delta and the Pearl River Delta to develop rapidly. The implementation of strategies including developing China's western region, revitalizing China's north-eastern areas, and promoting the rise of central part afterward, have stimulated the coordinated development between regions, and regional economic growth has continued to take on new vitality.

As the vanguard of regional economic development, the eastern coastal areas have made vital contributions to the growth of the national economy. After the 1990s, eastern areas such as the Pearl River Delta and the Yangtze River Delta expanded areas of development and promoted the economic development of surrounding areas while improving the ability of independent innovation and optimizing economic structure. The gross product of eastern regions accounted for 60.5% of GDP in 2007; their gross product per capita was RMB31,814, or 1.7 times the national average. Driven by the rapid development of eastern regions, the dynamic economic development in central and western regions was further enhanced. Since the strategy of developing China's west was implemented in 2000, the establishment of western regions' infrastructure has made a significant progress. The Yangtze River Three Gorges Project (*san xia*), the Qinghai-Tibet railway, and other major infrastructure have greatly improved the producing and living conditions of western regions. Since the implementation of the strategy of revitalizing the old north-eastern industrial base in 2003, the growth rate of economic development of the three north-eastern provinces has significantly improved, and their economic and social development has shown good momentum. Since the strategy of promoting the rise of central regions was carried out, central regions have entered a period of rapid growth, and major indicators of economic development have achieved double-digit growth. Overall, with a growing vitality of economic development, the potential for economic development of mid-western and north-eastern regions has constantly improved and the coordination of regional economic development has shown positive changes.

The improvement of people's livelihood

With the restructuring of economic growth and economic structure, people's living standards have constantly improved, shifting from having basic food and clothing to being well-off. The per capita GDP was only USD379 in 1978 and exceeded USD1,000 in 2002. It exceeded USD2,000 in 2006 and amounted to

Integrated Analysis of the Imbalance of China's Economic Structure

USD2,485 in 2007. According to standards of the World Bank, China has moved up to the rank of middle-income countries.

Due to the continuous increase in income, the structure of consumer spending has undergone significant changes. The per capita disposable income of urban households was RMB343.4 in 1978 and reached RMB13,785.8 in 2007, increasing by 39.1 times; the per capita net income of rural households in 2007 was RMB133.6 and increased to RMB4,140.4, by 30 times. In the same period of time, consumer spending rose from RMB184 to RMB7,016, an increase of 37.1 times. In fact, the consumer spending of urban residents increased from RMB405 to RMB11,777, an increase of 28.1 times; the consumer spending of rural residents rose from RMB138 to RMB3,210, an increase of 22.3 times. In addition, the structure of urban-rural consumer spending has made significant changes. The Engel coefficient of urban residents fell from 0.575 in 1978 to 0.363 in 2007, and that of rural residents dropped from 0.677 to 0.431. At the same time, there was a significant increase in housing, transportation, and consumption of enjoyment and development (such as culture and entertainment), in particular with a rapid rise in consumption such as transportation and communication, culture, education, entertainment, and medical care.

The rise of international economic status

With the continuous enhancement of the overall national strength, the contribution rate of China's economic growth to the world's economic growth is rising. The average contribution rate was 15.4% from 2002 to 2007, following only the U.S. In 2007, this contribution rate first surpassed the U.S. and reached 17.1% (see Table 10.2).

Table 10.2. Contribution of countries to the world's economic growth, 2002–2007 (%)

Country	2002	2003	2004	2005	2006	2007
China	20.1	15.6	11.4	14.3	14.0	17.1
The U.S.	27.0	29.9	31.4	28.0	25.3	14.0
Japan	1.1	9.2	7.9	10.3	7.6	4.2
Germany	0.2	−0.4	2.3	1.5	3.8	—
UK	5.0	4.2	3.5	2.4	3.1	—
India	3.1	4.6	3.3	4.4	4.1	4.7

Source: Database of the World Bank.

STRUCTURAL ECONOMICS IN CHINA

The rapid development of China's foreign trade not only promotes the thriving development of the world's trade, but to a large extent influences the pattern of the world's trade. China's total volume of import and export trade was only RMB35.5 billion and ranked No.27 in the world's trade in 1978; it reached RMB9.55 trillion and ranked No.3 in 2004; it amounted to RMB16.7 trillion and maintained at No.3. Moreover, huge imports of goods to some extent alleviate the increasingly serious contradiction between supply and demand in the world market, and promote the development of the global economy. In addition, labor-intensive and common technology-intensive products for export provide the world with many inexpensive, high-quality goods, and improve living standards of people worldwide.

China's huge market provides the world's capital with opportunities for investment. From 1979 to 2007, the accumulated foreign capital China actually used was USD969.75 billion, in which the accumulated capital of FDI was as high as USD775.42 billion. This has greatly contributed to the deepening of the international division of labor and increased trade, and has promoted the rapid development of China's economy. Investors across the world have also shared benefits introduced by that rapid development.

Measurement and Analysis of the Degree of Imbalance of China's Economic Structure

Previous chapters have conducted in-depth analyses of the imbalance of investment-consumption structure, industrial structure, financial structure, regional economic structure and the structure of international balance of payments, but do not discuss the overall unbalanced degree of economic structure. Under the guidance of theories of economic structuralism, this section makes a comprehensive measurement and analysis of the unbalanced degree of economic structure by establishing an index system of imbalance measurement.

Significance of the measurement of economic structural imbalance

Economic structure is a very complex system, involving economy, the society, resources and the environment, and other aspects; thus, the measurement of structural changes is much more difficult than the study on aggregate issues. In the research about complex socio-economic phenomena, it is a common method to establish a set of index systems and measure them. This method will eventually form an indicator, thus making a comprehensive evaluation of

Integrated Analysis of the Imbalance of China's Economic Structure

socio-economic phenomena. For example, the United Nations Commission on Sustainable Development proposes an index system of sustainable development comprised of the society, the environment, the economy and the institutions, in order to conduct a comprehensive assessment of the sustainable development of countries across the world; OECD proposes a set of index systems of structural policy evaluation consisting of indexes such as the labor market, the institutional reform, the age structure, human capital, and international trade and investment.[1] The Human Development Index (HDI), used by the United Nations, is one of the most widely used and influential indexes to measure and compare the relative human development of various countries. This index reflects the basic situation of a country's social and economic structure by measuring health status, access to knowledge, and the quality of life of residents in a country.[2] The construction method of indexes abovementioned provides us with methodological inspiration to establish the measurement method of imbalance of economic structure.

When measuring the economic structure imbalance, the representative measurement indexes are selected on the basis of relevant theories and empirical analysis, and used to assess the measurement indexes according to theories and international experience. Index values with different dimensions are changed into score values with the same dimension, and the index of economic structure imbalance is obtained by using a simple arithmetic of average method. The contents of this measurement are a major innovation for the existing research, though it follows the traditional ideas and methods of measurement. In fact, there is a lot of domestic and international research literature on economic structure, but no scholars have yet established the index system to measure the unbalanced degree of economic structure. Therefore, measuring the unbalanced degree of economic structure has a certain value of reference for the restructuring practice of China's economy.

First, measuring the unbalanced degree of economic structure can solve problems of China's economic structure concerning China as well as foreign countries. As the largest developing country, China's economic structure is affected by the global economy and consequently, it deeply affects the global economic structure. The international community is widely concerned about features of China's economic structure,[3] but China's policy makers and economists are more concerned about structural imbalance.[4] The measurement of economic structure imbalance not only calculates the total unbalanced index of economic structure and offers a comprehensive judgment to the degree of economic structure imbalance, but also calculates indexes of imbalance in all areas and makes a specific analysis of the unbalanced degree inside economic structure.

Second, the measurement of economic structure imbalance can reflect the dynamic features of changes in the economic structure. China's economic structure consists of investment-consumption structure, industrial structure, financial structure, structure of regional economy, structure of international balance of payments and other major areas. The continuous measurement of the unbalanced degree of economic structure can reflect basic features of structural evolution, and can better connect the unbalanced degree of economic structure and other aspects of economic operation. It also benefits the analysis of the formation mechanism of economic structure imbalance and the in-depth understanding of the formation of the economic structure imbalance.

Finally, the measurement of the unbalanced degree of economic structure can provide ideas for solving economic structure imbalance. In the future, an important strategic task for the Chinese government is to carry out economic adjustment. Thus, the measurement of the unbalanced degree of economic structure and the examination of economic structure imbalance help the government to grasp the basic situations of economic structure imbalance and changing trends, so that decision-makers directly find out that there are outstanding economic problems in economic structure imbalance. Meanwhile they can also reflect the effect of policies related to the economic structural evolution, which provides restructuring with useful decision-making references.

The establishment of the measurement index system

The establishment of a relevant index system under the guidance of theories of structural economics and on the basis of the reality of economic structure imbalance is the primary content of the measurement of economic structure imbalance, and is also the combination of qualitative understanding and quantitative analysis.

Principles

The evaluation index system of economic structural imbalance is not a simple summary of economic, ecological and environmental indexes, but a multi-level, comprehensive evaluation index system based on existing statistics.

When choosing measurement indexes, we need to adhere to four main principles. The first is the scientific principle. The measurement of the degree of economic structural imbalance requires various indexes which are interrelated and mutually constraining. The selection of indexes should ensure that each index in the evaluative system has a clear responsibility and a scientific explanation, thus avoiding overlapping and repetition among indexes. The second is the representative principle. Measurement indexes should be representative and should be the core or basic indexes for evaluating the imbalance within their reigns. Therefore, the representative principle actually reflects some essential requirements for the economic structure operation. The third is the principle of comparability. Indexes that are chosen share exactly the same meaning in different countries or regions, and the statistic ranges and sources of data come from the same place, in order to secure the comparability of the same index in different countries or regions. The fourth is the principle of data availability. Carrying out measurement and obtaining indexes reflects problems more directly, so the availability of each variable is considered and the continuity of data is ensured when indexes are selected, in order to ensure the operability of evaluation.

The selection of measurement indexes

In line with the basic principles of selecting indexes, the selection process can be segmented into three procedures.

An extensive selection

The main task of selecting measureable indexes widely is to initially screen indexes covered by various factors of measurement by discarding unrepresentative and unconvincing indexes to set up a foundation for the establishment of measurement indexes. The basic theoretical analysis and realistic economic analysis provide a basic framework for the selection of indexes, and various international statistical yearbooks, reports, and statistics provide a support for the selection of indexes. Aggregate index is generally not chosen for measurement index, because the aggregate index is directly related to the overall units and overall ranges, and it is an index of figures, not suitable for international comparison. Thus, structure index, proportion index, intensity index and average index are generally selected as the basic forms of measurement indexes.

Based on the analysis of investment-consumption theories and relevant statistical indexes, we can choose the growth rate of fixed assets, investment rate, consumption rate, ratio of incremental capital output, and other alternative indexes. Using the analysis of theories of industrial structure and relevant statistical indexes, we can choose industrialization rate, output ratio of the tertiary industries, employment ratio of the tertiary industries, comparative labor productivity, energy consumption coefficient, and other alternative indexes. According to the analysis of theories of financial structure and relevant statistical indexes, we can choose inflation rate, financial-related rate, the degree of banking market concentration, non-performing loans rate, price-earnings ratio, M2-to-GDP ratio, and other alternative indexes. Based on the analysis of regional economic theories and relevant statistical indexes, we can choose regional per capita GDP, per capita urban-rural income ratio, the Gini coefficient, coefficient of convergence of regional industrial structure, coefficient of convergence of regional economy, and other alternative indexes. In terms of the analysis of theories of international balance of payments and relevant statistical indexes, we can choose the ratio of balance of trade to GDP, ratio of foreign exchange reserves to M2 (representing money and "close substitutes" for money), the degree of dependence on foreign trade, debt service ratio, and other alternative indexes.

Assessment and comparison

Alternative measurement indexes provide a range for the selection of indexes, but indexes within the range are complex, lack of internal logic and connection, and need to be further processed. Therefore, after getting optional indexes, we need to sort and categorize indexes and choose the most appropriate indexes among those of the same category. This is a very delicate task that requires collecting literature and analyzing documents, and to make identification and verification on this basis. For example, when choosing unbalanced indexes between economy and the environment, we initially select the index of "the proportion of damage of particulate emissions in gross national income (GNI)" in *The World's Development Indexes* through analysis and comparison of various yearbooks, which is the result of a comparative analysis.; When assessing the degree of industrial structural imbalance, we need to select measurement indexes in energy consumption, and through the analysis of statistical data we find out that the coefficient of energy production elasticity, the coefficient of energy consumption elasticity, the ratio of energy consumption per unit GDP, and other indexes can all be used as alternative indexes, and finally determine the ratio of energy consumption per unit GDP as the most appropriate index. When evaluating the degree of structural imbalance of international payments, we need to determine an index which can reflect the adaptability between foreign exchange reserves and economic development, and we find out that the ratio of foreign exchange reserves to M2 is more indicative of what impact the growth of foreign exchange reserves has on the economy, by the comparison of the ratio of foreign exchange reserves to M2, the ratio of foreign exchange reserves to GDP, and other alternative indexes.

Integrated Analysis of the Imbalance of China's Economic Structure

The final determination

Through the primary selection and assessment of measurement indexes, we have some groups of measurement indexes which cover all the aspects of measurement of economic structure imbalance and constitute the fundamental basis for judging economic structure imbalance. According to the scientific principle, the representative principle, the principle of comparability, and the principle of data availability for selecting indexes, the index system initially screened is compared to finally determine 21 indexes as measurement indexes of China's economic structure imbalance (see Table 10.3).

Table 10.3. The index system of measuring China's economic structural imbalance

Number	Indexes
	Investment-Consumption Structure
1	Investment Rate
2	Consumption Rate
3	Incremental Capital Output Ratio
4	Ratio of Housing Price to Income
	Industrial Structure
5	Comparative Labor Productivity of the Primary industries
6	Ratio of Energy Consumption to per unit of GDP
7	Proportion of Output of the Tertiary industries
8	Proportion of Damage of Particulate Emissions in GNI
	Financial Structure
9	Proportion of Indirect Financing
10	M2-to-GDP ratio
11	Non-performing Loan Ratio
12	Price-earnings Ratio
13	Share of Private Loans
14	Inflation Rate
	Regional Economic Structure
15	Per Capita Income Ratio of Urban to Rural Residents
16	Ratio of Agricultural Expenditure to Incremental Value of the Primary industries
17	Ratio of Extreme Value of Inter-provincial per capita GDP
18	Gini Coefficient
	Structure of Balance of Payments
19	Ratio of Current Account Balance to GDP
20	Ratio of Foreign Exchange Reserves to M2
21	Share of Short-Term Debt

Note: Meanings and the calculation method of various indexes are cited in the Appendix 10.1.

Limitation of the measurement indexes

The quantification of the degree of economic structure imbalance is a very difficult task, and the design of the measurement index system is also innovative and exploratory, so the measurement index system of economic structure imbalance is still imperfect in its design.

First, the complexity of objects for measurement constrains the comprehensiveness of measurement. Economic structure refers to the form and interrelationships in a certain time and space among various parts of economic activities and various sections of the social economic operation. It is a complex system itself, including not only the various elements within the system, but also interrelationships of various elements. Therefore, economic structure imbalance is supposed to examine both the imbalance of elements inside the structure and the coordination of those elements. At the same time, change in structure is a dynamic process, and it is difficult to fully and accurately reflect the unbalanced state of economic structure with limited indexes.

Second, the difficult quantification of economic phenomena directly affects the measurability. Indexes are designed for the quantification of economic phenomena with data, but not all economic phenomena can be quantified and compared. For example, the problem of urban-rural income distribution and the income gap in regional structure is an objective reality in any country, but to what extent a country can bear the income gap is different. Many factors are determined by social psychology and by the traditional value of culture, so the evaluation can only be relative.

Finally, the denotation of economic structural imbalance affects the accuracy of measurement. Economic structure is the basic structure of the entire social system. It is not only related to the operation of the economic system, but also interactive with the political system, the demographic construction, cultural traditions and other aspects. Therefore, the imbalance of economic structure is bound to have significant effects on those aspects, have interactions with each other, and increase the complexity of the measurement of economic structure imbalance, thereby increasing the difficulty of the measurement and affecting its accuracy.

Scoring of the measurement indexes

When indexes of economic structural imbalance are calculated, different indexes cannot be compared and calculated directly, due to different units and dimensions of various indexes of evaluation. This is mainly reflected in two aspects: first, measurement units of different indexes are inconsistent in their economic terms, so indexes cannot be integrated directly; second, properties of these measurement indexes are inconsistent, thus they can be divided into positive index, inverse index and appropriate index.[5] Herein we usually select positive indexes or inverse indexes, instead of appropriate indexes. After obtaining the index values, we need to first eliminate dimensions[6] of indexes through certain transformation and then sum up directly to form integrated indexes. It is thus clear that the scoring of measurement indexes requires the dimensionless index values, which may change index values into abstract scoring values according to established scoring criteria. In the socio-economic measurement, there are various methods[7] for scoring index values, which includes grading of scores, determination of scoring ranges, and scoring of indexes.

Table 10.4. Classification principles of types of index imbalance

Types of Structural Imbalance	Normal	Mild Imbalance	Moderate Imbalance	Severe Imbalance	Potential Crisis
Scores	1	2	3	4	5
Attributes of Indexes	Index values are within the appropriate range and the economy operates well.	Index values exceed the appropriate range a little and it needs concerns.	Index values exceed the appropriate range largely and it needs more concerns.	Index values exceed the appropriate range substantially and it needs serious concerns.	Index values exceed the appropriate range severely and it risks economic crisis.

The grading of scores

Different measurement indexes have different economic connotations and index values are not comparable, but different index values often reflect the state of economic operation in a particular area—that is, whether the economic operation drives beyond the normal range. From this perspective, values of different indexes have a common attribute in reflecting the degree of structural imbalance in a particular economic area. According to the deviation of index values and the appropriate range,[8] this book adopts a *quintile approach* to the scoring of the degree of economic structure imbalance. Index values are divided into five grades, each of which corresponds to 1 point, 2 points, 3 points, 4 points and 5 points, respectively; and their corresponding types of economic structure are classified into: normal, mild imbalance, moderate imbalance, severe imbalance and potential crisis.[9] The scoring of indexes are based on pre-set criteria[10] in the process of measurement, and the general principles of index judgement of structural imbalance of different types are demonstrated in Table 10.4.

Criteria for determining the thresholds of the measurement ranges

In the quintile method, establishing the normal range and the range of potential crisis are the most important things. Once determined, the upper and lower limits of other ranges can be determined according to the features of distribution of the data of the index value. The following three factors are mainly taken into consideration for the criteria for classification of the normal range and the range of potential crisis. The first is the basic theory. For example, according to the theory of inflation, it belongs to the normal range when the inflation rate is within 3%, but belongs to the "Pentium-type" inflation when the inflation rate is over 10%, which may cause financial or economic crisis and can be defined as the lower limit of the range of potential crisis. The second is the international experience and access regulations. For example, it is generally regarded that when the Gini coefficient is over 0.45, the income distribution gap is very large and can be defined as the lower limit of the range of potential crisis. The third is the actual situation of the economic operation. China's actual situation should be taken into full account while drawing on the international experience. The point of the normal range and the range of potential crisis are determined according to the changes of the measurement indexes. Take the evaluation of the price-earnings ratio for example. The average price-earnings ratio fluctuates in the range of between 10 and 20 times in the U.S., UK and other developed markets, and in the range of between 23 and 25 times in the Japanese and Indian markets. China's stock market is in the developing period in which certain premium growth exists. The normal range of the price-earnings ratio of the stock market is defined as less than 30 times while the range of the potential crisis is over 45 times. Appendix 10.2 shows the criteria for determining the normal ranges and the range of potential crisis of the 21 unbalanced measurement indexes.

The ranges of the mild imbalance, moderate imbalance and severe imbalance are determined by the features of the distribution of the data of the index value after determining the normal range and the range of potential crisis of the measurement indexes. If the data is distributed relatively evenly, the principle of equidistance[11] can be adopted to determine the three ranges above; if the distribution of data is skewed, the principle of non-equidistance can be adopted to determine the thresholds of the intervals. Table 10.5 reflects the five grades and the criteria of the scoring of the measurement indexes.

Table 10.5. Criteria of the indexes measuring the imbalance of the economic structure

Name of the Index	Unit	Normal (1 point)	Mildly Unbalanced (2 points)	Moderately Unbalanced (3 points)	Severely Unbalanced (4 points)	Potential Crisis (5 points)
The Investment and Consumption Structures						
The Investment Rate	%	<38	38–40	40–42	42–45	≥45
The Consumption Rate	%	≥60	57–60	54–57	50–54	<50
The ICOR	—	<2	2–3	3–4	4–5	≥5
The Ratio of Housing Price to Income	—	<4	4–5	5–6	6–7	≥7
The Industrial Structure						
The Comparative Labor Productivity of the Primary Industries	—	≥0.5	0.4–0.5	0.3–0.4	0.2–0.3	<0.2
The Specific Energy Consumption of GDP	—	<1	1.0–1.1	1.1–1.2	1.2–1.4	≥1.4
The Proportion of the Output of the Tertiary Industries	%	≥50	40–50	30–40	20–30	<20
The Proportion of the Damage of the PM Emission to GNI	%	<0.8	0.8–1	1–1.2	1.2–1.4	≥1.4
The Financial Structure						
The Ratio of Indirect Financing	%	<70	70–75	75–85	85–90	≥90
The M2-to-GDP ratio Ratio	%	<1.4	1.4–1.5	1.5–1.6	1.6–1.7	≥1.7
The Rate of Non-Performing Loans	%	<5	5–10	10–15	15–20	≥20
The Price-Earnings Ratio	—	<30	30–35	35–40	40–45	≥45
The Share of the Private Loan	%	≥60	50–60	40–50	30–40	<30
The Inflation Rate	%	0~3	3–5 or -1–0	5–7 or -2–-1	7–10 or -3–-2	≥10 or <-3

STRUCTURAL ECONOMICS IN CHINA

(Cont'd)

Name of the Index	Unit	Criteria				
		Normal (1 point)	Mildly Unbalanced (2 points)	Moderately Unbalanced (3 points)	Severely Unbalanced (4 points)	Potential Crisis (5 points)
The Regional Economic Structure						
The Ratio of the Urban to Rural Per Capita Income	—	<2.3	2.3–2.7	2.7–3.1	3.1–3.5	≥3.5
The Ratio of the Agricultural Financial Output to the Output of the Primary industries	%	<11	11–9	9–7	7–5	≤5
The Ratio of Extreme Value of the Inter-provincial Per Capita GDP	—	<4.7	4.7–5.1	5.1–5.5	5.5–6.0	≥6.0
The Gini Coefficient	—	0.2–0.3	0.3–0.35	0.35–0.4	0.4–0.45	≥0.45
The Structure of the Balance of Payments						
The Ratio of the Balance of the Current Account to GDP	%	<5	5–6	6–7	7–8	≥8
The Ratio of the Foreign Exchange Reverses and M2	%	<12	12–15	15–20	20–25	≥25
The Ratio of the Short-Term Foreign Debt	%	<25	25–35	35–45	45–50	≥50

Note: The scoring range is in accordance with the general principles of statistical groups. The lower limit is included in the group, while the upper limit is not.

Results of index measurement

The measure of the degree of the economic structure imbalance literally is the estimate of the deviation between the real performance and the appropriate ranges of the economic structure. The statistics reflecting this bias are the index of the economic structure imbalance. Therefore, the measurement of the index of the economic structure imbalance is a function created on the relationship between the scores of the imbalance and the measurement index of the imbalance, i.e., I=F [f(V)].

In this function, V is on behalf of the variable value, I is the score of the structural imbalance. The process of "V → I" is the integrating process of:

the value of the measurement index → the score of the economic structure imbalance → the index of the imbalance of the economic structure.

Integrated Analysis of the Imbalance of China's Economic Structure

The index calculation methods

The comprehensive evaluations of the socio-economic phenomenon include the measurement approach including the comprehensive scoring, the method of composite index, the standardized treatment, and the method of efficacy coefficient, et cetera. Here, we use the method of composite index to measure the degree of the economic structure imbalance. The composite index of the economic structure imbalance is a process in which each score of the measurement is comprehensively averaged, which consists of two steps: the first step is to average each index rating value of each type of factor in order to get the index of imbalance for each factor. The second step is to average the indexes of five factors of measurement in order to get the overall index of imbalance. We take a simple arithmetic average method in calculating the index and the overall index for three main reasons: first, the overall measuring body of the economic structure imbalance is constituted of different measurement indexes whose importance is hard to distinguish. Second, there are some drawbacks of the index of neglect, or the differences between the factors exist in some objective methods, such as the analysis of the principal components. They are unreasonable to some extent. Third, as for the accuracy of the statistical measurement, none of the measurements are completely accurate, particularly the complex ones in the socio-economic areas; rather, they are relatively objective. The simple average of the treatment is feasible in order to achieve the basic symmetry of the options of the indexes and factors on all levels.

Scores of each measurement index

According to the scoring criteria of the measurement index, the scores of each index from 1992 to 2007[12] can be obtained after scoring the 21 measurement indexes of the five factors of the index system of the economic structure imbalance, as shown in Table 10.6. The scores of each measurement index show the following basic features:

First, the indexes within the normal range were few. The vast majority of indexes were unbalanced for a long time, but only some of the indexes were in the normal range for a few years. This indicates that the economic structure imbalance is an overall imbalance rather than a partial imbalance. For instance, the index evaluation scores of the share of the private loans and the extreme ratio of the inter-provincial per capita GDP were in the range of potential crisis for most of the years.

STRUCTURAL ECONOMICS IN CHINA

Table 10.6. Scores for measurement indexes of the economic structural imbalance, 1992–2007

Index	1992	1993	1994	1995	1996	1997	1998	1999	2000	2001	2002	2003	2004	2005	2006	2007
The Investment Rate	1	4	3	3	2	2	1	1	1	2	2	4	4	4	4	4
The Consumption Rate	1	2	2	2	2	2	2	1	1	2	2	3	3	4	4	5
The ICOR	1	1	1	1	2	3	5	5	3	3	4	3	2	3	4	3
The Ratio of Housing Price to Income	5	5	3	3	3	4	4	4	4	4	3	3	4	4	5	5
The Comparative Labor Productivity of the Primary industries	3	3	3	3	3	3	3	3	3	4	4	4	4	4	4	4
The Energy Consumption Per Unit DGP	—	5	5	5	5	5	4	5	4	4	4	5	5	4	4	4
The Proportion of the Output of the Tertiary industries	3	3	3	3	3	3	3	3	3	2	2	2	2	2	3	2
The Proportion of the PM Emission in the GNI	4	4	4	4	4	4	4	4	4	5	5	4	4	4	5	—
The Proportion of Indirect Financing	4	5	5	5	5	4	5	5	5	5	5	5	4	3	2	—
The M2-to-GDP Ratio	1	1	1	1	1	1	1	1	1	2	3	4	3	4	4	4
The Non-Performing Loans Rate	3	5	5	5	5	5	5	5	5	5	5	5	4	3	2	2
The Price-Earnings Ratio	—	4	1	1	2	4	2	3	5	3	3	3	1	1	2	5
The Share of the Private Loans	—	—	5	5	5	5	5	5	5	5	5	5	5	5	5	5
The Inflation Rate	3	5	5	5	4	1	2	3	1	1	2	1	2	1	1	2
The Ratio of the Urban to Rural Per Capita Income	2	3	3	3	2	2	2	2	3	3	4	4	4	4	4	4
The Ratio of the Agricultural Financial Output to the Output of the Primary industries	4	4	4	5	5	4	3	3	3	2	2	2	2	2	1	1
The Ratio of Extreme Values of the Inter-provincial Per Capita GDP	3	3	5	5	5	5	5	5	5	5	5	5	5	5	5	5
The Gini Coefficient	3	4	4	4	4	4	4	4	4	5	5	5	5	5	5	5
The Ratio of the Balance of the Current Account to GDP	1	1	1	1	1	1	1	1	1	1	1	1	1	4	5	5
The Ratio of the Foreign Exchange Reverses to the M2	1	1	1	1	1	2	1	1	1	1	2	3	3	4	4	5
The Ratio of the Short-term Foreign Debt	1	1	1	1	1	1	1	1	1	3	3	3	4	5	5	5

Integrated Analysis of the Imbalance of China's Economic Structure

Second, great differences exist in the scores of the indexes. From 1992 to 2007, the index with the lowest score, at 1.69 points, was "the ratio of the balance of the current account and GDP," while the index with the highest score, at 5 points, was the share of the private owner's loans. Specifically, there is one index whose average score was less than 2 points, i.e., the ratio of the balance of the current account and GDP. There are 10 indexes whose average scores were between 2 points and 3 points: the proportion of the output of the tertiary industries, the investment rate, the consumption rate, the ICOR, the M2-to-GDP ratio, the price-earnings ratio, the inflation rate, the ratio of the agricultural financial output to the output of the primary industries, the ratio of the foreign exchange reverses to M2, and the rate of the short-term foreign debt. There are three indexes whose average scores were between 3 points and 4 points: the comparative labor productivity of the primary industries, the ratio of housing price to income, and the ratio of the urban to rural per capita income. There are 7 indexes whose average scores were more than 4 points: the energy consumption per unit GDP, the proportion of the PM emission in the GNI, the proportion of indirect financing, the Gini coefficient, the ratio of the extreme value of the inter-provincial per capita GDP, the non-performing loans ratio, and the share of the private loans.

Third, as for the changing trend of the scoring index, the degree of the imbalance of most indexes from 1992 to 2007 was deteriorative. For instance, the three indexes of measuring the degree of the imbalance of the structure of the balance of payments were in the normal range before China's entry into the WTO, but in the range of potential crisis after 2007. Meanwhile, the scores of some individual indexes improved a lot; for example, the non-performing loans and the ratio of the agricultural financial output and the output of the primary industries.

Results of the index calculation

After determining the score of each measurement index, we use the simple arithmetic average of the measurement indexes in the five areas to get the index of the structural imbalance in the five areas. Then, we use the simple arithmetic average of the index to get the overall index of the imbalance. The index of the imbalance of each factor can be obtained through the simple arithmetic average method, as shown in Table 10.7.

As can be seen from Table 10.7, the degrees of the imbalance of each area in the economic structure are unbalanced. In the situation in 2007, the most unbalanced was the structure of the balance of payments, followed by the investment and consumption structures, the structure of the regional economy, the industrial structure, and the financial structure. In the average level from 1992 to 2007, the least unbalanced were the investment and consumption structures and the structure of balance of payments; the most unbalanced was the structure of the regional economy; in the middle were the industrial structure and the financial structure. However, the structure of regional economy, the industrial structure and the financial structure had suffered from moderately unbalanced to severely unbalanced.

Table 10.7. Index of the economic structural imbalance, 1992–2007

Year	Investment and Consumption Structures	Industrial Structure	Financial Structure	Regional Economic Structure	Structure of the Balance of Payments
1992	2.00	3.33	2.75	3.00	1.00
1993	3.00	3.75	4.00	3.50	1.00
1994	2.25	3.75	3.67	4.00	1.00
1995	2.25	3.75	3.67	4.25	1.00
1996	2.25	3.75	3.67	4.00	1.00
1997	2.75	3.75	3.33	3.75	1.33
1998	3.00	3.50	3.33	3.50	1.00
1999	2.75	3.75	3.67	3.50	1.00
2000	2.25	3.50	3.50	3.75	1.00
2001	2.75	3.50	3.50	3.75	1.67
2002	2.75	3.50	3.83	4.00	2.00
2003	3.25	4.00	3.83	4.00	2.33
2004	3.25	3.75	3.33	4.00	2.67
2005	3.75	3.50	3.00	4.00	4.33
2006	4.25	3.75	2.83	3.75	4.67
2007	4.25	3.75	3.33	3.75	5.00
Average	2.92	3.67	3.45	3.78	2.00

First, the imbalance of the investment and consumption structures has increased overall. The imbalance of the investment and consumption structures is closely related with the economic cyclical fluctuation. China's economy, in 1992, set off a construction boom with a rapid growth of the investment of the fixed asset. The investing rate was 43.5% in 1993, and the index of the imbalance of the investment and consumption structures worsened. Since then, the government adjusted the economy, adopting a series of controlling methods with decrease of investment and control of credit-releasing as the main measures. In 1996, the economy fundamentally achieved a "soft landing," but

Integrated Analysis of the Imbalance of China's Economic Structure

investment remained inefficient when the ICOR increased significantly. In 1998, in the industrial restructuring, the industries of textile, petrochemical and other key industries were compressed, closed and cleaned up appropriately, leading to a recovery of the index of the imbalance of the investment and consumption structures. But since 2001, China has entered a new round of investment-led economic growth while the residential consumption has still been crawling, causing the degree of the imbalance of the investment and consumption structures to deteriorate.

Second, the imbalance of the industrial structure has long been at the moderate level. The adjustment of the industrial structure has been the main content of the overall economic adjustment, which was previously featured an incremental adjustment and a flawed stock system, thus resulting in the recurring structural contradictions. During the late 1990s to the early 2000s, the government increased the enforcement of the industrial policy amendment and selected six industries, namely, textile, coal, building materials, steel, automobile, and petrochemical in which structural contradictions were prominent, as the focus of the industrial restructuring, reducing the degree of the imbalance of the industrial structure.

Third, the imbalance of the financial structure presents its own characteristics. Over the years, the indirect financing structure, which is dominated by the banking institutions (particularly the state-owned commercial banks), is the culprit of the severe imbalance of the financial structure. Moreover, disrupted by administrative intervention and other factors, the rate of the non-performing loans of the state-owned commercial banks has kept worsening, and hence forging a vicious circle which further exacerbates the imbalance of the financial structure. Since the 21st century, China's financial reform has accelerated significantly. The state-owned commercial banks have given great impetus to the reform of the joint-stock system. The structure of the marketization of finance has achieved great success. Thanks to comprehensive effects of the factors abovementioned, the imbalance of the financial structure has been calmed down to a mild level. The financial structure is fragile, in which some scores of the indexes fluctuate a lot, and some have long been on the verge of collapse. Influenced by the impacts of the inflation rate hike, the fluctuations of the asset price and the crawling international economy, there are still some uncertainties of the imbalance of the financial structure which cause concern.

Fourth, the structure of the regional economy fluctuates between the moderate level and the severe level. Since 1992, the imbalance of the structure of the regional economy continued to increase, reaching its peak in 1995 and gradually returned to a moderate level. But after 2002, the imbalance of the structure of the regional economy was aggravated again to the severe level and remained so until 2005. In 2007, the imbalance was slightly mitigated to the moderate level. Generally, the structure of the regional economy fluctuated between moderate and severe from 1992 to 2007. Since the 1990s, the economy in the eastern coastal area has developed rapidly with its inherent geographical advantage after being given the priority to efficiency in the non-equilibrium regional development strategy. But the radiating effect of the developed regions is expanding, as is the one between urban and rural areas. The Gini coefficient has continuously remained over the international warning line, indicating the fruits harvested from the economic growth have not been fully shared by the general public.

Fifth, the imbalance of the structure of the balance of payments has shifted from normal to severe. In the 1990s, the index of the imbalance of the structure of balance of payments had been in the normal range, but after 2000, the index soared dramatically and reached its peak of 5 in 2007. The main reason was the significant growth of the surplus of the current account and the short-term foreign debt in the capital account. Since China's entry into the WTO in 2001, the surplus of the trade has expanded substantially, leading to an increase of the ratio of the balance of the current account to GDP. Meanwhile, the short-term foreign debt in the capital has increased rapidly, bringing about a dramatic rise of the short-term foreign debt ratio.

The calculation of the indexes of the overall imbalance of the economic structure

The overall index of the economic structure can be obtained through the indexes of imbalance of each factor (see Table 10.8).

Table 10.8. Indexes of the imbalance of China's economic structure, 1992–2007

Year	1992	1993	1994	1995	1996	1997	1998	1999	2000	2001	2002	2003	2004	2005	2006	2007
The Overall Index	2.42	3.05	2.93	2.98	2.93	2.98	2.87	2.93	2.80	3.03	3.22	3.45	3.42	3.73	3.90	4.02

Integrated Analysis of the Imbalance of China's Economic Structure

The changes of the index of the overall imbalance of China's economic structure from 1992 to 2007 can be obtained from the data in Table 10.8. Fig. 10.1 shows that, along with the rapid economic growth, the imbalance of the economic structure increased from 2.42 in 1992 to 4.02 in 2007, and that the overall imbalance of the economic structure shifted from mild to moderate and has continued to increase. The results show that the imbalance of the economic structure is extremely urgent.

Fig. 10.1. Index of the overall imbalance of China's economic structure

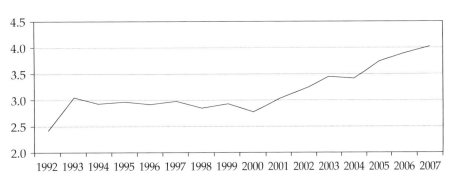

The reliability analysis of measuring the imbalance of the economic structure

It can be seen from the changes of the index of the imbalance that China's economic structure imbalance in the 1990s was mild, but began to intensify after 2001 and gravitate toward a severe imbalance. The reliability of this measurement can be proven by the analysis and studies of the authorities.

The *China Economic Quarterly*, released by the World Bank in December, 2007, stated clearly that the Chinese economy had maintained rapid growth and the surplus of trade had continued to expand, but the economic growth model had not been changed. The external imbalance remained the main macroeconomic issue. Although there was no serious demand or price pressure, there was a risk that the strong growth would overpass the growth of supply. The key challenge was still to rebalance the economy. The special economic report—*The Importance of China's Re-balance* by Morgan Stanley in March, 2005 pointed out that internally and externally, China faces a very urgent need to rebalance. The former refers to the investment and consumption, and the latter is mainly reflected in the huge foreign exchange reserves, the risks of

STRUCTURAL ECONOMICS IN CHINA

write-offs, the escalating tension of trade, and so on. The study group led by the Professor Oliver Blanchard from the Department of Economics, MIT, argued that the Chinese economy is facing quite a lot of internal and external imbalances, and the imbalance of the macro-economy is worsening. The imbalances, specifically, include the imbalance of the inter-provincial growth, the imbalance of the inter-skilled-labor, the imbalance of the growth of the different sectors in economy, the continuous reduction of the functions of the system of the social security, and the misallocation of investment.[13] On August 15, 2007, the British *Financial Times* drew the conclusion from the analysis of the inflation rate, the surplus of trade, and other data that "a real risk comes from the fact that China's economy seems to reach a very hopeless unbalanced situation."

Some Chinese scholars have concluded some understandings on the issue of the structural imbalance. *The Report of Economic Growth in 2008—the Harmonious Society and the Sustainable Development*, released by China's National Economic Accounting Center in Peking University, pointed out "the new imbalances in the operation of China's macro-economy requires the dedicated formulation of the macroeconomic policy."[14] In September, 2006, the research group of the State Information Center pointed out that "what the macro-economy faces is not only the imbalance of the total amount, but rather the structural imbalance. The objective requirement to solve the issue of the current main economic contradiction is to make the policies of the macro-regulating and controlling bias toward the economic adjustment."[15] In the press conference after the National People's Congress (NPC) and Chinese People's Political Consultative Conference in March, 2007, Premier Wen Jiabao publicly stated that "there are unstable, unbalanced and unsustainable structural problems in China's economy." He emphasized again in the government work report, in the 11th NPC, that "some prominent problems and deep-seated contradictions still exist. In recent years, there is excessive investment of the fixed asset and the money and credit. The balance of payments is unbalanced. The problems of the long-term structural contradictions and the extensive mode of growth remain serious. The rate of investment has been continuously high, which is uncoordinated with the consumption. The development of the primary industries, secondary industries and tertiary industries is unbalanced. The proportion of industry, particularly the heavy industry, in the entire economic structure is too large, while the service industry is squeezed. The independent innovation capability is not strong and the cost of resource environment is too large. The agricultural foundation is still weak, which results more difficulties in the steady development of agriculture and the steady increase of farmers' income. The gap between the urban and rural development is still enlarging." This is a precise description of the main aspects of the current imbalance of the economic structure.

Integrated Analysis of the Imbalance of China's Economic Structure

The domestic and international studies have shown that the development speed and potential of China's economic growth have been recognized by the world. At the same time, the issue of economic structure imbalance has been highlighted and become very serious. The domestic and international attention is mostly concerned with the imbalances of the structure of the balance of payments and the structure of domestic investment and consumption, followed by the structure of regional economy, the industrial structure, the financial structure, and so on. This is in accordance with the abovementioned results of the measurement of the imbalance of the economic structure.

The Overall Performance and Potential Risks of China's Imbalance of Economic Structure

The results of measurement show that since the 1990s, the imbalance of China's economic structure has grown, while the economic growth has been high. This seemingly paradoxical phenomenon, as called the phenomenon of "imbalance and growth," is the co-existence of the imbalance of the economic structure and economic rapid growth in some certain periods within the tolerant range of the risks of society, finance and resources, and environment. This section dissects the overall performance of the phenomenon of China's economic imbalance and growth and deeply analyzes the issue of risks implied by this phenomenon.

The "imbalance and growth"

Imbalance and growth is a paradox, but it embodies the complex and special formation mechanism. On the one hand, the rapid economic growth makes the structural imbalance continue to accumulate, but the accumulation of the structural imbalance will weaken the sustainability of the development of economy. On the other hand, the problem of the structural imbalance can only be solved during the process when the economy maintains rapid growth. For this reason, during the economic operation, some special performances derived from the phenomenon of "imbalance and growth" appear.

High economic growth, yet low employment rate

In theory, economic growth is an effective way to expand employment. But the actual situation of China's economic growth is that the increase of economy is disjointed with the expansion of employment, and the increase of employment is far behind the increase of economy. The imbalance of economic structure

STRUCTURAL ECONOMICS IN CHINA

impacts the employment from the following two aspects: first, the imbalance of the economic structure impacts the total employment. The growth of economy will be uncoordinated, unstable and unsustainable, which further leads to the instability of the total employment when the economic structure is unbalanced. Second, the imbalance of the economic structure will lead to the imbalance of the employment structure. For instance, irrationality of the structure of the primary, secondary, and tertiary industries, the imbalance of the structure of the regional industry, the imbalance of the rural-urban development, and other situations of the imbalance of the industrial structure hinder the rational flow of labor, which is not beneficial to the allocation of the labor among the primary, secondary and tertiary industries. Since the 1980s, the elasticity[16] of China's employment has been declining. In 2007, the elasticity was 0.07, but the average elasticity of development courtiers is between 0.3 and 0.4. Thus, the phenomenon of high growth but low employment in China requires profound attention.

Domestic demands give way to the foreign demands

Since the 1990s, China's foreign demand has continued strengthen while the domestic demand has not been developed simultaneously. In the export-oriented strategy, the export has grown rapidly, with an increase of over 13 times, from USD84.9 billion in 1992 to USD1,218 billion in 2007, and an average annual increase of 19.4% which was much higher than the growth of GDP. Affected by the widening gap of income and investment-oriented system, the investment and consumption structures were seriously unbalanced. The domestic consumer market has been in the doldrums. From 1992 to 2007, the total sales of the social retail had increases from RMB1.1 trillion to RMB8.9 trillion, with an increase of about 7 times and an average annual increase of 15%—4.8% lower than the annual growth rate of exports over the same period. It can be seen that the foreign demand was becoming heavy but the domestic demand was reserved. The imbalance between the heavy foreign demand and the light domestic demand made the national economy dependent more on foreign trades, leading to China's increased dependence on foreign trade; it increased from 34% in 1992 to 64% in 2007. The international experience and lessons have already shown that economic growth, which is highly dependent on the foreign demand, has found it difficult to optimize the domestic economy, but increases the international economic and political friction. Therefore, the imbalance of the structure of the foreign and domestic demands needs to be corrected urgently.

Integrated Analysis of the Imbalance of China's Economic Structure

Strong finance, yet weak social security

The basic targets of China's reform and opening include three aspects: to ensure people's life with contentment, stable consuming prices, and better social welfare. Nevertheless, due to the multi-impact of factors such as the inappropriate pattern of income distribution, unbalanced regional economics, disproportional balance of international payments, as well as the mismatch of financial structure and economic structure of entity, people's livelihood has improved with a much slower speed than economic development, while the comprehensive national strength increased rapidly. However, China's national financial power has been continually enhanced. By the year 2007, the total government revenue reached RMB5.13 trillion, or 14.7 times as much of that in 1992. The annual speed of economic increase went up to 19.6%, and the proportion of GDP rose from 12.9% to 17.9%. Tax revenue in 1997 was RMB4,561 billion, or 13.8 times of that in 1992, and the annual increase was 20.1%. However, prominent problems in people's livelihood emerged—particularly that the social security system is unwholesome. The covering of social insurance is still comparatively small. Hardest hit are those who live in the relatively isolated rural areas, as they have little to no access to endowment insurance. More than ten million elderly people who do not work anymore have no socialized pension. A strong financial system and weak social security defies the goal of economic development. If the situation stays as it is, it accumulates detrimental social risks in the long run.

Potential risks of an unbalanced economic structure

Economic imbalance leads to incongruity among factors in the economic system and among other systems. The operation of the economic system is thus with more uncertainty, which is displayed in potential risks. The potential risks mainly take shape in the following five aspects.

Intensifying economic fluctuation

As is shown in the Business Cycle theory, the economy constantly repeats the periodic cycle of "prosperity, recession, depression, and prosperity." For a long time, China's imbalanced economic structure has intensified the fluctuation of economy. First and foremost, the degree of correlation between investing growth and economic growth is higher than consuming growth. In the meantime, the fluctuation range of investment is much higher than that of consumption. As a consequence, over-investment or reduction in investment then becomes the

STRUCTURAL ECONOMICS IN CHINA

major reason of economic fluctuation. Moreover, secondary industries, which put manufacturing as the priority, are typical pro-cyclicality industries. Rapid increase in manufacturing in the rise phase of the economy promotes economic growth, and vice versa; both effects augment the fluctuation of the economy. In addition, over-dependence of foreign economy largely weakens China's power of resisting external financial risks. The international commercial crisis originating from America's subprime mortgage crisis in 2007 had a much greater influence on China than that from Asian financial crisis in 1998. A notable reason is that China's economy only depended 30% on foreign capital in 1998, whereas in 2007, China's economy depended nearly 70% on foreign capital. Finally, since investment is more effective than consumption, investing entities, including local governments, invested more during the course of economic expansion. More sources went to the fields of investment and foreign trade; thus, the backward reaction resulting from the macro-policy was ineffective. The government was forced to take a more strict deflation policy, and regulate with administrative measures, hence the economic fluctuation intensified.

Increasing financial risks

Finance is the core of the modern economy. Financial security directly affects the stable functioning of the economic system. Severe imbalance of a financial structure, to some extent, undoubtedly leads to financial risks, or even triggers a financial crisis. Judging from the previous experience of several international financial crises, the modern economic crisis usually takes shape in a financial crisis, with the structural imbalance being the cause of that crisis. For example, the Asian financial crisis in 1997 and 1998, triggered by Thai Baht's sharp currency devaluation was caused mainly by the respectively weak financial structure of South-east Asian countries, excessive openness of the capital market, the structural imbalance of convertible currency, and underdevelopment of the financial market. Russia's financial crisis in 1998 and 1999, though influenced by the Asian financial crisis and decline of oil prices, was basically a reflection of a defective internal financial system, an inappropriate external debt structure, and long-standing economic recession. Seemingly a result of over-creative finance, a burst real estate bubble, and absent financial supervision, the American subprime mortgage crisis since 2007 was fundamentally a consequence of imbalanced economic structure—an imbalanced financial structure led by disjunction between a fictitious economy and real economy—and by excessive consumption. In some sense, it is the lack of due attention of the imbalanced economic structure from most countries in the world in recent years that the American subprime mortgage crisis turned into a rare worldwide financial crisis.

Integrated Analysis of the Imbalance of China's Economic Structure

China established a modern financial system in the 1990s. Nevertheless, the financial system is still behind the real economic system reform. Recently, the emergence of problems including surplus monetary liquidity, artificially high asset prices, and fierce fluctuation in the capital market shows a relatively weak financial structure; the risk cannot be ignored. Generally speaking, the major financial risks faced at this stage include three aspects.

First, the asset prices are artificially high. Affected by excess liquidity and other factors, housing prices and stock prices were artificially high. Stock prices were inflated and the real-estate bubble continued to expand. With the sharp decline in the stock market, the stock bubble risks were significantly reduced; however, the enthusiasm of micro-economic agents involved in the financial market has been seriously damaged. Meanwhile, the housing prices remained high, and thus the potential risks in the real-estate market still demand attention.

Second, the risk of large-scale outflow of international capital has increased. Because RMB is in its anticipated appreciation period, and asset prices increased rapidly, among other factors, a large number of international capital flows into China through various channels. At the present time, China is faced with a rapid decline in the stock market, a downturn in the real-estate market, a slow-down of RMB appreciation, et cetera, which could lead to massive capital outflows, hence damaging the economic development.

Third, bank risk cannot be underestimated. The proportion of bank-based indirect financing is too large, so that the risk is highly concentrated in banking. Corporate governance in state-owned commercial banks has not been perfected. Dislocation exists in the bank credit allocation of resources, promoting a considerable number of enterprises with high energy consumption and low efficiency to expand. The incremental capital output ratio is too high, while investment efficiency is low and risk-control awareness is weak. All those factors may accumulate considerable credit risks.

Threatening social stability

Unbalanced regional economic development strategy has liberated productivity in the eastern region, promoting a swift boost to the national economy. However, the increasing regional imbalance of the economic structure has not shared the effect of economic growth within the whole society, and ultimately led to the expansion of regional disparity. If the Gini coefficient is used to determine the distribution of wealth of a country or a region, China's present Gini coefficient has exceeded the international alert level, and the indicators have no sign of significant reduction. Serious imbalance in the distribution of income and regional disparities continues to polarize the rich and poor, further weakening the intrinsic motivation of economic development and reform. The sustainability of reform and development is thus affected, and in the long run it will exacerbate social instability, or it may even lead to social shocks and crises. As has been warned in the *China's Human Development Report (2005)* by the United Nations Development Programme, China's constant widening wealth gap could threaten its social stability; in this regard there have been profound historical lessons. In the late 1960s, Latin America became a region with the most inequitable income distribution in the world because of the extreme wealth inequality, strict hierarchy, and ignored social equity in social differentiation, all of which eventually led to the outbreak of a decade-long social economic crisis. Therefore, the social instability and risks caused by polarization demand long-term attention.

The constraint of the "resource bottleneck"

The rapid development of the heavy industry which dominates iron and steel, nonferrous metals, building materials, and the chemical industry, led to irrational use as well as excessive consumption of resources. As a consequence, vital resources such as coal, steel, and oil are in short supply, and constraints in resources and environment have become increasingly evident. Large capacity and production formed by excessive and disorderly exploitation go far beyond the market demand, resulting in excessive supply, not only failing to properly give the best economic effects, but also causing serious pollution. The accelerated process of industrialization has increased the consumption of land resources. With the rapid progress of urbanization, a large number of the rural population have flooded into cities and towns, directly leading to increased demand for urban residential land and its supporting public infrastructure. Consequently, the protection of arable land resources is faced with great challenges. In some areas, illegal occupying of arable land often occurs, and usable land is in increasingly short supply, further exacerbating the imbalance between land supply and demand. With China's continuing population growth and its deepening process of urbanization and industrialization, the conflicts between shortages of land supply and the demands of social and economic development will become even more prominent.

Integrated Analysis of the Imbalance of China's Economic Structure

Deteriorating environmental problems

In recent years, although China has emphasized its environmental protection efforts, the environmental situation is still severe. With large emissions of pollutants, overall environmental pollution is still at a very high level. Environmental quality in some parts of China continues to deteriorate. Water, air and soil pollution in many cities is still very serious. This situation is spreading to rural areas, seriously threatening China's sustainable socio-economic development. In the environmental sustainability index rankings of 144 countries and regions, China ranked the 133rd. In 90% cities, the groundwater is contaminated, and more than half of the cities' urban area has heavily polluted groundwater (400 out 600 cities face a water shortage). 2006, seven major river systems were subject to different degrees of pollution; Liaohe river and Haihe river were seriously polluted. National total emission of waste water in that year was high up to 53.68 billion tons. In 2006, the air pollution and sulfur dioxide in air emissions reached 25.89 million tons, and the air quality in nearly two thirds of all cities failed to meet the secondary standard. In some cities, sulfur dioxide pollution was so severe that acid rain was of frequent occurrence. About 1.5 million *mu* of arable land was contaminated, accounting for almost 1/10 of the nation's total arable land. The soil pollution places threats on ecological environment, food security, and sustainable development in agriculture.

"China's population, resources, and environmental capacity have reached the limits of support."[17] Water pollution in Songhuajiang River, the "algae incident" in Taihu Lake, the "arsenic incident" in Hunan Yueyang, and other serious environmental damages continue. If the environmental problems are not actively responded to, risks today might turn into future disaster. As a matter of fact, climate conditions in China and other parts of the world are deteriorating. China's frequently encountered natural disasters, such as drought, floods, snowstorms and so on, have sounded the alarm of environmental crisis for China's economy.

STRUCTURAL ECONOMICS IN CHINA

Appendix 10.1 Implication and Calculation Method of 21 Measurement Indexes

Index	Implication	Computation Method
Investment Rate	It usually refers to the ratio of GCF to GDP quota formed in a period of time.	(GCF/Expenditure Approach GDP) × 100%
Consumption Rate	It usually refers to the ratio of final consumption expenditure to GDP quota formed in a period of time.	(Final Consumption Expenditure/Expenditure Approach GDP) × 100%
Incremental capital-Output Ratio	It is the inverse of marginal productivity of capital. Incremental capital-output ratio reflects efficiency of investment; the larger the figure, the lower the efficiency.	Total Social Fixed Asset Investment / Augmentation of GDP
Ratio of Housing Price to Income	It usually reflects the average payment capability of residential houses. To some extent, it measures whether the housing prices are too high for purchasers, or whether there is a bubble in the market.	(Floor Space Per Capita of Residential Buildings × Average Household Size × Unilateral Housing Prices) / (Average Household Size × Average Annual Salary Per Capita)
Comparative Labour Productivity in the Primary Industries	It refers to the ratio of output value proportion to employment proportion, indicating the benefit disparity of internal industrial structure and flowing trend of production factor in certain period of time.	Comparative Labour Productivity in the Primary Industries = Proportion of Output Value in Primary Industries / The Employment Rate in the Industry
Energy Consumption Per Unit of GDP	It refers to the ratio of China's energy consumption per unit to India's energy consumption per unit. GDP per unit refers to the energy consumed by every RMB10,000 of GDP. It is the main index indicating energy consumption level and energy saving condition.	China's Energy Consumption Per Unit of GDP/ India's Energy Consumption Per Unit of GDP
Productivity Ratio in Tertiary Industries	It reflects basic tendency of changes in every country's industrial structure, showing the adaptation level between production structure and demand structure.	Added Value in Tertiary Industries / GDP

Integrated Analysis of the Imbalance of China's Economic Structure

(Cont'd)

Index	Implication	Computation Method
Proportion of Particulate Emission Damage in Total GNI	The polluted damage of particulate emission is an estimated from evaluating the effect of exposure of particulate emission on human body.	Damage to the Environment Caused by Particulate Emission / GNI
Proportion of Indirect Financing Fund-Raising	It directly reflects the rationality of the financial system and indirectly indicates the level of financial risks.	The Amount of Fund-Raising in Loans / (The Amount of Fund-Raising in Loans + The Amount of Fund-Raising in Stocks + The Amount of Fund-Raising in Corporate Bonds)
M2-to-GDP Ratio	It measures the degree of excessive liquidity, namely the degree of the flow of money in economic development exceeding actual need.	M2 / GDP
Non-Performing Loan Ratio	Non-performing loan rate is calculated in home currency and foreign currency. It shows the allocation of funds in efficiency of banking system while indicating the focused risks in banking system.	(The Amount of Non-Performing Loans / Various Loans) × 100%
P/E Ratio	It reflects the level of risks in financial markets. Combining both cost and benefits in investment, it indicates the whole picture of stock market development.	Market Value of the Stocks / Earnings Per Share
Share of Loans in Private Enterprise	It indirectly reflects the proportion of loans from financial institutions to invest non-state enterprises.	The proportion of short-term loans to foreign-funded enterprises, private enterprises, individual short-term loans, and short-term loans to township enterprises in total short-term loans of financial institutions.
Inflation Rate	It directly reflects the changes in general price level and indirectly shows the stability of the macro-economic development.	Indicated by Consumer Price Index (CPI)

STRUCTURAL ECONOMICS IN CHINA

(Cont'd)

Index	Implication	Computation Method
Ratio of Urban-Rural Income Per Capita	It reflects the individual income differences between urban and rural residents. It is a comprehensive reflection of urban-rural dual economic structure.	Disposable Income of Urban Residents / Net Income of Rural Residents
Ratio of Agricultural Expenditure to the Added Value of the Primary Industries	It reflects the real standard of agricultural expenditure of each country.	Agricultural Expenditure / Added Value of the Primary Industries.
Ratio of Extremums of Inter-Provincial GDP Per Capita	It refers to the ratio of maximum value to minimum value. It is used to estimate the relative gap of economic development in different regions.	GDP of Three Provinces with the Highest Figures / GDP of Three Provinces with the Lowest Figures
Gini Coefficient	It indicates the quantitative measurement of the differences of income distribution.	Percentage of unequal income distribution among all residents
Ratio of Current Account Balance to GDP	It reflects the difference between import and export of commodities and services, as well as the difference resulting from the international flow of capital, labour and other production factors.	current account balance is the sum of trade balance in international payments and balance of income and current transfer
Ratio of Foreign Exchange Balance to M2	It indicates how the foreign exchange balance affects money supply. The higher the ratio, the more the foreign exchange balance takes in total money supply, which results in excessive liquidity.	Foreign Exchange Balance / M2 Balance
Ratio of Short-Term External Debts	It reflects the maturity structure of foreign debt of a country. Due to high mobility of short-term debt, a high index ratio indicates greater debt risks.	Short-Term External Debts of the Country / Total External Debt of the Country

Appendix 10.2 The Determination Basis of the Normal Range and the Range of Potential Crisis of the 21 Measurement Indexes

Among the five classifications, it is part-and-parcel of determining both the normal range and the range of potential crisis. According to general principles of the index grading classification, the two intervals of upper and lower limits can be determined based on basic theory, international experience, China's reality and some other factors. However, due to the different nature of each indicator, the methods for determining each are significantly different. Specifically, the determining basis of the normal range and the range of potential crisis for 21 imbalance indexes is as below.

In terms of the investment and consumption structures

1. *Investment rate.* According to international experience, the investment rates of a country have usually gone from a low point to a high point, and then dropped to a steady level. Judging from the effect of China's reform and opening-up, an investment rate of 36% to 38% is comparatively appropriate. Therefore, 38% should be set as the upper limit of the normal range, while 45% should be set as the lower limit of the range of potential crisis, considering the investment rates of other East Asian countries sharing similar geographical and cultural traditions with China.
2. *Consumption rate.* The determining principles of consumption and investment rates are quite the same. Both are closely linked, demonstrating a trade-off proportional relation. According to the effect of national economy since China's reform and opening-up, a percentage of over 60% is considered normal; according to the data regarding China's consumption rate, 50% should be set as the lower limit of the range of potential crisis.
3. *ICOR.* According to the trends of China's ICOR and its comparison with that of Japan's and Korea's, 2 should be set as the upper limit of normal range; the investment efficiency would be considered normal. The lower limit of the range of potential crisis is set at 5; any macro-investment exceeding 5 shall be considered extremely low in efficiency.

STRUCTURAL ECONOMICS IN CHINA

4. *Ratio of housing prices to income.* In developed countries, the ratio of housing prices income is normally three to four. In 1998, the State Council clearly stated in its housing reform document that when the ratio is over 4, the owner should have access to housing subsidies. Therefore, the ratio of housing prices income should be lower than 4 in the normal range; according to international experience, a ratio over 7 is classified as the range of potential crisis.

In terms of the Industrial structure

1. *The comparative labor productivity ratio in the primary industries.* In general, the higher the comparative productivity ratio, the greater the labour efficiency is. Judging from comparative labour productivity ratio in the primary industries, developed countries usually have a ratio of 0.5 to 0.7. Therefore, 0.5 distinguishes a normal range. If the comparative labor productivity ratio is above 0.5, it is considered normal. Taking China's high proportion of its agricultural labour force into account, the ratio of comparative labor lower than 0.2 is seen as in potential crisis, which means the economic development will be seriously affected.
2. *Ratio of GDP consumption per unit.* The ratio of GDP consumption per unit in developed countries is much lower than that in developing countries. Hence it would be a disparate comparison to evaluate China against developed countries; China should be compared to developing countries. Both China and India are developing countries with promise; therefore, it is appropriate to compare each with the other. To put it simply, the energy consumption of China and India per unit of GDP should set indicating 1 and below as the normal range, and then follow the 10% differential, respectively determining lower limits of mild, moderate and severe imbalanced ranges. The range of 1.4 times should be put as the lower limit of range of potential crisis.
3. *The proportion of tertiary industries.* Currently, the proportion of tertiary industries in developed countries is normally 60% to 80%, while in developing countries it is 50% to 60%, demonstrating that the level of developed countries is substantially more than the average level of developing countries. As a consequence, the proportion of tertiary industries above 50% should be considered normal, following the 10% differential; 20% should be seen as a critical point of potential crisis range.

Integrated Analysis of the Imbalance of China's Economic Structure

4. *Proportion of particulate emission damage in GNI.* Judging from different income levels of different countries, the higher the income, the lower the index value. According to statistics, middle- and low-income countries maintain an average ratio of 0.8%, with increases in recent years of around 1%, while the world average level maintains around 0.5 percent. Consequently, 0.8% is set as the upper limit of normal range, and according to distribution of international statistics, the range of 1.4% is the lower limit of potential crisis.

In terms of the financial structure

1. *The proportion of indirect financing.* The proportion of indirect financing in financial market-oriented countries is significantly lower than that in financial intermediate-oriented countries. For example, the proportion of indirect financing in the United States is around 50%, while in Japan it is about 70%. Considering the structural feature of China's financial system, concentration of financial risks, and the changing tendency, the range of proportion of indirect financing should be set at less than 70%, while proportion of over 90% should be the range of potential crisis.
2. *M2-to-GDP ratio.* Since the purpose of setting this index is to measure the degree of excessive liquidity, historical changes in the liquidity position should be taken into full account when determining the range of indexes. For example, China started having excessive liquidity in 2001. Coupled with the joint of WTO, the ratio of M2/GDP by the end of 2001 should be taken as the upper limit of the normal range. Since 2007, there has been a growing severity of excessive liquidity, which is mostly shown in the sharp rise in housing prices and over-estimation of the stock market. This has been putting an adverse impact on economic growth. Therefore, the ratio of M2/GDP by 2006 should be set as the lower limit of the range of potential crisis; the ratio below 1.4 should be considered in normal range, whereas the ratio above 1.7 is in the range of potential crisis.
3. *Non-performing loan ratio.* Recently, the non-performing loan ratio in advanced international banks has been less than 5%, thus the normal range of a non-performing loan ratio should be set lower than 5%. For developed countries, a ratio above 10% indicates it is in high-risk range. Considering the special nature of the transitional economy in China and its capability to resist financial risks and historical data in the Southeast Asian financial crisis, the potential crisis range of the NPL ratio should be set over 20%

STRUCTURAL ECONOMICS IN CHINA

4. *P/E ratio (PER)*. At the present time, the PER of the U.S., UK, South Korea, Hong Kong, and other mature markets are in the range of 10 to 20. The average PER of Japan and India is in the range of 23 to 25. Because China's stock market is in developing stage, and there is a certain premium growth, the PER of China's stock market should be set below a ratio of 30, while a ratio above 45 would be in the range of potential crisis.
5. *Ratio of private loan share*. From 1992 to 2007, the average proportion of the non-state economy dominated by private enterprises in industrial added value was above 60%. Considering that the share ratio and economic contribution should basically match, a ratio over 60% would be in normal range, while the ratio below 30% would be in the range of potential crisis.
6. *Inflation rate*. According to international experience, most countries are trying to limit the inflation rate to between 0 and 3%; hence the normal range is within 0 to 3%. In theory, however, an inflation rate higher than 10% is considered to be out of control; 10% is the threshold distinguishing whether the inflation rate is in the range of potential crisis. In addition, when serious deflation takes place, economic development would be severely hampered. Combined with historical experience of economic development, the inflation rate below -3% is also a threshold of a potential crisis range.

In terms of the regional economic structure

1. *Ratio of urban-rural per capita income*. The income gap in developing countries such as India and Brazil is within 2.3, so the threshold point of normal range should be set at 2.3 times. According to the Warning System of Income Distribution launched in 2005 by the Wages Institute of Ministry of Labour and Social Security, the income gap between urban and rural areas in 2003 was 3.23 times, a number which should cause concern. Therefore, the ratio of 3.5 is set to be the critical point of the potential crisis range.
2. *Ratio of agricultural expenditure to the added value in the primary industries*. The index excludes the impacts brought by different nations' industrial structures, generally reflecting the real level of agricultural financial investment of each country. This index in developed countries is normally over 25%, while in developing countries such as India and Brazil, the index is between 9% and 11%.[18] As a consequence, 11% is set as the threshold point of normal range; according to national statistics of low-income countries, less than 5% is considered in the range of potential crisis.

3. *Ratio of extremums of inter-provincial GDP per capita.* In the late American industrialization era, the GDP per capita ratio of 48 states differs from 4.3 times to 5.1 times. From 1992 to 2000, the GDP per capita ratio in 16 regions differs from 3.8 times to 5.6 times, of which the feature of numbers resembles that in the United States. Using India as a reference, a ratio of 4.7 times (the mean) is set as the threshold point of normal range and a regional GDP per capita ratio is at 5 to 6 times. If the relative gap of GDP per capita ratio exceeds the warning level, economic growth will slow down, social conflicts will increase, and political stability will also be affected. As a result, a ratio below 6 is set to be the lower limit of the range of potential crisis.
4. *Gini coefficient.* The Gini coefficient between 0.2 and 0.3 is comparatively even; the internationally recognized warning line of the Gini coefficient is 0.45.[19] Therefore, 0.3 should be the upper limit of normal range, while 0.4 is the critical point of moderate and severe imbalance, and 0.45 is the lower limit of the range of potential crisis.

In terms of the balance of payments

1. *Ratio of the current account balance to GDP.* IMF believes that the ratio of the current account balance to GDP should be below 5%, therefore a ratio less than 5% is set as the normal range. China's ratio of current account balance to GDP has seen a sharp increase since 2005, and by 2006 it reached 9.23%. However, Mexico's financial crisis broke when the ratio went to 7.5%. Consequently, combining changes in China's current account and international experience, a percentage over 8% is identified as the range of potential crisis.
2. *Ratio of foreign exchange balance to M2.* It is generally believed that the ratio of foreign exchange balance to domestic money supply over 25% causes crises. Therefore, a ratio over 25% is considered in the range of potential crisis, and according to relevant data of China's foreign exchange balance to M2, index below 12% is in the normal range.
3. *Ratio of short-term foreign debt.* According to international standards, 25% is the warning line of the ratio of short-term debt to the total foreign debt balance, so that a ratio below 25% belongs to the normal range. At the same time, judging from changes in the short-term foreign debt ratio in China and other countries as well as general international experience, a ratio above 50% is in the range of potential crisis.

Chapter 11

Strategic Orientation of China's Economic Structural Adjustment

STRUCTURAL ECONOMICS IN CHINA

Since the 1990s, while China's economy has maintained rapid growth, the overall imbalance of its economic structure has become increasingly severe and structural problems have attracted growing attention.[1] As the largest developing country, China has become an important driving force of the global economic growth. If economic structural imbalance is not resolved in time, China and even the global economy are likely to pay greater economic and social costs.[2] However, the complexity of China's economic structure predicts that the adjustment will be a very long, gradual, and difficult process, and will require strategies and initiatives in accordance with China's practices. Based on the comprehensive analysis of the evolution of China's economic structure, this chapter presents the overall ideas and strategic initiatives of economic adjustment, and looks ahead to the sustainable issues of economic development in the future.

The General Idea of China's Economic Structural Adjustment

The co-existence of high economic growth and structural imbalance is a unique phenomenon in the economic operation of modern China. It resulted in the decline in the quality and benefits of economic development, the significant increase in environmental costs and social risks, and the serious erosion of the basis of sustainable economic growth. In this complex situation, economic structural adjustment must have positive ideas of resolution.

Principles

Few per capita shares of resources and a fragile ecological environment are the basic characteristics of China's resources and environment. The basic national reality determines that China is supposed to develop in a resource-saving way; however, it has been taking a path of extensive economic growth. This rapid economic growth is achieved mainly though the wide-scale expansion of factors of production and a considerable amount is obtained at the sacrifice of the overload of resources and the excessive pollution of the environment. The predatory exploitation and use of natural resources not only accelerated the depletion rate of resources, but exacerbated the damage to the environment. The fact that investment rates were too elevated for too long, and the allocation tended to flow into capital, has lead to the low ratio of labor allocation and the delayed development of the tertiary industries. That affected the optimization

Strategic Orientation of China's Economic Structural Adjustment

and upgrading of the industrial structure, and ultimately influenced the stability and sustainability of macroeconomic growth. If this extensive mode of economic growth is not changed, it will be difficult to have sustainable development of China's resource environment, and people's livelihood issues will continue to be difficult to solve. In addition, the foundation of the coordinated evolution of economic structure will be damaged, which is bound to aggravate the imbalance of the economic structure. In this context, the goal of economic adjustment is to transform the mode of economic development, changing the extensive development mode of "high energy consumption, high emissions, high pollution" to the intensive development mode of "low energy consumption, low emissions, low pollution." While maintaining a stable and rapid economic growth, China should make efforts to eliminate potential risks in the economic operation and to promote sustainable and coordinated development of the economy, the society and the environment; that is, to achieve "three-dimensional balance." In order to realize the above goal, economic structure adjustment should follow the basic principles below.

First, overall planning and all-around consideration. China's economic structural imbalance involves not only endogenous variables such as investment, consumption, finance, technological progress, and institutional innovation, but also variables outside the economic system such as resources and the environment. The interaction among variables will form a complex, multi-layered network, which will require that economic adjustment adhere to the principle of overall planning and all-around consideration. This principle means that in the process of economic structure adjustment, we should consider both the main contradiction in the macroeconomic performance and the imbalance of all aspects of social reproduction, as well as domestic and international structural imbalance. We should strive to balance the focus adjustment and general adjustment, combine partial adjustment and full adjustment, and coordinate domestic economic adjustment and foreign economic policies.

Second, orderly classification. Economic structure imbalance tends to be the result of imbalance in many areas; the causes and degrees of imbalance in different areas are not the same. Therefore, in order to improve the relevance and effectiveness of the resolution, we should classify unbalanced problems and take different approaches according to different types of imbalance in the process of the resolution and correction of imbalance. As China's economic structure imbalance is a very complicated and systematic project, resolving the problem of imbalance will require enormous costs. Thus, we should also determine the priorities of treatments according to the nature and treatment target of imbalance. The structure imbalance, which affects the entire system and grows more serious, can be placed as the priority.

Third, self-adjustment. It implies: first, in the resolution of the dual imbalance in the domestic economic structure and the external economic structure, we should put the resolution of the domestic imbalance as the fundamental target, because China's external economic structural imbalance is mainly caused by the imbalance of the domestic investment-savings structure; second, in the process of the resolution of economic structural imbalance, China should initiatively promote various policies and measures of adjustment, rather than submit to foreign pressure or blindly copy the West. It is evident that we should also pay attention to international rules and emphasize coordination of the macro-economic policies of our country and other major countries, while stressing the principle of self-adjustment. From the Japanese experience in the 1980s, the appreciation of the yen cannot resolve the imbalance of international payments fundamentally, and may also exacerbate the degree of domestic economic structural imbalance, triggering economic recession. Therefore, China should take the initiative to undertake obligations of a large developing country in the global economic adjustment; however China should also adhere to the national interest as the fundamental starting point and firmly persist in the principle of self-adjustment.

Fourth, combination prevention and control. In the process of economic adjustment, we should consider not only what negative impacts the existing imbalance has on the economy, but what potential imbalance may occur in the future. The principle of combining prevention with control requires that we should have and use foresight to resolve the economic imbalance. For example, the economic growth should be organically combined with the adjustment of the structure, with a focus on handling the investment-consumption ratio. From China's successful experience of stimulating its economic growth after the Asian financial crisis, investment in fixed assets can indeed play a significant role in accelerating the pace of output and restoring economic growth. However, it should be noted that economic growth led by investment alone is not sustainable, and it often results in the imbalance of the investment-consumption ratio and the formation of a large excess capacity. Based on historical experience, it is relatively certain that China's investment will enter a new rapid growth cycle after the introduction of a series of measures to maintain growth. However, whether relevant measures can significantly stimulate consumption remains to be seen. Thus, stimulating domestic demand in the coming period cannot just focus on governmental investment, but must also focus on the promotion of residential consumption, especially the residential consumption in rural areas.

Strategic Orientation of China's Economic Structural Adjustment

Especially after the implementation of the investment policy of RMB4 trillion by the central government in 2008, China should firmly avoid economic growth that is based on the old path of extensive development of "high input, high energy consumption, high emission, and high pollution," and steadily avoid a new round of blind expansion and low-level repeated construction.

Patterns

Regarding adjustment patterns throughout the world, economic structure adjustment can be categorized into two kinds. One is the passive adaptive adjustment, which is a structural adjustment implemented when the imbalance of the economic structure becomes more serious and does severe harm to economic development. Most countries adopt this adjustment pattern amid an economic and financial crisis. The other is the positive strategic adjustment. In terms of features of the national economic structure and the new changing trend of the global economic structure, the country adjusts its economic structure with foresight, so as to bring new opportunities to its economic development. As for the adjustment pattern, whether it is strategic or adaptive, it generally covers industrial policy, fiscal policy, credit policy, labor policy, and legal and administrative measures. In terms of the effect of economic structure adjustment, the adaptive choice is generally remedial, and economic "hard landing" triggers more negative consequences; whereas the strategic adjustment caters to development trend, thus bringing more positive achievements with less efforts. This has been fully confirmed by changes in the development of both the U.S. and Japanese economies in the 1960s and the 1970s, and by the Asian financial crisis in 1997. In the 1960s, with the declining international competitiveness of the manufacturing sector, the U.S. had a serious structural contradiction and a significantly increasing trade deficit with Japan. However, the U.S. government did not pay enough attention to the economic structure adjustment, and continued following the demand expansibility under the guidance of the Keynesian theory, which did not solve the structural contradictions, but instead caused the intensification of aggregate contradictions with the structural contradictions, and the emergence of stagflation. Thanks to the active economic structure adjustment in the 1960s and the 1970s, and the formulation of policies of industrial restructuring in line with its reality, Japan's international competitiveness in knowledge-intensive industries significantly improved, thus promoting the Japanese economy to enter a golden era of growth. The reason for the Asian financial crisis in 1997 appeared to be the impact of international capital, but the root cause was actually that countries in crisis with unbalanced economic structure were unable to withstand the risks brought by the global economic structure adjustment. In reality, prior to the crisis, problems of domestic economic structure in countries such as Thailand, Malaysia and the Philippines were very prominent, but these governments did not pay serious attention to it. Only after experiencing the heavy blow of the financial crisis did Asian countries began to realize the importance of economic adjustment and take actions. However, the initiative and effect of economic adjustment during this time was greatly reduced, which lead to a stagnation in the Asian economy for a long period of time. It is thus clear that the strategic adjustment tends to provide a country's economic development with new vitality and the adaptive pattern tends to miss the opportunity for the economic development.

Since the 1990s, China's economic structure imbalance has turned from moderate to severe, and structural imbalance has become a large bottleneck constraining its economic development. In this case, economic adjustment should be the combination of adaptive restructuring and strategic restructuring. China is supposed to implement the adaptive restructuring in areas with a severe imbalance, while assuming the strategic adjustment to have a more vigorous and sustainable economic growth according to the goal of economic adjustment and the changing trend of the global economic structure. Therefore, whether it is from the perspective of China's present reality, or from international experience and lessons, China will have more costs to pay in the future if it does not seize this restructuring opportunity.

As the largest developing country and economy, the economic adjustment of China is related to the special background of industrialization and marketization; this restructuring has unprecedented complexity and difficulty. The strategic adjustment of economic structure includes broad contents and is a systematic project, rather than a problem of adjustment in a particular economic area. The core idea is to overall adjust and optimize investment-consumption structure, industrial structure, financial structure, structure of international balance of payments, and regional economic structure. We should ensure the combinations of short-term and long-term adjustment, the adjustment of real economy and virtual economy, and the adjustment of domestic economic structure and major economies' economic structure, so as to achieve the mutual coordination and promotion of the optimization of economic structure and economic growth. China's economic structure adjustment must integrate existing problems in the current economic structure with changes in the development of domestic and international environment, thus innovating the adjustment strategies in well-planned, steady steps.

Paths

Theoretically, economic growth has two path choices: positive growth and negative growth. And economic structure has two states: optimization and imbalance; the real economy is a state of combination of economic growth and economic structure. Thus, economic growth and adjustment constitute a two-dimensional coordinate system. The right part of the horizontal axis represents positive economic growth, and its left part represents negative economic growth; the vertical axis represents the optimization (or imbalance) of economic structure, the upper part represents the optimized degree of economic structure, and the lower part the degree of economic structure imbalance (see Fig. 11.1).

Fig. 11.1.   The path choice of the economic structure adjustment

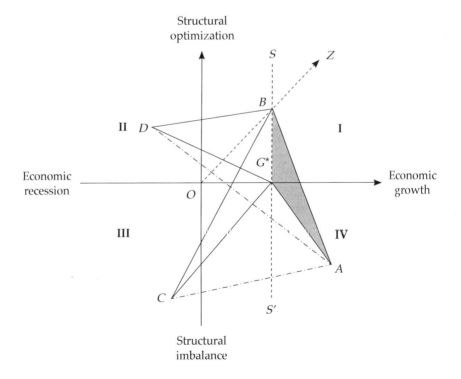

STRUCTURAL ECONOMICS IN CHINA

The plane shown in the Fig. 11.1 can be divided into four quadrants. Quadrant I indicates that economic growth is positive and structure is in the state of optimization,[3] which is an ideal state. *OZ*, the 45-degree line of Quadrant I, indicates that economic growth and structural optimization are in the path of the best balanced development. Quadrant II represents the economy is in recession but that the structure is in the optimized state, which is a transitional state. Quadrant III is the state in which economic recession and structural imbalance coexist; this does a great harm to the economic and social, aspects, among others, and is highly likely to trigger economic and social crisis. Quadrant IV refers to the economy in the positive growth and the structure in the unbalanced state, that is, the state of imbalance and growth. In this quadrant, economic growth is relatively low in efficiency and poor in quality. With a great economic risk, this quadrant is easy to transform into Quadrant III.

In the above coordinate system, assume a country's rate of potential economic growth is G^*. The vertical line of SS' through the horizontal axis of G^* and the best balanced developmental path of *OZ* intersect at Point *B*. Point *B* refers to the best binding point of economic growth and structural optimization, which means that economic growth is in the state of potential growth and economic structural optimization, and the efficiency and quality of economic growth are high. Suppose Point *A* represents that the economy is in the state of imbalance and growth; Point *C* represents the economy is in the state of imbalance and recession; Point *D* indicates the economy is in the state of economic recession and the relative optimization of structure. The adjustment and optimization of economic structure are to achieve the adjustment from Point *B* to Point *B*, from Point *C* to Point *B*, and from Point *D* to Point *B*. in other words, the vector lines of *AB*, *CB*, and *DB* are the optimal paths of economic adjustment. However, in the reality, economic structure cannot be fully adjusted along the optimal path, but can only be gradually optimized in an ideal range. In terms of the economic situations of Point *A* and Point *C*, their ideal *range* of adjustment should be within Triangle ABG^* and Triangle CBG^*. In terms of the economic situation of Point *D*, the pressure is mainly how to promote economic growth, and the ideal range of adjustment is Triangle DBG^*, because of the relatively optimal economic structure.

From the perspective of the economic reality, China's economy is currently in the imbalance-yet-growth state of Point *A*. The economic development in the future may have the following three states. The first state is within Triangle ABG^* and indicates that economic adjustment achieved the established objectives, which are that the rate of economic growth was close to the rate of target growth or the rate of potential economic growth, and economic structure has been optimized. Of course, achieving this path of objectives requires a long period of time. The second state is within Triangle ACG^*, and shows that the effect of economic adjustment was poor and that structural imbalance was increasingly serious, leading to the decline in economic growth or even recession, and the national economy was closer to Point C. That is the most harmful situation. The third state is within Triangle ADG^*, and shows that too much emphasis on optimization of economic structure and the ignorance of economic growth resulted in the rapid optimization of economic structure, but the rate of economic growth was lower than the rate of target growth, recession appeared, and the national economy moved closer to Point D. From the example above, in the dual pressure of domestic and foreign structural imbalance, the best path of China's economic adjustment is to achieve the two-way coordination of economic growth and structural optimization in Triangle ABG^*.

Strategic Measures of China's Economic Structural Adjustment

At this stage, China's economic structural imbalance is very serious, and could further deteriorate. Thus, we should deal with this problem in a positive manner. Following the basic principles of economic adjustment, and based on the accurate grasp of the crux of China's economic structure imbalance, the strategic adjustment of China's economy has been summarized into the following five basic areas.

Structural adjustment strategies of low-carbon economy

Implications

The environmental problem caused by the constant increase of the global population and economic scale has attracted great concern across the world. In this context, a new model of economic development—a low-carbon economy—comes into being. Low-carbon economy advocates the strategic adjustment of energy structure, industrial structure and technological structure. In July, 2007, the U.S. Senate proposed the *Low-carbon Economy Act of 2007*, which indicates that low-carbon economy may become an important strategic choice for the U.S. in the future.[4]

In December 2007, the United Nations Climate Change Conference decided to hold negotiations regarding climate change, and formulated the *Bali Roadmap* to deal with the climate change. It required developed countries

STRUCTURAL ECONOMICS IN CHINA

to reduce emissions of greenhouse gases by 25%–40% by 2020 and played a positive role in driving the world toward a low-carbon future.[5] In 2008, the UNEP established the theme of the World Environment Day as "Kick the Habit! Towards a Low Carbon Economy." This theme aimed to promote energy conservation and use clean energy resources, to reduce emissions of carbon dioxide and other atmospheric pollutants, to develop a low-carbon economy, and to promote sustainable economic and social development.

China's economy is now in its transitional period, but the growing mode of high input, high consumption, high pollution and low efficiency has not yet been changed greatly. Its economic development is confronted with challenges of resource depletion, environmental pollution, and ecological degradation. In December, 2007, the white book *China's Energy Conditions and Policies* highlighted the development of energy diversification and officially listed the development of renewable energy as an important component of the national energy development strategy; this, indicates that China has actively complied with the development of low-carbon economy based on low energy consumption and low pollution. China's future economic development has to seek a balance between industrialization and reduction of greenhouse gas emissions, and the final choice can only be the transformation of the mode of economic growth and active implementation of the restructuring strategy of low-carbon economy.

The so-called adjustment strategy of a low-carbon economy means that in the economic adjustment process, we should improve the quality and efficiency of the economy as a starting point, and continue to reduce the high-consumption and inefficient components in the industrial system through technological innovation and innovation of managing modes. We should also improve the efficiency of the use of resources and promote the sustained and coordinated development of the economy. The implementation of this strategy includes the following three basic contents. First, the restructuring strategy of a low-carbon economy is the fundamental shift in the concept of human survival and development, and it means that the industrial structure changes in an efficient, economical and ecological direction; second, measures of the restructuring strategy of a low-carbon economy are technological and institutional innovations, and it is a profound and extensive change; third, the key of the adjustment strategies of a low-carbon economy is to reduce industrial energy and material consumption, and to improve the quality and efficiency of the economy, thus achieving the optimization of industrial structure.

Strategic Orientation of China's Economic Structural Adjustment

Strategic measures

The adjustment strategy of a low-carbon economy is the internal requirement of a new round of international competitiveness. China should grasp the opportunity to gradually promote the implementation of the new strategy of development according to basic features of the structural imbalance. Through the formulation of industrial, financial, taxation, and other economic policies beneficial to the restructuring strategy of low-carbon economy, China will integrate this strategy into the planning of economic development and a new round of macro-control policies. Specifically, China can adopt the following strategic measures.

First, vigorously develop the circular economy. A circular economy has the principle of reduce, reuse and recycle; the core of improving the efficiency of use of resources; and the focus of resource saving, comprehensive utilization of resources, and clean production. It promotes the use of resources to shift towards the circular mode of "resource—product—waste—renewable resources." This development idea of low input, low consumption, low emission and high efficiency corresponds to the low-carbon economic growth of sustainable development. In order to develop a circular economy, China has to reduce the production of waste from the source, and realize the transformation from the end treatment to the prevention of pollution and the control of the whole productive process. China also has to further reduce the consumption of energy and natural resources, and begin waste recycling and the recovery and use of renewable resources. For example, Japan has enacted a very complete legislation of circular economy. It provides long-term loans at preferential rates through non-profit financial institutions, provides partial financial subsidies from the state treasury, offers encouragement through preferential tax policies, et cetera. China is supposed to learn from the successful experience abroad, and emphasize the development of technologies and equipment of reduction, reuse and recycling, while completing relevant legal and institutional measures to create conditions for the development of circular economy.

Second, improve the abilities of technological transformation and innovation. The implementation of development mode of a low-carbon economy depends on the core link of the improvement of technological transformation and innovation. Through technological innovation, we can gradually reduce the over-reliance of traditional industries on fossil energy, develop low-carbon industries and products with limitations, and eliminate high-carbon industries. The government can encourage the development of the low-carbon industry by the formulation of tax policies of high-carbon energy, high-carbon industry and high-carbon products, promoting the low-carbon industry to be an emerging industry from which entrepreneurs can benefit. The research and development of low-carbon technology is an important part of the innovation of industries and technology. The establishment of carbon funds can encourage the research and development of low-carbon technologies, help companies seek business opportunities involving low-carbon technologies, and develop and foster markets of low-carbon technology in order to promote long-term reduction of emission and fully realize low-carbon economic development. In countries with trade in carbon emission, governments provide businesses with licenses which all have emission standards permitted. If the actual emission is higher than the standard, companies must pay for the emission from other companies whose actual emission is lower than the standard, so they have two choices—increasing technological innovation to reduce emission or eating their own bitter fruits. Because transactional prices get higher and higher, most companies choose to innovate their technologies, so that the total amount of emission will gradually decrease and the energy efficiency of the whole society will gradually increase.

Third, establish the incentive mechanism of energy saving. Since there is a close relationship between the development of energy and environmental protection, most countries in the world set the environmental protection as an important goal for their strategy of energy. Carbon tax, sulfur dioxide tax, and other taxes of energy and environment implemented by western European countries are all formulated in accordance with their economic systems, resources, laws and regulations, and needs of social development. Those taxes can encourage consumers to conserve energy, stimulate the development and use of renewable energy and resources, optimize the structure of energy consumption, and reduce emissions of carbon dioxide and other environmental pollution. According to the Integrated Prevention of Pollution and Programs of Control, the British government and companies can enter into voluntary protocols of standards of carbon emission. If standards of companies' emissions reach standards regulated in protocols, companies can reduce the tax of energy consumption by 20%; if not, they have to pay 100% tax for energy consumption. On the contrary, if companies do not sign the protocol with the government, even if they reach the standards, they also have to pay 100% tax for energy consumption. China can learn from this practice, and accelerate the establishment of an energy-saving incentive system. In addition, China can also increase its support in major investment projects of resource conservation and environmental protection by providing discount loans, free financing, for example, and promote the commercialization of energy-saving technologies and their rapid spread by bulk purchases or government procurement.

Fourth, further optimize industrial structure and rationally allocate resources. China should develop a scientific and sustainable strategy of industrial restructuring, and guide the rational and optimized resource allocation. While upgrading technologies of the secondary industries, China should develop the primary and tertiary industries. Consolidating the basic status of agriculture, it should adhere to agricultural modernization with Chinese characteristics, and accelerate the construction of new a socialist countryside and the coordinated development of urban and rural areas, which provides continuous power for the expansion of domestic demand. Vigorously developing the tertiary industries, especially the development of high-value-added services, can not only expand channels of employment, but also benefit the optimization and upgrading of industrial structure and enhance the industrial competitiveness of the country.

Strategies of consumption-oriented economic structural adjustment

Implications

Judging from the developing process of the global economy, a consumption-oriented economic model in developed countries is rather obvious and prevalent; clearly most developing countries tend to move from an investment-oriented economy to a consumption-oriented economy. Practice has proven that consumption realizes values of products and services. On the other hand, the growth of consumer demand and the upgrading of a consumption structure provide new space for production and economic growth. Therefore, consumption in economic growth plays a fairly important role; only the high-growth, on the basis of sustained growth in consumption, is the stable pattern of economic development.

The overall idea of a consumption-oriented economic adjustment strategy is to promote the general consuming ability of society by adopting an active employment policy, income distribution policy, and social security policy. In this way, it promotes positive transformation from saving to consuming, thereby continuingly increasing the consumption level, upgrading the technology of products and services, improving overall social supply, and simultaneously realizing positive economic development and social progress by fully sharing the fruit of economic growth within the whole society. China's current GDP per capita has now exceeded USD2,000. When GDP per capita is between USD1,000 and USD3,000, development of entertainment-oriented consumption is on the rise. In fact, since the Asian financial crisis in 1997, China has been focusing on improving the level of domestic consumption, but it is not ideally effective.

STRUCTURAL ECONOMICS IN CHINA

The Party's 17th Congress has made it clear to adhere to the expansion of domestic demand (especially consumption demand), and to promote economic growth by transforming from being reliant solely on investment and exports to being reliant on coordinated consumption, investment and exports.[6] This idea has shed light on the direction of investment consumption adjustment. To fundamentally correct China's imbalanced investment consumption structure and growing model, implement the scientific concept of development, and realize sustainable socio-economic development, it is necessary to adopt the consumption-oriented economic structure adjustment strategies as guiding the ideology of the economic development and structural adjustment.

The so-called consumption-oriented economic structure adjustment strategy refers to establishing a consumption-oriented economy in the adjustment process of economic structure. It promotes consumption growth and increases the consumption capability of the whole society. At the same time, it keeps optimizing the investment-consumption ratio, advancing a sustainable and balanced macro-economy development. Those adjustment strategies include three aspects: first, consumption should be the starting point of production. Structure and investment scale should coincide with basic requirements of consumption scale and structure. Second, people's consumption capabilities should be enhanced, making consumption the pillar force of economic development. In addition, the investment-consumption ratio should be maintained with dynamic optimization. Consumption-orientation highlights the control of the total demand and keeps balance of social supply according to actual situation of national economy.

Strategic measures

Currently, China is in the ascending stage of industrialization and urbanization and is still some distance from establishing a fully-fledged economy. Investment continues to be rather important to economic growth. Therefore, the adjustment of the consumption-oriented economic structure adjustment still needs to experience a process in which consumption and investment are both developed. There should be more contribution of consumption in economic growth, and ultimately an efficient consumption-oriented economic development model will appear. Specifically, China can take the following strategic initiatives.

The first step is to implement employment promotion policies. Employment is the fundamental guarantee of consumption growth. China's implementation of active employment policy has achieved positive results, but the employment problems are still rather severe. Judging from past international experience,

Strategic Orientation of China's Economic Structural Adjustment

increasing employment policies is a great asset. The Clinton administration took the policy of enhancing labor market flexibility and promoting employment, and remarkable achievements were made. Unemployment rate fell from 7.5% in 1992 to 4.5% in 1998. Learning from this observation, China should effectively establish a unified national labor market system. Various forms of employment should be encouraged and workers' ability and quality should be improved.

The second step is to diminish the gap of income distribution of the whole society. In theory, the more unequal a country's income distribution, the lower the consumption level. Higher income means lower marginal consumption propensity. That is, with the increase of income, the proportion of consumption gets smaller, thus decreasing the balanced national consumption level. China's current income distribution gap has reached the internationally recognized warning line. The government needs to adjust the income and wage levels through tax levers, gradually setting up a mechanism of the labor price market and stable income, enhancing the living allowance for low-income groups. The government also needs to raise the threshold of personal income tax, yet lower the tax burden of the middle class people. For example, in the United States, 1% of the population possesses 25% of the savings, but pays 28% of personal tax income. Relying on improving the income distribution gap to promote consumption is an important strategic practice, which will bring more than one promising effect.

The third step is to improve the social security system. Improving the social security system is important to enhance the stability of consumption expectations and promote consumption growth, and it is also important to strengthen social security. Both developed countries and developing countries have attached great importance to the building of the social security system. At present, China's social security system coverage and level of protection are still relatively low. China should accelerate the improvement of public finances and establish a healthy social security system. In particular, China should explore social the security system in rural areas, focusing on a minimum living standards guarantee of groups of landless people in rural areas. Also, the government should establish a rural endowment insurance system as soon as possible, strengthening basic medical care in rural and remote areas. In the meanwhile, China should establish an unemployment insurance system, an industrial injury insurance system and a medical security mechanism for migrant workers, as well as improve their actual spending power.

The fourth step is to reduce the proportion of government savings. At present, the Chinese government still has a comparatively large saving scale. Government's investment is of high proportion, which is not conducive to

STRUCTURAL ECONOMICS IN CHINA

improving investment efficiency and quality. Currently, the Chinese government's savings takes about 6% of the total GDP. Compared to 0.3% in France, 1.5% in India, -0.9% in the United States, and -2.2% in Japan,[7] China's savings' share in the GDP is rather high. Consequently, some investment spending should shift to investing in the construction of public goods, social security, poverty alleviation, education, healthcare, and environmental protection. Thus, it can help boost consumption and enhance consumers' confidence.

The fifth step is to foster the consumption growth pole. With the gradual improvement of economic development and income levels, people's upgraded consumption will improve the production structure and supply structure of the whole society. As a result, technology will improve and the society will develop. In different period of different countries, an appropriate growth pole of consumption is fostered. For example with the entry of the 21st century, digital consumption has become the mainstream in Japan, promoting relevant consumption and industry to develop. Currently, China has entered into an entertainment-oriented consumption stage, but the level of consumption still varies widely. Therefore, there should be positive service consumption that orients toward a higher income class, promoting new spending consumption development. The consumption growth pole in rural areas, especially in central and western China, should also be fostered, so that it can promote the balanced development of urban and rural consumption.

The sixth step is to improve the consumption environment. Consumption environment promotes the growth of consumption. Different countries have different consumption culture. South Korea raises the slogan "healthy consumption is virtue" to encourage residents to expand consumption. China has a traditional culture of being thrifty. However, in this new era, an outdated consumption concept should be replaced by modern and civilized consumption habits. The culture of consumption should have more values and meanings, advocating a modern consumption behavior. Additionally, certain legislation and systems in this field should be constructed as soon as possible, particularly the system of personal credit evaluation. In this way, a positive atmosphere of integrity can be created, and consuming credit can be promoted and consumption will become more convenient and more efficient.

Strategies of market-oriented financial structural adjustment

The implication of the strategies of market-oriented financial structural adjustment

There are no simple similarities between the level of economic development and financial structure. Some developed countries are financial-market-oriented with direct advanced financing, such as the U.S. and UK. Some are bank financing–oriented with indirect advanced financing, such as Germany and Japan. That is also the case in developing countries. Both models of financial development have examples of success and failure; there is really no clear comparison between market-oriented financial structure and intermediary-based financial structure. The key is whether it is possible to balance financial structure and economic development. For developed countries, since the market economic structure is not yet completed, bank-oriented financial structure is comparatively more advanced than market-oriented financial structure. For countries with a mature market, the advantages of market-oriented financial structure are better presented because of the strong function of error-correction and financial discovery.

Currently, financial industry is at a turning point. On the one hand, with the deepening of financial globalization and financial innovation, the world's financial markets are more closely linked. International financial competition has become increasingly fierce, calling for adjusting and optimizing the financial structure with an international perspective. On the other hand, with the deepening and completing of the market economic system, financial reform needs improvement and innovation needs to speed up. Those two aspects are related to financial market problems, so that the market has become the basic orientation of the stage of financial restructuring. It is also worth emphasizing that compared to countries with a mature market economy; China's economic market still has a long way to go. The financial market exists to make financial transactions so that both sides continue to "bargain" and interest rates can fully reflect the situation of capital market supply and demand. To make sure both trade bodies are motivated to "bargain" and follow the principle of market-based price, an incentive system should be established to adapt to the market-oriented reform. In this case, the financial restructure should employ a market-oriented financial restructuring strategy.

The market-oriented financial structure adjustment strategies imply that financial reform must adhere to the markets' orientation. An incentive system that fits the market rules should be set up in order to improve the guidance of the interest and exchange rate. The ability to fix prices should be improved in the financial market, so as to encourage financial innovation. A multi-layer financial market system should be established and perfected. The market-oriented financial restructuring strategy includes three aspects: first, financial trading subjects enjoy decision-making autonomy. Financial trading subjects should have the right to bargain over the scale, interest rate, repayment period, and method of guarantee of the financial transaction. In particular, the term structure and risk structure should be decided by market behavior. Second, the basic function of market mechanisms for the interest rate and exchange rate should be given full play. The sensitivity and flexibility of the interest rate and exchange rate should be gradually increased. Third, market-oriented financial restructuring strategy does not propose to give up government's financial regulation, but to emphasize the inner requirement of financial control fitting in market economic development. That means more financial regulation should be adopted as economic levers to regulate the economy. In the abovementioned three aspects, financial institutions' price-setting is the micro-foundation of the market-oriented financial restructuring strategy. Interest rate and exchange rate are at the core of market mechanism, and financial macro-control is the basic guarantee of the restructuring progress.

Strategic measures of the market-oriented financial structure adjustment

According to market-oriented financial restructuring strategy, financial restructuring and optimization at this stage should continue to adhere to a gradual approach in the reform. In the course of deepening banking reform, the financing system should be accelerated and market-oriented interest reform should be steadily promoted. The RMB exchange rate mechanism needs improving. Specifically, China at this stage should take the following strategic initiatives.

The first step is to accelerate the establishment of the financing market system. With the improvement of the economic market, the bank-oriented system of indirect financing can no longer meet the needs of economic development; it requires accelerated construction of the relevant financial market system to promote stocks, bonds and other directing financing development. Market-oriented financing restructuring strategy does not mean that China has to build up a financial system based on the financial market, but that market system shall play an important role in adjusting the financial structure. In fact, with the advancement of information technology, financial innovation, and the progress of financial globalization, the evolution of the world's financial structure is not a substitution problem of the dominant model of financial intermediation and the financial-market-driven model anymore. The key is how to promote finance and economy to develop coordinately within the market system. In reality, those two models are constantly developing together. In countries with developed banking industries such as Germany and Japan, the power of the financial market is evidently increasing. However, in countries with developed markets such as Britain and America, financial intermediary institutions are changing. For example, the U.S. banking industry increases its ability in all-around strength; the importance of banking is emphasized. It is obvious that to accelerate the establishment of the financing market system does not mean to substitute an intermediary with a financial market, but to perfect the balanced development of finance and economy. Therefore, China's deepening financial market reform also calls for financial innovation, focusing on the bond market, and enriching the levels of the financial market. And thus the balanced development of financial market and financial intermediary can be realized.

The second step is to steadily promote the marketization of interest rates. The process in the United States took 13 years, while the process in Japan took nearly 20 years. It is evident that the marketization of interest rates is a long-term process. China's financial system is still rather fragile and the potential risk of financial reform is higher than expected. Consequently, this reform must follow an incremental pattern. On the basis of liberating the upper limit of loan interest rate and lower limit of saving interest rate, China gradually established the Shibor of the benchmark interest rate market position. In this way, the formation of the system that decides by market demand and supply, and is manipulated by the central bank, can be established and perfected. The financial institutions' ability of setting interest rate prices should be enhanced. The focus of marketizing the interest rate should be transferred from regulating agencies to market subjects who participate in deciding on the market interest rate.

The third step is steadily promoting exchange rate formation and foreign exchange management market-oriented reform. Since the RMB exchange rate formation mechanism reform, the RMB exchange rate fluctuations gradually increased, reflecting the market supply, demand and expectations. However, with the changes in domestic and international economic situation and China's deepening economic integration into globalization, the function of RMB's exchange rate as the main tool for regulating needs improving. At the present time, due consideration of the strategy should be given to stabilize the expected appreciation of the fundamental role of RMB exchange rate formation. But, China's current mandatory exchange settlement system increases the central bank's sterilized intervention in foreign exchange pressure and operational costs, although it is conducive to the unified management of foreign exchange revenue and expenditure. The risks of enterprises and banks should be shifted to the state. Thus China should gradually promote an exchange settlement system, so that businesses and citizens can hold and use foreign exchange more conveniently. Doing so would enable the foreign exchange supply and demand to be rationalized, turning from "foreign exchange possessed by the government" to "foreign exchange possessed by the people."

The fourth step is to steadily promote financial institutional integrated operations. Since the 1980s, international financial institutions have seen the traditional commercial banking business and securities, insurance and other financial products grow in a convergence trend. For example, Japan is a typical representative country that has separate operations. On October 1, 2005, Mitsubishi Tokyo Financial Group and UFJ merged into a financial holdings company called Mitsubishi UFJ Financial Group (MUFG). Until then, Japan's financial institutions achieved a formation turning from independent financial institutions to integrated financial institutions. Nowadays, China can explore integrated business organizations such as financing holding companies and other appropriate organizations. Financial institutions can also be encouraged to develop integrated businesses. At the same time, in the process of promoting the integrated management, certain systematical arrangement and coordinate mechanisms should be perfected. Possible cross-sector risks and cross-market risks should be prevented; conflicts of interest that may exist should be properly handled and coordinated.

Strategies of coordination-oriented regional economic structural adjustment

Implications

Coordinated regional development is a major socio-economic development issue that all countries in the world face. In order to diminish the economic development gap between regions, countries usually support the economic development of less-developed regions through legislative, fiscal, and financial approaches, so that wrong market mechanisms in space allocation of resources can be corrected and inter-regional equity can be maintained. For instance, the U.S. government adopted a "public land" policy in the implementation of the development of its western regions. Land was a type of bait to attract a large number of European and eastern U.S. capital, driving off a heated wave of western migration, thereby contributing to western economic development. Japanese government established the Hokkaido Development Finance Corporation in 1956, specifically providing financial support for the Hokkaido region's economic development. The European Union established the European

Strategic Orientation of China's Economic Structural Adjustment

Regional Development Fund in 1975, dedicated to assist the less-developed areas.

Regional economic development theory has fully demonstrated that, along with the continuous development of the regional economy, these based on the theory of a non-equilibrium model of development of regional priorities (such as growth pole theory and theory of point-axis) will face two major bottlenecks in the development process: First, some of the limitations of the region itself will gradually expose, such as the rising labor costs and insufficient supply, et cetera. Second, if the surrounding areas cannot keep up the pace of development, these areas may become isolated economies that find it difficult to maintain long-term sustainable development. Therefore, in order to maintain long-term viability of regional economic development, the original non-equilibrium model of development should be upgraded to a non-balanced and coordinated development model. It must adhere to some of the regional economic development priorities, and adopt a positive approach to conduct imbalanced regulation in order to achieve an overall rapid, healthy and sustainable development of the economy.

As a developing country, China has long had a serious urban-rural dual structure, so the problem of unbalanced regional economic development is rather conspicuous. In recent years, China has continued to promote the regional development among urban and rural areas by drawing economic policies. But the win-win cooperation mechanism among urban and rural areas has not been fully established; rural economic development is weak and the gap between developed areas and less-developed areas is still large. In some regions, social conflicts are even intensified. In this context, the implementation of the coordinated development of regional economic structure adjustment has become an inevitable choice.

The strategies of coordination oriented regional structure adjustment center on the basic principles of market-orientation, thus motivating the whole region, especially the less-developed ones, by methods of legislation, tax, and finance, so that regional differences can be maintained in a stable manner, ultimately realizing their co-development. The strategy includes three meanings: first, the coordinated development of regional economies should be based on the market principles. Policies, measures and instruments must comply with market rules. The areas of market failure should include policy intervention, and this government intervention must be transparent and efficient. Second, the regional economic development should fully realize its comparative advantages, achieving rational division of labor, complementary advantages and common development in different regions of the whole economy. Third, coordinated regional economic development does not mean the absolute elimination of the economic gap, but emphasizes the gap in socio-economic stability and development being controlled in bearable range, gradually narrowing down the gap and eventually achieving coordinated development.

Initiatives

According to the basic premise of the coordinated regional development of economic adjustment strategy, combined with the degree and trends of imbalanced regional economic structure, the adjustment and optimization of China's regional economic structure at the present stage should promote the equalization of basic public services, enhance the economic development ability, improve functions of district compensatory mechanism, and guide the rational flow of production factors. Specifically, China can take the following strategic initiatives.

The first step is to improve the financial transfer payment system in less-developed areas. Targeted subsidies of national transferred payments are mainly the less-developed areas with a lower-than-average GDP per capita. For example, in the implementation process of the German transfer payments, the federal and state financial departments first estimated "average tax amount of the national residents" and "average tax amount of the state residents." If the "average tax amount of the state residents" exceeds 2.0% more than the "average tax amount of the national residents," the state is a wealthy state. If the ratio is less than 95%, it is a less-developed state. Accordingly, the wealthy states are obliged to hand over part of the revenue to the federal government, and the less-developed states have the right to obtain federal funding from the wealthy ones. In 1994, after China adopted the reform of the tax system, although the central government focused on the significant increase in revenue, financial resources used to adjust the gap between regions were still limited, so that the financial transfer payment system cannot effectively control the widening gap of fiscal ability among regions. Therefore, in order to reduce regional differences of financial resources and to achieve regional equalization of basic public services, the scope of government powers at all levels should be scientifically divided. The financial and taxation system should continuously improve, and the focus should be to improve the proportion of the central government transfer payments on less-developed areas, making the less-developed regions have sufficient financial resources to provide roughly the national average of public services.

The second step is to improve the industrial transfer and inter-regional coordination mechanism of interest. China initially formed the eastern industrial region, and although the central and western regions' capacities of undertaking industrial gradient transfer are relatively weak, there has been a move toward those areas. This is due in part to the rising costs of eastern coastal areas' land and labor, and reducing capacity of the environment. However, due to relatively independent regional interests of inter-provincial and city-level districts, the interest demands of industrial area and transitional area often could not reach agreement in the transfer process, and instead would resort to conflicts of interest, blocking effective transfer of the industry. Thereby, China should establish and improve the inter-regional and regional industrial gradient transfer mechanism between the economic interests of coordination mechanisms, in an attempt to build a good public service platform for the industries in the transferred areas.

The third step is to improve the supporting measures of "the main functional areas," a new concept proposed in the national eleventh five-year plan. As the concept denotes, the Chinese territory is divided into four main functional areas: the optimized development area, the key development areas, restricted areas, and prohibited development areas. The classification of main functional areas indicates that not all the regions should make efforts to promote economic development, which would help coordinate resources and the environment and economic development. On the basis of reasonable division of main functional areas, China should primarily accelerate the establishment of related legislation, determining the legal range and standard of the main functional areas. In fact, developed countries generally have certain laws of national land development. For example, Germany's content and principles of its national land space planning responsibilities are all deliberated by the "Spatial Planning Law" and "Building Code." In addition, developed countries take measures such as the tax incentives, financial subsidies, and financial support to back up the economic development of less-developed areas. During the mid-1950s to the mid-1970s, Italy established an income tax preferential policy for new plants settled in the southern area, which promised a ten-year exemption from income tax. This policy helped Italy to promote economic development and industrialization process in the southern areas. In 1964, France established a regional development award to financially reward enterprises that carried out business activities in less-developed areas. China can learn from the experience and practices of those developed countries in promoting economic development, exploring the means to establish market-oriented ecological compensation patterns and regional co-ordination of ecological compensation, and directing all walks of society to become involve in environmental protection and ecological construction.

The fourth step is to establish and improve a sound and long-term supporting mechanism of rural socio-economic development. While China makes efforts to increase government support in agricultural sector, the national income distribution and expenditure structure should be rationalized, forming the financial-support agriculture policy system and stable growth mechanism of funds for supporting agriculture. A public finance system of the establishment of rural education, healthcare and other social development should be accelerated in the construction of public service system. The management system and input mechanism of rural compulsory education should be adjusted to and improved. In agricultural subsidy policies, rural economic development should not only be supported by direct means such as financial subsidies, transfer payments and other direct means, but also by indirect means such as financial discount policy, establishment of politically guaranteed funds, agriculture-related tax preferential and, other indirect means. The *Rural Economic Development Promotion Act* should come out as soon as possible, so as to provide legal protection for rural economic development.

Balanced-management structural adjustment of the balance of payments

Implications

According to the theory of international balance developmental stage,[8] with the development of a country's economy, its international revenue and expenditure structure generally go through four stages: the first is immature stages of the debtor countries, the main features of which are more imports than exports, and there is strong demand for foreign capital. In this stage, current account deficit and financial account surplus co-exist. The second is a mature stage of the debtor countries, the main features of which are falling foreign trade deficit which gradually turns into a surplus. Foreign demand declines, export of capital increases, international balance of payments is roughly even, or the amount of current deficit and a capital and financial account surplus co-exist. The third is immature creditor stage, the main features of which are increasing foreign trade and international capital inflows becoming net outflow. The structure of international balance is the co-existence of current account surplus and capital and financial account deficit. The fourth is mature creditor stage, the main features of which are deficit in goods trade, surplus in investment income and service income, a relatively large amount of capital inflow and outflow, and the international revenue and expenditure structure is roughly double-balanced or co-exists of a small current account surplus and a capital and financial account deficit. Using the above criteria, China's current international balance is on the transition from the second stage to the third stage. Therefore, for a long period of time in the near feature, the structure of international balance will be gradually moved from the balance of payments current account and the capital and financial "double surplus" to "surplus deficit."

However, transition in the structure of international balance is not solely an issue of foreign economic adjustment, but also an issue of domestic economic adjustment. Therefore, the adjustment of the international balance structure must rely on the domestic economic adjustment, and keep in accordance with investment and consumption structures, industry structure, and financial structure. At the present time, China's imbalanced international balance structure is widening, continually accumulating external financial risks. Under this kind of circumstance, the international balance structure should take a balanced managerial adjustment strategy.

The balanced-management-type strategy of restructuring of the balance of payments means that the restructuring of China's balance of payments should adhere to the self-oriented basic principle to achieve an appropriate scale of the surplus of the balance of payments and the structural optimization. This should be done on the basis of reasonable control of the excessive growth of the "double surplus" of the balance of payments by adjusting the policies of industry, trading, foreign capital, and by using the means of legality, price, credit, tax, and control. It has two meanings: first, the balanced-management-type strategy of restructuring of the balance of payments means the neither the balance of a simple amount nor in a simple sense, but the adaption of the balance of the balance of payments to the domestic economic development. Second, the balanced-management-type strategy of restructuring of the balance of payments is a managed one. During the process of achieving the balance, the government should take active encouragement or restriction.

Initiatives

In the situation of the changes of the present balance of payments, despite the turmoil in the international finance and the increase of the downside risks to the global economic growth, the external conditions for supporting China's export growth have not undergone fundamental changes; therefore, it is difficult to change the surplus of trade in a short time. At the same time, due to the positive trend of economic growth and a continuous appreciation of RMB, China is still one of the most attractive countries for long-term international capital. There will be a surplus between China's capital and the financial account in the short term; however, once the appreciation of RMB has reached its maximum and the exchange rate has entered the period of two-way fluctuation, those with international capital in pursuit of the interests of the appreciation of RMB will flow out of China. Moreover, coupled with the expansive scale of foreign

STRUCTURAL ECONOMICS IN CHINA

investment, a deficit of China's capital and the financial account may occur. Based on the balanced-management-type strategy of restructuring of the balance of payments, China's adjustment and optimization of the balance of payments should aim to solve the imbalance of the domestic economic structure, adjusting the import and export strategies and foreign trade policy while bringing the exchange rate into the adjustment of the balance of payments, actively and orderly expand the foreign direct investment, and continuously strengthen the management of capital in order to achieve a balanced balance of payments. Specifically, China can take the following strategic initiatives.

The first is to change the concept and the implementation of the "double balance" management strategy, which means the balance in both the foreign trade and the capital flows. The concept of "the larger the balance of payments and the scale of the foreign exchange reverse, the better" should be changed. The surplus in large scale and for a long term is also a manifestation of imbalance. On the one hand, the management strategy of "heavy export but light import" should gradually be changed to the balanced management strategy of "heavy export and import." On the other hand, the balance management strategy of the inflow and outflow of capital should be gradually established. The management strategy in the area of direct investment of "easy inflow but hard outflow" should be changed to "hard inflow but easy outflow" in order to further deepen the management strategy of "controlled inflow and no outflow" to the international capital.

The second is the active use of the industrial policy and price to adjust the structure of the current account. China needs to restrict the export of the goods of "two highly and one type" (highly polluted, highly energy-consumptive and the resource-type), gradually reduce the export tax rebate rate of the commodities with low added value or those that are simply processed, offer more favorable terms to the export of the products with the capability of independence, innovation and creation, and take full use of the price signals and the industrial policies to adjust the structure of export commodities. Additionally, China should further improve its import tax policy, speed up trading facilitation, establish the import trade developing funds, and encourage the enterprises to expand the scale of importing the advanced technology, the key equipment, the insufficient domestic energy, and the raw materials. With regard to the service trade, China has to put forth efforts for the development of tourism and transport, finance and insurance, and information and technology services in order to become internationally competitive.

The third is the optimization of the direct investment structure. The key to solving the surplus of the capital account is to adjust the structure of direct

Strategic Orientation of China's Economic Structural Adjustment

investment, thereby enhancing the efficiency of the direct investment. The direct investment here includes two aspects: the foreign direct investment in China, and China's foreign direct investment. On the one hand, China needs to strengthen the macro-control of the scale of the foreign direct investment in China to optimize the structure of the foreign direct investment. The aim of China's absorption of the FDI should not be only for the capital, but more importantly, to develop the market competition mechanism and to introduce the advanced foreign technology and management experience. For this reason, China should cancel the super-national treatment to foreign investors, but reasonably guide the foreign direct investment into the high-tech industry and the modern service industry, and give full play to the active role of the foreign direct investment in the upgrading of China's industrial structure. China should also continue to develop its strategy of "going out" to improve the enterprises' voices in the global economy. Meanwhile, China has to actively explore the operation of the investment of the sovereign wealth fund to innovate the models and channels of China's foreign direct investment.

The fourth is the continuous strengthening of the supervision of capital. China should establish the formal coordination mechanisms involving the relevant departments, strengthen the inter-departmental communication and exchange of information, restrict the management of the inflows and outflow of the capital (especially the short-term capital), strengthen the statistics, monitoring, and punishment of the violations of the cross-border capital flows the. At present, China needs to pay extra attention to the large-scale outflows of foreign capital, while continuously preventing the influx of speculative capital. There are no reliable statistics regarding the inflows of short-term capital, but the scale of China's inflows of short-term capital in recent years has been expanded by the impact of the soaring stock market, the dramatic increase of the real estate prices, and the continuous high exchange rate of RMB/USD. The stock market's rapid decline, the downturn of the real estate market, and the expectation of the devaluation of RMB in 2008 resulted in the outflows of capital in a large scale. Although China has such massive foreign exchange reserves that even a large-scale capital outflow will not result in the crisis of the balance of payments, this may undermine the stability of China's economic growth; therefore, preventing the large-scale outflow of capital in a short period of time should be the focus of capital control in the future.

The fifth is the strengthening of the inter-governmental communication and collaboration of the balance of payments. Currently, the formation of the "double surplus" of the balance of payments is the result and reflection of the fundamental global economic structural imbalance, rather than a completely inevitable result of the domestic economic imbalance. In this case, it is unfair for some developed countries to blame China's exchange rate system for the adjustment of the global economic imbalance. It is not the solution either. In fact, forcefully adjusting the exchange rate may change the distribution of the global imbalance in different countries and inter-regions, but it cannot change the overall global imbalance. The adjustment of the balance of payments is related to the vital interests of all countries, but different countries have a certain consensus on the issue of adjustment, i.e., the adjustment of balance of payments should obey the method of symmetrical adjustment. All the countries have to bear the obligation of the adjustment of the balance of payments, regardless of surplus or deficit.

To sum up, China's economic adjustment is a very complex, difficult and long-term task. The five major restructuring strategies above are not isolated, but are an organic whole—the requirements of China's realization of the "three-dimension balance."[9] In the strategic system above, the aims of the low-carbon economic adjustment strategy are to achieve the rational development of resources, control the pollution within the environmental capacity, maintain the growing power of the economy, and achieve the coordinative development of economy and environment. The aims of the consumption-led type of economic adjustment strategy are to maintain the dynamic optimization of the ratio of investment and consumption and to promote the sustainable and balanced macroeconomic development. The coordinately developing regional economic adjustment strategy is related with the rational allocation of income, the aims of which are to share the fruits of economic development with the residents, and prevent the gap between rich and poor. The market-oriented financial restructuring strategy and the balanced-management-type strategy of balance of payments are related with the stability of finance, the aims of which are to prevent financial risks and to create a stable financial environment for the development of economy. Thus, the five restructuring strategies should be united in the framework of the coordinated development of economy, environment and society.

Prospects for China's Future Economic Sustainable Development

The strategy of economic adjustment has a far-reaching effect on China's sustainable economic development. At present, the opportunities for China's economic development coexist with the challenges. The momentum of economic growth remains strong and is in the strategic opportunities of development; however, economic development faces dual pressures home and abroad. The external pressure is the adverse impact of the international financial crisis and the internal pressures are the uncertainty and potential risks of the economic growth due to the formation of the economic structure imbalance as well as the great pressure of the environment and resources. To determine China's future sustainable economic development, we should first have an international perspective and observe China's economic trends in the context of economic globalization. Second, we must use a strategic vision to comprehensively assess and balance the positive and negative forces[10] affecting economy, society, and environment and resources, looking ahead of the developing trend of economy and society and planning for the future developing strategies. Lastly, we must think dialectically, employ the thoughts of general contact and motional changes to analyze the deep-seated contradictions of the current economic operation, and fully consider the profound impacts of the economic sustainable development brought by the economic adjustment. Based on the overall analysis of China's economic structure and economic development, we make the following basic judgments of the performances of China's future economic sustainable development.

Sufficient momentum of growth

First, the process of industrialization provides important support for the economic growth. According to the basic law of industrialization and the experiences and facts of developed countries, combined with the evolution of industrial structure, we can determine that China, overall and currently, is still at the middle stage of industrialization. In other words, China's process of industrialization is far from over. A huge demand from the domestic market and the effects of industrial upgrading will stimulate the economy and maintain a high growth rate.[11] Meanwhile, there are great differences in the degrees and structures of industrialization in China's different regions. The transfer of this industry will be beneficial to the potential of the economic growth and to reach a new point of the economic growth.

Second, the high savings rate provides a capital base for the high growth rate. The savings rate has a significant impact on the macro economy. A high savings rate leads to a rapid increase in capital stock, which provides a sufficient guarantee of capital for China's rapid economic growth. The statistics show that since 1992, China's savings rate has been rising, and reached 50% in 2007. Thus, the high savings rate is hard to reverse in the short term. China's high savings rate is not only the internal driving force supporting economic growth in the near future, but also provides the material base for development in the long run.

It will not be changed due to the adjustments of the short-term policy.

Third, there is still a large space for promotion of economic growth by the urbanization. The former vice president of the World Bank, the Nobel Laureate Joseph Stieglitz, said that the two most important factors affecting the contemporary global economy are the U.S. high-tech industry and China's urbanization.[12] During the 30 years since the reform and opening-up, China's urbanization has developed rapidly, but room remains. In 2006, the world's average level was 49%, and 78% for the high-income countries. In 2007, the level of China's urbanization was only 44.9%, indicating that the level of urbanization was still relatively backward.[13] China's increase of the urbanization process in the future is bound to drive the developments of infrastructure, real estate, transportation, and the electric power industry, leaving a positive lasting effect on economic growth. Moreover, the process of urbanization makes the labor continuously transform from rural to urban areas, which not only improves the primary industries and promote the non-agricultural industries, but also accelerates the upgrading of industrial structure.[14] The rapid growth in the demands of the urban investment and the consumption demand drive the growth of society as a whole, offering support for the rapid economic growth.

Finally, the information communication technology (ICT) has become an important factor in promoting economic growth. The rising level of information will inevitably lead to a further development of the industrialization, and the development of the industrialization in turn will facilitate ICT. This will form a cycle in which the ICT will facilitate rapid economic development. China's overall ICT is still relatively low and different regions are at different levels of ICT. There is a giant gap between the levels of ICT and large room for the development of the future ICT. The ICT will become an important factor promoting the economic growth and upgrading the economic quality.

Acceleration of the structural adjustment

The external shocks of the international financial crisis and domestic economic structural imbalance have accelerated China's economic adjustment. China's continued adjustment and optimization of the economic structure adjustment will further promote the productive factors transfer from a low efficient sector to a high efficient sector, injecting new vitality to the economic growth. In this way, China can improve the quality of economic growth and the relationship between economy, society, environment, and resources.

First, economic adjustment will be the main goal of the improvement of the market economy. Since the reform and opening-up, China's system of

Strategic Orientation of China's Economic Structural Adjustment

the market economy has been established and the basic role of the market mechanism in the resource allocation has been reinforced. With the opening-up expanding, China has integrated into the global market system more actively. At present, the reform of China's market economy still holds great potential; the comprehensive and assorted reform will continue to develop. In the near future, the government functions will be changing and improving; reform of the monopoly industries will continue to be promoted in order to increase the economic efficiency; the market-oriented reform of the productive factors will deepen and the efficiency of the factor allocation will be improved; a breakthrough will occur in the financial and fiscal sectors and the capacity of the macro-control will be strengthened; the urban and rural reform will become the new focus and will seriously promote the development of various rural undertakings, and so on. Thus, the future economic structure adjustment will be further developed, directly involving a series of core areas and deep-seated issues of China's economy operation and injecting new vitality into China's future economic growth.

Second, the economic structural adjustment will help improve the quality of the economic growth. Since the reform and opening-up, China achieved a rapid economic growth resulting in a significant increase of the overall national strength and a great improvement of people's living standards in general. However, the massive economic and social transformation has also brought profound economic and social contradictions, as well as bottlenecks in resources and environment, and the prominent imbalance of the development. The basic aim of the future economic adjustment is to change the traditional development approach and solve the unstable, uncoordinated and unbalanced problems in economic development. Through the implementation of the strategies of the low-carbon economic structure adjustment, the consumer-led economic structure adjustment, the market-oriented financial structure adjustment, the coordinated regional economic structure adjustment, and the balanced-management-type structural adjustment of the balance of payments, the economic structure can be reversed from severe imbalance to the area of optimization: the area of the target adjustment. While optimizing the economic structure, a steady economic growth can be achieved, and the pressure on resources and environment can be reduced to promote social harmony. If the above goals can be achieved, the overall quality of China's economic growth will be improved.

STRUCTURAL ECONOMICS IN CHINA

Revitalization of agricultural development

In the 30 years since the reform and opening-up, China has made great contributions to its economic and social development, but the unbalanced development of urban and rural areas has increasingly become a major practical problem. In recent years, the Party Central Committee and the State Council have made it a priority to resolve the issues of agriculture, rural areas, and farmers. The pilot reform of rural taxes has been implemented across the nation since 2003. The policy of "giving more, taking less and getting free" has been discussed, focusing on the fundamental change of the urban-rural dual structures and an overall co-ordination to solve the rural issues. In 2004, the capital used by the central government to solve the issues of agriculture, rural areas and farmers reached RMB262.6 billion, which is more than 3 times that of 1997. Since January, 2006, agricultural tax has been completely abolished throughout the nation to reduce the burden for farmers, at an annual average of RMB120 billion.[15]

But it is undeniable that China's agricultural development and rural development is still at a difficult climbing stage. Agriculture is still the weak link in national economic development. Inadequate investment and a fragile foundation have not changed. The widening gap between urban and rural economic and social development is prominent. The deep-seated contradictions constraining the agricultural and rural development have not been eradicated. Therefore, solving the issue of the agriculture, rural areas and farmers is an arduous task, which offers a lot of room for China's future economic and social development. In fact, with the accelerating pace of traditional agriculture's transformation, the continuous implementation of the policies and measures benefiting the farmers, the continued development of public utilities' construction in rural areas, and an increase of the establishment of the modern rural financial system, China's future rural development will be greatly revitalized.

Rising contribution rate of human resources

The modern economic competition is the competition of the quality of human resources. The quality of human resources provides important protection for sustainable economic and social development. Rich human resources are vital for China's economic development. However, the size and structure of human resources should be coordinated with the level of economic and social development. Only when the human resource synchronizes with the accumulation and development of economic and social development can China secure its sustainable economic development. With China's aging population, the "demographic dividend" will gradually disappear. It is essential to continuously improve the quality of human resources and build a strong human-resources and innovation-oriented country and is possible to achieve from the current developing trend.

The per capita years of education increased significantly. In recent years, government increased their investment in education, and the years of a national education significantly increased. The average years of schooling increased from 7.8 years in 2000 up to 8.4 years in 2007.[16] China's scale and quality of national education has been rapidly improved. This means that China's human capital is at a period of a relatively fast growth, which will offer a strong intellectual support and an increasing contribution rate for future sustainable economic and social development. The quality of human resources will also be effectively improved. Since the reform and opening-up, China's systems of household registration and the labor and personnel have seen a fundamental change. The labor force rapidly flows between urban and rural areas, inter-regions, inter-industries and between different forms of ownership and the marketization of the labor force will continue to increase. In the future, with a gradual establishment of the unified labor market, the quality of the human resource will be improved significantly.

Improvement of social security

Social security is the fundamental system securing the stability of the state.[17] In recent years, China's social security system has been rapidly developed. Till the end of 2007, more than 200 million people have been holders of the national basic pension and the basic medical insurance.[18] But it should be noted that there is a flaw in China's social security system. A rural-urban unified system of social security has not been established; in fact, it has not been established in most rural areas. Except for a trial of the rural social security system in some developed regions, most rural areas have yet to establish the social security system, and a considerable number of workers are excluded from the social security system, which seriously impacts the social equity.

At present, China has made the establishment of a sound social security system as an important livelihood project. The coverage and content of the future social security will be more encompassing, especially the major changes in the systems of rural endowment insurance, the new rural cooperative medical, and the urban and rural minimum living security. The constant improvement of the social security system will help stabilize and improve the income expectations and propensity to consume, and will help stimulate the

STRUCTURAL ECONOMICS IN CHINA

domestic demands—in particular, the consumer demands. The consumption growth will improve the state of people's social welfare and the investment and consumption structures, and will ensure the normal operation cycle of social reproduction, further having a significant positive impact on China's future sustainable economic and social development.

Enhancement of macro-control capability

The strength of the government's macro-control is an important factor for the stable and rapid economic growth, playing an important role in fueling the economic development and preventing relevant risks. In the early 1990s, China began to establish the goals of a socialist market economic system and explore the corresponding macro-control system. After years of effort, the strength and ability of China's macro-control has gradually increased, providing an important safeguard to the steady and rapid development of the national economy.

At this stage, the Chinese government has a strong macro-control, primarily in the following three aspects. First, the government's experience of macro-control has become richer. Since the mid-1990s, China has successfully withstood the Asian financial crisis, and the macro-control system has successfully prevented and overseen the recurring economic overheating and inflation. In recent years, China has organically combined the adjustment of volume and structure, has grasped the development direction, and has therefore guaranteed a rapid economic growth. Second, financial resources have significantly increased, and the scale of revenue has come to a new level. From 1992 to 2007, the average annual growth rate of China's fiscal revenue was up to 19.6% and the portion of GDP was increased from 12.9% to 20.8%, which enabled the country to strengthen the control of the structure imbalance. The significant increase in the expenditure of the environmental protection, the issues of "agriculture, rural areas and farmers," and the less developed regions strengthen the effects of the government's macro-control. Third, the foreign exchange reserves have continued to increase substantially. Until the end of 2007, the national foreign exchange reserves were up to USD1,528 trillion. The substantial increase in foreign exchange reserves makes the Chinese government able to calmly deal with a variety of external shocks and has greatly increased the ability to withstand financial risks. It is foreseeable that China's future ability and strength of macro-control will continue to be consolidated and the ability to withstand the financial and economic risks will continue to be improved.

Strategic Orientation of China's Economic Structural Adjustment

Opportunities and challenges brought by new changes in the international economic environment

Since the 1990s, affected by the new technological revolution, the state transition of the planned economy, and other factors, the world economic order has been undergoing major changes and adjustments, and the trend of multi-polarization is apparent. Especially after the international financial crisis, developing countries have become important forces in the global economic development and new changes in the international economic environment have brought China unprecedented opportunities and challenges.

The financial problems caused by the U.S. subprime mortgage crisis not only exposed that the Western countries, especially the United States, have seriously uncoordinated and unbalanced problems, but also exposed that the international financial system has many deep-rooted disadvantages. Therefore, it is necessary to reform the international financial system. As Chinese Premier Wen Jiabao pointed out at the third China-Russia Economic Forum in Moscow in 2008, "the establishment of new international financial order is a priority and is also at the right time."[19] In the restructuring of the new international financial order, the ample liquidity and rapid stability of the economic development gave China more right to speak and also gave China an indispensable new role in the reconstruction of the world financial order. China can seize the opportunity to size up the situation, to follow the flow and to actively enhance China's rights to know, to speak, and to make rules in foreign trade, economic, and political exchanges.

The international financial crisis is also a serious challenge whose seriousness of the impact cannot be underestimated by China. Since the second half of 2008, affected by the deterioration of the international economic situation, the downward pressure on the Chinese economy has been increased. According to the recent data, the industrial growth declined significantly; the real growth of the investment and export has slowed down; the negative growth has turned up in the revenue; the corporate sales have been sluggish, and the profits have been reduced from the coast areas, the middle sized and small enterprises, and the export industries to the interior, the large enterprises, and other industries. There are indications that the China's economy is likely to experience a U-shaped, moderate adjustment. From a positive perspective, this also provides an opportunity for China's economic adjustment and deep-seated economic reform. For a long time, the economic adjustment could not enter into a substantively strategic change due to the lack of urgency and breakthrough, but the economic downturn provides a reversed transmission of pressure. Only if China has enough sense of potential danger, takes careful measures, grasps

STRUCTURAL ECONOMICS IN CHINA

opportunities from the changing situations, accelerates the transmission of the developing approaches and the structural restructuring, and enhances the ability of sustainable development can they turn "danger" to "security" and change "crisis" to "safety."

In summary, the negative forces hindering the sustainable domestic economic development include of the low efficiency of production, high risk of financial operations, a large gap between the distribution of income, an imperfect system of social security, an inadequate capacity of innovation, and the increased pressures on resources and environment, which can be summed up as a weak foundation of the "three-dimensional balance" of the sustainable economic development. However, the comprehensive judgments of the positive and negative forces affecting China's future economic and social sustainable development show that opportunities and the potential of China's future development outweigh the challenges and difficulties. In fact, most of China's current major problems in the process of development are double-edged swords. On the one hand, there are contradictions and problems existing in the process of realization, which require attention and need to be solved properly. On the other hand, it also shows that there is room and potential for China's economic and social development. Only if we respond actively we can turn the negative forces to the positive forces. Objectively speaking, wishing to achieve the "three-dimensional balance" in economy, society, and environment and resources, as well as maintenance of the sustainable economic development, China has to not only overcome many difficulties but also actively respond to various domestic and foreign issues, conflicts, and risks. This requires us to change the concept of development, innovate and develop models, enhance the quality of development, continue to develop economic adjustment, accelerate technological progress, and build an innovative country to comprehensively promote the harmonious development between nature and human and between human and society.

Notes

Chapter 1

1. Xiang Junbo, "On the Establishment of Structural Economics," *Guangming Daily*, April 7, 1990.
2. Xu Chongwen, *Structuralism and Post-Structuralism* (Shenyang: Liaoning People's Publishing House, 1986), 16.
3. Lance Taylor, *Structuralist Macroeconomics* (Beijing: Economic Science Press, 1990), 1.
4. Jan Tinbergen, *International Economic Integration* (Amsterdam: Elsevier Press, 1965).
5. *Selected Works of Marx and Engels* (Beijing: People's Publishing House, 1972), vol. 2, 82.
6. Dixin Xu, ed., *Dictionary of Political Economy* (Beijing: People's Publishing House, 1980), vol. 2.
7. Joseph Stiglitz, *Economics*, 3rd ed. (Beijing: China Renmin University Press, 2005).
8. Rodrigo de Rato, speech delivered at the Foreign Policy Association Financial Services Dinner, New York, February 23, 2005.
9. "Water Crisis Facing the World," http://big5.xinhuanet.com/gate/big5/news.xinhuanet.com/world/2006-03/16/content_4309747.htm, March 16, 2006.
10. Xiang Junbo, "On the Establishment of Structural Economics," *Guangming Daily*, April 7, 2008.
11. William A. Lewis, *The Economic Growth Theory* (Shanghai: Shanghai Joint House Press, 1994).
12. Raúl Prebisch, "Commercial Policy in the Underdeveloped Countries," *American Review* (1959).
13. Paul Narcyz Rosenstein-Rodan, "Problems of Industrialization of Eastern and South-Eastern Europe," *The Economic Journal* (1943).
14. Ragnar Nurkse, *Problems of Capital Formation in Underdeveloped Countries* (New York: Oxford University Press, 1953).
15. Luigi L. Pasinetti, *Structural Economic Dynamics* (Cambridge University Press, 1993).
16. Irma Adelman, "Beyond Export-Led Growth," *World Development*, 12 (1984).
17. Francois Bourguignon, Branson, W. and de Melo, J., "Adjustment and Income Distribution: A Micro-Macro Model for Counterfactual Analysis," *Journal of Development Economics*, 38 (1992).
18. The computable general equilibrium model is an application model involving multiple sectors and it assumes that no excess, in demand and supply of goods and services exists in the competitive market. It combines production, demand, international trade, and price into an organic unity through the introduction of the optimized behavior of economic agents, depicting the response to the changes in relative price by different industries and consumers in a mixed economic situation.
19. Faye Duchin, *Structural Economics: Measuring Change in Technology, Lifestyles, and the Environment* (Island Press, 1998).
20. Raa, T. T., *Structural Economics* (London: Routledge, 2004).
21. Arnold J. Toynbee, *Mankind and Mother Earth* (Shanghai: Shanghai People's Publishing House, 2001).
22. Report of the World Commission on Environment and Development (WCED), *Our Common Future*, 1987.

Notes

23. Wen Jiabao, "On Important Issues in Current Development," *Qiushi*, 11 (2008).
24. SAM is an economic accounting table in a form of matrix using single-entry bookkeeping to reflect double-entry bookkeeping contents. Using the input-output table, which describes production, national income, and production accounts, SAM depicts the economic cycle of production creating income which results in demand, which leads to production, to express the economic structure and social structure of a country or a region.
25. Neo-institutional economics has three innovations on its original version. The first is an innovation in its analysis method. Old institutional economics employs on the whole the psychological method, while the new version primarily adopts the approach of neo-classical economics. The second innovation is in its basic categories. The old institutional school offers many valuable ideas, but there are no strict theoretical categories, while the new puts forward many new theoretical categories and strictly defines them. The third is an innovation in research fields. The research of the old institutional economics is essentially limited to the micro-economic field, whereas the new institutional school basically covers all the areas of social economy.
26. "Game" means that individuals, teams, or other organizations, under certain environmental conditions and rules, and relying on the information available, choose from and implement, at the same time or successively, actions or strategies for them specifically, and from which they obtain their own, again specific, benefits.
27. See note 23 above.
28. IMF, *China Rank First among Economies that Should Reduce Imbalance of Global Trade*, August 9, 2007, http://www1.cfi.net.cn/newspage/20070809000133.

Chapter 2

1. *Ci Hai* (Shanghai: Shanghai Dictionary Publishing House, 2002), 2953–4.
2. Richard Nelson and Winter, Sydney, *Evolutionary Theory of Economic Change* (Beijing: Commercial Press, 1997), 20.
3. Douglas North, *Structure and Change in Economic History* (Shanghai: Shanghai Joint Publishing Company, 1991), 1–2.
4. Ma Jiantang et al., *The Theory, Application and Policy of Economic Structure* (Beijing: China Social Sciences Publishing House, 1991), 10.
5. C. Rosin and Belew, R., "New Methods for Competitive Co-Evolution," *Evolutionary Computation*, 1 (1997): 1–29.
6. Polarization effect means that because advanced industries owned by the growth cluster itself have a strong appeal to factors of production, factors of production around the areas and economic activities continue to gather around the cluster, thereby speeding up its own development but simultaneously widening the inter-regional imbalance.
7. Chen Chunxin, *Exploration of Technological Innovation*, (Beijing: China Economic Publishing House, 1997), 234.
8. Joseph A. Schumpeter, *Theory of Economic Development*, (Beijing: Commercial Press, 1990), 73–74.
9. J. Metcalf, "Technological Innovation and the Competitive Process," *Technology Innovation and Economic Policy* (1984).

Notes

10. R. Solow, "A Contribution to the Theory of Economic Growth," *Quarterly Journal of Economics*, 70 (1956): 65–94.
11. Zhao Yulin, *Innovation Economics* (Beijing: China Economic Publishing House, 2006), vol. 5.
12. Uzawa Hirofumi, "Optimal Technological Change in an Aggregative Model of Economic Growth," *International Economic Reviews*, 6 (1995).
13. P. Stoneman, *Technological Diffusion and the Computer Revolution* (Cambridge University Press, 1976).
14. E. Mansfield, *The Economics of Technological Change* (W. W. Norton and Company, 1971).
15. R. Romer, "Endogenous Technological Change," *Journal of Political Economy*, 8 (1990): 71–102.
16. R. Lucas, "On the Mechanics of Economic Development," *Journal of Monetary Economics*, 22 (1988): 3–42.
17. S. Kuznets, *Economic Growth of Nations: Total Output and Production Structure* (Beijing: Commercial Press, 1985), 366.
18. R. Coombs et al., *Economics and Technological Progress* (Beijing: Commercial Press, 1989), 108–120.
19. Zhao Feng, "Promoting Innovation Is the Core of Optimization and Upgrading of Industrial Structure," *Finance and Trade Economics*, 10 (2005).
20. T. Hagerstrand, *Innovation as a Spatial Process* (Chicago: Chicago University of Press, 1967), 12–14.
21. R. Morrill, "The Shape of Diffusion in Space and Time," *Economic Geography*, 7 (1970): 259–68.
22. Li Jian et al., *Structural Problems in China's Financial Development* (Beijing: China Renmin University Press, 2004), 326–8.
23. D.C. North, *Structure and Change in Economic History* (Shanghai: Shanghai Joint Publishing Company, 1991), 225.
24. T. Veblen, *The Theory of Leisure Class* (Beijing: Commercial Press, 1964), 139–40.
25. J.R. Commons, *Institutional Economics (I)* (Beijing: Commercial Press, 1962), 87–89.
26. D.C. North, *Institutions, Institutional Change and Economic Performance* (Shanghai: Shanghai Joint Publishing, Shanghai People's Publishing House, 1994), 3.
27. D.C. North, *Structure and Change in Economic History* (Shanghai: Shanghai Joint Publishing Company, 1991).
28. Evolutionary game is a theory which combines the analysis of the game theory and the dynamic process of evolution. Using rational individuals and groups as the research object, the theory holds that in the reality individuals are not fully rational, and their decisions are made through dynamic processes such as imitation, learning and mutation among groups.
29. Aoki Masahiko, *Analysis of Comparative Institutions* (Shanghai: Shanghai Far East Press, 2001), 28.
30. L. Davis and North, D.C., "The Theory of Institutional Change: Concepts and Reasons," in *Property Rights and Institutional Change* (Shanghai, Shanghai Joint Publishing, Shanghai People's Publishing House, 1994), 277–286.
31. Lin Yifu, "Economic Theory on Institutional Change: Induced Institutional Change and Mandatory Institutional Change," in *Property Rights and Institutional Change* (Shanghai: Shanghai Joint Publishing, Shanghai People's Publishing House, 1994), 371.
32. Tu Yongshi, *Outline of Institutional Structural Innovation* (Shanghai: Shanghai Joint Publishing Company, 2006) 12.
33. D.C. North, Roberts, T., *The Rise of the Western World* (Beijing: Huaxia Publishing House, 1999), 189.

Notes

34. Liang Jiagen, *Labor Division, Institutional Change, and Economic Development* (Tianjin: Nankai University Press, 1999), 169.
35. Yang Xiaomeng, "Analysis of Regional Differences in Marketization Measurement of Transitional Countries, Design and Evaluation Based on Industrial Restructuring Indexes," *World Economy*, 1 (2006).
36. Zhang Zongxin, "Optimization of Economic Structure: An Analysis Based on Innovation of Financing System," *Economic Review*, 5 (2002).

Chapter 3

1. Yuan Zhigang, *Non-Walrasian Equilibrium Theory and its Application in China's Economy* (Shanghai: Shanghai Joint Publishing Company, Shanghai People's Publishing House, 1997), 14–15.
2. Wei Jie, *An Introduction to Imbalance Economics* (Beijing: China Renmin University Press, 1991), 71.
3. Karl Marx, *Das Kapital* (Beijing: People's Publishing House, 1975), vol. 2.
4. Hao Shouyi and An Husen, *Regional Economics* (Beijing: Economic Science Press, 1999), vol. 5.
5. P. Krugman and Obstfeld, M., *International Economics* (Beijing: China Renmin University Press, 2002).
6. Consumer preference is a psychological state, often depending on a number of non-economic factors.
7. T. Malthus, *An Essay on the Principle of Population*, 1798.
8. J. Sismondi, *New Principles of Political Economy* (Beijing: Commercial Press, 1977).
9. Chen Leyi, "Comments on the Theory of the Traditional Western Economic Cycle," *Financial Studies*, 2 (1996).
10. Yan Zhijie, *The History of Theories of the Western Market Economy* (Beijing: Commercial Press, 1999).
11. J. Kornai, *Shortage Economics* (Beijing: Economic Science Press, 1986).
12. E.S. Shaw, *Deepening Finance in Economic Development* (Shanghai: Shanghai Joint Publishing Company, Shanghai People's Publishing House, 1988).
13. R.I. McKinnon, *Currency and Capital in Economic Development* (Shanghai: Shanghai Joint Publishing Company, Shanghai People's Publishing House, 1988).
14. H. Minsky, *Stabilizing an Unstable Economy* (New Haven: Yale University Press, 1986).
15. M. Carter, "Financial Innovation and Financial Fragility," *Journal of Economic Issues*, 3 (1989): 779–93.
16. Lin Yifu, Zhang Qi and Liu Mingxing, "Financial Structure and Economic Growth: The Manufacturing Sector," *The World Economy*, 1 (2003).
17. R. La Porta, López-de-Silanes, F., Shleifer, A. and Vishny, R., "Investor Protection and Corporate Governance," *Journal of Financial Economics*, 58 (2000): 3-28; R. La Porta, López-de-Silanes, F., Shleifer, A. and Vishny, R., "Law and Finance," *Journal of Political Economy*, 6 (1998): 1113–55.
18. G. Myrdal, *Economic Theory and Underdeveloped Regions* (London: Duckworth, 1957).
19. R. Prebisch, *Peripheral Capitalism: Crisis and Reform* (Beijing: Commercial Press, 1990).
20. P. Krugman, *Geography and Trade* (Boston: MIT Press, 1991).
21. A. Venables, "Equilibrium Locations of Vertically Linked Industries," *International Economic Review*, 36 (1996).

Notes

Chapter 4

1. Fang Fuqian, "The Evolution of the Theory of Sustainable Development in Western Economics," *Contemporary Economic Research*, 10 (2000): 14–22.
2. Li Jiatu, *Principles of Political Economy and Taxation* (Beijing: The Commercial Press, 1972).
3. M. John, *Principles of Political Economy* (Beijing: The Commercial Press, 1991).
4. The static economy described by Mill is actually the balance of zero growth.
5. Zhuo Chenglin and Guan Hua, *Environmental Economics* (Beijing: Science Press, 2004), 22–23.
6. Available online at http://www.unep.org/geo/yearbook/yb2008.
7. T. Panayotou, "Economic Growth and Environment, Center for International Development," Harvard University CID Working Paper, 56 (July 2000).
8. G.M. Grossman, Krueger, A.B., "Environmental Impacts of a North American Free Trade Agreement," National Bureau of Economic Research Working Paper, Cambridge, MA, 3914 (1991).
9. G.M. Grossman, Krueger, A.B., "Economic Growth and the Environment," *Quarterly Journal of Economics*, 2 (1995): 337–53.
10. N. Shafik, "Economic Development and Environmental Quality: An Econometric Analysis," *Oxford Economic Paper*, 46 (1994): 757–73.
11. T. Selden and Song, D., "Environmental Quality and Development: Is There a Kuznets Curve for Air Pollution Emissions?," *Journal of Environmental Economics and Management*, 27 (1994): 162–8.
12. A. Xepapadeas and Amri, E., "Environmental Quality and Economic Development: Empirical Evidence Based on Qualitative Characteristics," *Nota di Lavoro, Fondazione Eni Enrico Mattei*, 15 (1995).
13. G.M. Grossman and Krueger, A.B., "Economic Growth and Environment," *Quarterly Journal of Economics*, 4 (1995): 357–78.
14. See note 12 above.
15. Chen Huawen and Li Kangbing, "Economic Growth and Environmental Quality: An Analysis of the Experience of the Environmental Kuznets Curve," Fudan University Journal, 2 (2004).
16. Grossman & Krueger (1991) were pioneers in decomposing the impact of economic development or revenue change upon environmental pollution with scale effect, structure effect, and technology effect. They also estimated the size of these three effects through empirical research. Panayotou (1997) also identified three effects of economic development upon the environmental pollution; his were economic scale effect, economic structure effect, and the effect of income upon the supply and demand of efforts to reduce pollution. Panayotou analyzed the impact from each effect on environment pollution as well.
17. J. Andreoni and Levinson A., "The Simple Analytics of the Environmental Kuznets Curve," *Journal of Public Economics*, 2 (2001): 269–86.
18. T. Panayotou, "Empirical Tests and Policy Analysis of Development," ILO Technology and Employment Programme Working Paper 238 (1993).
19. D. Stern, "The Rise and Fall of the Environmental Kuznets Curve," *World Development*, 32 (2004): 1419–39.
20. S. de Bruyn, "Explaining the Environmental Kuznets Curve: Structural Change and International Agreements in Reducing Sulphur Emissions," *Environment and Development Economics*, 4 (1997): 485–6.

Notes

21. T. Panayotou, "Demystifying the Environmental Kuznets Curve: Turning a Black Box into a Policy Tool," *Environment and Development Economics*, 2 (1997): 465–84.
22. R. López, "The Environment as a Factor of Production: The Effects of Economic Growth and Trade Liberalization," *Journal of Environmental Economics and Management*, 1 (1994): 84–116.
23. A. Jean and Duane, C., "A Dynamic Approach to the Environmental Kuznets Curve Hypothesis," *Ecological Economics*, 28 (1999): 267–77.
24. I. David, "Explaining Changes in Global Sulfur Emissions: An Econometric Decomposition Approach," *Ecological Economics*, 42 (2002):201–20.
25. P. Markus, "Technical Progress, Structural Change, and the Environmental Kuznets Curve," *Ecological Economics*, 4 (2002): 381–9.
26. F. Antonio, "Empirical Evidence in the Analysis of Environmental and Energy Policies of a Series of Industrialized Nations, 1960–1997," *Energy Policy*, 31 (2003):333–352.
27. See note 20 above.
28. Li Guozhu, *The Analysis of Measurement of Economic growth and the Development of Environmental Coordination* (Beijing, China Economics Publishing House, 2007), 51.
29. H. de Groot, "Structural Change, Economic Growth and the Environmental Kuznets Curve: A Theoretical Perspective," OCFEB Research Memorandum 9911, *Environmental Policy, Economic Reform and Endogenous Technology*, Working Paper Series 1, 2000.
30. Cited in Lu Chuanyi, *Resources and Environmental Economics* (Beijing, Tsinghua University Press, 2004), 163.
31. S. Grepperud, "Population Pressure and Land Degradation: The Case of Ethiopia," *Journal of Environmental Economics and Management*, 30 (1996): 18–33.
32. N. Shafik and Bandyopadhyay, S., "Economic Growth and Environmental Quality: Time Series and Cross Country Evidence," *The World Bank*, Washington DC, 1992.
33. R. Lopez, "The Environment as a Factor of Production: The Effects of Economic Growth and Trade Liberalization," *Journal of Environmental Economics and Management*, 27 (1994): 163–84.
34. V. Suri and Chapman, D., "Economic Growth, Trade and Energy: Implications for the Environmental Kuznets Curve," *Ecological Economics*, 25 (1998): 195–208.
35. B. Copeland and Taylor, M., "North-South Trade and the Environment," *Quarterly Journal of Economics*, 109 (1994): 755–85.
36. See note 11 above.
37. L. Magnus, "An EKC-Pattern in the Historical Perspective of Carbon Dioxide Emissions, Technology, Fuel Prices and Growth in Sweden, 1870–1997," *Ecological Economics*, 42 (2002): 333–47.
38. B. Kristrom, "Growth, Employment and the Environment," *Swedish Economic Policy Review*, 7 (2000): 148–55.
39. W. Brock and Taylor M., "The Green Solow Model," NBER Working Paper Series, No.10557.
40. Gao Hongye, *Western Economics*, 3rd ed., (Beijing, China Renmin University Press, 2005).

Notes

Chapter 5

1. Data from 1985 to 1995 were obtained from National Bureau of Statistics, vol.7, "Analysis Reports of the New China: Rich Fruits of the Construction of Investment," available online at http://www.stats.gov.cn/tjfx/ztfx/xzgwsnxlfxbg/t20020605_21424.htm, September 18, 1999.
2. See *China Statistical Yearbook*, 2008.
3. Investment rate usually refers to the proportion of gross capital formation in the using amount of GDP in a period of time. Gross capital formation consists of two parts. One is the gross fixed capital formation and the other is the increase in stock. Consumption rate, also known as the rate of final consumption, usually refers to the proportion of the final consumption in the using amount of GDP in a period of time. It is generally calculated based on current prices. In addition to these methods, there are many other methods in the society to calculate investment rate and consumption rate. The most representative methods are as follows. Investment rate is calculated by using the proportion of the finished amount of investment of fixed assets of the whole society to production-based GDP; consumption rate is calculated by using the proportion of the total retail sales of consumer goods to production-based GDP. These indicators do not meet international standards.
4. Due to the existence of the rate of net exports, investment rate plus consumption rate is not equal to 1; thus, the proportion of investment to consumption is clearer to reflect the relationship between investment flows and consumption flows.
5. There are two flaws in the current unemployment statistics, which is the registered urban unemployment rate: on the one hand, it is not the level of unemployment in the whole society; on the other hand, it's just the nominal unemployment rate, far from the actual unemployment rate.
6. The calculation formula is shown as follows: ICOR = total social fixed capital investment increased volume/GDP increment; the larger the ICOR, the lower the investment efficiency.
7. P. Krugman, *The Return of Depression Economics* (Beijing, China Renmin University Press, 1999), 62–78.
8. Yang Xueting et al. "Academic Interpretation of China's Economic Hot Spots," *Beijing Commercial Daily*, July 30, 2007.
9. The data are taken from *China Green National Accounting Study Report 2004* offered by National Bureau of Statistics and Environmental Protection Administration in September, 2006.
10. Available online at http://www.cin.gov.cn/habitat/indicators/cn/00605.doc.
11. There are some differences between the arithmetic mean and the median, which is a form of average; the difference will be very small when the statistical distribution tends to be normal.
12. "Multi-pronged Suppression of Prices of House," *Guangming Daily*, October 22, 2007.
13. Chenery, Robinson and Syrquin, *Comparative Study of Industrialization and Economic Growth* (Shanghai, Shanghai Joint Publishing House, 1995).
14. Li Wenfeng, "Management of Economic Imbalances: the Promotion of the Reform of the Price of Production Factors," *China Economics Times*, June 14, 2007.
15. Wang Xueli, "The Status of the Labor Costs, problems and countermeasure of the China," *Economic Research Reference*, 44 (2006).
16. Zhang Dongsheng, *The Annual Report of China's Income Distribution 2007*, (Beijing, China Financial and Economic Publishing House, 2008).

Notes

17. Zhang Yanhua and Li Binglong, "The Quantitative Study of the Income Gap and Consuming Demand between Urban and Rural Residents in China," *Rural Economy*, 7 (2004).
18. Yan Xianbo, "Consumer Fault Affects the Release of the Potential of the Consumer Market," http://archive.cn.biz.yahoo.com/biz/020827/99/17v67.html.
19. Social Security Research Institute of Labor and Social Security Ministry, "Perfecting Social Security System and Promoting Consumption Growth," *Social Security Research* 14 (2007).

Chapter 6

1. Contribution rate of the primary, secondary and tertiary industries refers to the incremental value of each industry divided by the incremental value of GDP.
2. Industrial pulling rate refers to the growth rate of GDP multiplied by each industrial contribution rate.
3. In this table, industries whose total output accounted for less than 2% in the gross industrial output are omitted, and industries whose proportions were around 2% and were relatively stable are also omitted.
4. National Bureau of Statistics China, "Series on China's economic and social development during the 30-year reform and opening-up," http://www.stats.gov.cn/tjfx/ztfx/jnggkf30n/t20081029_402512864.htm.
5. S. Kuznets, *Economic Growth in Each Country*, (Beijing: Commercial Publishing House, 1985).
6. The comparative productive labor refers to the ratio of the proportion of one industrial output of the labor in the same industry. This indicator reflects the relative changes in the relationship between the structures of output and employment as well as the deviation between the structures of industry and labor force.
7. The energy consumption refers to the consumption of energy when the enterprise generates RMB10,000 of GDP. This indicator reflects the levels of the consumption and saving of energy. It is also an indicator of the efficiency of energy consumption, explaining a country's utilization of energy in economic activities. This reflects changes in the economic structure and the efficiency of energy consumption.
8. In accordance with the present general classification, the service industry can be divided into consumer services providing services to the consumers, and producer services providing pre-production, mid-production, and post-production services to the producers. The original division of the service industry was not as detailed; therefore, such a classification reflects the practical needs of the industrialization process. The producer services industry has become increasingly important in the development of modern manufacturing, because the service activities of producer services are not only key investments in modern manufacturing, but also the key factors and basic sources for the efficiency improvement and industrial upgrading of the modern manufacturing industry.
9. People's Daily Online, "Ten World Economic Entities China Should Be Concerned about," http://www.people.com.cn/GB/jingji/1037/3092378.html.
10. The "Smile Curve" was first put forward by Stan Shih in *Recreation of Acer: Creation, Growth and Challenge* in 1992. The curve became popular for being like smiling lips. See Stan Shih, *Recreation of Acer: Creation, Growth and Challenge*. (Beijing: CITIC Publishing House, 2005).

Notes

Chapter 7

1. See *China Financial Stability Report* (2007).
2. Yi Rongxian, "China's Year of Bonds," http://finance.sina.com.cn/t/20030129/1023307666.shtml.
3. M. Aoki and Patrick, H, eds., *The Japanese Banking System*, (Oxford University Press, 1994), 36.
4. See *China Banking Regulatory Commission Annual Report* (2007).
5. See *China Financial Market Development Report* (2007).
6. See *Report on International Financial Markets* (2007).
7. Refer to related contents in Section 2 of Chapter 3.
8. See *China Capital Markets Development Report*.
9. See *The People's Bank of China Statistics Quarterly Reports*.
10. CRn Index refers to the proportion of the operations in several of the largest banks in one country or region. The formula is (X_i refers to the operations of *i*. Generally, the larger the CRn Index is, the more monopolized the industry is).

$$CR_n = \sum_{i=1}^{n} X_i \Big/ \sum_{i=1}^{All} X_i$$

11. See note 4 above.
12. See note 8 above.
13. See note 8 above.
14. In fact, the increase of the profitability of state-owned commercial banks originated from the huge non-performing loans by the country.
15. See note 4 above.
16. See *The Banker* (2007).
17. Cited in "The Report of the Analysis of the Way out of China's Banks," http://new.china-review.com.
18. We take the stock market as the example to analyze the capital market due to the its leading position in China's capital market.
19. Includes the transactions of inter-bank repo, inter-exchanges repo and the outright inter-banks repo.
20. Cited in *China Bond*, http://hqtj.chinabond.com.cn/chinabond/hqtj/index.
21. The price impact index is the level of impact on the market price, when a certain amount of or a certain number of stocks are traded. It is usually calculated against the level of impact of RMB100,000 on the market price. Base point is its unit, and 1 basis point=0.01%.
22. See note 8 above.
23. The turnover rate is the ratio of total trading value and total market value.
24. The calculation is based on the relevant data of *China Statistical Yearbook* (2008) and *Quarterly Statistical Bulletin* of People's Bank of China.
25. The data comes from *Distribution Atlas of the Rural Financial Services in China's Banking Industry 2008* on the official website of the China Banking Regulatory Commission, www.cbrc.gov.cn.
26. The data comes from *Report of China's Rural Financial Service 2008* on the official website of People's Bank of China, www.pbc.gov.cn.
27. See note 25 above.
28. China Rural Finance Association, *Thirty Years of Rural Financial Reform and Development*, (Beijing: China Financial Publishing House).
29. See note 26 above.
30. See note 26 above.

Notes

Chapter 8

1. Ten eastern cities and provinces refer to Beijing (municipality), Tianjin (municipality), Hebei Province, Shandong Province, Jiangsu Province, Shanghai (municipality), Zhejiang Province, Fujian Province, Guangdong Province, and Hainan Province. Six central provinces refer to Shanxi Province, Henan Province, Anhui Province, Jiangxi Province, Hubei Province, and Hunan Province. Twelve western provinces refer to Chongqing (municipality), Sichuan Province, Guizhou Province, Yunnan Province, Tibet Province, Shaanxi Province, Gansu Province, Qinghai Province, Ningxia Province, Xinjiang Province, Inner Mongolia Province, and Guangxi Province. And Liaoning Province, Jilin Province, and Heilongjiang Province are the Three Provinces in the northeastern part.
2. National Bureau of Statistics, "The Project of the Analysis of 30 Years of Reform and Opening Up," www.stats.gov.cn/tjfx/ztfx/jnggkf30n.
3. The data of Chongqing is included in Sichuan.
4. Among which, general transfers payment refers to the financial subsidy and expenditure for finance by the central finance to compensate for the financial gap in areas where the fiscal solvency is weak, to balance the regional disparities of the financial resources, and to achieve equalization of the inter-regional capacity of basic public services.
5. The coefficient of the variation is a statistic to measure the variable degree of the variable value. It equals to the ratio of the standard deviation and average.
6. The calculation is based on the RMB/USD exchange rate of 1:7.3046 at end of 2007.
7. The classification of national income per capita in 2004 is obtained according to the World Bank Atlas method. The criterion of classification is: Class A: low-income (USD825 and less); Class B: lower-middle income (USD826–3,255); Class C: higher-medium income (USD3,256–10,065); Class D: high income (USD10,066 and more).
8. Han Zhaozhou, *The Theory of the Measurement and Statistical Methods of Regional Economic Development*, (Guangzhou: Jinan University Press, 2003).
9. Modernization Research Center of China Academy of Sciences, *China Modernization Report* (Beijing: Peking University Press, 2004), 53.
10. Lu Yunhang et al., "Causes of China's Inter-provincial Differences in Income: Factor Accumulation or Productivity," *Modern Finance*, 4 (2007).
11. Fan Gang et al., *China's Market Index—The 2006 Report of the Relative Process of Regional Market* (Beijing: Economy and Science Press, 2007), 79.
12. Engel coefficient refers to the proportion of the amount of household food expenditure of total household consumption. Engel's coefficient is often used internationally to measure the living standard of people within a country or region. The smaller the Engel coefficient, the higher the living standard. According to the Food and Agriculture Organization's standards, when the Engel coefficient is over 59%, it means destitute; between 50% and 59%: survival; between 40% and 50%: well off; between 30% and 40%: wealthy; less than 30%: the wealthiest.
13. The intensity of dual economic structure is the ratio of non-agricultural comparative labor productivity to agricultural comparative labor productivity. In economics, the index of the intensity of dual economic structure reflects the transformation speed of the dual economic structure. If this coefficient gets larger, it indicates that the structural contrast between the two sectors is greater and the dual economic structure is more noticeable.

Notes

14. The Gini coefficient is an important indicator to reflect the average level of income distribution and gap of residents. It refers to the proportion of income of social members that account for a certain percentage of the total population in the total income of all residents. According to the regulations of relevant organizations of United Nations: if the Gini coefficient is lower than 0.2, it indicates that income of residents in a country is absolutely average; if the Gini Coefficient is between 0.2 and 0.3, it indicates that the income is relatively average; if the Gini Coefficient is between 0.3 and 0.4, it indicates that the income is relatively reasonable. Meanwhile, 0.4 is internationally often set as the "warning line" of the income gap between the rich and the poor; the figure between 0.4 and 0.5 indicates a large income gap; the figure above 0.6 indicates a sharp income gap.
15. Data of the Gini Coefficient in 1991–2005 is obtained from *China Human Development Report (2007)*; data of 2006 is obtained from: He Ya, "Gini Coefficient: The Deconstruction of Urban and Rural Historical Policy," *China's National Conditions and Strength*, 4 (2007).

Chapter 9

1. Accordingly, the follow-up analysis in this chapter will start from the formation of the pattern of the "double surplus" in 1994.
2. Because of the adjustment of the statistics, the specific contents of China's current accounts in the balance of the payments table varied a lot before and after 1997. Before 1997, the current accounts included the foreign trade, the non-commercial trade, and the free transfer account. Since 1997, the current accounts have included the goods and services, the profits, and the current transfer account. The foreign trade before 1997 equals to the goods item in the goods and services since 1997. The non-commercial trade includes not only the services item but also the income. The free transfer account is almost the same as the current transfer account in the new table.
3. The import and export use the statistical caliber of the Customs.
4. Only the capital account, not the financial account, existed in the table of the balance of payments before 1997. Since 1997, the statistics of the original capital have changed and been renamed the "capital and financial accounts". Of this, the financial account is the major part while the capital account is simple and minor.
5. In addition to the commodity trade and direct investment, the balance of other balance of payments is also a source of foreign exchange reserves. As the balance of these projects shows a surplus in some years and a deficit in some others, the balance owns a positive proportion of the increase in foreign exchange reserves when the accumulated balance shows a surplus; it shows a negative proportion when the accumulated balance shows a deficit. Thus, the total proportion of commodity trade and direct investment of the increase in foreign exchange reserves is less than 100% in some years but more than 100% in others.
6. The so-called short-term external debt ratio is the ratio of short-term external debt to the entire external debt in a country. This index reflects the term structure of external debt in a country. The higher this index, the greater risk a country's debt takes.
7. Data obtained from *China's International Balance of Payments Report 2007*, compiled by the State Administration of Foreign Exchange (SAFE). The data time of this international comparison is 2006.

Notes

8. Macro-economic Research Department of Development Research Center of the State Council of P.R.China, "On Several Problems Associated with China's Expansion of FDI," http://www.drcnet.com.cn/DRCnet.common.web/DocViewSummary.aspx?version=Integrated&docid=1349777&leafid=3079&chnid=1034&gourl=/DRCnet.common.web/docview.aspx.
9. Wei Houkai and Changquan, Liu, "The Negative Effect of China's Foreign Investment and Adjusting Strategy," *People's Daily online*, http://theory.people.com.cn/GB/49154/49155/4741564.html.

Chapter 10

1. OECD, "Economic Policy Reforms: Going for Growth," (2007).
2. United Nations Development Programme, "Human Development Report," various years.
3. The World Bank's *China Quarterly Update* in September, 2007 stressed that the main challenge for China's economy is still the economic restructuring (available at www.worldbank.org/china); reports by Morgan Stanley and other leading international institutions repeatedly studied China's economic structural imbalance, cited in Morgan Stanley's official website.
4. In the first meeting of the 11th National People's Congress in 2008, Premier Wen Jiabao, in his government work, reported, "Some outstanding problems and deep-seated contradictions in economic operation still exist. In recent years, investment in fixed assets has grown too fast and monetary credit has been too much; international balance of payments has been unbalanced. Long-term structural contradictions and the extensive mode of growth have remained serious."
5. Positive indexes mean statistical index values and index values are positively correlated, which indicates the higher index values are, the higher degree serious economic structural imbalance has; inverse indexes mean statistical index values and index values are negatively correlated, which indicates the higher index values are, the lower degree economic structural imbalance has; appropriate indexes mean there is no direct positive or negative correlation between statistical index values and the degree of economic structural imbalance.
6. Dimension is the unit of measurement. Being dimensionless is transforming values of variables with dimensions into ones without dimensions. This transformation should be based on scoring criteria set beforehand, which refers to establishing a fitting function between scoring values of the degree of economic structural imbalance and measuring indexes.
7. The processing includes percentile, 5-point scale, 10-point system, etc. Although each method has different scales, the different scales can be compared and transformed, due to no specific corresponding economic meanings.
8. What is called "appropriate range" is a range of index value normally operating in a certain stage of development; this range is proven by theoretical and empirical analysis.
9. What is called 'potential crisis' does not mean that the index has reached the degree to trigger an economic crisis, but refers to a range in which this index is more possible to trigger economic crisis or financial crisis.
10. Pre-set criteria refer to scoring values of different grades corresponding to different measuring index values and each range of index value corresponding to a scoring value.

Notes

11. The so-called principle of equidistance refers to the criteria where either the distances between the ranges are equally divided by the index value. If this is not the case, it is the principle of non-equidistance.
12. Due to the lack of most data in the years 1990 and 1991, the results of the scores of the overall economy and each factor after 1992 are presented here.
13. "Three Major Strategies to Resolve Six Main Imbalances in China," *Shanghai Securities News*, June 19, 2006, also available online at http://news1.jrj.com.cn/news/20060619/000001528503_004.html.
14. "Macro-control Should Focus More on Economic Restructuring," *Securities Times*, April 5, 2007, also available online at http://www.steel5696.com.
15. Cited in *China Securities Journal*, September 6, 2006.
16. The elasticity of employment refers to the ratio of the growth rate of employment to the growth rate of GDP.
17. "China's Five Questions for Social Risks—Are Social Risks Exaggerated?", *China Network*, January 28, 2006, in *China Comment*, http://www.china.com.cn/chinese/sy/1108410.htm.
18. He Zhenguo, *Research on the Scale and Structure of Financial Support to Agriculture* (Beijing: China Financial and Economic Publishing House, 2005), 139.
19. The World Bank, 2003.

Chapter 11

1. Xiang Junbo, "The Measure and Analysis of China's Economic Structure Imbalance," *Management World*, 9 (2008).
2. Xiang Junbo, "On the Creation of Structural Economics," *Guangming Daily*, April 7, 2008.
3. Structural optimization is a state in which the economic structural system experiences coordinated development in its internal proportional relationship and promotes economic growth, social equity and environmental optimization.
4. Zhang Honghe, "A Low Carbon Economy: The Only Way of Sustainable Development," *China's Information News*, July 22, 2008.
5. See *Xinhua Net*, http://news.xinhuanet.com/world/200712/13/content_7243707.htm.
6. Hu Jintao, Work Report, the 17th Cong., October 15, 2007.
7. "Face with the "Excess Liquidity": Predicament and Way out," *Financial Times*, September 12, 2006.
8. P. Samuelson, *Economics* (Beijing: Commercial Press, 1991).
9. Please refer to Chapter 1 for the concept of the "three-dimension balance." The "three-dimension" refers to the three aspects of economy, society and resource environment.
10. The positive force affects the economic sustainable development actively, while the negative force is the passive force. These two concepts were defined in Chapter One of this book.
11. Chen Jiagui, Huiqun, Huang, and Tao, Zhang, "China Economy Form Rapid Growth to the Harmonious Development," *China Industrial Economy*, 7 (2007).
12. Li Jingwen, "The Major Trends of China's Urbanization: the Emergence of Urban Group and the Demand for Investment," *Xinhua Digest*, 10 (2008).
13. Ma Jiantang, "How to Correctly Judge the Situation of China's Economic Development," *Qiushi*, 12 (2008).
14. R. Shen and R. Jiang, "The Empirical Research of the Mechanism of the Impact on Economic Growth of China's Urbanization," *Statistical Research*, 6 (2007).

Notes

15. See *China Statistical Yearbook* (2007).
16. The National Bureau of Statistics, "The Statistical Monitoring Report of China's Building a Well-off Society in 2007," http://www.stats.gov.cn.
17. Wen Jiabao, "Several Major Problems on the Thorough Application of the Scientific Outlook on Development," *Qiushi*, 21 (2008).
18. Cited in *China Pension Net*, www.cnpension.net/index_lm/20080820/378118.html.
19. See *China News Net*, October 28, 2008.

References

English Materials

Allen, F. and G. Douglas. 2000. *Comparing Financial Systems*. Cambridge, MA: MIT Press.

Beck, T. and R. Levine. 2000. *External Dependence and Industry Growth: Does Financial Structure Matter?* World Bank Mimeo. Feb.

Faye, Duchin. 1998. *Structural Economics—Measuring Change in Technology, Lifestyles, and the Environment*. Covelo, CA: Island Press.

Krugaman, P. 1991. Increasing Returns and Economic Geography. *Journal of Political Economy* 99: 183-199.

———. 1991. *Geography and Trade*. Cambridge, MA: MIT Press.

North, D. 1971. *Institutional Change and Economic Growth in the United States*. Cambridge: Cambridge University Press.

Panayotou, T. Environmental Degradation at Different Stages of Economic Department. In Ahmed, I. and J. Doeleman eds. 1995. *Beyond Rio: The Environmental Crisis and Sustainable Livelihoods in the Third World*. London: Macmillan Press.

Thijs ten R. 2004. *Structural Economics*. London: Routledge.

United Nations. 2007. *World Economic Situation and Prospects 2007*. New York.

Chinese Materials

Cai Fang 蔡昉. 2007. "Zhongguo jingji mianlin de zhuanzhe jiqi dui fazhan he gaige de tiaozhan" 中國經濟面臨的轉折及其對發展和改革的挑戰 (At the Turning Point of the China's Economic Development and Reform). *Zhongguo shehui kexue* 中國社會科學 (Social Sciences in China), 3.

China Development Research Foundation. 2005. *Renlei fazhan baogao* 人類發展報告 (Human Development Report). Beijing: China Translation and Publishing Corporation.

China Modernization Research Center of China Academy of Sciences. 2004. *Zhongguo xiandaihua baogao, 2004* 中國現代化報告2004 (China's Modernization Report, 2004). Beijing: Peking University Press.

Dai Li 戴利. 2006. *Chaoyue zengzhang kechixu fazhan de jingjixue* 超越增長可持續發展的經濟學 (Sustainable Economics beyond the Growth). Shanghai: Shanghai Translation Publishing House.

References

Fan Gang 樊綱 et al. 2007. *Zhongguo shichanghua zhishu—gediqu shichanghua xiangdui jincheng 2006 nian baogao* 中國市場化指數—各地區市場化相對進程2006年報告 (China's Market Index—The 2006 Report of the Relative Progress of Regional Markets). Beijing: Economic Science Press.

Guo Kesha 郭克莎. 2001. *Jiegou youhua yu jingji fazhan* 結構優化與經濟發展 (Structure Optimization and Economic Development). Guangzhou: Guangdong Economic Publishing House.

Hao Shouyi 郝壽義 and An Husen 安虎森. 1999. *Quyu jingjixue* 區域經濟學 (Regional Economics). Beijing: Economic Science Press.

He Liping 賀力平. 2007. "Zhongguo guoji shouzhi de changqi bianhua qushi ji yingxiang yinsu" 中國國際收支的長期變化趨勢及影響因素 (Long-term Changing Trend and Influencing Factors of China's International Balance of Payments). *Zhongguo waihui* 中國外匯 (China Foreign Exchange), 1.

Headquarter of People's Bank of China, Shanghai. 2008. *Zhongguo jinrong shichang fazhan baogao 2007* 中國金融市場發展報告2007 (Report of China's Financial Market Development, 2007). Beijing: China Financial Publishing House.

Hong Yinxing 洪銀興. 2005. *Fazhan jingjixue yu Zhongguo jingji de fazhan* 發展經濟學與中國經濟的發展 (Development Economics and Economic Development in China). 2nd ed. Beijing: Higher Education Press. Also available online at http://www.022net.com/2007/26/33434316233449.html.

Hu An'gang 胡鞍鋼. 1997. "Diqu chaju de guoji bijiao ji guoji jingyan" 地區差距的國際比較及國際經驗 (The International Comparison and Experience of the Regional Disparities). *Jingji yanjiu cankao* 經濟研究參考 (Review of Economic Research), 3.

Hu Jintao 胡錦濤 and Wen Jiabao 溫家寶. 2007. Speech Drafts. Central Economic Work Conference, Beijing. http://news.xinhuanet.com/newscenter/200712/05/content_7205171.htm.

Hu Jintao 胡錦濤. 2007. Government Work Report. 17th Cong. http://news.xinhuanet.com/politics/200710/24/content_6939223.htm.

———. 2006. Ba jieyue nengyuan ziyuan fangzai geng tuchu de zhanlue weizhi 把節約能源資源放在更突出的戰略位置 (Highlighting the Energy and Resource-Saving's Strategic Function). http://news.xinhuanet.com/politics/200612/26/content_5534918.htm.

Hua Min 華民. 2007. Shijie jingji jiegou shiheng yu Zhongguo de xuanze 世界經濟結構失衡與中國的選擇 (Imbalance of the World's Economy and China's Choice). http://www.022net.com/2007/26/33434316233449.html.

Jiang Boke 姜波克. 2005. *Guoji jinrong xinbian* 國際金融新編 (New Edition of International Finance). 3rd ed. Shanghai: Fudan University Press.

References

Jiang Xiaojuan 江小涓. 2001. "Shiwu woguo duiwai touzi qushi yanjiu: quanqiu beijing, touzi guimo yu zhongdian xuanze" "十五"我國對外投資趨勢研究：全球背景、投資規模與重點選擇 (Research on the Trend of China's Foreign Investment during the Tenth-Five-Year-Plan Period: Global Influence, Investment Scale and Development Focus). *Guanli shijie* 管理世界 (The Management World), 1.

Jing Tihua 景體華. *2006–2007 nian Zhongguo quyu jingji fazhan baogao* 2006–2007年中國區域經濟發展報告 (Report on China's Regional Economic Development, 2006–2007). Beijing: Social Sciences Academic Press.

Li Guozhu 李國柱. 2007. *Jingji zengzhang yu huanjing xietiao fazhan de jiliang fenxi* 經濟增長與環境協調發展的計量分析 (Quantitative Analysis on the Economic Growth and the Development of Environmental Coordination). Beijing: China Economic Publishing House.

Li Shi 李實. 2003. "Zhongguo geren shouru fenpei yanjiu huigu yu zhanwang" 中國個人收入分配研究回顧與展望 (Review and Outlook of China's Income Distribution). *Jingjixue* 經濟學 (Economics), 2. Published quarterly.

Li Shantong 李善同 et al. 2005. "Zhongguo diqu chaju biandong de weilai" 中國地區差距變動的未來 (The Future of the Movement of China's Regional Differences). In *Zhongguo fazhan yanjiu 2005* 中國發展研究2005 (Study on China's Development, 2005). Beijing: China Development Press.

Liu He 劉鶴. 2006. "Cujin nongcun laodongli zhuanyi de wuda duice" 促進農村勞動力轉移的五大對策 (Five Major Measures for Promoting Rural Labors Migration). *Zhongguo jingji shibao* 中國經濟時報 (China Economic Times). March 21.

Liu Renwu 劉仁伍. 2003. "Jinrong jiegou jianquanxing he jinrong fazhan ke chixuxing de shizheng pinggu fangfa" 金融結構健全性和金融發展可持續性的實證評估方法 (Empirical Evaluation Methods of the Completeness of Financial Structure and Sustainability of Financial Development). *Jinrong yanjiu* 金融研究 (Journal of Financial Research), 3.

Liu Runkui 劉潤葵. 1994. *Jiegou jingjixue* 結構經濟學 (Structural Economics). Chengdu: Sichuan Science and Technology Press.

Liu Shijin 劉世錦. 1998. "Jiegou zhuanhuan quekou: Zhongguo jingji mianlin de wenti yu xuanze" 結構轉換缺口：中國緊急面臨的問題與選擇 (Gap of the Economic Transition: Problems and Choices of China's Economy). *Guanli shijie* 管理世界 (Management World), 6.

Liu Wei 劉偉 and Li Shaorong 李紹榮. 2005. *Zhuangui zhongde jingji zengzhang yu jingji jiegou* 轉軌中的經濟增長與經濟結構 (Economic Growth and Economic Structure in the Transition). Beijing: China Development Press.

References

Lu Chuanyi 魯傳一. 2004. *Ziyuan yu huanjing jingjixue* 資源與環境經濟學 (Resources and Environmental Economics). Beijing: Tsinghua University Press.

Lu Jianjie 陸劍傑. 2005. *Guangyi jingji jiegou lun* 廣義經濟結構論 (Generalized Economic Structuralism). Beijing: Social Sciences Academic Press.

Lu Zhongyuan 盧中原. 2005. "Weilai 5–10 nian Zhongguo jingji shehui fazhan de ruogan zhongda wenti" 未來5–10年中國經濟社會發展的若干重大問題 (Problems of China's Economic and Social Development in Next 5–10 Years). *Caimao jingji* 財貿經濟 (Finance and Trade Economics), 7.

Ma Jiantang 馬建堂 et al. 1991. *Jingji jiegou de lilun, yingyong yu zhengce* 經濟結構的理論、應用與政策 (Theories, Application and Policies of the Economic Structure). Beijing: China Social Sciences Publishing House.

National Bureau of Statistics. Xin Zhongguo xilie fenxi baogao 新中國系列分析報告 (Series of Analyses Reports on New China). http://www.stats.gov.cn/tjfx/ztfx/xzgwsnxlfxbg/index.htm.

———. Cong Shiliuda dao Shiqida jingji shehui fazhan huigu xilie baogao 從十六大到十七大經濟社會發展回顧系列報告 (Series of Review of Economic and Social Development from the Sixteenth to Seventeenth Party Congress). http://www.stats.gov.cn/tjfx/ztfx/sqd.

———. 2001–2006. *Zhongguo tongji nianjian* 中國統計年鑒 (China Statistical Yearbook). Beijing: China Statistics Press.

Sina Finance 新浪財經. Dierci ZhongMei zhanlue jingji duihua 第二次中美戰略經濟對話 (Second Sino-U.S. Strategic Economic Dialogue). http://finance.sina.com.cn/focus/zmjjt.

Sohu Finance 搜狐財經. 2006. Conference Memoir. International Conference of Global Imbalances. http://business.sohu.com/20060713/n244248392.shtml. July 14.

Song Chengxian 宋承先. 2005. *Xiandai xifang jingjixue—hongguan jingjixue* 現代西方經濟學—宏觀經濟學 (Modern Western Economics—Macroeconomics). Shanghai: Fudan University Press.

Sun Jiuwen 孫久文. 1999. *Zhongguo quyu jingji shizheng yanjiu—jiegou zhuanbian yu fazhan zhanlue* 中國區域經濟實證研究—結構轉變與發展戰略 (Empirical Research on China's Regional Economy—Structural Changes and Development Strategies). Beijing: China Light Industry Press.

Tan Chongtai 譚崇台. 2002. *Fazhan jingjixue de xin fazhan* 發展經濟學的新發展 (New Development of the Development Economics). Wuhan: Wuhan University Press.

References

Tang Min 湯敏 and Yushi, Mao 茅於軾. 2005 *Xiandai jingjixue qianyan zhuanti* 現代經濟學前沿專題 (At the Frontier of the Modern Economics). Beijing: Commercial Press.

The Discussion Group of Development Strategy and Regional Economic Research Department of the Development Research Center of the State Council. *China Regional Science Development Research*. Beijing: China's Development Press, 2007.

The Economic Department of the Chinese Academy of Social Sciences. *The Global Economic Imbalances and China's Economic Imbalances*. Beijing: Economic Management Press, 2006.

Wang Luolin 王洛林 and Xiangyang Li 李向陽. 2006. *2005–2006 shijie jingji xingshi fenxi yu yuce* 2005–2006年世界經濟形勢分析與預測 (Analysis and Forecast of World Economic Trend, 2005–2006). Beijing: Social Sciences Academic Press.

Wang Mengkui 王夢奎. 2005. *Zhongguo zhongchangqi fazhan de zhongyao wenti 2006–2020* 中國中長期發展的重要問題2006–2020 (Major Issues of China's Medium and Long–term Development, 2006–2020). Beijing: China Development Press.

Wang Xiaoguang 王小廣. 1999. "Shiwu shiqi gongye cong shiyingxing jiegou tiaozheng xiang zhanluexing jiegou tiaozheng zhuanbian" 十五期間工業從適應型結構調整向戰略型結構調整轉變 (Industry Tranformed from Adaptive Structural Adjustment to Strategic Structure Adjustment during the 10th Five-year-plan). *Zhongguo gongye jingji* 中國工業經濟 (China Industrial Economics), 10.

Wang Yiming 王一鳴. 2007. "Jingji neiwai shiheng he hongguan jingji zhengce—dui dangqian jingji xingshi de jidian renshi" 經濟內外失衡和宏觀經濟政策—對當前經濟形勢的幾點認識 (Internal and External Economic Imbalances and Macro-economic Policies—Understandings of Current Economic Situation). *Hongguan jingji guanli* 宏觀經濟管理 (Macro-economic Management), 6.

Wei Houkai 魏後凱. 2006. *Xiandai quyu jingjixue* 現代區域經濟學 (Modern Regional Economics). Beijing: Economic Management Press.

Wei Jie 魏傑. 1991. *Shiheng jingjixue daolun* 失衡經濟學導論 (Introductory of Unbalanced Economics). Beijing: China Renmin University Press.

Wen Jiabao 溫家寶. 2007. Zhengfu gongzuo baogao—dishiji quanguo renmin daibiao dahui diwuci huiyi shang 政府工作報告—第十屆全國人民代表大會第五次會議 (Government Working Report—at the 5th Meeting of the 10th National People's Congress). http://news.xinhuanet.com/misc/2007-03/17/content_5859480.htm. March 17.

References

Wu Jinglian 吳敬璉. 2006. *Zhongguo zengzhang moshi jueze* 中國增長模式抉擇 (Choice of China's Growth Pattern). Shanghai: Shanghai Far East Press.

———. 2003. *Yujing Zhongguo jingji fengxian* 預警中國經濟風險 (Warning China's Economic Risks). http://finance.sina.com.cn/roll/20031024/0906487994.shtml. October 24.

Wu Xiaoling 吳曉靈. 2007. Jingji jiegou shiheng shi goucheng jingji weiji zhongyao yuanyin 經濟結構失衡是造成經濟危機重要原因 (Economic Structural Imbalance Is an Important Cause for Economic Crisis). http://www.sina.com.cn. April 15.

Xiang Junbo 項俊波. 2007. "Zhengfu ruhe zhichi ruoshi jinrong" 政府如何支持"弱勢"金融 (How does the Government Support the "Weak Finance"). *Zhongguo jingji zhoukan* 中國經濟週刊 (China Weekly Economy), 2.

———. 2007. *Xiandai jinrong shichang zhishi shouce* 現代金融市場知識手冊 (Handbook of Modern Financial Market). Beijing: China Financial Publishing House.

———. 2006. Jiejue quanqiu jingji shiheng xu geguo gongtong nuli 解決全球經濟失衡需各國共同努力 (Joint Efforts in Addressing Global Economic Imbalances). http://www.cs.com.cn/xwzx/200609/t20060903_987099.htm. September 3.

———. 2005. Jiaqiang jinrong wending, cujin jinrong fazhan de zhongqi zhanlue 加強金融穩定、促進金融發展的中期戰略 (Strengthen Financial Stability and Promote the Mid-term Financial Strategy of Financial Development). Speech Draft. 7th Asian Institute of International Finance Summit. http://www.pbc.gov.cn/detail_frame.asp?col=4200&id=193&isFromDetail=1. October 26.

Yin Jianfeng 殷劍峰. 2006. *Jinrong jiegou yu jingji zengzhang* 金融結構與經濟增長 (Financial Structure and Economic Growth). Beijing: People's Publishing House.

Yu Yongding 余永定. 2006 "Quanqiu jingji jiegou shiheng: Zhongguo shijiao" 全球經濟結構失衡：中國視角 (Global Economic Structural Imbalance: In China's Perspective). *Guoji jingji pinglun* 國際經濟評論 (International Economic Review), 9–10.

Zhang Shuguang 張曙光 and Liu Xiahui 劉霞輝. 2000. Jinrong jiegou tiaozheng yu zhengquan shichang fazhan 金融結構調整與證券市場發展 (Financial Restructuring and the Development of Securities Market). http://www.drcnet.com.cn/DRCNet.channel.web.

Zhang Xiuzhong 張秀生. 2007. *Quyu jingjixue* 區域經濟學 (Regional Economics). Wuhan: Wuhan University Press.

References

Zhou Li 周立 and Hu An'gang 胡鞍鋼. 2002. Zhongguo jinrong fazhan de diqu chaju zhuangkuang fenxi, 1978–1999" 中國金融發展的地區差距狀況分析1978–1999 (Analysis of the Regional Disparities of China's Financial Development, 1978-1999). *Qinghua daxue xuebao* 清華大學學報 (Journal of Tsinghua University (Philosophy and Social Sciences)), 2.

Zhou Xiaochuan 周小川. 2007. Zhizhi jinrong shichang sida ruanlei 直指金融市場四大軟肋 (Analysis on Four Major Soft Spots of the Financial Market). *Shanghai zhengquan bao* 上海證券報 (Shanghai Securities News). September 4.

———. 2006. Zhongguo huobi zhengce de tedian he tiaozhan 中國貨幣政策的特點和挑戰 (Characteristics and Challenges of China's Monetary Policy). *Caijing* 財經 (Finance), 26.

Zhou Zhenhua 周振華. 1995. *Xiandai jingji zengzhang zhong de jiegou xiaoying* 現代經濟增長中的結構效應 (The Structural Effects of Modern Economic Growth). Shanghai: Shanghai Joint Publishing House.

Translated Materials

Bourguignon, Francois (弗朗索瓦·布吉尼翁). 2007. *Jingji zhengce dui pinkun he shouru fenpei de yingxiang—Pinggu jishu he fangfa* 經濟政策對貧困和收入分配的影響—評估技術和方法 (Effects of Economic Policies on Poverty and Income Distribution—Techniques and Methods of Assessment). Beijing: China Renmin University Press.

Burns, Tom R. (湯姆·伯恩斯). 2000. *Jiegou zhuyi de shiye* 結構主義的視野 (From the Perspectives of Structuralism). Beijing: Social Sciences Academic Press.

Chenery, Hollis B. (霍利斯·錢納里) et al. 1989. *Gongyehua he jingji zengzhang de bijiao yanjiu* 工業化和經濟增長的比較研究 (The Comparative Study of Industrialization and Economic Growth). Shanghai: Shanghai Joint Publishing House.

Goldsmith, R (戈德史密斯). 1990. *Jinrong jiegou yu jingji fazhan* 金融結構與經濟發展 (Financial Structure and Development). Shanghai: Shanghai Joint Publishing Company.

Hirschman, Albert O. (赫希曼). 1991. *Jingji fazhan zhanlue* 經濟發展戰略 (Strategies for Economic Development). Beijing: Economic Science Press.

IMF. 2005. *Shijie jingji zhanwang—Quanqiuhua he duiwai shiheng* 世界經濟展望—全球化和對外失衡 (World Economic Outlook: Globalization and External Imbalance). Beijing: China Financial Publishing House.

References

———. 2004. *Shijie jingji zhanwang—Tuijin jiegou gaige* 世界經濟展望—推進結構改革 (World Economic Outlook: Promoting Structural Reforms). Beijing: China Financial Publishing House.

Krugman, Paul R. (保羅·克魯格曼) et al. 1999. *Guoji jingjixue* 國際經濟學 (International Economics). Beijing: China Renmin University Press.

Kuznets, Simon S. (西蒙·庫茲涅茨). 1989. *Xiandai jingji zengzhang: Sudu, jiegou yu kuozhang* 現代經濟增長：速度、結構與擴張 (Modern Economic Growth: Rate, Structure and Expansion). Beijing: Beijing Economic College Press.

Kweilin, M. E. (莫迪查·克雷林). 2004. *Guoji jingjixue: Yizhong zhengce fangfa* 國際經濟學：一種政策方法 (International Economics: A Policy). Beijing: Peking University Press.

Lewis, William A. (路易斯). 1990. *Jingji zengzhang lilun* 經濟增長理論 (Theory of Economic Growth). Shanghai: Shanghai Joint Publishing Company.

Metcalfe, Stanley J. (梅特卡夫). 2007. *Yanhua jingjixue yu chuangzaoxing huimie* 演化經濟學與創造性毀滅 (Evolutionary Economics and Creative Destruction). Beijing: China Renmin University Press.

Nelson, Richard (理查·納爾遜) and Sydney Winter (悉尼·溫特). 1997. *Jingji bianqian de yanhua lilun* 經濟變遷的演化理論 (Evolutionary Theory of Economic Change). Beijing: Commercial Press.

North, Douglas (諾斯·道格拉斯). 1999. *Jingjishi zhong de jiegou yu bianqian* 經濟史中的結構與變遷 (Structure and Change in the Economic History). Shanghai: Shanghai Joint Publishing, Shanghai People's Publishing House.

Nurkse, Ragnar (納克斯). 1996. *Bufada guojia de ziben xingcheng wenti* 不發達國家的資本形成問題 (Capital Formation in Underdeveloped Countries). Beijing: Commercial Press.

Organisation for Economic Cooperation and Development. 2006. *Zhongguo gonggong zhichu mianlin de tiaozhan: Tongwang geng youxiao he gongping zhilu* 中國公共支出面臨的挑戰：通往更有效和公平之路 (Challenges of China's Public Spending: A Road to be More Effective and Fair). Beijing: Tsinghua University Press.

Perkins, Dwight H. (波金斯) et al. 2005. *Fazhan jingjixue* 發展經濟學 (Development Economics). Beijing: China Renmin University Press.

Prebisch, Raúl (普雷維什). 1990. *Waiwei zibenzhuyi: weiji yu gaizao* 周邊資本主義：危機與改造 (Peripheral Capitalism: Crisis and Reform). Beijing: Commercial Press.

Renne, Roland R. (熱若爾·羅蘭). 2002. *Zhuanxing yu jingjixue* 轉型與經濟學 (Transformation and Economics). Beijing: Peking University Press.

References

Romer, David H. (大衛·羅默). 2003. *Gaoji hongguan jingjixue* 高級宏觀經濟學 (Advanced Macro-economics). Shanghai: Shanghai University of Finance and Economics Press.

Rostow, Walt W. (羅斯托). 1988. *Cong qifei jinru chixu zengzhang de jingjixue* 從起飛進入持續增長的經濟學 (The Take-Off into Self-Sustained Growth). Chengdu: Sichuan People's Publishing House.

The World Bank. 2007. *Shijie fazhan zhibiao* 世界發展指標 (World Development Indicators). Beijing: China Finance and Economy Publishing House.

———. 2004. *Zhongguo: Tuidong gongping de jingji zengzhang* 中國：推動公平的經濟增長 (China: Promoting a Fair Economic Growth). Beijing: Tsinghua University Press.

World Commission on Environment and Development. 1989. *Women gongtong de weilai* 我們共同的未來 (Our Common Future). Beijing: World Affairs Press.

Index

Agricultural Bank of China (ABC) 171
agricultural economy 4-5, 124, 137
asset-liability ratio 158-9

bad loan ratio 171-2
balance of payments 59, 62, 64, 71, 108, 214, 216, 221, 223-4, 226-7, 257, 260, 262-3, 302-6, 325
banking system 68, 183-4, 271
Beijing 106, 113, 190, 193, 196-7, 315-24, 327, 329-37
bond financing 158, 160, 163-5
Brazil 114-16, 140, 145-7, 230, 276
buy-back operation 173-4

Cambridge 319, 329
capital account 70, 216, 219, 221, 224, 226-7, 236, 260, 304, 325
China Construction Bank (CCB) 170
China Statistical Yearbook 100, 105, 109, 125-8, 130, 133, 141-2, 157, 169, 191, 193, 203, 205, 207, 321
China's consumption rate 99, 273
China's reform 26, 220, 265, 273
classical economics 10, 12, 27, 74, 76
commodity trade 225, 228-9, 325
commodity trade surplus 225, 228
comparative labor productivity 133-4, 247, 249, 253, 256-7
comparative labor productivity ratio 274
comprehensive economic strength 240
computable general equilibrium (CGE) 12, 24, 315
consumer price index (CPI) 109, 271
consumption level 25, 103, 119-20, 291, 293-4
consumption rate 99-100, 113-16, 121, 236, 247, 249, 253, 256-7, 270, 273, 321
contribution rate 128, 131, 154, 199, 243, 322

corporate bond financing 159-60
corporate equity financing 160
current account balance 59, 227, 249, 272, 277
current account surplus 216, 227-8, 302
current transfer account 218-19, 325

debtor countries 302
deficit rate 109-10
direct financing 160, 163-4
direct investment 59, 91, 117, 221, 223, 225, 231-2, 236, 304-5, 325
direct investment surplus 221, 223, 225
double surplus 214-16, 223-4, 228, 232, 234, 302-3, 305, 325

economic agents 22-3, 182, 315
economic disparities 195-6, 199
economic liberalization 8, 198
economic recession 61, 121, 282, 285-6
employment structure 127, 139-40, 264
Engel coefficient 202, 324
Environmental Kuznets Curve (EKC) 79-82, 84, 319-20
evolutionary economics 30
evolutionary game theory (EGT) 23, 44
exchange repo market 173
external imbalances 261-2, 335
extreme value ratio 196, 198, 249, 254, 256

fictitious economy 18, 266
financial account surplus 214, 216
financial accounts 214-16, 219-21, 231-2, 237, 303, 325
financial assets 67, 154, 156-7
financial bonds 157, 164-5, 176
financial instruments 57, 163, 168
financial intermediaries 67, 182-3, 297
financial repression 65
fixed assets 48, 98, 203, 247, 258, 262, 282, 321, 326

Index

foreign capital 8, 149-50, 236-7, 266, 302-3, 305
foreign direct investment (FDI) 37, 216, 220, 223, 228, 231-3, 236-7, 244, 304-5, 326
foreign exchange balance 272, 277
foreign exchange reserves 54, 214-16, 223-5, 232-4, 241, 248-9, 261, 312, 325

Germany 121, 140, 158, 177, 230-1, 240-1, 243, 295, 297
gross national income (GNI) 248, 253, 256-7, 271
goods trading 216, 232
Green Solow Model 93, 95
gross capital formation (GCF) 104-5, 270, 321
Guangdong 190, 193-4

Heilongjiang 190, 193-4
household deposits 194-5
housing price earnings ratio 107, 112-13
human development index (HDI) 245

Industrial and Commercial Bank of China (ICBC) 170, 184
increment capital output ratio (ICOR) 110-11, 253, 256-7, 259, 273, 321
incremental value 131-2, 249, 322
India 115, 121, 145-7, 164, 169-70, 177, 198, 208-9, 224, 230-1, 234, 243, 274, 276-7, 294
indirect financing 159, 249, 253, 256, 296
inflation rate 107-8, 248-9, 252-3, 256-7, 262, 271, 276
innovation diffusion 36, 48-9
institutional equilibrium 45-6
international division of labor 2, 54, 64, 70-1, 91, 146, 149-51, 233, 236, 244
inter-regional economic structure 188, 195, 198
investment efficiency 106-7, 110-11, 267, 270, 273, 321

Jiangsu 190, 193

Krueger 79-80, 90, 319

labor productivity 10, 63, 86, 132, 139, 145, 149
Liaoning 190, 193-4
low-carbon economy 287-9

Malaysia 111, 115-16, 119, 208, 224, 230-1, 284
Malthus 61, 75, 318
market liquidity 176
marketization 175, 185, 199, 211, 259, 284, 311
Mexico 114-16, 139-40, 145, 147, 230, 277
modern economics 13, 30, 333
modern economic structure 17-18, 55, 59

National People's Congress (NPC) 262, 326, 333
neo-institutional economics 22, 316
neoclassical economics 13, 22, 28, 76
non-agricultural output 189
non-performing loan ratio 249, 271, 275

Organization for Economic Cooperation and Development (OECD) 36, 245, 326
operational efficiency 136-7, 145-6, 169
output value 40, 134, 137, 139-40, 143, 270

Panayotou 81, 84-5, 319-20, 329
Pearl River Delta 188-9, 242
per capita income 41, 69, 81-3, 90, 96, 98, 132-3, 143, 182
price-earnings ratio 178, 248-9, 252-3, 256-7
primary industries 124-8, 131-4, 137-41, 148, 189, 249, 253-4, 256-7, 262, 270, 272, 274, 276, 308

Qualified Domestic Institutional Investors (QDII) 161

Index

Qualified Foreign Institutional Investors (QFII) 161, 167

real estate investment 104-5, 107, 112
removal effects 81-3, 85
residential consumption 259, 282
resource allocation 3-6, 18, 35, 41, 43, 66-7, 136, 162, 169, 185, 199-200, 309
Robert Solow 37, 94
rural consumption 101-2, 120, 294
rural economy 200, 204-5, 210, 322
rural investment 203
rural households 98, 180, 202
Russia 114-15, 145, 147, 230, 266

social accounting matrix (SAM) 21, 316
soft budget constraint (SBC) 62-3
scale effects 81-7, 319
secondary industries 84, 125, 127-8, 131-4, 137-41, 148, 189-90, 235, 262, 266, 291
Shaanxi 190, 193-4
Shandong 190, 193-4
Shanghai 106, 113, 190, 193, 196, 315-18, 321, 324, 329-30, 332, 334-7
Shanxi 190, 193
Shibor 175-6, 297
short-term external debt ratio 230-2, 272, 325
Sichuan 190, 193-4, 324
social security system 121, 206, 265, 293, 311
South Korea 111, 114-16, 119, 140, 147, 164, 177, 208, 224, 230-1, 276, 294
special economic zones 188, 200
structural adjustment 84, 283, 292, 302, 308-9
structural changes 12, 27, 34, 79, 85-7, 143, 219, 244, 320
structural economy 4-6, 9
structural effects 81-7
structural imbalance 7, 10, 24-6, 55, 60, 62, 65-8, 71, 118, 154, 204-5, 227-8, 251-2, 262-3, 284-7
structuralism 2, 10, 12, 315, 335

technological diffusion 37, 39-40, 317
technological effects 84, 86
tertiary industries 25, 57, 125, 127-9, 131-4, 137-41, 143-4, 148, 189-90, 235, 247, 256-7, 264, 270, 291
the Philippines 116, 119, 208-9, 230-1, 284
three-dimensional balance 14-16, 281, 314
Tianjin 190, 193, 196-7, 318, 324
transfer payments 121, 192, 302

UK 121, 140, 158, 160, 163, 168, 177-8, 230-1, 241, 243, 252, 276, 295
United Nations Environment Program (UNEP) 14, 78, 288
urbanization 107, 115-16, 119, 131, 148, 211, 240, 268, 292, 308

vertical economic structure 28
virtual economy 62, 67, 284

Xiang Junbo 315, 327, 334
Xinjiang 190, 193-4

Yangtze River Delta 188-9, 242

Zhejiang 190, 193-4